The
Politics
of Sin

Bureaucracies, Public Administration, and Public Policy

Kenneth J. Meier
Series Editor

THE STATE OF PUBLIC BUREAUCRACY
Larry B. Hill, Editor

THE POLITICS OF DISSATISFACTION
Citizens, Services, and Urban Institutions
W. E. Lyons, David Lowery, and Ruth Hoogland DeHoog

THE DYNAMICS OF CONFLICT
BETWEEN BUREAUCRATS AND LEGISLATORS
Cathy Marie Johnson

THE POLITICS OF TELECOMMUNICATIONS REGULATION
The States and the Divestiture of AT&T
Jeffrey E. Cohen

WOMEN AND MEN OF THE STATES
Public Administrators at the State Level
Mary E. Guy, Editor

ETHICS AND PUBLIC ADMINISTRATION
H. George Frederickson, Editor

ENVIRONMENTAL PROTECTION AT THE STATE LEVEL
Politics and Progress in Controlling Pollution
Evan J. Ringquist

THE POLITICS OF SIN
Drugs, Alcohol, and Public Policy
Kenneth J. Meier

Bureaucracies, Public Administration,
and Public Policy

The Politics of Sin

DISCARDED

Drugs, Alcohol, and Public Policy

KENNETH J. MEIER

M.E. Sharpe
Armonk, New York
London, England

Library of Congress Cataloging-in-Publication Data

Meier, Kenneth J. 1950-
The politics of sin: drugs, alcohol, and public policy / Kenneth J. Meier.
p. cm. — (Bureaucracies, public administration, and public policy)
Includes bibliographical references and index.
ISBN 1–56324–298–2 (C). — ISBN 1–56324–299–0 (P)
1. Drug abuse—United States—Prevention. 2. Drug abuse—Government policy—
United States. 3. Alcoholism—United States—Prevention. 4. Alcoholism—
Government policy—United States 5. Narcotics, Control of—United States.
I. Title. II. Series.
HV5825.M375 1994
362.29'0973—dc20

93–14454
CIP

Printed in the United States of America

The paper used in this publication meets the minimum requirements of
American National Standard for Information Sciences—
Permanence of Paper for Printed Library Materials,
ANSI Z 39.48-1984.

∞

BM (c)   10   9   8   7   6   5   4   3   2   1
BM (p)   10   9   8   7   6   5   4   3   2   1

To Dwight Waldo and Lloyd Nigro

Contents

List of Tables and Figures   ix

Preface   xiii

Chapter

1. Politics and Morality Policies: A Theory   3

2. The Policy History of Government Antidrug Efforts:
   Or, "It's Déjà Vu All Over Again"   20

3. Reefer Madness: A Quantitative Historical Analysis of
   Drug Enforcement Policy   66

4. The State Politics of Drug Abuse   103

5. A Historical Review of Public Policies Regarding Alcohol   135

6. One for the Road: A Quantitative Historical Analysis
   of U.S. Alcohol Policies   176

7. Dealing with the Devil: State Regulation of Alcohol   209

8. The Politics of Sin   242

Bibliography   256

Index   273

List of Tables and Figures

Tables

2.1   Revenues Collected under the Harrison Act, 1915–45   28
2.2   Violations of the Harrison Act, 1915–30   29
2.3   Discretion and Morality Law Violations, 1922–28   31
2.4   Federal Drug Prosecutions after the Marijuana Tax Act,
      1938–90   38
2.5   The Rise in Salience of Marijuana: Number of Magazine
      Articles per Year, 1959–75   44
2.6   Racial Distribution in Drug Arrests, 1950–90   45
2.7   The Salience of Drug Abuse in the 1980s: Number of
      Magazine Articles   52
2.8   Median Age of Individuals Arrested for Drug Violations,
      1950–90   58
2.9   Percentage Distributions of Arrests for Drug Violations   59
3.1   Determinants of Federal Drug Agency Budgets   74
3.2   Determinants of Drug Agency Personnel   75
3.3   Determinants of Federal Drug Enforcement   77
3.4   Determinants of Federal Marijuana Enforcement   79
3.5   Impact of Legislation on Drug Penalties   81
3.6   Impact of Legislation on Marijuana Penalties   83
3.7   Determinants of State Drug Arrest Rates   85
3.8   Determinants of State Marijuana Arrest Rates   86
3.9   Determinants of Federal Prison Population   88
3.10 Determinants of State Prison Population   89
3.11 Determinants of Drug Prices   91
3.12 Determinants of Drug Use   94

3.13 Impact of Drug Arrests on Violent Crime   96

4.1   Determinants of State Marijuana Laws   111

4.2   Determinants of State Controlled-Substance Laws   113

4.3   Determinants of Drug Arrest Rates I   115

4.4   Determinants of Drug Arrests II   117

4.5   Drug Arrest Rates by Race   120–121

4.6   Determinants of Drug Arrest Rates by Race   122

4.7   Impact of Laws on Arrest Rates   124

4.8   Impact of Drug Enforcement on Prisons and Treatment   125

4.9   Impact of Drug Enforcement on Crime Rates   128

5.1   Alcohol Taxes and the Federal Budget (in millions of dollars),
      1910–20   140

5.2   Prohibition Enforcement Activities, 1920–33   143

5.3   Prohibition Enforcement Activities in Federal Court, 1920–33   144

5.4   Prohibition Penalties and Agency Efficiency, 1922–33   147

5.5   The Salience of Alcohol: Articles in Periodicals, 1910–40   152

5.6   Federal and State Alcohol Tax Revenues, 1920–90   157

5.7   Federal Tax Rates for Distilled Spirits and Beer, 1934–90   158

5.8   Enforcement of the Alcohol Tax Laws after Prohibition,
      1934–44   159

5.9   Arrest Rates (per 100,000 persons) for Alcohol-Related
      Problems, 1950–90   165

5.10 Trends in Alcohol Consumption, Cirrhosis, and Traffic
      Fatalities, 1950–90   166

6.1   Historical Determinants of Alcohol Taxes   182

6.2   Historical Determinants of Alcohol Taxes   185

6.3   Federal Prosecutions for Liquor Law Violations   186

6.4   Impact of Policies on Alcohol Consumption   188

6.5   Impacts on the Consumption of Beer, Wine, and Spirits,
      1934–90   190

6.6   Determinants of State Alcohol Enforcement   192

6.7   Determinants of State Alcohol Enforcement—Status Crimes   193

6.8   Impact of Policies on Jail Population   195

6.9   Impact of Policies on Cirrhosis Death Rates   197

6.10 Impact of Policies on Suicide Death Rates   199

6.11 Impact of Alcohol Policies on Traffic Fatalities, 1920–90   200

6.12 Impact of Alcohol and Policies on Crime Rates   202

6.13 Impact of Alcohol and Policies on Arrest Rates   203
7.1   Determinants of State Alcohol Policies   217
7.2   Determinants of State Drunk Driving Laws   221
7.3   Determinants of Alcohol Law Enforcement   224
7.4   The Influence of Drunk Driving Laws on Enforcement   226
7.5   The Influence of Alcohol Policies on Alcohol Consumption   228
7.6   The Influence of Alcohol Policies on Cirrhosis and Suicide
      Rates, 1988   230
7.7   The Influence of Alcohol Policies on Traffic Fatalities   232
7.8   The Influence of Alcohol Policies on Reported Drunk Driving
      and Binge Drinking   234
7.9   The Influence of Alcohol Policies on the Prison Population   235
7.10 Impact of Alcohol Enforcement on Crime Rates   236

Figure

1.1   A Model of the Policy Process   6

Preface

My initial interest in drug policy can be concisely explained by the following table:

Estimated Deaths and Death Rates, by Drugs

Drug	Users	Deaths per year	Deaths per 100,000 persons	Status
Tobacco	60 million	390,000	650	legal
Alcohol	100 million	150,000	150	legal
Heroin	500,000	400	80	illegal
Cocain	5 million	200	4	illegal
Marijuana	9.7 million	0	0	illegal

Source: Adapted from Ostrowski, 1989: 47.

Extremely dangerous drugs are legal and, in the case of tobacco, so lightly regulated that virtually everyone has access to them. Other drugs with far fewer negative consequences are illegal, and prohibition is aggressively enforced. The United States' war on drugs during the 1980s spawned an escalation in restrictive policies for illegal drugs while drug repression became the motherhood issue of the decade. Politicians competed with each other to see who could be the most antidrug. Striking in its absence was any rational assessment of policy options, especially given that this was not our first war on drugs.

The Politics of Sin has two objectives. The first is to provide an empirical assessment of the content, politics, implementation, and outcomes of U.S. policies on illicit drugs and alcohol. (Tobacco will not be considered; that would take another book-length manuscript by itself.) The second is to illustrate a multimethod approach to public policy analysis. Within political science three distinct approaches to public policy exist—descriptive historical studies, quantitative historical studies, and cross-sectional quantitative studies. Each approach has a full literature with little cross-fertilization among them. The theoretical argument of the book is that all three approaches are compatible.

In chapter 1 a general theory of public policy is introduced that portrays public policy as resulting from the interaction of political institutions, interest groups, and citizen forces subject to environmental constraints. Chapter 2 then uses this theory to guide a historical study of illicit drug policies in the United States from 1900 to 1992. Chapter 3 employs the same theory to structure a quantitative historical analysis of illicit drug policies. Also relying on the theory presented in chapter 1, chapter 4 presents a cross-sectional quantitative analysis using the 50 states. Chapters 5, 6, and 7 repeat the process for U.S. policies toward alcohol. Chapter 8 discusses the theoretical and substantive conclusions of the study.

Although reviewing all the theoretical and substantive findings of the book is not possible in a short preface, a recap of some of the more important findings will provide the flavor of the book. First, the major argument is that all three approaches to public policy are theoretically compatible, even though they rely on vastly different methods. Each approach often provides some insight that is lacking in the other two, so that using all three simultaneously provides a better assessment of drug control policies. My hope is that other students of public policy will follow my lead and write similar analyses of other policy areas. Second, the book argues that policy implementation and policy outcomes are integral parts of the policymaking process and must be studied to obtain an accurate view of a policy. Only by determining the impact that public policies have on the public can we get an accurate portrayal of the politics of public policy. Third, drug policies can be divided into two types—those with advocacy coalitions on both sides of an issue (e.g., the regulation of alcohol sales) and those with only one "acceptable" position (e.g., widespread opposition to drunk driving and drug abuse). Political systems handle the two-sided drug policies similarly to redistributive policies, with high levels of partisan conflict and decisionmaking by the major political institutions. The one-sided policies reflect entrepreneurial politics, whereby an entrepreneur pushes for new policies, and the policies adopted come from a grab bag of whatever is available. Proposals rarely face serious challenges. This book shows that generally the former policies tend to be effective and the latter policies usually have no impact.

Several substantive findings are presented in the book. First, drug law enforcement (not drug use per se) is associated with greater levels of violence and more crime; enforcement disrupts drug markets, and such markets can be established only by force. Second, the enforcement of drug control laws (including those for alcohol) disproportionately falls on minorities and immigrants, even though their use of these drugs rarely exceeds the norm. Third, federal enforcement of illicit drug laws responds quickly to actions taken by Congress and the president when they seek to exert control over drug policies; drug policies are adopted for political reasons. Fourth, state implementation of illicit drug laws is determined almost exclusively by federal enforcement efforts. Even though state and local law enforcement officials enforce different laws, the levels of enforcement closely track the efforts of the federal government. Fifth, controlled-substance laws and enforcement of those laws have little impact on either the price or the use of illicit drugs (except for marijuana). Sixth, the bottom line is that current U.S. drug policies are irrational. They provide few benefits, and those benefits that do occur are paid for through extremely high costs in law enforcement, corrections, crime, and violations of civil rights.

The research for this book took place over a five-year period. Numerous scholars in other social sciences examined drug policies before I did; the intellectual debt that I owe them can be seen in the extensive references and documentation. The data sets for this book were collected from a diverse set of sources; I suspect that no one has attempted a study such as this one, because simply gathering and verifying the data was a difficult undertaking. The federal Office of Justice Programs is without a doubt the most useful government agency ever created for disseminating data. The Federal Bureau of Investigation provided me with additional unpublished information on drug-related arrests.

Some of the preliminary work on alcohol policies was done with Cathy Johnson; she deserves my thanks for her ideas and her contributions. Paul Sabatier and Kathy Kemp were gracious enough to comment on fragments of this manuscript. Jeff Cohen read the entire manuscript and provided helpful comments. Gene Medford made a serious effort to convince me that Cabernet Sauvignon should be my drug of choice. The University of Wisconsin–Milwaukee provided me with a sabbatical leave for the purpose of finishing this book. Michael Weber and the people at M. E. Sharpe demonstrated why everyone should publish with M. E. Sharpe. Robin Whitaker deserves my special thanks for her usual superior work as copy editor. As is now tradition in public policy, any remaining errors of omission or commission should be attributed to Paul Sabatier.

Kenneth J. Meier

The
Politics
of Sin

1

Politics and Morality Policies: A Theory

Three approaches to the study of public policy flourish in political science—case studies, quantitative state politics studies, and quantitative historical studies. Although each occasionally cites works from the others, each field has developed in isolation to claim a separate niche as *the* study of public policy. Of the three, the case study approach is the most common (see Anderson, 1990; Skocpol and Finegold, 1982; Derthick and Quirk, 1985). Case studies use a variety of theoretical approaches, and some eschew theory simply to tell a substantive story. Within the case study approach, substance is king. To learn the detail of defense policy, agricultural policy, or environmental policy, reading the case studies is a necessity. Other approaches often shortchange substance in quest of other goals. The stress of substance does not mean case study approaches are devoid of theory; many, including the growing theory of the state literature (Skowronek, 1982), the more recent socioeconomic literature (Etzioni, 1988), and the policy-learning literature (Sabatier, 1988), are driven by complex policy theories.

Quantitative cross-sectional studies, primarily focused on politics and policy in the American states, are the next most common approach and have come to dominate the study of state politics in the political science journals (Dye, 1966; Hofferbert, 1969; Barrilleaux and Miller, 1988; Lowery and Gray, 1990). From a substantive perspective, state policy analysis began as a primitive effort to explain variations in state expenditures regardless of the policies that made use of those expenditures. Measurement problems, a common lament in public policy, forced the field to devote substantial time to questions that were not especially interesting (e.g., which state spends more for highway construction?). Gradually these measurement problems are being solved with studies now focusing on policies that are measured in a myriad of ways other than the simple expenditure of funds (Lowery and Gray, 1990; Meier, 1988). Theories within the cross-sectional literature have evolved from open-system views of the policy process to more complex political economy approaches (Barrilleaux and Miller, 1988).

Historical quantitative studies of policy are the newest growth area in policy

3

studies. Such studies usually focus more on implementation than policy adoption and often examine only a single agency. Studies of environmental policy, labor relations, antitrust policy, transportation safety, and other areas appear prominently in the literature (Wood, 1988; Wood and Waterman, 1991; Moe, 1985; Eisner and Meier, 1990). Although much of this literature uses a principal agent theory borrowed from economics and focuses almost exclusively on federal regulatory policies, the approach is applicable to other jurisdictions and other areas of public policy.

Despite the separate development of these three approaches to public policy and the implicit hostility of the approaches to one another, they are simply different ways of observing the same phenomena. The theoretical objective of this book is to demonstrate that the three approaches to public policy can be applied fruitfully to the same policy area.[1] Although such a demonstration may not unify the study of public policy, it will illustrate to each of the warring factions that the literature in the other fields has something to offer.

Perhaps the lesson of this effort is that each of the three approaches has some advantages over the other two. Bureaucratic leadership, for example, is much easier to study in a case study format than in a quantitative historical or cross-sectional approach. The impact of public policies on citizens is better informed by quantitative cross-sectional and quantitative historical approaches. Throughout the book, the strengths of one approach will compensate for the weaknesses of the others. The result is a mosaic of public policy that, I think, is more revealing of the politics of drug policy in the United States than the results of any single approach.

The substantive policy under consideration is drug policy. Why drugs? Theoretically drugs—as well as alcohol, abortion, sex education, gambling, school prayer, and so on—are a part of what can be termed morality politics. Morality politics involves interesting policy areas, because one segment of society attempts by governmental fiat to impose their values on the rest of society (see Gusfield, 1963). As such they are a form of redistributive policy that is rarely viewed as redistributive because the policies redistribute values rather than income (Ripley and Franklin, 1991). Along with the redistribution of values, government policies also attempt to change behavior (e.g., put a stop to the use of drugs or to driving while intoxicated). Such policies tend to be highly salient and permit little role for expertise; information that challenges the position of one party or the other is often ignored (Sharp, 1992). This suggests a fatal flaw in many morality policies: they are extremely popular but rarely effective.

The second reason for studying drugs is that political science has ignored them in at least two of the three major public policy approaches. To be sure, some political scientists contribute to the case study literature and seek to influence current drug policy (Nadelman, 1988), and the study of drugs and U.S. foreign policy is mushrooming (see Lewis, 1992; Lee, 1985–86). Except for the preliminary research that spawned this book, however, no quantitative cross-sectional or quantitative historical studies have appeared in political science or in other disciplines.

Included in the study are both illicit drugs and alcohol. Initially both were selected because one was illegal and one was legal yet highly regulated, suggesting a difference in government approaches that would make an interesting policy study. The historical focus adds additional variation; during the twentieth century all of America's favorite recreational drugs have been, at various times, legal and unregulated, legal yet regulated, illegal but with little enforcement, and illegal with massive enforcement. My initial belief was that the study of one drug policy area could inform the study of the other drug policy area.

A Theory of Public Policy

Theories of public policy abound (see Dye, 1966; Etzioni, 1988; Hofferbert, 1969; Sabatier, 1988). Rather than introduce a new theory of public policy, this study will use a theory that underlies many previous studies of public policy. Each analyst emphasizes the parts of the theory most relevant to his or her study, but the general contours tend to be remarkably similar.[2]

The basic premise of the theory is that public policy results from the interaction of political actors within an environment that constrains their choices. An outline of the basic theory appears in Figure 1.1. Three clusters of political actors are included—political system forces, industry forces, and bureaucratic forces. Each of these forces or sets of actors is aided or restricted by the citizen forces in the model. The process results in the adoption of policies, the implementation of policies, and perhaps some policy outcome that in turn affects the citizens' environment.

Before discussing each set of forces, some of the more pertinent aspects of this theory should be discussed. First, the theory views the political elite and the general public in similar terms. Each has preferences, and each rationally attempts to enact its preferences as public policy. Morality politics presents virtually no barriers to citizen participation in the policy process. Morality, in political terms, can always be viewed as black and white. Everyone is an expert, so citizens require little policy-specific knowledge to demand action from government. Some of these demands take place through interest groups (broadly defined), and some result from the direct action of individuals.

Second, legislatures, chief executives, and bureaucrats do not merely ratify the preferences of citizens and interest groups; they have their own policy preferences and seek to influence policy accordingly (see Nordlinger, 1981). Their institutional positions give them the resources and time to exert policy influence long after citizens have gone on to the next salient issue. Government actors, however, are only quasi-autonomous. To accomplish their public policy goals, they need the support of citizens if for no other reason than to remain in office. Such a position suggests responsiveness to citizen demands within the constraints of the government actor's own policy position.

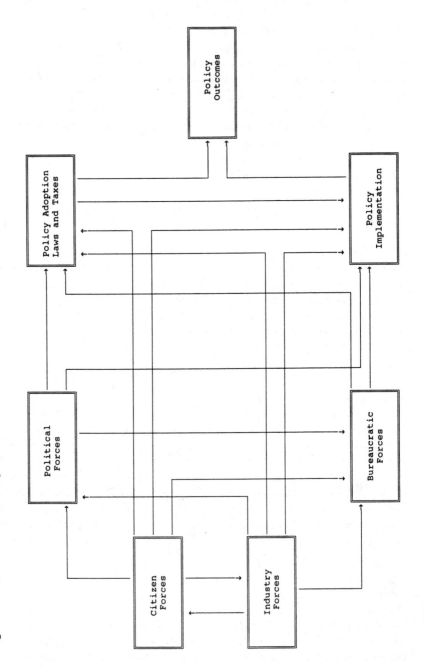

Figure 1.1 **A Model of the Policy Process**

Third, the theory is outcome focused. Most political scientists stop their studies with the adoption of public policies; implementation questions are deemed to be part of public administration and policy outcomes to be the realm of economics or specialists in program evaluation. Such a nearsighted perspective limits one to studying only part of the policy process, and in many cases it is the least interesting and least important part of the process. This theory includes as part of the proper study of public policy both the implementation of public policies and the impact that those policies have on citizens and their environment.

Fourth, this theory pays little attention to what is often termed environmental constraints. Many scholars treat variables such as income, education, industrialization, and urbanism as exogenous constraints on the policy process (see Dye, 1966). This study does not for two reasons. First, many of these environmental constraints may be nothing more than surrogates for the political demands of citizens. In their pathbreaking work, Wright, Erikson, and McIver (1985), for example, argue that state differences in income are really surrogates for differences in political ideology. Income or education in such a view generates different policy demands by different groups of citizens. Urbanism increases the contact among citizens with similar demands. The demands and the contact are what are important, not the income or the level of urbanism. Second, in the long run such constraints are manipulable. A great many policies are targeted at levels of income, education, industrialization, and so on. Some of them work, especially in a nation with the resources to fund public policy decisions (see Lowery and Gray, 1990; Schwartz, 1988). Environmental constraints in this view may be only short-term restrictions on policy options.

Finally, the model in Figure 1.1 treats many relationships as unidirectional. This is a simplification for the purposes of this study. In reality public policy is a far more complex process than is displayed here. At a minimum the model has a feedback loop, because policy implementation affects outcomes, which are then translated into new citizen demands. The great unknown in the study of public policy is this feedback loop; we know it exists but rarely venture out to examine it. From a long-term perspective, however, the model is even more complex; all the relationships might be reciprocal. The linkage between bureaucracy and political actors, for example, is a linkage that both institutions influence and that each institution structures in its own responses to the other (see Rourke, 1984). Finding a way to separate out such reciprocal influences is a promising area of study in public policy; it is not the subject of this book, however.[3]

Citizen Forces

Morality politics is made to order for citizen participation in the policy process (see Gormley, 1986). Whenever morality issues are placed on the public agenda, the issues are generally highly salient and presented in a simple manner. The issues are salient because few things motivate citizens more than threats to their deeply held values (see Sabatier, 1988, on deep core beliefs). Although many morality issues can be complex, efforts are made to simplify them to avoid losing control over them to technocrats. Abortion, for example, can be highly complex, especially when issues of family planning, fertility control, health consequences, and reproductive technologies are at stake. Both sides of this issue, however, have attempted to simplify it, portraying abortion as either an individual's right to choose or the murder of an innocent human being. Policies that are both salient and not complex see greater citizen involvement, because salience makes it easier to attract other citizens to the issue, and because citizens need not invest a great deal of time in learning the nuances of public policy.

Five citizen forces will be included in the theory of morality politics— demand, attitudes, race, salience, and self-help organizations. These forces are not conceptually distinct; many indicators of one force could also be indicators of another force. Anti-alcohol forces, for example, could well be the product of attitudes, demand for alcohol, race, and salience. An effort has been made to be inclusive and suffer some conceptual overlap rather than to omit any key variables. Each of the citizen forces merits separate discussion.

Demand

This study assumes that citizens have a demand for recreational intoxication, be it through alcohol, illicit drugs, or glue. Intoxication provides an escape from the problems of everyday life, and whenever demand for a product exists, some individual will attempt to supply it. One major citizen influence on public policy is the extent of demand for drugs or alcohol. Such demands are affected by a wide variety of forces, including costs, perceived risks, available resources, and so on. Actual demand curves for intoxication do not exist, so surrogates for demand must be created. One frequently used surrogate is income or per capita gross national product under the assumption that as discretionary resources increase so will demand. In other cases demand can be measured more directly. Demand has two possible influences in the theory. First, demand should generate some citizen support for access to drugs, be they alcohol or other drugs. Second, greater demand might also mean more visible drug problems, so it will be associated with calls for more government action to resolve drug problems.

Attitudes

Individuals have deeply held attitudes that frequently explain their position on drug policy issues and also reinforce demand or the lack of demand. Because drugs and alcohol are morality issues, the source of these attitudes is often religion. Religious pressures mean different things for illicit drugs and for alcohol. For illicit drugs virtually all religions are in opposition (the Native American church and Timothy Leary's former church are exceptions). Alcohol is another matter. Many religions tolerate the consumption of alcohol in moderation while others advocate a bone-dry parish and perhaps polity. This difference means that religious influences will need to be specified somewhat differently in the alcohol and the illicit drug chapters.

Churches also play another role in drug politics. By clustering like-minded individuals, they ease the problems of interest aggregation. Prohibition support came directly from many churches (see chapter 5). Those churches with a history of political activism will be more likely to spawn the interest groups that pressure political institutions. The guiding hypothesis is that policies should reflect the relative strengths of the churches that favor or oppose more restrictive drug policies.

Attitudes toward drugs also have an urban-rural dimension. Gusfield (1963) interprets prohibition as having been an attempt by white rural Protestants to impose their values on urban Catholic immigrants. Urban environments expose individuals to more varied lifestyles and are likely to generate greater levels of tolerance. Such tolerance could well generate libertarian attitudes concerning drugs. Urban areas, however, also increase the visibility of problems, and drug abuse is unlikely to be an exception. Given the greater visibility and the greater contact of individuals with like-minded views, urbanism could also generate more support for tough drug laws and stricter enforcement.

Race

Race is one of the most enduring forces in American politics (Carmines and Stimson, 1989). Of all the demographic factors in public policy, none is more persistent and more influential than race. Race is more than the sum of attitudes of minorities, however. Race is also the reaction of others to minorities. In morality politics, policies are often targeted at individuals different from oneself. Race, ethnicity, and immigration foster differences. As many historians have argued, we should expect morality policies to be targeted at immigrants and minorities (see chapters 2 and 5). Accordingly, if minorities are able to consolidate sufficient political power to influence politics, then the presence of larger numbers of minorities or immigrants is likely to result in policies favorable to the minority population. If minorities and immigrants are unable to consolidate political power, the predominant relationship will be that more minorities or immigrants will be associated with policies detrimental to their communities.

Self-Help Groups

With the rise of Alcoholics Anonymous, self-help groups have played an important role in drug policies. Self-help groups are not really interest groups in that they do not directly participate in the political process; they exist primarily to assist in treatment (although off-shoots of these groups might well become interest groups; see the discussion of the National Council on Alcoholism in chapter 5). Membership in such groups, however, suggests a pool of individuals with attitudes that support a medical rather than a morality approach to drugs. Large participation in self-help groups should be associated with less punishment-oriented approaches to drug abuse, although such groups might also support additional enforcement so that individuals become aware of their problems.

Salience

Although drug issues are generally salient, they go through periods of time when few individuals are concerned about them. Alcohol problems in the 1970s before the rise of Mothers Against Drunk Driving were generally unsalient, as was illicit drug abuse during the 1950s. Drugs must compete with other issues for space on the political system's agenda. Wars, depressions, and similar major events tend to blow drugs off the political agenda. At other times drugs can be a major, perhaps even dominant, agenda issue. Elections from 1912 through 1932 often focused on the role of alcohol. Elections in the 1980s had a similar drug component after the drug-related death of Len Bias. Salience generally assists the forces of prohibition and enforcement. When the salience of drug issues declines, other political issues become increasingly salient and should draw resources away from drug issues.

Salience may be either a citizen force or a political elite force. Although most theories interpret salience as a citizen pressure that the political system must respond to, some literature argues that mass attitudes about the importance of drug issues were created by political elites acting as policy entrepreneurs (Jensen, Gerber, and Babcock, 1991). By focusing public attention on drug issues, the politicians can draw public scrutiny away from other, less consensual issues (e.g., the federal deficit).

Industry Forces

Morality policy by necessity has an element of regulation in it. No current theories of regulatory policy exist without a major role for the regulated industry (see Reagan, 1987). The regulated industry is the one stable force in a regulatory policy area, regardless of the salience of the public policy, because the industry's livelihood depends on favorable policies. Morality policy is an interesting type of regulatory policy because at times the industry is declared illegal. When this occurs, the industry goes underground and is prohibited from using the normal methods of political participation to influence public policy. This legality dimension means that industry forces can be examined only in the alcohol policy chapters.

Even in the most regulated of industries, monolithic industries do not exist. The alcohol industry, similar to some other industries, is divisible into the production industry and the consumption industry. Firms that produce alcoholic beverages have an interest in selling them, but they have only minor interests in restrictions placed on retailers. Although distillers might prefer that liquor be sold through private liquor stores, they certainly can live with it being sold from government-owned stores. The retail side of the industry, however, is very interested in efforts to regulate retail sales. This distinction means that policies must be examined to determine if there is a production industry interest or a sales/consumption industry interest or both. If industry can mobilize its political resources, policies should become more favorable to it as the industry itself becomes larger.

Many industry-related policies are regulatory, and in these issues the regulated industry is usually opposed by a relatively weak collection of public interest advocates. Morality policy is more akin to redistributive policy than to regulatory policy in this regard. At times the regulated industry will be opposed by an active and aggressive set of citizen groups. A reasonable counterhypothesis to the industry-influence hypothesis is that, given the likely divisions in the industry, the alcohol industry will have little or no impact on alcohol policies, especially when policies become salient.

In some areas of public policy, policies are structured so that one industry is a competitor of other industries (e.g., railroads and the trucking industry). The drug industry could be one such industry. If there is a general demand for intoxication, then alcohol and illicit drugs are substitutes for each other. Several historians argue that the alcohol production industry played a role in banning other drugs (see chapter 2). During current debates, the alcohol industry could play a behind-the-scenes role to encourage stronger drug control laws and greater law enforcement. If this competitor hypothesis is valid, we would expect a powerful alcohol industry to be associated with restrictive drug policies.

Political Forces

Morality policies, whether symbolic or with real impact, have to be adopted or imposed by political institutions. These institutions are perceived as quasi-autonomous. The individuals who occupy positions of political influence have their own values regarding morality issues and will seek to influence policies to be consistent with those values. The theory of public policy will incorporate three elements of political forces—institutions, political values, and political competition.

Institutions

Political institutions include Congress (the legislature at the state level), the president (the governor at the state level), and the courts. Each has a variety of ways it can influence the direction of morality policy. Congress and state legislatures use legislation as their main policy option. Laws establish how the individual drug will be treated, ranging from prohibition to regulation to an unregulated free market. All laws clearly are not equal; some are ambitious efforts to establish major policies, and others are mere tinkering with current policy or perhaps even window-dressing to provide the appearance of action. Accordingly legislation needs to be examined to determine its scope and intent before providing specific hypotheses about the impact of an individual law on drug policy. This specification will be done in the empirical chapters.

Legislation is not the only activity that Congress and state legislatures use to influence drug policy. Policies have to have resources attached to them (money, personnel authorizations, etc.) to be effective. Morality policies are rarely funded at a level necessary to achieve complete prohibition; nor is it likely that the American public would tolerate the other costs imposed by a complete prohibition policy. The key question is whether or not sufficient resources are attached to provide some deterrence and make the policy feasible. Where possible, the budgeted resources of the drug enforcement agency will be included in the models.

When legislative policy declares certain drugs legal, legislatures still have the option to make access to drugs more or less easy. Restrictive regulation can limit access to drugs, as can the imposition of higher tax rates. Such policies, however, have inherent limitations because excessive restrictions create incentives for black markets in the regulated drug.

Presidents and governors can play a role in the legislative process; they also appoint the administrators who head drug control efforts. A large literature documents the influence of executive appointees on the policy actions of an agency (see Wood and Waterman, 1991; Meier, 1993). Elected chief executives can also establish higher priorities for drug enforcement by emphasizing drug policies (as recent presidents have done) and by providing organizational status. One method of providing organizational status is through reorganizations (Seidman and Gilmour, 1986). Presidents propose reorganizations when they perceive that current drug control efforts are not working. With the reorganization often comes greater resources and more "political support" for aggressive law enforcement efforts. Reorganizations can also de-emphasize law enforcement strategies, so that specific hypotheses can be generated only for each specific reorganization.

Courts affect drug policy by ratifying decisions made by the other political branches of government. Courts are often asked to evaluate drug policies in terms of constitutional restrictions and generally respond to such requests. Courts also have an implementation role in drug policies, because individuals charged with drug-law violations must be tried in courts. The importance of courts is in the cues that they provide the law enforcement bureaucracy. A court system that is willing to sanction agency methods and uphold agency arrests should generate a more aggressive enforcement of drug laws. A restrictive court will have the opposite impact.

Values

Drug policies should reflect the political values of the politicians who hold office. Surveys of specific drug policy values are impossible in a study of this nature with its historical focus. The primary measure of values, therefore, is partisanship. Although drug policy goes through periods of bipartisan support, law enforcement approaches to drug abuse are generally more characteristic of Republicans than Democrats. The use of partisanship means that values can be determined for both legislatures and elected chief executives. The hypothesis is that drug control policies will become more law enforcement oriented when Republican elected officials are in control of the government.

In some cases a more precise assessment of values is possible. In case studies, individual statements of values are often available. At the state level, several measures of political ideology have been created (see Holbrook-Provow and Poe, 1987). As the values of government elites become more conservative, we should also expect policies to reflect greater law enforcement emphasis.

Party Competition

Few political variables have a longer or more mixed empirical history than party competition. Party competition affects certain types of policies but not others (Hofferbert, 1969). V. O. Key (1964) stressed that competitive party systems are more likely to produce redistributive policies. Key, of course, was concerned only with redistributive issues involving money, not with those involving values. His argument, however, should also apply to drug issues. Literally hundreds of issues compete for the political agenda. Single-party governments have no real incentive to be responsive to all claims from citizen groups in the environment. After all, the probability of being ousted from political control is remote; therefore, elected officials in uncompetitive regimes will pursue their own agenda items rather than those advocated by others. Although some political elites may have drug control issues as part of their personal political agendas, in normal political times such priorities are rare. With two competitive parties, however, not only can citizen groups appeal to both political parties, but also elected officials should be more attune to public demands. This logic suggests that, when party competition increases, policies will be adopted that stress law enforcement strategies to drug control.

Bureaucracy

To be effective, policies must be implemented.[4] Although some might claim that drug control policies are symbolic, most drug control policies do more than just redistribute values. Individuals are arrested and prosecuted; entire industries are declared illegal. For long periods of time when the legislature is not actively making drug policies and even during times when it is, bureaucracies play a dominant role in drug policy by enforcing the existing laws. Bureaucracies exercise discretion and, therefore, must be considered policymaking entities in their own right (Rourke, 1984). Four variables will be included in the analysis—bureaucratic capacity, bureaucratic leadership, federalism relationships, and bureaucratic competitors.

Bureaucratic Capacity

If historians such as Gusfield (1963) are correct about drug control policies being primarily symbolic, the implementing bureaucracies will have little capacity to implement public policy. Capacity can be thought of as both autonomy and resources (see Meier, 1993; Rourke, 1984). In some public policies bureaucracies are given little autonomy. They are restricted by very detailed laws (e.g., the social security retirement program) or by required procedures (e.g., the Consumer Product Safety Commission of the 1970s; see Meier, 1985). Drug control agencies generally have not had this problem. Although early federal laws appeared to limit federal drug agents to tax collection functions, permissive interpretations of those laws by the courts allowed full-fledged law enforcement actions. Because drug control bureaucracies have extensive discretion, autonomy will not be considered directly in this theory of public policy.

Resources include both personnel and budgets. Drug control efforts are personnel intensive, at least in the way they are conducted in the United States. Enforcement consists of undercover agents buying drugs, making arrests, and convincing arrested persons to implicate others. Such tactics do not lend themselves to high-level technology. As a result, a constraint on the agency's activities is the total personnel available and the total dollar resources of the agency. As these resources increase, the total law enforcement effort of the agency should also increase.

Bureaucratic Leadership

The role bureaucracy plays in the policy process can be greatly enhanced by effective bureaucratic leadership (Rourke, 1984). As director of the Federal Bureau of Investigation, J. Edgar Hoover was able to fashion one of the most powerful agencies in the federal government. Hoover's successors have lacked his bureaucratic and political talents and, thus, have presided over an agency that has been more subject to political control. Bureaucratic entrepreneurs (from Harry Anslinger to William Bennett) have sought to establish control over drug policies. Because bureaucratic leaders have a variety of goals, a specific hypothesis concerning leadership is not possible. Many bureaucratic leaders have aggressively attempted to expand the agency, and others have tried to limit the agency's policy sphere to a narrower one in order to retain control over public policy.

Federalism

Drug control policies are an example of the shared powers of federalism. Both the federal and state governments adopt laws and enforce them with their own agencies. In theory, the federal law enforcement agencies operate separately from the state and local agencies, but in practice that is not possible. Federal agencies rarely have sufficient personnel to operate nationwide without some local assistance. Heads of federal law enforcement agencies often perceive themselves as providing encouragement and support for all law enforcement personnel, not just federal officials.

Because individual law enforcement agencies have a great deal of discretion in the priority that they give various crimes, especially morality crimes, federal agencies can attempt to encourage local agencies to invest more resources in drug control efforts. Influence might also be indirect. When state and local agencies see federal enforcement priorities change, they might also adjust their own enforcement. The specific hypothesis under consideration is that an increase in the level of federal law enforcement agencies' drug law enforcement will stimulate a similar increase in the efforts of state and local law enforcement agencies.[5]

Bureaucratic Competitors

Bureaucracies often must compete with other bureaucracies for control of a policy area (Downs, 1967). Such competition might occur directly for funds or indirectly to influence the direction of public policy. In drug abuse policy, the major competitor of the law enforcement bureaucracies is the health care–drug abuse treatment bureaucracies. These agencies advocate medical rather than law enforcement approaches to drug control. They will attempt to reallocate funds from law enforcement to treatment.

The best interests of the treatment bureaucracy, however, might not be obvious. One research hypothesis is that, as treatment bureaucracies grow, fewer resources will be allocated to law enforcement agencies, and the enforcement of drug control laws will decline. A more complex hypothesis is also possible. Drug treatment agencies need clients to operate, and addicts may not voluntarily seek treatment. In such a situation, a drug treatment agency might advocate greater law enforcement efforts to "notify" potential clients of their treatment needs. In such a situation, the relationship between treatment resources and law enforcement would be positive. Such a hypothesis, however, also suggests that treatment bureaucracies want access to these clients, so that the laws should either involve modest penalties or permit individuals to opt for treatment in lieu of punishment.

Policy

Drug control policies follow a general hierarchy. The first decision, or perhaps nondecision, is whether or not the drug will be legal. If the determination is that the drug will be declared illegal, then laws need to be passed declaring this illegality. Such laws not only make a declaration of illegality but also specify what offenses shall be punished. A major policy distinction is between use/possession and trafficking (trafficking consists of manufacture and/or sale of drugs). The legality of use can be independent of trafficking (e.g., federal alcohol prohibition), and declaring use illegal is considered a more stringent drug policy. At times this distinction is finessed by declaring possession illegal. Because using drugs without possessing them is impossible, such policies are targeted at drug users. In some instances both possession and use are declared illegal; this policy is simply a way to increase penalties by creating two crimes out of one. Therefore, two policy measures included in this study will be whether or not a substance is illegal and the range of offenses that is covered by the law.

Once offenses are specified, the question of punishment must be considered. Punishments, particularly for drugs other than alcohol, vary dramatically, both historically and geographically, from long jail terms to routine citations. In some states marijuana has been decriminalized. Despite a wealth of literature rejecting the connection between severe punishment and deterrence, drug abuse policy frequently responds to perceptions of increased use with more severe punishments. The severity of punishment for drug law violations will be a major measure of public policy in this study.

If the policy decision is made to permit legal sales of a drug, the policymaking institutions face several questions. First, should the drug be taxed? The answer is almost always yes. Governments tax drugs for a variety of reasons. On the one hand, they might perceive that higher taxes reduce the level of consumption and thus any ill effects of consumption. On the other hand, sin taxes are a source of revenue that is relatively painless to raise in comparison to other sources. The level of taxes on the legal drug will be the fourth policy measure.

The second question involving a legal drug is, Should it be regulated? Again, the decision, at least in twentieth-century America, has always been yes. Regulation, however, varies in strictness. Under regulatory systems, the regulations themselves will be analyzed to determine how far the policy moves away from a totally free market. This assessment will be used to create a measure of regulatory stringency.

Enforcement

The policy implementation literature strongly advises that public policy can be only understood by examining policy implementation as well as the adoption of public policies (Mazmanian and Sabatier, 1989; O'Toole and Mountjoy, 1984). Bureaucratic agencies change policies to adapt them to the problems that they face; problems often change faster than policies do. Standard operating procedures of agencies may emphasize one aspect of a policy and completely ignore another. Bureaucratic agencies, particularly those in law enforcement, have far more responsibilities than resources. Accordingly, the agencies will exercise some discretion in how enthusiastically they implement various policies.

Although implementation is problematic for all public policies, the study of morality policy in particular must go beyond the study of policies that are adopted by legislatures or regulations that are issued by regulatory agencies to include an examination of enforcement. Enforcement of morality laws is even more discretionary than the enforcement of other laws. Victims of morality crimes do not demand that the police take action; most "victims" would prefer to avoid contact with law enforcement officials. The degree of enforcement may well be the most crucial aspect of the public policy. A strict law without any enforcement will soon be treated as a policy without content. A moderate law strictly enforced can have more impact than a stringent law with sporadic enforcement.

The primary measure of enforcement used in this analysis will be arrests for drug law violations. From an academic perspective, one advantage of studying drug control policies is that law enforcement agencies are very systematic about keeping enforcement records. Arrest data exist for long periods of time, and some effort has been made to collect uniform data from the various law enforcement agencies. In some cases actual punishment data also exist. Both federal and state/local law enforcement will be examined.

In addition to examining the politics of policy implementation by using models similar to those for public policy adoption, this study will also directly link policies to policy implementation. By determining if policies affect the extent of implementation, we can determine if policymakers control factors that can be used to structure the implementation process and get results that are desired. A lack of relationship between public policies and public policy implementation suggests a policy area that is either dominated by bureaucratic discretion or poorly designed.

Policy Outcomes

Public policies are adopted to affect some perceived problem. Analyzing public policy without some attempt to assess whether or not policies affect the problem they were intended to affect would be an incomplete analysis. Policy is government's attempt to shape its own environment, to create a polity with more advantages or fewer disadvantages than it currently has. Assessing policy outcomes is rarely easy, but the theoretical and policy advantages of doing so (in order to specify better policy theories or better public policy) far outweigh the problems of doing it.

The prime outcome variable of drug policy is the consumption of drugs. When the policy under consideration permits legal sale of drugs, consumption figures are readily available. When the drug is illegal, consumption data are difficult to gather and estimates tend to be biased. The importance of estimating drug consumption, however, requires analysis of even biased data as long as the biases are made clear and adjusted for if possible.

Drug consumption is not the only policy outcome of drug policy. Drug use affects a wide variety of other factors that should produce some evidence of the success or failure of drug policies. Such results are termed second-order consequences. The consumption of licit and illicit drugs is often associated with health consequences that can be measured. For alcohol consumption, health measures include deaths from cirrhosis of the liver, nighttime automobile fatalities, and suicides. For illicit drugs, fewer reliable measures are available.

The final policy outcome will be levels of crime. Few concepts are more intertwined than drugs and crime. Drug use and crime rates are positively correlated, but the nature of their relationship is one of the major disputes in the field. Using both historical data and cross-sectional data, this study will attempt to determine if the relationship between drugs and crime is caused by the drug usage itself or by drug law enforcement.

A Roadmap for the Book

The next six chapters address drug policy questions using the theory developed in this chapter. Owing to the difficulties in using a single theory in two different policy areas with three different approaches to public policy, each chapter begins with some specified modifications of theory. To make the chapters as comparable as possible, however, such modifications will be kept to a minimum. Each chapter will also conclude with an assessment of how well the theory performed and the important substantive findings.

Chapter 2 is a historical case study of nonalcohol drug control policies in the United States. Covering such drugs as heroin, cocaine, and marijuana, the chapter examines the evolution of twentieth-century drug policies primarily at the federal level. Chapter 3 is a quantitative historical analysis of nonalcohol drug control policies. Both federal and state policies are included, with substantial emphasis on policy outcomes and second-order consequences. Chapter 4 is a quantitative cross-sectional study of nonalcohol drug control policies by state governments.

The next three chapters repeat the process for alcohol policies. Chapter 5 is a historical case study; chapter 6 is a historical quantitative analysis; and chapter 7 is a quantitative cross-sectional analysis of the 50 states. Chapter 8 returns to the theory to assess its performance in the six studies. The chapter also integrates the substantive conclusions regarding drug policy in the United States and makes some modest suggestions for a more rational drug control policy.

Notes

1. The book is the second step in the process. In Meier, 1988, I used both historical case studies and quantitative cross-sectional analysis to examine the politics of the insurance industry. Jeff Cohen (1992), in his study of telecommunications policy, makes a similar effort.

2. Others have labeled this approach a variety of things from systems theory, to bureaucratic politics, to socioeconomics, to neoinstitutionalism. None of these terms is

incompatible with my theoretical approach. Rather than discussing such theoretical issues in the study of public policy, I would prefer just to move ahead with the study. Some might object to my use of the word *theory* to describe the framework presented here. They might merely substitute the word *model* whenever the word *theory* appears.

3. People who insist that all problems be solved before undertaking a study are unlikely to finish any studies. The current book may already be too ambitious. I will solve these other problems tomorrow at Tara.

4. The separation of bureaucracy from political institutions should not be taken to imply that bureaucracy is not a political institution. It is. The distinction between bureaucracy and political institutions is useful because the form of politics varies from one to the other.

5. This relationship could be reciprocal. That is, state and local agencies, by refusing to work with federal law enforcement personnel, could limit the activities of the federal government. The refusal of many states to enforce alcohol prohibition laws made the federal efforts a guaranteed failure. My analysis suggests that the causal relationship for illicit drug control issues is from the federal government to state governments (see chapter 3).

2

The Policy History of Government Antidrug Efforts: Or, "It's Déjà Vu All Over Again"*

The federal government periodically undertakes a systematic effort to restrict the use of illegal drugs such as heroin, cocaine, and marijuana. Varying by length and by illegal substance, these drug wars are presented with good intentions; but their timing relative to elections and electoral strategies implies that political considerations are never far from any antidrug campaign. Antidrug campaigns are ahistorical; by ignoring past efforts at drug control, they continue to address policies in ways that have been tried before and found lacking.

Theoretical Modifications

Chapter 1 discussed the seven clusters of variables used to study morality policy. Policy (laws, implementation, and outcomes) results from an interaction among citizen groups, industry groups, political forces, and bureaucracies. Using this theory to study illicit drug abuse policies requires one major modification. Because drugs are illegal, the industry is not permitted to participate in the policy process. A modest organization of drug consumers exists (the National Organization for the Reform of Marijuana Laws), but generally this and other consumer organizations can be disregarded. Industry groups can influence public policy only through extralegal methods (e.g., bribes, violence). Although substantial evidence suggests such influence at various points in policy history, without some formal right to participate in open politics, such efforts are not consistently visible. Accordingly, this chapter will pay little attention to "industry forces."

The case study methodology will also affect the assessment of citizen groups, political forces, and bureaucratic actors. Concepts that are difficult to measure quantitatively, such as leadership or entrepreneurial ability, can easily be incor-

---

*With apologies to Yogi Berra.

porated into a historical case study. Many bureaucratic and political forces will be nothing more than the efforts of individuals to exert some influence over drug abuse policy. Questions of bureaucratic capacity and partisan competition will receive less attention.

Substantive Themes in Drug Abuse Policy

Five themes permeate twentieth-century efforts to combat the use of drugs. First, drug politics inevitably involves foreign affairs.[1] Because most of America's favorite drugs are imported, a general policy of blaming the supplier is adopted.[2] This policy contends that drug problems exist because other countries supply drugs to the United States, not because Americans demand them. Pressure is exerted on foreign countries to restrict the production and export of drugs or even to change traditional farming practices. Pressure is administered both bilaterally and multilaterally. The United States has sought a variety of multilateral agreements to restrict the flow of narcotics and other drugs. In turn, these foreign agreements are often used to justify the adoption of strict laws in the United States.

Second, drug politics is frequently linked to issues of race and social class. Harsh drug policies are often passed in response to perceived drug use by immigrants, minorities, and working-class individuals. When drugs become a problem for middle-class whites, sanctions are relaxed. Protecting white middle-class young people, however, from the evils of drug abuse is paramount. Arguments are repeatedly made that harsh methods are necessary because drugs are threatening to destroy America's youth.

Third, drug politics and policy are marked at times by aggressive bureaucratic imperialism by agencies with a stake in drug control. Although bureaucratic imperialism is a common political phenomenon (see Holden, 1966; Downs, 1967; Niskanen, 1971) and has some beneficial results, in drug control policy bureaucratic imperialism produces three bureaucratic pathologies that seriously constrain effective policymaking—information distortion, corruption, and abuse of citizens. Bureaucracies will portray the drug problem in ominous terms; historically law enforcement bureaucracies have generated major propaganda efforts distorting the information available to policymakers. Corruption is frequent because law enforcement personnel have vast amounts of discretion, and the drug trade has access to large amounts of untraceable cash (Wilson, 1966). Drug control agencies also have a long history of violating the civil rights of American citizens. Agencies have often justified illegal activities by reference to the serious nature of the drug problem as demonstrated by the agency's own propaganda.

Fourth, drug control policies in the United States show an excessive concern with marijuana. Many drugs are potentially harmful to the user or are implicated in crimes committed for the purpose of obtaining drugs. Marijuana often suffers from guilt by association. Because marijuana is more widely used than other illegal drugs, enforcement strategies, no matter how they are targeted, always seem to fall heaviest on marijuana.

Fifth, our wars on drugs have been remarkably unsuccessful. Accurate data on drug usage are difficult to obtain and agency-gathered data are subject to systematic distortion, but available evidence suggests that drug wars neither reduce the supply of illegal drugs nor have much impact on the demand for them. Perhaps the best illustration of the policy failure of drug wars is that the nation perceives a recurring need to fight them. After all, a successful war on drugs would eliminate the need for future wars.

This chapter examines the political history of drug control policies in the United States. Within this historical examination, these five drug policy themes will be stressed. Because the focus is on the political aspects of drug control, medical and sociological issues will not be discussed unless they are directly relevant to the politics of drug abuse control.

The Pure Food and Drug Act of 1906

In the nineteenth century narcotic[3] and hallucinogenic drugs were sold openly. Medicine, lacking the scientific base it would develop in the twentieth century, relied heavily on the use of pain-killers, many of which contained various opiates. In 1910 morphine was the fourth most frequently used medical drug; alcohol was number five (Grinspoon and Bakalar, 1985: 75). The Bayer chemical company of Germany successfully synthesized heroin in 1898 and sold the drug over the counter as a "nonaddictive" substitute for codeine and morphine (Walker, 1979: 13) and as a sedative for coughs (Bellis, 1981: 7). Cocaine, marketed aggressively by the Parke-Davis Company, was touted as a cure for hay fever and sinus problems (Musto, 1973: 7).[4] Cocaine was also used as a food additive; Coca-Cola revised its secret formula in 1903, substituting caffeine for cocaine (Musto, 1973: 3).[5] Addiction was common; widespread drug use was facilitated by the growth of large-scale industrial organizations using mass production and distribution techniques (Musto, 1981: 5). Many physicians and pharmacists maintained a lucrative practice by supplying opiates to drug addicts.

Marijuana has perhaps the longest history of any drug in the United States. The hemp of the marijuana plant was widely used in the manufacture of rope, cloth, and other goods. First introduced to the colonies in Virginia in 1611, marijuana hemp rapidly became a major cash crop. George Washington's diaries reveal that our first president grew marijuana, although probably not for "medical" purposes (Grinspoon, 1971: 12). Over 100 medical articles on the use of marijuana in treatment were published between 1839 and 1900, even though its use as a medicine declined when opiates and stronger pain-killers entered the market (Grinspoon, 1971: 13). Used as a treatment for coughs, insomnia, convulsions, asthma, opiate addiction, and menstrual cramps, marijuana was listed as a recognized medicine from 1850 to 1942 in the *United States Pharmacopeia* (Himmelstein, 1983: 22).

Both cocaine and opiates continue to have key functions in modern-day medical practice. Morphine, an opium derivative, was used as the prime pain-killer during the U.S. Civil War and is still used to reduce the discomforts of extreme pain (Bellis, 1981: 5). Heroin, also an opium derivative, does not have medical uses in the United States but is used medically in Great Britain and other countries (Lindesmith, 1981: 340). Cocaine's early medical popularity was established in 1884, when Karl Koller discovered it could be used as a local anesthetic and Sigmund Freud published the first of his papers advocating cocaine as a treatment for a variety of physical and mental ills (Grinspoon and Bakalar, 1985: 22). Although novocaine replaced cocaine for many anesthetic uses, cocaine is still used as a local anesthetic for some operations (Grinspoon and Bakalar, 1985: 23).

The use of drugs was first addressed at the national level in the Pure Food and Drug Act of 1906. Congress passed this law in response to organized consumer groups aided by muckraking journalists. Industry groups (that is, food producers and pharmaceutical manufacturers) joined the coalition when it appeared that consumer demand for certain foods and drugs dropped in response to the negative publicity (see Nadel, 1971; Feldman, 1976). The Pure Food and Drug Act had a direct effect on drug usage. The act prohibited misbranding of pharmaceuticals; patent medicines that contained heroin, opium, cocaine, or marijuana could still be sold, but the medicines had to list these ingredients by name. Although the Pure Food and Drug Act did not make the use of narcotics illegal in patent medicines, Musto (1973: 94) argues that accurate labeling greatly reduced sales. Individuals, aware of the problems of addiction, avoided patent medicines containing narcotics. As a result, patent medicine producers generally eliminated the use of opiates and other narcotics.

Although the Pure Food and Drug Act did not address the nonmedical use of drugs, addiction was reasonably prevalent. Reliable estimates of the number of drug addicts in 1915 ranged from 200,000 to 275,000 with concentrations in the South and among the upper and middle classes (Walker, 1979: 13). The first federal effort to restrict nonmedical use, however, was aimed not at these users but rather at the Chinese immigrant population. Racial tensions in California exacerbated by economic problems in the 1870s produced local ordinances and then a state law in 1881 prohibiting the smoking of opium (Morgan, 1978: 59). The intent to target Chinese persons was clear from the law because opium consumption by means other than smoking remained legal; smoking opium was perceived to be a working-class Chinese habit. Seventeen other western states with some Chinese population also passed laws prohibiting the smoking of opium (Bonnie and Whitebread, 1970: 985–986). Racially targeted regulation continued in 1909, when the federal government banned the importation of smoking opium but permitted its importation for other purposes (Musto, 1973: 2).

The U.S. ban of smoking opium was also influenced by its participation in international opium politics. The Opium Wars of 1838–42 were fought by the British to force China to accept the importation of opium. The opium trade was highly profitable for the British colonial empire; the British government of India raised one-half of its operating revenues from the export of opium to China (Lowinger, 1981: 616). The United States took a strong position against opium trade for economic reasons: elimination of the opium trade would erode the European domination of the China trade and open trade opportunities for the United States (Brunn, Pan, and Rexed, 1975: 9). In pursuit of this goal, the United States was influential in organizing the Shanghai Convention to restrict trade in smoking opium; the U.S. ban on importation was passed while the convention was in session as a method of showing the United States' good faith in opium politics (Musto, 1981: 7). Because a variety of states had already banned opium smoking, the national legislation entailed few political costs.

The Harrison Act

Specific regulation of narcotics by the United States government began with the Harrison Act of 1914. The Harrison Act resulted from the actions of bureaucratic entrepreneurs with some minor support from public opinion. Hamilton Wright, the Department of State's opium commissioner, was the first to blame America's drug problems on the willingness of producing nations to supply the drugs (Musto, 1981: 8). Seeking limitations on foreign production of drugs, the United States was instrumental in calling for the Hague Convention of 1912 with its agenda to control the international traffic in opium and cocaine.

Domestically, commitments made by the United States at the Hague Convention provided both a justification for and a legitimation of federal efforts to restrict narcotics. Because the Harrison Act was framed as part of U.S. obligations under a foreign treaty, state government concerns about growing federal power were swept aside by the federal government's supremacy in foreign policy (Musto, 1981: 8; Dickson, 1968: 148). Public support for this drug legislation came from an unlikely source. King (1972: 23) attributes the growth in public support for drug legislation to a rivalry between the current Mrs. Cornelius Vanderbilt and the former Mrs. Vanderbilt. The former Mrs. Vanderbilt was an active crusader for women's suffrage. Seeking an equally prominent issue on which to do good, the current Mrs. Vanderbilt organized women in support of restrictive drug legislation. Her organizations were credited with encouraging New York State to adopt a fairly restrictive drug control law in 1914.[6] This public pressure was then used to support federal legislation.

Francis Harrison, a New York Democrat, mediated between foreign policy advocates and domestic interest groups to produce the law that bears his name. He made a series of changes in the proposed legislation to gain the support of pharmacists and physicians (Musto, 1973: 60). Part of the initial sparring over the law was a dispute between these two professions over which would control the dispensing of drugs (Musto, 1973: 15).[7] Marijuana was included in the early drafts of this law but was dropped in response to opposition from the pharmaceutical industry. Because marijuana was used only in corn plasters, veterinary medicine, and other nonintoxicating uses, little purpose was seen in including it with the more dangerous opiates and cocaine (Musto, 1972: 101).

Race appears to have played a role in the adoption of the Harrison Act. Kinder (1991: 473) documents law enforcement claims that cocaine gave blacks superhuman strength and contributed to assaults on whites. Cocaine was also used as a stimulant by white overseers in order to get higher production from black farm workers (Zimring and Hawkins, 1992: 59). These arguments might have been more persuasive in the 1914 Congress with its Democratic majority, because the Democratic party was overrepresented among southern members of Congress.

The legislative intent of the Harrison Act was fairly clear from the statute itself. It required that persons and firms selling the regulated drugs register with the federal government, pay a small tax, and keep records of all transactions (Lindesmith, 1965: 4).[8] Nothing in the act referred to addicts or addiction (Dickson, 1968: 148). The use of drugs in medical treatment was specifically exempted: "Nothing contained in this section . . . shall . . . apply . . . [t]o the dispensing or distribution of any drugs mentioned . . . to a patient by a physician" (26 U.S.C. 4705c, cited in Dickson, 1968: 148).

Because the Harrison Act was framed as a revenue act, enforcement was assigned to the Treasury Department. A narcotics division was created in the department's Bureau of Internal Revenue to administer the law. Rather than implement a law that was primarily record keeping, the Bureau of Internal Revenue began a systematic effort to expand its powers. The effort took place on three fronts. First, the bureau launched a public relations campaign using government reports and friendly newspaper reporters to paint narcotics as a major threat to society (Dickson, 1968: 149). Their 1919 annual report claimed there were 1 million addicts nationwide and that extensive addiction occurred among children (see Dickson, 1968: 150).[9] This effort conveniently ignored evidence that opium consumption, as well as the use of other narcotics, was declining even before the passage of the Harrison Act (Musto, 1973: 4).

Second, the bureau issued a series of regulations that went far beyond the powers authorized by the Harrison Act. In January of 1915, regulations prohibited consumers from registering under the act, thus requiring that addicts procure their drugs through a physician, pharmacist, or veterinarian (Musto, 1973: 122). On May 11, 1915, regulation TD 2200 required that physicians treating addicts systematically reduce the dosage provided so as to wean the addict from dependence (Trebach, 1982: 133). Although the Treasury Department had no authority to regulate the practice of medicine, in effect it declared drug addict maintenance to be an illegal medical practice under Treasury regulations.

Third, the Bureau of Internal Revenue began a major campaign of arresting physicians and pharmacists who supplied addicts with maintenance dosages. These arrests generated a series of court cases that defined the enforcement authority of the bureau. In *United States* v. *Jin Fuey Moy* (241 U.S. 394, 1916) the U.S. Supreme Court dealt harshly with the bureau's expansion of powers. The court rejected the bureau's arguments that the Harrison Act provided broad police powers that allowed the bureau to prosecute physicians engaged in drug treatment (see Musto, 1973: 129). The court implied that provisions applying to possession would be unconstitutional and, therefore, the act could not apply to mere possession (Bonnie and Whitebread, 1974: 20).

The Treasury Department did not passively accept the Supreme Court's restrictions on its efforts to expand its powers. In annual reports to Congress in 1916, 1917, and 1918, the department requested legislative amendments to the Harrison Act granting such powers (Musto, 1973: 130). Congress declined to act. Rather than abandon their bureaucratic imperialism, the bureau undertook additional enforcement and brought new test cases. In *United States* v. *Doremus* (249 U.S. 86, 1919), a more sympathetic Supreme Court held that the Harrison Act did permit control over the manner in which physicians prescribed narcotics. In a companion case, *Webb et al.* v. *United States* (249 U.S. 96, 1919), the Supreme Court upheld indictments of a physician and a pharmacist for providing drugs to an addict for maintenance purposes. The Supreme Court went so far as to refer to such treatment as a "perversion" of the meaning of the word.[10] With these cases, the Internal Revenue Bureau had legal authority to prosecute physicians and pharmacists who used maintenance as a treatment for addiction.[11]

With renewed powers the Bureau of Internal Revenue (and its successor, the Narcotics Division of the Prohibition Unit) cracked down hard on physicians and pharmacists. In *United States* v. *Behrman* (258 U.S. 280, 1921), the Supreme Court refused to accept the defense that a physician had acted in "good faith."[12] Vigorous law enforcement after this court case seemed to provide few alternatives for physicians who treated addicts except either to adopt gradual withdrawal as a treatment or to get out of the addict treatment business. By implementation, therefore, the Bureau of Internal Revenue had successfully limited the practice of medicine and had been able to brand addicts as criminals under federal law (Clausen, 1977: 27). In 1922 Congress assisted this effort by making possession without a prescription presumptive evidence of concealing illegally imported drugs (Bonnie and Whitebread, 1974: 20).

In *Linder* v. *United States* (268 U.S. 5, 1924), the U.S. Supreme Court reinterpreted the Harrison Act more consistently with the act's original intent. The Court noted that the act did not refer to addicts at all and that nothing in the act permitted the Treasury Department to regulate the good faith practice of medicine. In theory, the *Linder* decision was to remove the Treasury Department from medical regulation and permit physicians to reestablish maintenance forms of drug treatment (Trebach, 1982: 137). In practice, it did not. The Treasury Department simply refused to recognize the court case in its regulations or its enforcement. It continued an all-out campaign against physicians and publicized its arrests and convictions. Arrests under the Harrison Act jumped from 1,700 in 1919 to over 10,000 in 1925 and subsequent years (Walker, 1979: 20; see Table 2.2 below). As a result, the few physicians who still engaged in addict maintenance abandoned the practice (King, 1953: 744).

The federal government also played a role in ending a short-lived experiment with narcotic treatment clinics. These clinics were established in a variety of cities in 1919 to provide outpatient treatment for addicts. The Bureau of Internal Revenue, in fact, proposed in the Treasury Department's annual reports of 1916 and 1917 that such clinics be established. When legal rulings provided authorization for greater enforcement actions, the Treasury Department changed its position and conducted a concerted effort to close these clinics. At least one clinic in Shreveport, Louisiana, appeared to be fairly successful in reducing some of the ill effects of addiction. Federal officials maintained that the clinics were a failure and used this example to oppose similar medical efforts for the next 40 years (see Trebach, 1982; Musto, 1987).

Despite the law enforcement emphasis in the Bureau of Internal Revenue's implementation strategy, the Harrison Act was a revenue act. Often forgotten in the historical analysis of the act is that appreciable revenues were collected. During each year from 1915 to 1918 approximately a quarter of a million dollars in taxes were collected and another $75,000 in fines (see Table 2.1). In 1919 along with other powers, taxes were increased on narcotics. In 1920, tax revenues increased to $1.5 million with over $270,000 in fines. After 1920, tax collections gradually declined when the Bureau of Internal Revenue was able to restrict maintenance treatment for addicts. The revenue provisions of the Harrison Act continued to collect at least half a million dollars a year until 1948, when the Treasury Department ceased to report narcotics taxes as a separate item.

The Treasury Department's implementation strategy established a pattern of drug enforcement that would be repeated several times. In addition to bureaucratic imperialism, the implementation strategy relied on four tactics. First, the department generated a great deal of propaganda to portray the drug problem as more dangerous than it actually was. During the 1920s the Internal Revenue Bureau claimed that the nation had 1 million addicts, with a growing number of addicts among young people (Musto, 1981: 9); studies by the Public Health Service in the mid-1920s estimated that the nation never had more than 250,000 addicts during this time period (see Kolb, 1962). The bureau also distorted the results of its enforcement actions by referring to the total dollar amount of drugs seized; because these estimates used the maximum street price rather than an average, they dramatically overestimated the volume of drugs (King, 1972: 25). Supplementing these "statistics" in annual reports was a series of anecdotes detailing dangerous crimes committed by addicts whom the bureau had subsequently arrested. Second, the bureau shaped its information to show that, al-

Table 2.1

Revenues Collected under the Harrison Act, 1915–45

Year	Fines/penalties	Tax collections	Marijuana Tax Act
1915	NR	250,474	NA
1916	78,865	245,072	NA
1917	67,033	227,165	NA
1918	86,525	185,359	NA
1919	144,930	726,137	NA
1920	273,790	1,513,920	NA
1925	539,999	1,090,932	NA
1930	292,879	588,682	NA
1935	174,732	580,613	NA
1940	226,401	610,098	4,702
1945	131,649	756,019	23,581

Source: U.S. Department of the Treasury, *Annual Report of the Secretary of the Treasury.*
NR = not reported.
NA = not appropriate.

though the drug problem was massive, the bureau was having an impact on it. The prime technique for this was to add together the prison sentences of all individuals convicted of drug violations and announce that bureau actions had resulted in drug users sentenced to 3,600 years in prison.

Third, enforcement of the law was characterized by abusive treatment of citizens and little concern with procedural rights. Massive accusations and arrests were an end in and of themselves. Physicians were specifically targeted. Enforcement of the Harrison Act relied on two types of charges—technical and serious. Technical charges were for failure to register or failure to pay small amounts to the tax. Table 2.2 lists the number of technical violations of the Harrison Act. Compliance with the law was clearly resisted; technical violations rarely dropped below 20,000 per year. In 1927 the Internal Revenue Bureau ceased reporting technical violations in its annual reports.

Serious violations reveal the discretionary nature of Harrison Act enforcement. Treasury agents frequently threatened physicians with arrest; in fact, the technical violations are an example of minor harassment in this regard. If the

Table 2.2

Violations of the Harrison Act, 1915–30

Year	Technical violations	Compromises	Average fines	Serious arrests	Convictions	Percent Wins	Percent Doctors
1915	4,058	NR	NR	1,027	131	NR	10.4
1916	21,249	584	$ 62.48	2,568	663	31.9	25.6
1917	20,996	411	61.72	1,434	445	37.6	41.6
1918	14,701	297	118.06	1,290	392	44.4	31.2
1919	23,595	519	103.84	1,767	582	47.0	43.0
1920	46,663	546	NR	3,277	908	30.7	41.9
1921	37,189	304	NR	4,014	1,583	60.8	32.6
1922	40,055	515	108.04	6,651	3,204	64.7	22.3
1923	29,776	750	64.68	7,201	4,194	61.9	21.8
1924	27,439	758	110.59	7,301	4,242	57.6	22.1
1925	27,535	1,107	NR	10,297	5,600	59.3	29.8
1926	23,506	2,019	71.35	10,207	5,058	56.0	35.3
1927	NR	2,083	50.00	10,342	4,469	51.6	30.9
1928	NR	1,221	55.05	8,851	4,725	53.2	27.1
1929	NR	1,036	58.09	8,833	5,193	54.6	26.0
1930	NR	1,114	51.24	9,266	4,958	51.7	24.0

Source: U.S. Department of the Treasury, *Annual Report of the Secretary of the Treasury*; and author's calculations.
NR = not reported.

physician was charged with a serious violation, agents might have offered to resolve it as a technical violation, or they might have pressured the physican into a "compromise" whereby he or she would pay a small fine and the charges would be dropped. Compromises were not taken to court but rather negotiated by the Bureau of Internal Revenue. From 1916 to 1930, 12,868 cases against registered users (e.g., physicians, dentists, pharmacists, etc.) were compromised while only 3,131 such users were convicted in court. Addicts rarely were given the opportunity of negotiation. During this same time period, 43,216 nonregistered persons (e.g., addicts) were convicted of violations and only 396 were granted compromises (see Table 2.2). Registered persons were the focus of approximately 40 percent of enforcement efforts until the closing of the clinics. After that time, enforcement shifted to target addicts (see Table 2.2).

The arbitrary nature of enforcement is perhaps best illustrated by the lack of good quality cases among the serious violations. If individuals are charged in order that they be coerced into paying fines, then the government's actual winning percentage in court is likely to be fairly low. Table 2.2 shows both the number of arrests for serious cases each year and the number of convictions. Since many of the cases remained pending at the end of a year, these cases were deleted and a percentage of conviction rate was calculated in the table. Not until 1921 was the government able to win over one-half of its Harrison Act cases; after a brief surge, the win percentage dropped back to around 50 percent by the turn of the decade. In comparison, during the 1980s the federal government routinely won over 80 percent of its drug-related cases.

Another indicator of the poor quality of arrests can be found in Table 2.3, which compares the conviction rate for liquor law violations and Harrison Act violations. In five of the seven years, liquor violations had a higher conviction rate than drug law violations. This is especially interesting given the perceived lack of expertise in the Prohibition Unit and in the relative ease of obtaining a conviction. During this time period possession of drugs was a crime (and one fairly easy to prove), whereas possession or consumption of alcohol was not. Under such circumstances, conviction rates for drug offenses should have been significantly higher than for liquor offenses; in fact, they were lower.

Fourth, the massive threatening of arrests plus the lucrative nature of the drug business created the potential for corruption. The first federal narcotics agent was convicted of bribery in 1917 (King, 1972: 22). By the end of the 1920s, a major corruption scandal had rocked the drug enforcement effort (see below).

From a policy perspective, in addition to proscribing one form of medical treatment and using the Harrison Act to prosecute addicts, the Treasury Department's bureaucratic entrepreneurship had three other consequences. First, it had a major impact on the composition of the federal prison population. By 1928 almost one-third of all inmates in federal prisons were imprisoned for Harrison Act violations. The criminalization of drug addiction also had the impact of driving the narcotics business underground, thus generating higher drug prices and the need to commit crimes to support a drug habit.

Second, the Harrison Act and its enforcement also served as an example to state governments. By 1931 every state had passed stronger restrictions on the sale of cocaine, and all but two states had similar laws restricting opiates. Those states with laws predating the Harrison Act responded by sharply increasing penalties (Bonnie and Whitebread, 1970: 1028). Enforcement by state officials,

Table 2.3

Discretion and Morality Law Violations, 1922–28

	Liquor violations		Drug violations	
Year	Arrests	% convicted	Arrests	% convicted
1922	42,223	53.9	6,701	46.7
1923	66,936	50.9	7,201	58.2
1924	68,161	54.5	7,301	58.1
1925	62,747	62.3	10,297	54.4
1926	58,391	70.5	10,342	49.5
1927	64,986	56.2	8,851	50.5
1928	75,307	78.1	8,653	55.8

Source: Schmeckebier, 1929; and author's calculations.

however, was limited; federal arrests appear to have outnumbered total state-level arrests at this time (see Bonnie and Whitebread, 1970: 1029).

Third, the Narcotics Division greatly benefited from its bureaucratic entrepreneurship. The division's budget increased from approximately $300,000 in 1916 to $1.7 million in 1932. Agency employment at the same time grew to 450 persons.[13]

The success of the Internal Revenue Bureau and the Narcotics Division of the Prohibition Unit provided a blueprint for future drug enforcement agencies to follow. Rather than passively administer laws, these agencies could creatively interpret and enforce legislation; this coupled with a well-orchestrated public relations campaign would lead to a growth in agency resources and power. Although this pattern of actions has repeated itself several times in the history of drug politics and policy, agencies have rarely been as successful as the Internal Revenue Bureau and its successor were with the Harrison Act.[14]

The 1920s also saw a major focus on the international side of drug control, with the United States gradually losing its leadership role in the international community. In an effort to control importation of narcotics, the Narcotic Drugs Import and Export Act of 1922 banned the importation of refined narcotics. Only crude narcotics could be imported, with the final refining done by U.S. firms. The logic behind this act was to prevent drugs from being diverted from legal to illegal sources (Musto, 1981: 12).

With the Treasury Department generating information on the continuing problems of drug abuse, these actions were perceived as insufficient. In 1923 Congress passed a resolution that enjoined the president to exert pressure on opium- and coca-producing nations (Brunn, Pan, and Rexed, 1975: 14).[15] In 1924 the importation of opium for the purposes of making heroin was banned. At the second Geneva Convention in 1925 the U.S. delegation failed to effect greater restrictions on the production of drugs and walked out in response. The 1925 walkout, along with the nonparticipation of the United States in the League of Nations, greatly reduced U.S. influence in international drug policy (Brunn, Pan, and Rexed, 1975: 202).

The Marijuana Tax Act of 1937

Problems in international arenas were matched by domestic problems in enforcement. With the advent of Prohibition, the Narcotics Division was established within the Treasury Department's Prohibition Unit to enforce the Harrison Act regulations. When the illegal drug business became profitable, efforts to bribe law enforcement officers occurred. A federal grand jury in New York documented the corruption and the frequent falsification of arrest records by federal agents. From January 1920 to February 1929 a total of 752 drug enforcement agents, fully 28 percent of all agents employed, were dismissed for "collusion, dereliction of duty, submitting false reports, perjury, illegal disposition of liquor, embezzlement, and other charges" (McWilliams, 1990: 34). Of an equally serious nature, Levi G. Nutt, the administrator of the Narcotics Division, was implicated in illegal activity. Nutt's son and his son-in-law both had lucrative business ties with Arnold Rothstein, a known gambler reputed to have dealt in narcotics (Walker, 1979: 68).

This scandal provided the momentum to reorganize the federal drug control effort; the reorganization removed the Narcotics Division from the Prohibition Unit and created the Federal Bureau of Narcotics. Appointed as commissioner of the Federal Bureau of Narcotics (FBN) was Harry J. Anslinger, who would serve in that position until 1962.[16] More than anyone else Anslinger, as a bureaucratic politician, would dominate federal drug policy with his attempts to create a secure policy niche for his agency.

Anslinger's background before becoming commissioner of narcotics provides two clues about how he would handle the job. First, Anslinger supported the enforcement of drug laws against consumers. Entering a national contest in 1928 on how to enforce prohibition, Anslinger argued for reducing smuggling through international agreements and making the use of alcohol a crime so that users as well as sellers could be prosecuted (Musto, 1987: 211). Although the consumption of alcohol was not made a criminal offense, the use of drugs was (see above). Second, Anslinger was a career diplomat who participated in efforts to limit the smuggling of alcohol (Musto, 1981: 13). Anslinger's interest in foreign policy foreshadowed his effort to regain U.S. leadership in international drug control arenas.[17] By 1931 Anslinger had some success in this area; the Geneva Convention of that year (at U.S. urging) provided agreements to police the diversion of drugs from legal sources (Brunn, Pan, and Rexed, 1975: 137).

The affiliation of the FBN's precursors with the Treasury Department's Prohibition Unit had implications for the FBN's future policy initiatives. Prohibition was clearly a failure from a law enforcement standpoint. It created a highly profitable criminal industry, and large portions of the general public not only opposed the law but also refused to obey it. Never was the Prohibition Unit given sufficient resources to enforce the law. The lesson of prohibition to bureaucratic entrepreneurs was that the expansion of agency functions brings a greater risk of failure. This lesson was not lost on Anslinger and the FBN; it was reflected in the FBN's strategy of dealing with marijuana.

The Marijuana Tax Act of 1937 had its origins in the Uniform State Narcotic Drug Act. Marijuana was not covered by the Harrison Act, although regulations under the Pure Food and Drug Act prohibited its importation except for medical purposes (Musto, 1972: 102). Notice of marijuana use began in the South and West when the recreational use of marijuana increased with the influx of Mexican agricultural workers (Musto, 1973; Helmer, 1975).[18] Police in New Orleans in the early 1920s claimed that marijuana use was responsible for a large number of crimes, particularly among the city's black population (Walker, 1979: 100). That racial tension was a concern in adoption of legislation prohibiting nonmedical uses of marijuana is well illustrated by the governments that first adopted such laws.[19] El Paso, Texas, outlawed the use of marijuana in 1914 (Himmelstein, 1983: 23); similar legislation was passed by California in 1915, Texas in 1919, Louisiana in 1924, and New York in 1925, all states with large black or Hispanic populations (Sloman, 1979: 30). Sixteen of the 22 western states, all with some Hispanic population, banned sale or possession of marijuana before 1930 (Bonnie and Whitebread, 1970: 1012).

The Federal Bureau of Narcotics in the 1930s faced an unfavorable political environment. Criticism of the bureau as the result of earlier scandals was common; the election of Franklin Roosevelt, a Democrat committed to ending prohibition, also might have created a hostile environment for an FBN commissioner appointed by a Republican president. In addition, the depression had greatly restricted the bureau's budget when funds were reallocated to more crucial programs. The bureau's budget dropped from $1.7 million in 1932 to $1.0 million in 1934. Within this context, the advocacy of state laws targeted at marijuana use provided the FBN with some opportunities. By participating in the process of drafting and adopting such laws, the FBN could retain hegemony over the drug policy process and at the same time not be burdened with the responsibility for enforcing the laws because enforcement would remain a state function (Himmelstein, 1983: 57). Since the prospects for adequate funding were remote, the bureau rationally sought policy control rather than implementation authority.[20]

Commissioner Anslinger and the bureau assisted in drafting the new Uniform State Narcotic Drug Act in 1931. Although marijuana was not included in the original version of the law owing to opposition from physicians, hemp growers, and pharmaceutical companies, it was included in the final version as the result of FBN efforts (Bonnie and Whitebread, 1974: 83–90; Himmelstein, 1983: 57–58). FBN influence on the model law is perhaps best illustrated by the provision that state and local law officers have a duty to cooperate with federal drug enforcement personnel (King, 1972: 153). FBN support for the Uniform State Narcotic Drug Act initially took the form of offering testimony, lobbying by FBN agents, and enlisting the Women's Christian Temperance Union, the YMCA, the PTA, and other organizations to support the legislation (Bonnie and Whitebread, 1974: 95; Goldman, 1979: 91). When such indirect efforts resulted in only 10 states adopting the act by the end of 1934, Anslinger and the bureau changed tactics.

In 1935 the Federal Bureau of Narcotics made a concerted effort to influence public opinion by publicizing the "marijuana menace" (Himmelstein, 1983: 58). By using horror stories collected in bureau files, Anslinger attempted to "educate" legislators about the dangers posed by marijuana. Marijuana was portrayed as an addicting drug that led to insanity and violent crime (often on the part of blacks and Hispanics; see McWilliams, 1990: 52). The bureau claimed that "fifty percent of the violent crimes in districts occupied by Mexicans, Spaniards, Latin-Americans, Greeks, or Negroes may be traced to this evil" (quoted in Bonnie and Whitebread, 1974: 100).[21] Anslinger's efforts to portray marijuana as a major cause of crime paid off in the popular press. Becker (1963: 142) in an analysis of marijuana literature from 1937 to 1939, found 17 articles; 10 specifically acknowledged the help of the bureau in furnishing facts and figures. Several other articles also appear to have been influenced by the bureau, because many of the same anecdotes were used. In a more extensive analysis, Himmelstein (1983: 69) contends that 16 of the 22 marijuana articles published from 1935 to 1940 were influenced by the FBN point of view. And propaganda efforts were not limited to print media; the 1936 movie *Reefer Madness* presented a similarly misleading portrayal of marijuana (Goldman, 1979: 90).

Dickson (1968: 147) argues that the Federal Bureau of Narcotics' effort was successful because the public's attitudes toward marijuana were weakly held. By tying marijuana to the evils of narcotics, the bureau painted a picture of marijuana as far more dangerous than it was, claiming that the drug was the "assassin of youth" (Anslinger with Cooper, 1937). Stories of young people committing vicious crimes under the influence of marijuana could not help but persuade legislators to support the Uniform State law, especially given its endorsement by federal drug regulators. As with all good propaganda, the picture was one-sided. Ignored in the bureau's effort were studies by the Indian Hemp Commission in 1894, the U.S. Canal Zone Committee in 1926 and 1933, and Walter Bromberg's (1934) assessment of marijuana and crime. All these studies challenged the linkage between marijuana and crime (see Himmelstein, 1983: 70).

Commissioner Anslinger's propaganda campaign was a major success. By 1936 all 48 states had adopted legislation governing the sale or possession of marijuana (Dickson, 1968: 154). All but two had adopted the harsh provisions of the Uniform State Narcotic Drug Act (Grinspoon and Bakalar, 1985: 42). The bureau was in an enviable position; it had achieved policy control over marijuana yet would not be burdened with enforcement responsibilities.[22]

Unfortunately for the bureau, its highly successful public relations campaign not only alerted people to the need for state laws, but also convinced them that the danger was so great that a federal law was necessary as well. The bureau opposed the passage of federal legislation; as late as January of 1937, Anslinger stated that marijuana was an intrastate problem and that states were well equipped to handle it (Musto, 1972: 105; Sloman, 1979: 80). The perceived danger of marijuana, however, was so great that Anslinger's position was over-ruled by others in the Treasury Department.

Herman Oliphant, general counsel for the Treasury Department, is credited with the idea of using the federal taxing power to restrict the consumption of mari-juana (Walker, 1979: 103). The Supreme Court had recently upheld a federal law using taxation to control the interstate spread of gangster weapons. Danger-ous drugs seemed analogous to dangerous weapons. The specific proposal was to tax the transfer of marijuana at $1.00 per ounce for registered persons (e.g., physicians) and $100.00 per ounce for unregistered persons.[23] Tax evasion charges could result in fines of up to $2,000 or imprisonment for up to five years.

After losing the internal Treasury Department battle to seek a new law, Com-missioner Anslinger became a team player and used his political skills to secure passage of the proposed legislation. The Treasury Department presented a solid front by making sure only supporters of the legislation appeared at congressional hearings. The absence of the Public Health Service, despite its expertise in drug abuse, was especially noticeable (Musto, 1973: 225). The star of the hearings was Commissioner Anslinger, who repeated his horror stories linking marijuana use to insanity, murder, suicide, and child abuse (Goldman, 1979: 88–89; Slo-man, 1979: 62). Especially stressed was the impact of marijuana on impression-able youth, turning obedient children into ruthless killers (Himmelstein, 1983: 65). Anslinger was a stunning success; the one nonsupporting witness was treated with skepticism; and the Marijuana Tax Act of 1937 was passed with little debate.[24]

In his analysis of federal marijuana policy, Himmelstein (1983) correctly argues that Anslinger and the Federal Bureau of Narcotics were the victims of their own aggressive advocacy of state marijuana laws. Passage of the Marijuana Tax Act was an unintended consequence of the public pressure Anslinger had generated for new state laws. Commissioner Anslinger consistently resisted fed-eral legislation within the Treasury Department. Only after the decision was made to "tax" marijuana did Anslinger become an enthusiastic advocate of a larger federal role.[25] The passage of the act, however, had the potential to create major problems for the bureau. Because the marijuana crisis was manufactured by the bureau, action had to be taken so that the bureau would not be blamed for the policy's failure.

The Federal Bureau of Narcotics' post-1937 strategy was designed to retain FBN control over drug policy yet position the bureau so that it would not be blamed for potential failures of the federal law. This strategy had three aspects— toning down the marijuana public relations campaign, trying to remain the sole source of reliable information on marijuana, and implementing the tax act. Each of these aspects was designed to provide an environment where the FBN would survive and perhaps flourish.

Because continued publicity about the evils of marijuana would suggest that the Federal Bureau of Narcotics had failed to eliminate the problem, after 1937 the bureau avoided the scare tactics that worked so successfully in gaining legislation. One particular concern was the rise of the "marijuana defense" with criminal defendants pleading not guilty to crimes as a result of marijuana-induced insanity (Sloman, 1979: 111). The FBN reacted quickly to reduce the salience of marijuana as an issue. FBN annual reports from 1937 to 1940 no longer exaggerated the threat of marijuana; rather, marijuana was presented as a serious problem that was being brought under control (Himmelstein, 1983: 77). FBN opposition was instrumental in withdrawing a "Killer Drug Marijuana" poster marketed in Chicago (Musto, 1972: 107) and in discouraging religious campaigns against the drug (Sloman, 1979: 106).

While the Federal Bureau of Narcotics de-emphasized the threat of marijuana, it continued to portray the drug as dangerous and challenged opinions to the contrary. Perhaps the best illustration of this tactic was the response to the LaGuardia Commission. Fiorello LaGuardia, mayor of New York, commissioned the New York Academy of Medicine to under take a sociological and scientific study of marijuana use. One article from this study was published in the *American Journal of Psychiatry* in 1942 (Allentuck and Bowman, 1942); this article and the final report released in 1945 challenged the view that marijuana is addictive or causes violence. Anslinger criticized the 1942 article as flawed and unscientific. Federal government pressure, in fact, might have been the reason the LaGuardia report was not released for three years after its completion (Walker, 1979: 114).

When the final report of the LaGuardia Commission was released in 1945, the editors of the *Journal of the American Medical Association,* who had supported the earlier findings published in 1942, reversed their support for that work. An editorial attacked the study as unscientific. Historians Richard Bonnie and Charles Whitebread (1974: 201) contend that this editorial was written by Commissioner Anslinger himself. Although the editorial made several incorrect statements about the study and its findings, it did serve to discredit the research in the eyes of the policy community (Himmelstein, 1983: 82). In a similar vein, Anslinger was able to convince Dr. Ernest Fullerton Cook, the chairman of the Commission on Revision of the *United States Pharmacopeia*, to remove marijuana from the *Pharmacopeia* in 1941 (Hamowy, 1987a: 24). This removal ended the use of marijuana as a medical treatment and halted any reason for medical research on marijuana.

Finally, the Federal Bureau of Narcotics implemented the Marijuana Tax Act in a manner designed to continue the bureau's hegemony over drug policy. The act did not ban either commercial or private use of marijuana; it merely made transfer subject to a tax, albeit a prohibitive tax for nonphysicians. The FBN, however, issued regulations in the spirit of the Harrison Act regulations. The rules for physician compliance with the law were incredibly complex, requiring a great deal of documentation and supervision by law enforcement officers. Not only did these regulations serve to restrict the use of marijuana, but they also hamstrung any medical research that might have challenged the FBN's portrayal of marijuana (Schaller, 1973: 220). The FBN then enthusiastically enforced these laws; in 1941, 39.8 percent of federal drug prosecutions involved marijuana (see Table 2.4). During the early 1950s over one-half of federal drug cases involved marijuana.[26]

The Federal Bureau of Narcotics' post-1937 strategy was successful in controlling the marijuana issue and drug policy in general until the 1960s. Although the FBN gained policy dominance, this should not be taken to imply that the agency became one of the predominant bureaucratic powers of the federal government. It did not. The bureau was unsuccessful in expanding its budget. In 1944 the FBN budget ($1.33 million), in fact, was about one-third less than it had been in 1932; in actual purchasing power, the budget had dropped by 46 percent. The number of personnel also dropped from 452 to 320 over this time period. The bureau also resisted any efforts to expand its role outside that of influencing overall policy (see below).

The Period of FBN Hegemony, 1937–62

After the passage of the Marijuana Tax Act in 1937, the predominance of the Federal Bureau of Narcotics remained unchallenged for 25 years within the narrow policy sphere it had defined. In 1942 the Opium Poppy Act regulated the legal cultivation of opium poppies in the United States for commercial purposes. During World War II smuggling patterns were disrupted, and domestic consumption declined. The end of the war brought renewed smuggling, and the return of U.S. soldiers provided potential customers (Musto, 1973: 230).

Capitalizing on the perceived change in drug flows, Commissioner Anslinger began a quest for new legislation. Bureau publicity claimed a major increase in the number of drug addicts, including a large number of young people (King, 1972: 109). Race played a role in this effort, with the bureau reporting an increase in drug addiction by blacks and Puerto Ricans in many northern cities (Musto, 1973: 230). Nationwide at this time, FBI data (Federal Bureau of Inves-

Table 2.4

Federal Drug Prosecutions after the Marijuana Tax Act, 1938–90

Year	All drug violations	Marijuana violations	% marijuana
1938	3,820	846	22.1
1939	3,742	1,062	28.4
1940	3,906	871	22.3
1941	2,790	1,111	39.8
1942	2,199	1,159	52.7
1943	3,398	776	22.8
1944	3,230	902	27.9
1945	1,413	603	42.7
1950	2,400	1,752	73.0
1955	2,166	896	41.4
1960	1,846	556	30.1
1965	2,078	523	25.2
1970	3,420	2,082	60.9
1975	10,901	3,852	35.3
1980	6,393	1,690	26.4
1985	11,208	3,894	34.7
1990	19,271	5,139	26.7

Source: Administrative Office of the U.S. Courts, *Annual Report.*

tigation, 1951) showed that about one-half of the persons arrested for drug violations were black. The reason for the growth in drug use, according to Anslinger, was soft judges who refused to punish drug users. The solution was harsh minimum sentences for drug offenses (Kolb, 1962: 110). Anslinger was able to claim that harsh minimum sentencing was supported by both the old League of Nations and the United Nations; this support was in part the result of Anslinger's successful activities in international arenas.[27]

By linking narcotics trafficking to the new communist government in China, the bureau was able to take advantage of the McCarthy-era red scare to increase drug crime penalties at the federal level (Sloman, 1979: 188; Musto, 1973: 231).[28] The Boggs Act of 1951 provided uniform penalties for violations of the Narcotic Drugs Import and Export Act and the Marijuana Tax Act. The minimum sentence for the first offense was 2 years; for the second offense, 5 years; and for the third, 10 years (Sloman, 1979: 189).[29] As part of the negotiations over the Boggs Act, the Federal Bureau of Narcotics was offered legal control over barbiturates. Consistent with past efforts to avoid expansion of responsibility, Anslinger declined this power, contending that barbiturates were not a problem. As a result, the Food and Drug Administration was left to regulate barbiturates through its regulation of prescription drugs; this assignment left a gap in the federal narcotics laws, given the limited law enforcement capacity of the Food and Drug Administration (Bakalar and Grinspoon, 1985: 96).

Encouraged by the Federal Bureau of Narcotics, state legislatures also increased penalties commensurate with the federal increases. Seventeen states passed "little Boggs acts" within two years of the federal law; 11 more did so by 1956 (Bonnie and Whitebread, 1970: 1074).

Commissioner Anslinger was also a key witness in the Kefauver hearings on organized crime that preceded the Boggs Act. FBN agent George White was loaned to the Kefauver committee and in this role greatly influenced the evidence presented. Both in testimony and in a book published in 1954 (Anslinger and Thomkins, 1953), Anslinger argued again that the People's Republic of China was the major source of narcotics in this country, thus linking domestic drug problems to the international communist menace (Woodiwiss, 1988: 109–111). Anslinger's contention was clearly a distortion. Within a year of achieving power in 1949, the People's Republic of China began a major campaign against opium use in China. Using harsh methods of punishment and control going well beyond what would be permitted in the United States, China eliminated its domestic problem by 1953 (Lowinger, 1981: 616). The reduction of Chinese opium production, in fact, disrupted the worldwide markets in opium during the 1950s, a disruption already evident when Anslinger published his book (Simmons and Said, 1974a: 21). In fact, during World War II and the Chinese civil war, evidence suggests that the Nationalist Chinese, not the Communists, used the drug trade to finance their efforts (Simmons and Said, 1974a: 5; McCoy, 1974: 115).[30]

A second effort to increase narcotics penalties occurred in 1956. Senator Price Daniel held hearings on drug problems, particularly the linkage between drugs and crime. The drugs–crime linkage appears frequently in the policy history of drug control. Such a linkage exists, although it is generally more complex than is portrayed. Anslinger in particular often alleged a direct linkage; that is, a person will consume drugs, and the drugs will cause him or her to commit some serious crime. Some drugs do have a direct linkage to crime; the research literature has clearly established such a link for alcohol and a reasonable link for cocaine and barbiturates (Anglin, 1983: 639; Fagan, 1990: 243). Because both marijuana and opium act as sedatives, their direct association with crime is rare (Chaiken and Chaiken, 1990).

An indirect linkage between crime and drug use, however, clearly exists. Drug users frequently engage in crime to finance their drug habits, particularly drug habits involving expensive drugs such as heroin and cocaine (Anglin, 1983: 641). This indirect linkage exists, not because taking drugs causes crime, but rather because laws making drugs illegal greatly increase their price. Not all users finance their habits with street crime; some are employed and others sell drugs.

The second theme of the Daniel hearings was the explosion in the number of users. Anslinger contended that drug addiction was contagious, that addicts encouraged others to take drugs; he often stated that one drug addict will create four more.[31] Although such a relationship was disputed by experts in the treatment field (see Kolb, 1962: 164), Anslinger was treated as credible by the Daniel committee. Anslinger's control over information was such that he could contend without challenge at this time that he had a list containing the names of every active drug user in the United States (King, 1972: 122).

Convinced that the drug problem was serious, the Daniel committee discussed some radical enforcement policies. The committee considered eliminating constitutional restrictions on the FBN in regard to search and seizure limits, authorizing the FBN to tap telephones, permitting FBN agents to arrest individuals without warrants, and authorizing higher bail for individuals arrested for drug offenses. The Narcotics Control Act of 1956 did not authorize such actions, but it did significantly increase penalties for drug violations. The 1956 act also required drug users to register with the immigration authorities on entering or leaving the country (Bonnie and Whitebread, 1970: 1078). Marijuana was treated no differently from narcotic drugs; federal law not only included tough minimum sentences but also prohibited probation or parole (Himmelstein, 1983: 90).

State governments, with federal encouragement, also increased drug penalties under state law (see Bonnie and Whitebread, 1970: 1074). Ohio, for example, increased the penalty for possession to 2–15 years for the first offense, 5–20 for the second, and 10–30 for the third (King, 1972: 154). Approximately one-fourth of the states went so far as to declare that drug addiction (not use, but addiction) was illegal. These drug addiction laws were later declared a violation of the Eighth Amendment to the Constitution, which prohibited cruel and unusual punishments (see *Robinson* v. *California,* 370 U.S. 660, 1960).[32]

Enforcement of the Narcotics Control Act of 1956 (also called the Boggs–Daniel Act) proceeded as if the law granted the Federal Bureau of Narcotics the proposed authority to override constitutional restrictions. Selective enforcement against prominent individuals was common; entrapment, violation of Fourth

Amendment restrictions on searches and seizures, and harsh penalties applied to minorities were documented in court cases (Kolb, 1962: 156–158; McWilliams, 1990: 121). The passage of state laws patterned after the Boggs Act of 1951 and the Narcotics Control Act of 1956 provided federal narcotics agents an interesting option. Federal agents could turn evidence and arrested individuals over to state courts for prosecution. The advantage of this action was that the U.S. Supreme Court had not yet applied many of the constitutional protections regarding search and seizure, confessions, right to counsel, and entrapment to the state courts (King, 1972: 155). As one legal historian of drug policy notes, "A disproportionate number of the worst Constitutional abuses have always arisen in narcotics cases, and the Anslinger forces were always prominent among the protesters" (King, 1972: 155).

Any efforts to suggest that such harsh penalties were unnecessary were strongly opposed by Commissioner Anslinger and the Federal Bureau of Narcotics. A joint study of narcotics by the American Bar Association and the American Medical Association in the mid-1950s was critical of the punishment approach and suggested the potential of drug clinics that relied on maintenance dosages and eventual rehabilitation (Musto, 1973: 232). The Federal Bureau of Narcotics responded with a vigorous attack and grouped the nation's physicians and attorneys with the other "crackpots" who sought more lenient treatment for drug abusers.

Not content to criticize the ABA–AMA report, the FBN undertook an effort to restrict access to it. The study commission had been promised funds for publication by the Russell Sage Foundation. After a visit by Treasury agents (employed by the department which oversees the tax status of foundations), the Sage Foundation decided not to provide funds (King, 1972: 170). The Federal Bureau of Narcotics printed a rebuttal to the ABA–AMA report; the rebuttal was made to resemble the report physically and, in fact, was often mistaken for the original ABA–AMA report. This misperception was especially a problem when the ABA and AMA quickly ran out of copies but the FBN did not (King, 1972: 171).

The FBN's attempt to control policy information in regard to the ABA–AMA report was not unique. In 1958 a National Institutes of Health symposium was highly critical of the law enforcement approach to drug abuse; FBN intervention in the federal bureaucracy prevented the subsequent printing of the symposium. A similar effort was taken against sociologist Alfred Lindesmith, a frequent critic of the Federal Bureau of Narcotics. Treasury agents on at least two occasions visited administrators on Lindesmith's campus (Indiana University) in an effort to limit Lindesmith's activities (King, 1972).

The FBN derived some financial benefits from its association with the Cold War. The bureau's budget increased from $1.6 million in 1950 to $4.0 million in 1959 (employment increased by 50 percent during the same time), and it was able to control the flow of information on drug policy. The bureau later manipulated its own data to show that the number of drug users was dropping, an impact attributed to the tough new laws passed by Congress (see Woodiwiss, 1988: 137).

Commissioner Anslinger's domestic successes were matched by his successes in international activities. As one analysis of comparative drug laws has noted, drug laws are fairly uniform in content (though not in punishments) from nation to nation as a result of U.S. influence on multilateral agreements (Bakalar and Grinspoon, 1985: 68). The peak of U.S. influence was reached in 1961 with the adoption of the Single Convention on Narcotics. The Single Convention attempted a comprehensive effort to control the traffic in all illicit drugs. The convention placed drugs in different classes, with stronger controls imposed on drugs perceived to be the most dangerous. One reflection of the influence of Harry Anslinger (the U.S. representative to the Single Convention) was the placement of marijuana with heroin in the most dangerous class (Chayet, 1972: 532; Brunn, Pan, and Rexed, 1975: 201).

The Decline of the Federal Bureau of Narcotics

The Federal Bureau of Narcotics made an effort to maintain a monopoly on information relevant to drug policy, but it was eventually bound to be challenged. The FBN played no role in treatment, considering drug abuse a law enforcement problem rather than a health problem. Government agencies involved in treating addicts interpreted drug abuse as a disease that required health measures rather than punishment. Federal drug treatment clinics trained personnel, who saw firsthand how unsuccessfully the punishment approach to drug addiction worked. Eventually these mental health professionals became an alternative source of information in the drug policy debates (Musto, 1973: 235).

President John F. Kennedy provided a forum for these debates with the White House Conference on Drug Abuse and a study group, the Commission on Narcotic and Drug Abuse. President Kennedy sponsored the White House conference for political reasons according to Rufus King (1972). Richard Nixon, in 1962, was still perceived as the likely Republican nominee in 1964. In his 1962 campaign for governor of California, Nixon painted incumbent governor Edmund G. Brown as soft on drugs and crime. To provide Brown with a national forum to demonstrate his opposition to drugs, the White House Conference on Drug Abuse was scheduled with Brown as a featured speaker (King, 1972: 232; see also Woodiwiss, 1988: 165–166).

The president's Commission on Narcotic and Drug Abuse issued its final report in 1963, and the report reflected the inability of the Federal Bureau of Narcotics to control policy information. The report recommended the relaxation of minimum mandatory sentences, increased appropriations for research on drug abuse, and increased funding for drug treatment (Musto, 1973: 238). The report was critical of grouping marijuana with narcotics and suggested that the drug be treated differently because it was nonaddictive (Himmelstein, 1983: 90). The triumph of health care professionals was perhaps best illustrated by the recommendation that the Federal Bureau of Narcotics be abolished and its functions transferred to the Department of Justice and the Department of Health, Education, and Welfare (Musto, 1973: 238–239). In 1966, an amendment to federal drug laws permitted marijuana violators to be paroled. Although this was a minor change in policy, it was a harbinger of future changes.

The fight of mental health professionals to redefine drug abuse as a health problem was greatly aided by the rise of marijuana as a political issue in the 1960s. Marijuana, with its ties to the counterculture and to opposition to the Vietnam War, became a symbol for the political differences between generations. Table 2.5 shows the rapid rise of marijuana as a salient issue; from 1959 to 1966 only 4 articles were published on marijuana in the periodical literature; in 1967 alone, 27 articles appeared. Initially the public response to marijuana was greater law enforcement. From 1965 to 1974 arrests for marijuana violations increased nationwide from 18,800 to 445,600 (Federal Bureau of Investigation, 1975). Massive arrests threatened not only minorities and lower-class users but also a great many middle-class sons and daughters. Table 2.6 shows this change in the racial distribution of drug arrests. Racial changes in drug arrests for minors were even more striking; in 1970, 87.5 percent of those under age 18 arrested for drug violations were white (Federal Bureau of Investigation, 1971). The criminal stigma attached to individuals who were not generally perceived in those terms created pressure to change public policies (see Rosenthal, 1977; Himmelstein, 1983; Grinspoon, 1971: 348).

The initial successes of the drug reform movement were at the state level. In 1968 Alaska, California, and Vermont reduced penalties for possession of marijuana (Rosenthal, 1977: 62). By the end of 1970, 32 states had reassessed their marijuana laws and reduced the penalties for possession. The federal government continued to influence state drug policy even as the policy trend turned to the relaxation of penalties. In 1970 Congress repealed virtually all prior drug legislation, including the Harrison Act and the Marijuana Tax Act, replacing them with the Comprehensive Drug Abuse Prevention and Control Act. The law attempted to live up to its name, covering stimulants, depressants, barbiturates, and hallucinogens, as well as narcotics. The law reduced possession of any controlled drug to a misdemeanor for the first offense with a maximum penalty of one year in jail and/or a $5,000 fine (Rosenthal, 1977: 63). Other federal penalties for trafficking and distribution were also reduced. Federal narcotics officials initially opposed these changes by repeating many of the arguments that had worked so well since the 1930s; but without the leadership of Anslinger (who was forced to retire in 1962) and with a broad-based coalition favoring reform, this opposition was overwhelmed (Himmelstein, 1983: 103). By the time legislation had passed, federal narcotics officials were reluctant supporters of lessened penalties (Himmelstein, 1983: 104).

Table 2.5

The Rise in Salience of Marijuana: Number of Magazine Articles per Year, 1959–75

Year	Number of articles
1959	0
1960	0
1961	0
1962	0
1963	1
1964	0
1965	2
1966	1
1967	27
1968	31
1969	41
1970	41
1971	46
1972	26
1973	11
1974	20
1975	21

Source: Reader's Guide to Periodical Literature (annual).

The federal Comprehensive Drug Abuse Prevention and Control Act stimulated additional state efforts to reduce drug penalties.[33] By 1977 over 40 states enacted drug control legislation modeled after the federal act or a similar proposed uniform state law (Rosenthal, 1977: 63). The federal law also created the National Commission on Marijuana and Drug Abuse to study existing marijuana laws.[34] Its report, *Marijuana: A Signal of Misunderstanding,* evaluated the existing knowledge concerning the potential harms of marijuana. The report stressed the symbolic nature of marijuana as a political issue, linking it to the rejection of certain values in society (Nahas, 1973: 41). While the report rejected legalizing

Table 2.6

Racial Distributions in Drug Arrests, 1950–90

Year	Total	% white	% black
1950	8,539	46.1	49.9
1960	16,370	52.0	46.2
1970	415,600	77.8	21.0
1980	580,900	75.6	23.6
1990	1,089,500	58.5	40.7

Source: Federal Bureau of Investigation, *Uniform Crime Reports* (annual).

marijuana, it supported only "partial prohibition," a policy that would decriminalize the possession of small amounts of marijuana (Rosenthal, 1977: 64). At the national level, the National Commission's report found an unsympathetic audience. President Richard Nixon rejected the report and proceeded with his national war on drugs.

The National Commission's report, however, had a major influence on state governments. In 1973 Oregon decriminalized the possession of marijuana. The decriminalization movement, spearheaded by the National Organization for the Reform of Marijuana Laws (NORML), was intense and short lived.[35] By 1978 and the adoption of the Nebraska law, it was over. A total of 11 states, also including Alaska, California, Colorado, Maine, Minnesota, Mississippi, New York, North Carolina, and Ohio passed decriminalization statutes. These states contained one-third of the nation's population. Many other states further reduced penalties for possession, cultivation, or sale of marijuana but did not go so far as to decriminalize its use. At its peak, decriminalization was supported by 60 percent of the population in a 1978 Gallup poll and endorsed by President Jimmy Carter in 1977 (Goldman, 1979: 5).

At the federal level, attention ostensibly shifted from marijuana to narcotics. President Richard Nixon, as part of his crime control effort, declared in 1969 that drug abuse was the most important problem facing the United States. The propaganda tactics previously used by law enforcement agencies were adopted by the White House. Estimates of the number of heroin addicts increased from 69,000 in 1969, to 322,000 in 1970, to 560,000 in 1971, even though all three estimates were based on figures from a single study done in 1969 (Woodiwiss, 1988: 171). The impact of drug use on violent crime was also exaggerated. A reanalysis of the White House data found that the number of thefts the White House associated with drugs in New York City was 10 times the total number of thefts that actually occurred (Singer, 1971: 9).

On the basis of the threat to the nation's safety, President Nixon declared a war on heroin and supported large increases in federal law enforcement agency budgets (Goldman, 1979: 91). Again the threat to white middle-class youth was used to generate support for drug programs. Nixon portrayed heroin abuse as radiating out from the cities and threatening to invade the suburbs (Bellis, 1981: 23). Election returns were a prime consideration in this effort; as presidential advisor John Erlichman noted, "Narcotics repression is a sexy political issue" (quoted in Bellis, 1981: 23).

The Nixon administration presided over a series of high-profile drug operations. Operation Intercept in 1969 attempted to seal off the U.S.-Mexican border for a week; the action raised massive protests by both Americans and Mexicans residing along the border (Goldman, 1979: 99). Only a small amount of marijuana was discovered by Operation Intercept, and the effort was canceled. Operation Buccaneer succeeded in reducing the marijuana traffic from Jamaica (Goldman, 1979: 101–109). The "Heroin Hotline" generated 33,000 calls in three months; unfortunately few calls led to any drugs. Expenditures of $260,000 on the Heroin Hotline netted only a few dollars worth of heroin.

Foreign policy efforts were a key part of the heroin drug war. Turkey was paid to destroy its opium poppy crop (Bellis, 1981: 71). The result was some minor shortages on the East Coast and the stimulation of opium production in Mexico to meet the demand. In 1974, Turkey lifted its ban on growing opium poppies. In Mexico a controversial effort to control opium and marijuana involved use of the pesticide paraquat (Woodiwiss, 1988: 172).[36] The dangers from ingesting paraquat while smoking marijuana were conceded to be greater than the dangers of marijuana itself.

Other foreign policy tools were also used. The Foreign Assistance Act was amended to permit the president to suspend U.S. aid to countries that traffic in illegal drugs (Quinn, 1974: 51). Passage of this legislation was greatly aided by conservative members of Congress, who charged once again that the People's Republic of China was the major source of drugs coming to the United States. Despite the announced policy, pressures on drug control were clearly subservient to other foreign policy concerns. During this time period the United States maintained a variety of alliances in Southeast Asia with anticommunist drug traffickers, and some evidence exists that the Central Intelligence Agency acquiesced, if it did not actively participate, in the drug trade (McCoy, 1972: 360; 1974: 115; Bellis, 1981: 80).

These and other high-profile efforts, particularly those based on domestic law enforcement, were doomed to failure, however, for bureaucratic reasons. Although the Federal Bureau of Narcotics and its successor, the Federal Bureau of Narcotics and Dangerous Drugs (created in 1968), maintained policy control over drug issues for an extended period of time, they never were particularly effective agencies. The Bureau of Narcotics and Dangerous Drugs initially used the increased funding to improve the quality rather than the quantity of their arrests (Woodiwiss, 1988: 173). Displeased with this low-profile approach, Nixon created the Office of Drug Abuse Law Enforcement (ODALE), which organized crime strike forces to provide high-profile drug arrests.[37] ODALE's creation during an election year (1970) was probably not a coincidence (Musto, 1987: 257). Using "no-knock" provisions then existing in federal law, ODALE strike forces waged a reign of terror; ODALE was implicated in widespread violations of citizens' rights, beatings, terrorism of innocent persons, and even murder (see Woodiwiss, 1988: 174–175).

The Bureau of Narcotics and Dangerous Drugs fared no better. Congressional hearings in 1975 documented corruption in the agency and a lack of trust by local law enforcement agencies (Goldman, 1979: 94). In 1970 one-half of all federal drug agents in New York City were fired or indicted for corruption (Kaplan, 1983: 641; McWilliams, 1990: 184). In response to the lack of success early in his administration, President Nixon consolidated all federal drug control efforts (the Federal Bureau of Narcotics and Dangerous Drugs, ODALE, and the drug units of the Customs Service) into the Drug Enforcement Administration (DEA) of the Department of Justice in 1973 (Rachal, 1982: 53). The president also created the Law Enforcement Assistance Administration to funnel federal funds to local police departments (Bellis, 1981: 31). The input side of the drug war was a success. In 1974 federal drug abuse expenditures were 10 times the size of federal expenditures in 1969.[38]

The output side of the drug war, however, was a failure. The Drug Enforcement Administration proved no more competent than the Bureau of Narcotics and Dangerous Drugs. Heavy media criticism followed DEA's mistakes and errors, including unauthorized entry, harassment of innocent citizens, the luring of narcotics suspects into sex traps, and the compiling of a catalogue of assassination devices (Bellis, 1981: 180). Nor was the DEA immune to corruption and political abuse.[39] Watergate-like problems were revealed in 1976 congressional hearings, when agents testified that drug smuggling investigations which led to Robert Vesco (a well-known political contributor to Richard Nixon's campaigns) were called off by superiors in the agency (Goldman, 1979: 97). Arrests designed to harass political opponents were also documented (see Woodiwiss, 1988: 176).

Abuse of citizens was perhaps the most common charge levied at the Nixon drug effort. Hellman (1975: 107) examined a variety of public court documents to establish that drug enforcement agencies frequently used trickery to gain access to houses to search for drugs. Exceptions to search and seizure restrictions were often claimed as a result of drugs being "in plain sight" or "abandoned" by the suspect (Hellman, 1975: 113–118). Abandonment usually meant that the suspect dropped drugs on the ground when a police officer approached. New York State judge Irving Younger, noting the frequency of fumbles among drug suspects, concluded, "Surely not in *every* case was the defendant unlucky enough to drop his narcotics at the feet of a policeman. It follows that at least in some of these cases the police are lying" (quoted in Hellman, 1975: 152).

The abuse of citizens resulted in poor quality arrests. A study of six cities in the early 1970s showed that only 14 percent of individuals arrested for drug violations went to jail; most cases were dropped by prosecuting attorneys for lack of good evidence (Johnson and Bogomolny, 1973). A New York City study of the same time period found that 70 percent of misdemeanor and 33 percent of felony drug cases that were taken to court were dismissed by the courts because of faulty police procedures (Cooper, 1973).

Despite the public emphasis on heroin and the decriminalization of marijuana at the state level, marijuana bore the brunt of the Nixon drug wars. Statistics from the Federal Bureau of Investigation's *Uniform Crime Reports* show that only 14,327 persons (about one-third of all drug arrests) were arrested for marijuana offenses in 1965. By 1974, the number of marijuana arrests had skyrocketed to 445,600 (increasing to 69 percent of all drug arrests; see Federal Bureau of Investigation, 1975; 1966). The flood of arrests coupled with the harsh sentences permitted in some states (e.g., 700 persons in Texas were serving penalties of 10 or more years for marijuana possession) had a significant impact on the decriminalization movement as noted above.

The brief presidency of Gerald Ford had little lasting influence on drug abuse policy. No significant legislation was passed. Ford administration policy was generally to admit that law enforcement had a limited impact on drug abuse and to downplay the issue (Musto, 1987: 263). In particular, marijuana enforcement was de-emphasized by the president, although not by state and local governments, which had most of the enforcement responsibility. Approximately 70 percent of all state drug arrests from 1974 to 1976 were for marijuana (Federal Bureau of Investigation, 1977).

President Jimmy Carter initially tried to continue the effort to liberalize drug laws. Administration witnesses, including those for law enforcement agencies, testified before Congress in 1977, supporting the federal decriminalization of marijuana (Musto, 1987: 266). The movement to liberalize marijuana laws ran out of steam, a casualty of the election of conservative politicians and the perception of a growing conservative trend in the electorate (Himmelstein, 1983: 5). President Carter had little impact on drug policies as a result of his single term, a series of crises in foreign policy, and a drug-related political scandal.[40] The scandal involved Dr. Peter Bourne, President Carter's appointee to head the White House Office of Drug Abuse Policy. Bourne was an advocate of treatment-based strategies and decriminalization of drugs (including heroin). Bourne was discredited and resigned after evidence surfaced that he supplied prescriptions under false names to White House staff members and might have used illicit drugs himself (see Bellis, 1981: 84).[41] Keith Stroup, president of NORML, leaked information to the *Washington Post* that Bourne had snorted cocaine at a NORML-sponsored party (Anderson, 1981: 7; Musto, 1987: 269). The leak was perceived to be in retribution for continued use of paraquat to spray marijuana crops. The resignation of Bourne played a major role in the resurgence of law enforcement agencies. Bourne, using his close ties to President Carter and his expertise in drug abuse, was able to maintain control over drug policies while he was in the White House. After he left, however, law enforcement agencies returned to their earlier positions (Musto, 1987).[42]

"Just Say No": The Reagan War on Drugs

In the 1980 presidential election, Ronald Reagan defeated Jimmy Carter. The change in political leaders set the stage for the Reagan war on drugs and a return to the policies of grouping distributors and users together in punitive-oriented policies. By 1980 both the political environment and the bureaucratic environment for drug policy had changed substantially. In political terms, it was clear that drug abuse was a useful electoral issue; being soft on drugs became equivalent to being soft on communism as a major electoral charge. Drug abuse became a partisan issue, with Republicans favoring greater law enforcement and Democrats advocating greater treatment and education.

Bureaucratically the situation had changed even more. The 1973 report of the National Commission on Marijuana and Drug Abuse warned that America had developed a drug-abuse industrial complex. The rapid growth of drug abuse funding during the Nixon administration had created large bureaucracies with a vested interest in additional drug abuse funding. Gone were the days when the Federal Bureau of Narcotics employed a mere 300 agents worldwide. The largest among the bureaucracies were, of course, the law enforcement agencies led at the federal level by the Drug Enforcement Administration. The prime information agency, the National Institute on Drug Abuse (NIDA), was viewed as being more of a propaganda agency than an information agency (Woodiwiss, 1988: 198).[43] Drug abuse treatment and education had also become big business. Many private-sector treatment organizations greatly benefited from the emphasis on drug abuse. These organizations mobilized politically, with approximately 3,000 organizations supporting greater law enforcement, more research, more education, or more treatment. Drug abuse policies had been effectively institutionalized (see Bellis, 1981).

Although the Reagan administration focused on drug abuse as part of its commitment to the family and to ending moral decay,[44] the most visible program initially was Nancy Reagan's "Just Say No" campaign. Created as a way to counter Nancy Reagan's negative image, the program relied on voluntary activity and little public money. Such a program provided a visible set of symbols and cost a budget-conscious president little in terms of actual outlays. The effort built on a variety of private-sector advocacy groups that had started in the late 1970s. Many of these were parent organizations such as the National Federation of Parents for Drug-Free Youth and PRIDE (Parent Resources Institute on Drug Education; see Musto, 1987: 271).[45]

In 1982 the Reagan administration expanded its drug program efforts beyond rhetoric. The South Florida Task Force was organized under the auspices of Vice President George Bush to interdict drugs smuggled into Florida (Woodiwiss, 1988: 199). Drug interdiction makes good politics because it provides for ample media opportunities to photograph piles of seized contraband. Unfortunately, given the size of the nation's borders and the volume of drug traffic, such policies are unlikely to have any impact on the supply on drugs entering the country (see Reuter, 1988).[46]

Reagan, in late 1982, announced 12 additional regional task forces to coordinate drug interdiction in other parts of the country. The National Narcotics Border Interdiction System was created under Vice President George Bush to coordinate the sealing of U.S. borders to drug traffic. The effort had little impact. From a bureaucratic perspective, the most interesting aspect of this new program was that it recognized the ineffectiveness of the Drug Enforcement Administration. After years of resistance, the Federal Bureau of Investigation was incorporated into the fight against drugs. In recognition of its perceived expertise, overall policy leadership shifted from the DEA to the FBI (Woodiwiss, 1988: 203). Despite these changes, in 1984 the General Accounting Office concluded that drug seizures had affected only a small portion of the supply and that drugs were actually more available than they had been before the interdiction effort (Reuter, 1988; Woodiwiss, 1988: 201).

Failing to stop supply, federal law enforcement efforts were refocused on drug users. The Reagan administration announced a policy of "zero tolerance" and targeted drug users for major enforcement efforts. At the state and local levels, this required little change in policy because, in 1982, 80 percent of all drug arrests were for possession rather than for sale or production (Federal Bureau of Investigation, 1983: 162). Although marijuana was not specifically targeted by the Reagan administration, the relative ease of marijuana arrests compared with those for other drugs meant that marijuana would bear a great deal of the enforcement burden. In 1982, 72 percent of all drug arrests were for marijuana (Federal Bureau of Investigation, 1983: 165). A Department of Justice policy recommendation contending that increased enforcement of marijuana laws would have at best marginal impacts on drug usage and perhaps negative consequences on the violence associated with the drug trade was ignored (see Kleiman, 1989).

Hoping to avoid President Reagan's dominance of the drug issue in an election year, Democrats in Congress included drug provisions in a major anticrime measure passed in 1984 (PL 98-473). The legislation reversed the previous trend toward lighter sentences for drug-related crimes; major drug offenses had their penalties substantially increased, and federal prosecutors were given the authority to seize the assets and profits of drug traffickers. The increase in penalties, however, was focused on the manufacture and sale of drugs rather than on possession.

The entry of Democratic members of Congress into drug policy created a competition between the parties over which could be the hardest on drugs. The bureaucracy benefited from this competition by receiving greater funds and responded by increasing the number of federal drug arrests by 40 percent from 1982 to 1986 (Lawrence and Gettinger, 1988: 1713). Foreign policy was reinserted into the debate when the Reagan administration linked drug trafficking to the communist menace. In March 1985, Vice President Bush claimed "communist Cuba and Nicaragua are definitely in bed with drug smugglers"; and on national television on March 18, 1986, President Reagan claimed that top Nicaraguan officials were involved in drug trafficking (see Woodiwiss, 1988: 218).[47] The role of Panamanian strongman Manuel Noriega, a Reagan administration supporter, was not mentioned by either Reagan or Bush. As early as 1984 reports circulated in Washington regarding Noriega's role in drug trafficking. Despite these reports both the DEA and Attorney General Ed Meese sent letters to Noriega commending him for his role in drug enforcement (Walker, 1989: 216). Other American allies with ties to drug trafficking included the governments of Honduras and Pakistan and the Afghan resistance (Bagley, 1988b: 189).

The salience of drug abuse received a major push in 1986, when Len Bias, the first-round draft choice of the Boston Celtics, died of a cocaine overdose. Media focus on drug usage first by athletes and then by children added more fuel to the perception that drug usage was increasing. Table 2.7 shows the explosion in media coverage on drug abuse in 1986; 113 magazine articles appeared, six times the number of articles appearing in 1985. This perception was augmented by the entry of a "new" drug, crack, a form of cocaine that could be smoked. Crack houses and especially crack babies generated the impression of a drug epidemic, even though later evidence would imply that overall drug usage was dropping at this time (see *Milwaukee Journal,* 1990c; Johnston et al., 1989: 49).

The increased salience of drugs, along with a midterm election that had the potential of returning control of the Senate to the Democratic party, provided a highly partisan environment for the passage of the $1.7 billion Anti-Drug Abuse Act in 1986. Penalties for violating federal drug laws were increased yet again, including mandatory minimum sentences for individuals convicted a second time for major drug crimes. Users were not neglected in the federal law. Possession of a controlled substance was subject to a mandatory minimum fine of $1,000 for the first offense, $2,500 for the second offense, and $5,000 along with at least a 90-day jail term for the third offense. At the federal level, the liberalization of drug possession laws had clearly been reversed. No distinction in this provision was made that separated marijuana from any other drugs. Other provisions banned drug paraphernalia from interstate commerce, restricted designer drugs, and provided authorization to combat money laundering.

One sign of a bill's legislative popularity is that individuals will seek to link pet proposals to it, thinking that no one would dare to vote against the bill (or consider vetoing it). This occurred with the 1986 drug bill. Some of the riders

Table 2.7

The Salience of Drug Abuse in the 1980s: Number of Magazine Articles

Year	Number of articles
1980	16
1981	10
1982	11
1983	9
1984	12
1985	18
1986	113
1987	51
1988	64
1989	85
1990	44

Source: Reader's Guide to Periodical Literature (annual).

linked to this bill were related to the general problem of drug abuse. For example, one prohibited the president from allocating any of the nation's sugar import quotas to any nation involved in the trade of illicit narcotics; it also contained a "sense of Congress" support for a $500,000 bounty on indicted drug trafficker Jorge Luis Ochoa Vasquez. Others of these riders were unrelated to drug abuse. One provision reversed a Supreme Court ruling and permitted Norfolk Southern Railroad to purchase North American Van Lines; another required a study by the Environmental Protection Agency on the use of cyanide; yet another spelled out new procedures for licensing bus and truck drivers. The final bill had something for everyone.

The Reagan administration's commitment to implementing the 1986 Anti-Drug Abuse Act was less than its commitment to antidrug rhetoric. The president's fiscal 1988 budget proposal included $1.0 billion in cuts from drug programs authorized by this law (Moore, 1987: 2954). Money intended for local governments was slow to be allocated. At the federal level, the numerous bureaucracies involved in drug abuse control (e.g., DEA, FBI, Customs, Coast Guard, Border Patrol) staged turf battles for control over interdiction (Moore, 1987: 2955). The result, according the congressional Office of Technology Assessment, was a few major seizures but almost no impact on the supply of drugs entering the country (Moore, 1987: 2956).

The fervor of the 1986 legislation was exceeded in 1988. One candidate for the Democratic nomination, Jesse Jackson, made drug abuse a major component of his campaign. Jackson criticized the Reagan administration for failing to mount an all-out attack on the problem of drugs, in short, of being soft on drugs. Vice President George Bush, who received the Republican nomination, was embarrassed by reports of his relationship with Manuel Noriega and Noriega's role in drug trafficking.[48] Both Bush and Jackson testified before Congress on the need for new legislation. Bush advocated a federal death penalty for drug dealers convicted of murder; Jackson called for the appointment of a federal drug abuse czar to coordinate policy. The partisan competition meant that a harsh new drug law was a certainty in 1988; the only question was the form it would take.

The 1988 omnibus antidrug law again resembled a Christmas tree with something for everyone. Democrats advocated and received funding increases for drug treatment and drug education. Republicans supported and received more money for interdiction, law enforcement, and prisons.[49] Users were targeted for new penalties. Individuals convicted of drug offenses could be denied public housing, federal grants, loans, contracts, and federal occupational licenses. Only veterans' benefits and social security were specifically exempted. Penalties were increased for offenses involving crack; three-time drug offenders could be sentenced to life in prison without parole; and the death penalty was authorized for certain crimes committed by major drug traffickers. Because penalties had been increased both in 1984 and 1986, the search for greater penalties reached the point of absurdity. One provision focused on penalties for killing a police dog engaged in investigating drug-related crime.

Perhaps the section with the greatest focus on users was the requirement of a "drug free" workplace for all organizations receiving more than $25,000 in federal funds. Regulations implementing this section required employers either to discipline or to arrange for treatment of employees arrested for drug offenses (including possession). Failure to comply with the law meant a loss of federal funds. The federal government has seemed very pleased with its efforts to force drug users into unemployment; drug czar Bob Martinez in 1992 noted that only 58 percent of drug users were gainfully employed compared with 70 percent a few years earlier (Skiba and Dresang, 1992).[50] The use of drug testing in the workplace has played a key role in this policy, and the federal government has continued its pressure in this area.

Other provisions of the bill provided for increased funding for law enforcement, treatment, and education. The military's role in drug interdiction (something the Defense Department had strongly resisted) was expanded. The bill also provided for the appointment of a federal drug czar, required the White House Conference on a Drug Free America, and required the president to send a plan for drug control to Congress once a year.

Nondrug issues were also prevalent on this Christmas tree bill. Truck and bus safety rules that were unrelated to drugs were added. A large section of the bill dealt with federal regulation of both child and adult pornography; a provision of this section banned "dial-a-porn" operations for commercial purposes.[51] Another section reversed a Supreme Court decision in a mail fraud case unrelated to drug abuse.

By requiring the president to send an annual "state of the drug war" address to Congress, the 1988 drug law institutionalized the politics of drug abuse. The president, of course, used this opportunity to generate publicity concerning his effort to control drug abuse. Members of Congress from the other party then criticized the president for not going far enough. The process continued to build competition between the president and Congress for more restrictive legislation until economic problems displaced drugs as the major agenda issue.

President Bush's 1989 drug message illustrated just this process. Billed as a $7.9 billion effort to combat drugs, the president's proposal requested approximately a 10 percent increase in drug abuse funding. Setting a goal of a 10 percent reduction in drug use in 2 years and a 50 percent reduction in 10 years, the plan stressed law enforcement by allocating about 73 percent of monies to drug interdiction, domestic law enforcement, and prisons (Biskupic, 1989: 2312). Bush called for no tolerance for casual users, proposing that casual users should have their names published in local papers, their driver's licenses suspended, their employers notified, and their automobiles seized. In a response to the president's first prime-time television address, Senator Joseph Biden presented the Democratic party's criticisms. Biden called the plan "not tough enough, bold enough, or imaginative enough," and likened it to Vietnam as a limited, unwinnable war (Biskupic, 1989: 2312). As an alternative, he proposed that funds be reallocated from law enforcement to treatment and education.

The implementation of the 1980s drug war was marked by three bureaucratic characteristics common to previous drug wars—abuse, corruption, and failure. Bureaucratic abuse of citizens was common. In a highly publicized case, former automaker John DeLorean was acquitted on charges of smuggling cocaine in 1984. DeLorean's arrest resulted from a cooperative drug sting operated by the FBI, the DEA, the U.S. Customs Service, and local law enforcement agencies. Court testimony revealed that the government had falsified evidence, rewritten investigative notes after the fact, and relied on highly questionable tactics (Woodiwiss, 1988: 205).

Many drug cases allow individuals to escape punishment in exchange for implicating others. Such deals have the potential for substantial abuse. The Noriega case involved 15 plea bargains whereby major drug charges were dropped in exchange for testimony against Noriega (Cohn and Reiss, 1992). The combined role of these individuals who copped pleas was probably substantially greater than the role Noriega played in drug trafficking.

The DeLorean and Noriega cases are only two of the most publicized of similar cases. In an Arizona case, DEA agents using a squad of armed local deputies ransacked a house, held two children at gunpoint for several hours, and found no drugs (Woodiwiss, 1988: 207). Local California drug enforcement programs were cited for similar abuses of innocent citizens, including armed searches and harassment by law enforcement officers (Woodiwiss, 1988: 208).

Officers in New York City were convicted of using electric stun guns to convince suspects to confess to drug crimes. The U.S. Supreme Court acquiesced in the kidnapping of a Mexican citizen in Mexico by U.S. narcotics agents so that the person could be tried in the United States for drug-related crimes (*Milwaukee Journal,* 1992d: A1). The failure to use extradition proceedings was even more embarrassing when the trial court judge ruled that federal prosecutors had insufficient evidence to try this individual (*Milwaukee Journal,* 1992c).

Perhaps the greatest threat to civil rights was the application of the federal law that permitted the government to seize assets acquired with drug profits (passed as part of the 1984 crime bill). Although such a law is reasonable if applied by the courts after a conviction, the law was implemented in quite a different matter. Property and money seizures were done administratively where the standard of proof was "a preponderance of the evidence" rather than "beyond a reasonable doubt" (*Milwaukee Journal,* 1990d); in the process individuals charged with drug crimes were often forced to rely on public defenders because they no longer had funds to pay an attorney. The quality of legal defense available from the federal public defenders office was perceived to be significantly less than the quality that could be purchased in the private sector. The most prominent case of this nature involved Manuel Noriega, when private attorneys refused to work at the rates specified by the government. In some cases assets were seized, but no criminal charges were brought. In 1989 $580 million in assets were seized in this manner (*Milwaukee Journal,* 1990d). Volusia County, Florida, seized $8 million in cash and property from motorists between 1989 and 1992; in most cases no drug charges were filed but in only 4 of 262 cases were assets returned (*Milwaukee Journal,* 1992a).

Asset seizures not only were applied before any determination of guilt but in many cases also affected individuals who were not involved in drug trafficking. In New York City apartment buildings owned by drug traffickers were seized, and individuals who lived there were evicted. In a Florida case, an individual who sold a business to a person subsequently convicted of drug trafficking was denied payments for the business, and the business itself remained in government hands (Katel, 1990). Law enforcement agencies were especially aggressive in seizing assets because the proceeds from the sale of these assets were split between local and federal law enforcement agencies.

Along with abusive treatment, drug enforcement was again characterized by corruption. In 1982, a county sheriff, a police chief, and a judge in Henry County, Georgia, were convicted of providing an escort service for drug smugglers. In May 1984, the Harrison County, Mississippi, sheriff received a 20-year sentence for drug-related crimes. The Drug Enforcement Administration lost several agents to convictions for bribery or participation in drug trafficking. Perhaps the most interesting case of corruption concerned San Jacinto County, Texas. The sheriff operated a marijuana trap where nonlocal cars were stopped, and some 90 percent were "found" to possess marijuana. The operation was able to raise approximately one-fifth of the county's total budget. The sheriff eventually received a 10-year sentence for operating the scam (Woodiwiss, 1988: 215). Such examples of corruption were not isolated cases (see Johns, 1992: 20–22). The Justice Department's annual report on corrupt public officials listed several cases a year involving drug-related corruption charges (Public Integrity Section, 1988; see also Wisotsky, 1990: 145–150).

The drug abuse control program has had almost no impact on the supply of drugs in the United States. The marijuana enforcement program is a prime example. One highly publicized part of that program is the Domestic Cannabis Eradication Program, a federally funded program that pays local law enforcement officers to destroy domestic marijuana crops. This program in 1982 was able to claim that it destroyed 138 percent of the estimated U.S. crop; recognizing the impossibility of this, crop estimates were increased dramatically for subsequent years (Woodiwiss, 1988: 208). In 1988 this program destroyed 107 million marijuana plants; most of these were clearly low-quality plants and ditch weed (Drug Enforcement Administration, 1989: 5). At the same time another analysis suggests that the domestic marijuana industry is profitable and thriving (Kleiman, 1989).

Mark Kleiman (1989: 109), a former Reagan administration analyst, contends that the marijuana crackdown had perverse consequences. Cracking down, he argued, benefited those producers who were most experienced and resistant to law enforcement efforts. These organizations were more prone to violence and more likely to be able to bribe local officials. A Wharton Econometrics study in 1985 estimated that illegal drugs produced $20 billion or about one-half of all revenues going to organized crime (Godshaw et al., 1985). The interdiction program, in turn, benefited the domestic producers by causing a shift from foreign marijuana to the more potent domestic marijuana (Kleiman, 1989: 119). The domestic industry doubled production from 4.6 million pounds in 1986 to 9.6 million pounds in 1988 (see *Milwaukee Sentinel,* 1989). The overall program had little impact on supply and caused only marginal increases in price. In short, the program accomplished little of what it was intended to do.

Marijuana is only the best studied of the drug industries. In regard to other drugs, there is far less information on the market and the effects of the drug war on that market. What indicators exist, however, suggest that supplies of drugs have not decreased. Despite record seizures of 150 tons of cocaine in 1989, the street price of cocaine was unaffected, thus causing drug officials to increase dramatically the estimated supply of cocaine (*Madison Capital Times,* 1990). Street prices for one gram of cocaine dropped from $780 in 1979 to $100 in 1987

(Office of Justice Programs, 1989: 372). At the same time the average purity of that gram increased from 12 percent to 60 percent.[52] Retail prices for heroin also remained fairly constant during the 1980s, and purity increased from 3.9 percent in 1983 to 6.1 percent in 1986 (Nadelmann, 1988: 7; Office of Justice Programs, 1989: 372).[53] A 1990 survey of high school seniors reported that nearly 85 percent said they knew where to purchase marijuana if they desired to get some (even though the percentage of users had actually declined; Maguire and Flanagan, 1991: 200). Other "market" percentages in this 1990 survey were 41 for LSD, 55 for cocaine, 32 for heroin, and 60 for amphetamines.

In sum, the drug policies of the 1980s appear to be no more successful than the drug policies of earlier times. The illicit drug market remains huge; the National Institute on Drug Abuse estimates that 60 million Americans spend $150 billion annually on illegal drugs (cited in Moore, 1989: 2693). Interdiction programs in particular generate a great deal of media attention when seizures occur, but they contribute little to solving the problem. Interdiction programs are unlikely to be a success for three simple reasons. First, marijuana and opium can be grown cheaply in a wide variety of locations; coca plant cultivation, once considered to be limited geographically, has recently succeeded in what were thought to be unfavorable locations (Nadelmann, 1988: 9). Second, the costs of drugs on the street level are many times the cost required to produce them; as a result, high profits and multiple sources of supply will encourage people to smuggle drugs even in the face of major penalties. Third, the potential supply of drugs greatly exceeds the current demand. Reuter (1988: 57) estimates that if 50 percent of the world's cocaine production were seized, the street price of drugs would increase by only 3 percent. Reuter (1988: 56) contends, "No one seriously claims now that interdiction can control the amount of drugs physically able to reach this nation. There are simply too many experienced drug smugglers, and too many producers and refiners, for that to be feasible."

Despite the general failures of drug control policy, two promising trends exist. First, survey data suggest that the number of persons who use illegal drugs is declining. The percentage of high school seniors who said they used marijuana in the previous year dropped from 50.8 percent in 1979 (the peak year) to 23.9 percent in 1991 (Flanagan and Maguire, 1992: 346). Cocaine use also dropped from 12.4 percent in its peak year of 1981 to 3.5 percent in 1991; only alcohol use appeared to be resistant to this trend. The decline in drug usage by high school students is also reflected in national statistics on drug arrests. The median age of individuals arrested for drug crimes in 1980 was 21.9; this age increased to 27.1 by 1990 (see Table 2.8). The exception to these declines was an increase in cocaine use in 1991 among older persons and a possible increase in cocaine-related hospital emergency room visits (Isikoff, 1992).

Second, drug arrests are beginning to reflect a concern with more serious drugs. Table 2.9 shows the percentage of total drug arrests in the United States for marijuana and for cocaine and heroin. As late as 1982, 72 percent of drug

Table 2.8

Median Age of Individuals Arrested for Drug Violations, 1950–90

Year	Age
1950	25.3
1960	25.1
1970	20.7
1980	21.9
1990[a]	27.1

Source: Federal Bureau of Investigation, *Uniform Crime Reports* (annual).
[a] Median age for all serious crimes in 1990 was 22.9.

arrests in the United States were for marijuana and only 13 percent for cocaine or heroin. By 1990 the pattern showed marijuana was involved in 30 percent of arrests, whereas cocaine or heroin was involved in 54 percent. These figures do not mean fewer persons are being arrested for marijuana. In fact, the annual number of marijuana arrests has remained fairly constant since 1973 at about 400,000 per year. What has occurred is that the total number of arrests has increased, and this increase has focused on cocaine and heroin.

The shift in arrests from marijuana to cocaine (primarily) and heroin is associated with a slight shift away from arresting users. The proportion of arrests that target users has dropped from 82 percent in 1980 to 68.4 percent in 1990 (Maguire and Flanagan, 1991). Despite the change in percentages, the figures indicate that users rather than traffickers still bear the brunt of enforcement. Even though the percentage of possession arrests has dropped in the last eight years, the actual number of persons arrested for possession has increased by 76 percent. In addition, many states have defined possession of more than a given amount of drugs as "possession with intent to deliver," so that some possession cases are counted as trafficking cases.

Enthusiasm for the war on drugs appears to have waned by 1993. Economic problems have pushed drug abuse down on the list of national priorities. Commensurate funding cuts, however, have not been made, so that the high levels of law enforcement activity of the 1980s have continued.

Substantive Conclusion

The policy history of drug abuse control in America repeats itself in a series of cycles that involve the same actors, the same tactics, and the same results. Five common patterns were found in these cycles of public policy. First, foreign policy has played an important role in domestic drug abuse policy. Efforts have

Table 2.9

Percentage Distributions of Arrests for Drug Violations

	% of total for:		% involving:[b]	
Year	Possession	Sale[a]	Marijuana	Heroin/cocaine
1990	68.4	31.6	30.0	54.0
1989	67.6	32.4	31.9	52.9
1988	72.6	27.4	33.9	51.9
1987	74.0	26.0	40.0	40.6
1986	75.0	25.0	44.0	41.0
1985	76.0	24.0	55.0	30.0
1984	78.0	22.0	59.0	26.0
1983	78.0	22.0	61.0	23.0
1982	80.0	20.0	72.0	13.0
1981	78.0	22.0	69.0	12.0
1980	82.0	18.0	70.0	12.0

Source: Federal Bureau of Investigation, *Uniform Crime Reports* (annual).
[a] Includes both sale and manufacturing arrests.
[b] Percentages in this set of columns do not add up to 100 because of other drugs involved in arrests.

continually been made to blame the countries that produce drugs for the drug problems in American society. In 1919, the 1950s, and the 1980s this foreign threat to the United States was even linked to communism despite a lack of supporting data.

Second, drug policy cycles are characterized by bureaucratic pathologies; drug enforcement agencies have consistently gone beyond legislative intent in implementing policies. Bureaucratic agencies have used propaganda effectively to portray the problem as greater than it actually has been. Unfortunately, these same bureaucratic agencies have been characterized by corruption, abuse, and the inability to solve drug abuse problems. Each of these pathologies can be viewed as resulting from rational behavior by the bureaucracy (see Downs,

1967). Bureaucracies seek to manage information so that they can portray themselves in a favorable light. A rational bureaucracy, therefore, will paint problems to seem as severe as they possibly could be and exaggerate its successes. Corruption is inevitable because drugs generate a great deal of money, especially in comparison to salaries of law enforcement officers. Given the harsh penalties involved in drug trafficking, the arrested person has little to lose by trying to bribe the law enforcement officer. Citizen abuse is to be expected in areas where the agency endorses an extreme view of the problem and places a great deal of pressure on employees to produce numbers.

Third, race and class have played a prominent role in drug control legislation. When minorities have been involved in drug usage, harsh laws have resulted, as illustrated by opium laws and Chinese immigrants, marijuana laws and Mexican workers, and blacks and the Boggs Act. When white, middle-class persons have been involved with drugs, policies have become more lenient. Fourth, marijuana has taken on mythical proportions in U.S. drug policies. Given its modest threat as a drug, it has received an excessive amount of policy attention and relatively far more enforcement than other drugs. Finally, the history of drug abuse policy is the history of failure. America repeatedly tries policies that have not worked in the past. Only when reasoned debate produces new public policy options will we be likely to see any chance of success in combating drug abuse.

A Theoretical Recapitulation

Of the three major groups participating in drug abuse policy (citizens, politicians, and bureaucrats), citizens have been the least active. Individual citizen groups, however, have played a role in drug abuse policy. The Harrison Act saw Mrs. Cornelius Vanderbilt mobilize citizens in support of drug legislation. During the legislative debates over the Marijuana Tax Act, the Women's Christian Temperance Union, the parent–teacher association, and other groups supported the legislation. Parent groups were active in supporting the Reagan war on drugs, and one historian rates them as a highly effective force (see Musto, 1987). Overall, however, citizen groups have probably been the least active of the participants (the linkage to race is also a citizen impact; see the previous section).

Political forces have influenced drug policy in a wide variety of ways. For much of the policy history, individual entrepreneurs used the drug abuse issue as a way to establish political reputations. Francis Harrison, Hale Boggs, and Price Daniel are examples of congressional entrepreneurs who were able to pass legislation; some evidence from the state level also suggests that individual entrepreneurs were active in marijuana decriminalization (see Anderson, 1981). At some point during the 1960s and 1970s, however, drug abuse became a partisan issue. President Kennedy reputedly supported a reassessment of drug policy to hinder the career of Richard Nixon. Nixon initiated the drug war of the 1970s and claimed success for it. The 1980s saw partisan divisions over strategies, with Republicans endorsing law enforcement strategies and Democrats advocating treatment-based strategies. Clearly some element of party competition was involved. In both 1970 and 1984 major drug legislation was passed during election years when one party held control of the presidency and the other controlled at least one house of Congress (Boggs–Daniel also passed in similar circumstances).

Among political institutions, courts have also played a major role. During the initial implementation of the Harrison Act, the Supreme Court first endorsed and then rejected the implementation procedures of the Federal Bureau of Narcotics. Many of the cases of citizen abuse in recent times have come to public attention because appellate courts have rejected or endorsed law enforcement activities. The court's role, however, has been primarily passive in drug abuse policy.

The historical case study revealed that bureaucracy has been a major player in drug abuse policy in three ways—advocacy, the influence of federalism, and the influence of bureaucratic competitors. The advocacy role of the bureaucracy in supporting new legislation is well documented. From Wright's advocacy of the Harrison Act to William Bennett's efforts as President Bush's drug czar, bureaucrats have forcefully sought new drug laws. Much of the influence of bureaucracy has been felt through the process of federalism. Federal agencies, because they recognize that state agencies are the major implementors of drug policy, seek to influence state activities. The Federal Bureau of Narcotics was active in support of state marijuana laws in the 1930s and stricter penalties in the 1950s. Similar pressure was exerted in the 1980s, and the states responded with significant increases in drug crime penalties. The influence process also works in reverse; state efforts to rationalize drug control laws during the 1960s and 1970s provided a blueprint for the federal effort. Competitors of the law enforcement bureaucracies have been institutionalized; but except for the brief period of time during the 1970s, they have not been able to win many battles at the federal level. Sharp (1992), in her assessment of congressional testimony, contends that treatment bureaucracies have been unable to offer solutions to the drug problem with any degree of certainty. Although law enforcement strategies do not appear to work by objective standards, the law enforcement agencies are convinced that they do and strongly advocate them.

This chapter also had a brief assessment of policy outcomes with a discussion concerning the effectiveness of law enforcement strategies. The discussion was primarily argumentative with only a modest amount of empirical evidence. The major assessment of policy outcomes will be included in the next two chapters.

Notes

1. This study will examine only those aspects of foreign policy that are directly related to important drug questions in domestic policy. As a result, a wide variety of foreign policy efforts in regard to drug control will not be discussed. For an analysis of the foreign policy of drugs see Walker, 1989.

2. The United States is self-sufficient in what is termed dangerous drugs. These include amphetamines, barbiturates, and hallucinogens.

3. Generally the term *narcotics* refers to both opiates and cocaine, although cocaine is

not a narcotic; it is an anesthetic and central nervous system stimulant. This book will use the term *narcotics* in a way that is consistent with other uses which include cocaine as a narcotic. This study will also use the term *marijuana* rather than the term *cannabis*.

4. Parke-Davis was also a major importer of marijuana for medical purposes at this time (see Bonnie and Whitebread, 1974: 55).

5. Grinspoon and Bakalar (1985: 28) note that in 1909 there were still 69 available imitations of Coca-Cola that did contain cocaine.

6. From 1897 to 1912 every state but Delaware adopted laws to regulate the sale of opiates and/or cocaine. These laws were relatively modest so that the New York law appears at the time to have been a significant change from current policy (Kolb, 1962: 145; King, 1972: 152).

7. Pharmacists were attempting to establish control over their profession. One of the major threats that they perceived was the physician who dispensed drugs directly to patients. The actions of pharmacists should be viewed as consistent with the actions of physicians, who were also in the process of asserting professional control over the practice of medicine at this time (Kessel, 1959).

8. Bonnie and Whitebread (1974) feel that there was a legislative consensus to ban narcotics at this time. Trebach (1982: 122) also comes to a similar conclusion by examining the legislative debates. On the other hand, if the wording of the law is clear, and in this case it is, seeking legislative intent in legislative debates hardly seems necessary. If legislative intent had been to ban narcotics or ban the use of certain medical treatments, then a specific exemption for medical practice would not have been included.

9. The threat-to-children argument has surfaced periodically in federal public relations efforts. See the discussion below on the Marijuana Tax Act of 1937 and the Nixon and Reagan drug wars.

10. The record shows that Webb was fairly free with his prescriptions. It is unclear if he actually practiced "medicine" in his interactions with addicts or simply provided drugs (see Trebach, 1982: 128).

11. Why the Supreme Court changed its mind in only three years is unclear. Musto (1973: 133) argues that the red scare of 1919 was a factor. The argument is consistent with later efforts to link drug trafficking with international communism. The general hesitance of courts to overrule executive power during time of war might be another factor.

12. Behrman prescribed large amounts of narcotics to individuals. Trebach (1982: 130) suggests that the court could have held that his practice was not in good faith rather than rejecting the good faith defense.

13. Data on budget and employment are taken from the Office of Management and Budget, *Budget of the United States Government* (Washington, DC: U.S. Government Printing Office, annual).

14. Zimring and Hawkins (1992: 60) contend that the decline in cocaine consumption at this time was compensated for by a rise in amphetamine consumption and after 1932 by an increase in alcohol consumption.

15. Some evidence suggests that a major propaganda campaign was conducted by the State Department in regard to foreign policy and drugs. My examination of articles appearing in the periodical literature at this time reveals a dramatic increase in 1920 and 1921. The overwhelming majority of these articles focus on the opium trade, with many looking at the opium problem in China.

16. The appointment of Anslinger did not end the corruption in the Federal Bureau of Narcotics; see McWilliams, 1990: 81.

17. Anslinger's diplomatic background also allowed him to play a role in the development of U.S. counterintelligence capacity. Because the Federal Bureau of Narcotics had

agents in foreign countries, Anslinger and key aides were able to assist the United States in later efforts to develop intelligence networks. See Block and McWilliams, 1989.

18. Enforcement of prohibition led to the establishment of marijuana "tea pads." An estimated 500 were operating in New York City in 1930 (Zimring and Hawkins, 1992: 71).

19. The argument presented here differs somewhat from that presented by Musto (1972; 1973). He contends that the federal legislation was in response to concerns about Mexican and black use of the drug. Himmelstein (1983: 44), however, clearly demonstrates that use by minorities played no role in the hearings and the actual adoption of the federal statute. Himmelstein goes too far, however, in concluding that racial tensions played no role. I argue that racial tensions affected state actions in regard to state laws, a position supported by Bonnie and Whitebread (1974: 52). By the time of federal passage, these fears were translated into the impact of marijuana on youth rather than on minority groups (see Himmelstein, 1983: 65).

20. McWilliams (1990: 86) provides some evidence that Anslinger also pursued a clientele strategy by granting licenses to import drugs for medicinal purposes to companies in exchange for political support.

21. Anslinger's use of race may have reflected his own racial biases. A 1934 memo on an informer refers to the person as a "ginger-colored nigger" (McWilliams, 1990: 84).

22. Some individuals have speculated that the rapid adoption of the Uniform State Narcotic Drug Act was the result of the demise of prohibition. The argument contends that the liquor industry feared that cheap drugs might provide an alternative to alcohol for purposes of intoxication. Similarly in 1919 a Public Health Service study contended that prohibition was a major cause of drug addiction (Bonnie and Whitebread, 1974: 55). Although little evidence of activity on the part of the liquor industry is evident, the issue has not been fully studied, so the influence of the liquor industry remains an interesting policy question (see Grinspoon, 1971: 16; Sloman, 1979: 202). Similarly, the tobacco industry would also have had an interest in the strict regulation of marijuana.

23. Bonnie and Whitebread (1974: 124) contend that the difference between the Harrison Act and the Marijuana Tax Act is that the Harrison Act provided for a small tax, so its function as a revenue measure could be justified. The Marijuana Tax Act provided for a prohibitory tax and as a result did not generate any revenue. Table 2.1 shows the small amounts collected by the marijuana tax in 1940 and 1945. The total collected in one year never exceeded $75,000. Since the amount collected was so small, the Treasury Department did not release separate figures for the marijuana tax after the first few years.

24. I could find no evidence in the historical records that there was a partisan dimension to the Marijuana Tax Act.

25. There is one flaw in Himmelstein's argument. My own examination of marijuana articles published in the literature shows that 1938 was the peak year. Many of the inflammatory articles on marijuana, therefore, were published after the passage of the act, not before. In fact, in the years preceding the tax act, articles on marijuana were quite rare.

26. These figures might underestimate the concentration on marijuana because they are figures for persons actually taken to court. More individuals were arrested than charged. As a result, the enforcement emphasis on different drugs might have varied somewhat from these figures.

27. The law was opposed by the Federal Bureau of Prisons and its director James Bennett. The Federal Bureau of Narcotics did not take opposition lightly. FBN agents were assigned by Anslinger to follow Bennett and gather possible evidence of wrongdoing (see Bonnie and Whitebread, 1974: 211).

28. Woodiwiss (1988: 139) describes the close relationship between Anslinger and Joe McCarthy. He also presents evidence that Anslinger and the FBN provided McCarthy with morphine to treat his addiction.

29. This was the first time that marijuana was grouped with other drugs by the federal government (see Bonnie and Whitebread, 1974: 204).

30. Anslinger also charged without substantiating evidence that Japan was a leading trafficker in drugs during World War II (McWilliams, 1990: 98). For other examples of Anslinger's xenophobia, see Kinder, 1991.

31. Anslinger supported this position as late as 1961, when he published an article in a popular magazine that made this contention; see Anslinger, 1961.

32. The U.S. Supreme Court has not extended this ruling. In *Powell* v. *Texas* (392 U.S. 514, 1968) the Court declared that imprisonment for public intoxication was not a cruel and unusual punishment. In *United States* v. *Moore* (414 U.S. 980, 1973) the Court held that addicts could be convicted of possession of heroin. The possibility of being an addict without possessing drugs was a situation the court did not clarify.

33. The 1970 federal act should not be interpreted as a complete victory for advocates of liberalization. The act places drugs in ranked categories similar to those in the Single Convention on Narcotics. As it was in the Single Convention, marijuana is placed in a category that portrays it as far more dangerous than it actually is (Musto, 1987: 261; Kaplan, 1983: 645).

34. The commission was created as the result of efforts by Ed Koch, then a member of Congress from New York and a future mayor of New York City (Anderson, 1981: 63).

35. NORML had the image of being the driving force behind changes in marijuana laws, but in many cases others were more influential. NORML, for example, was not involved at all in the Oregon law. Republican entrepreneurs using libertarian arguments were the key to gaining passage in Oregon (Anderson, 1981: 122), Colorado (Anderson, 1981: 162), and Ohio (Anderson, 1981: 163). The one exception appears to be California. Changes in marijuana laws were often part of omnibus drug reform laws, so that the marijuana issue was not as visible as it might have been.

36. Some decline in heroin supplied to the United States was apparent by 1973. Bellis (1981: 80) attributes this to the end of the Vietnam War. The end of the war, he contends, resulted in the withdrawal of the CIA from the opium transport business in Southeast Asia. The drop in operating efficiency without the CIA is suggested as a reason for the decline in heroin in the United States.

37. McWilliams (1991: 373–374) contends that ODALE was part of a Nixon effort to exert control over federal law enforcement activities. ODALE in McWilliams's view was part of the White House plumbers operation rather than a drug enforcement operation.

38. Musto (1987: 258) notes that drug treatment budgets also grew dramatically at this time. In fact, the fiscal year 1975 budget allocated 52 percent of federal drug funds to treatment compared with 48 percent to law enforcement, figures much different from those in the late 1980s (Trebach, 1982; 233).

39. For a documentation of the corruption in the famed New York City unit that was responsible for the French Connection case, see Woodiwiss, 1988: 182.

40. The Carter administration was, however, able to approve the use of THC pills for medical use. THC is the active ingredient in marijuana and is used as an antinausea drug for cancer patients undergoing chemotherapy (Trebach, 1982: 239).

41. There was also the widely publicized but undocumented incident concerning presidential assistant Hamilton Jordan and the use of cocaine in the White House.

42. Anderson (1981), also an aide to President Carter, presents Bourne as an individual with little influence in the White House, especially after his early efforts on drug issues. Anderson contends that the policy changes were the result of shifts by Carter, not the departure of Bourne.

43. NIDA has permitted parent groups to review its publications and has revised or removed from circulation documents that might portray drugs in a favorable light (Musto,

1987: 272). Good quality information on drugs and drug abuse is desperately needed to make informed drug policy. By confining its role to presenting only one side of various drug issues, NIDA is seriously undermining any efforts to make effective pubic policy.

44. Of all the family–morality issues such as school prayer, abortion, and teenage pregnancy, drug abuse was the least controversial. No one supports drug abuse. Selecting this as the moral issue for the Reagan administration turned out to be an effective political strategy, because it allowed Reagan to empathize with his Moral Majority constituents and not alienate other Republican voters who would not be supportive of efforts to permit school prayer or to curb abortions.

45. Botvin (1990: 504) provides some data that suggest such groups have very few members and rarely last for any period of time.

46. In February of 1990, the administration indirectly admitted as much. With nearly 150 tons of cocaine seized, including 20 tons in a single raid in California, 1989 was a record year for drug seizures. If these seizures had limited supplies, the street price of drugs should have risen. Prices remained stable, however, forcing the administration to revise its estimates of worldwide drug production upward by 40 percent.

47. Subsequent hearings by Senator John Kerry revealed that the Contras rather than the Sandanistas were involved in drug trafficking (Walker, 1989: 218). On Cuban involvement see Lee, 1985–86: 156.

48. Bush claimed he was out of the loop and denied knowledge of any involvement by Noriega in drug trafficking at this time. Walker (1989: 217) notes that Bush was actively involved in drug interdiction and thus implies that skepticism is in order about Bush's denial of knowledge.

49. These partisan divisions on the appropriate means to combat drug abuse date back to at least the 1972 election. In contrast with President Nixon's major emphasis on law enforcement, Democratic candidate George McGovern advocated that drug abuse be treated as a health problem. McGovern was highly critical of the hard-line approach to drug abuse (see Lawrence and Gettinger, 1988: 1712).

50. The logic of such a policy completely escapes me. Drug users who are gainfully employed are not likely to be committing crimes to support their habits. The punitive nature of the drug-free workplace policies is likely to exacerbate the level of drug-related crimes.

51. It is unclear whether anyone would establish such an operation for noncommercial purposes.

52. In May of 1990 federal reports claimed that the purity of cocaine had dropped from 65 percent in the previous year to 55 percent for the first four months of 1990. This drop in purity was claimed to be the result of successful interdiction. Dealers were perceived as having reduced the purity rather than increasing the price of cocaine.

53. The Drug Enforcement Administration in 1989 began releasing drug prices only in ranges rather than in specific figures. At times these ranges were enormous. The reason for this change was the claim by local law enforcement officials that drug prices varied a great deal from dealer to dealer and from time to time.

3

Reefer Madness: A Quantitative Historical Analysis of Drug Enforcement Policy

In 1989 and 1990 public opinion polls, the American public stated that drug abuse was the single most important problem facing the nation (Maguire and Flanagan, 1991: 152). President George Bush's drug control program had annual expenditures of $12.7 billion for law enforcement, treatment, and education in fiscal year 1992. Congress, in an effort to claim the issue, has pushed for even greater funding. Lost in the political feeding frenzy over drug abuse policies is any concern with systematic policy analysis. As chapter 2 demonstrated, state and federal drug policies date to the nineteenth century. Data on drug policies exist back to 1916. Since then periodic drug wars have been fought, yet little analysis from these earlier efforts has penetrated the current policy debates. This chapter attempts to remedy this failing by providing a quantitative, historical analysis of drug control policies in the United States.

The analysis takes place in six parts. First, our theory of policy will be adapted to the quantitative historical approach. Second, politics and political institutions will be related to the allocation of resources used to combat drug abuse. Third, the resources devoted to drug control will be linked to implementation efforts by federal law enforcement agencies. Fourth, federal law enforcement efforts will be tied to state law enforcement efforts. Fifth, whether or not law enforcement efforts affect the price or use of drugs will be investigated. Finally, second-order consequences will be examined by assessing the impact of drug control policies on crime rates.[1]

Theoretical Modifications

Most of the dependent variables in this chapter will measure policy implementation. The passage of laws is a fairly rare event in federal drug policy. Such events are more profitably considered either in a historical case study or in quantitative cross-sectional analysis of the content of individual laws (but see Berry and Berry, 1990). Accordingly, the major concern of this chapter will be with the policy outputs and the second-order consequences of drug enforcement policy.

For the historical quantitative analysis, several modifications of our theory will be made. Citizen forces are easier to measure in quantitative historical terms and will be fully represented in the models. Political forces can be included in rich detail with emphasis on political values and partisan competition. Bureaucratic forces such as capacity, leadership, and the federalism aspects of bureaucracy can be included. Because there is no legitimate industry producing illicit drugs, industry forces will be lacking, although a measure of the influence of the alcohol production industry will be included. Policies such as laws will generally be included as independent variables in the attempt to explain policy outputs and policy outcomes.

A Policy Model

Political Institutions

The examination of bureaucratic implementation of policy means a decided focus on the interactions between government bureaucracies and other political institutions (see Rourke, 1984; Meier, 1993). The fragmented nature of American politics permits government bureaucracies to exercise discretion in implementing public policies (Rourke, 1984). A major debate in the literature concerns the extent of this discretion. Proponents of the congressional dominance view of bureaucracy hold that legislative bodies dominate bureaucracies and completely control their outputs (Weingast and Moran, 1983). Principal–agent theorists contend that political institutions (principals) can exercise substantial control over their agents (bureaucracies; see Moe, 1985; Wood and Waterman, 1991). Others find that bureaucratic agencies are able to influence policy independently of political institutions (Wood, 1988; Eisner and Meier, 1990).

Congressional Control of Policy

Congress has four means of influencing any bureaucracy including drug control agencies—legislation, budgets, oversight, and legislative vetoes (Key, 1959; Cohen, 1985). Historically, however, Congress has used legislation as its prime control over drug abuse policy. Regulation of illicit drugs became a federal policy concern after Congress passed the Harrison Act of 1914 (Musto, 1987). Responding to a political scandal in 1930, Congress created a separate law enforcement agency for drugs, then called the Federal Bureau of Narcotics (Walker, 1989: 68).[2] Marijuana came under federal purview with the passage of the infamous Marijuana Tax Act of 1937 (Himmelstein, 1983). During the Cold War, Congress increased drug penalties significantly with the Boggs Act of 1951 and the Boggs–Daniel Act of 1956 (King, 1972). The Comprehensive Drug Abuse Prevention and Control Act of 1970 was an effort to provide a consistent, logical policy toward drugs; its major impact was the separation of use or possession from other drug violations in federal law enforcement (Himmelstein, 1983). The Crime Control Act of 1984 substantially increased penalties for drug trafficking and drug use as part of the 1980s war on drugs. Additional drug legislation was passed in 1986 and 1988, but these laws may be viewed as extensions of the 1984 legislation.

Congress can also control bureaucratic actions through the budget process, and federal law enforcement agencies are highly sensitive to budget allocations. The major policy output of these agencies is drug arrests. Because the arrest process is personnel intensive, budget changes are quickly reflected in policy outputs. Budget cuts virtually require layoffs, which will reduce arrests because there are few ways to make individual employees more efficient to compensate.

The best surrogate for Congress's predisposition to use political controls—budgets, informal contact, and so on—is the values of the members of Congress. One good way to summarize political values of politicians over time is party affiliation. The measure will be the percentage of seats in Congress held by the Republican party. Because Republicans have generally been more aggressive advocates of drug policy, our expectation is that Republican gains will be associated with more vigorous enforcement of drug laws. An alternative hypothesis might be that Democrats are more likely to support active government; therefore, the relationship between Republican lawmakers and drug policy will be negative.[3]

The use of legislation to control drug enforcement policy will be operationalized as a series of dummy variables coded 0 before Congress took action and 1 thereafter (see Lewis-Beck, 1980). The impact of each action was coded so that the first year of impact was the first year that the legislation was in effect, not necessarily the year that the legislation passed. The congressional policy variables are (1) the creation of the Federal Bureau of Narcotics in 1930, (2) the Marijuana Tax Act of 1937, (3) the Boggs Act of 1951, (4) the Boggs–Daniel Act of 1956, (5) the Comprehensive Drug Abuse Prevention and Control Act of 1970, and (6) the Crime Control Act of 1984.[4]

Presidential Control of Policy

Presidents also have several ways to exert control over the bureaucracy (Moe, 1985; Meier, 1993). Although intervention of presidential aides in drug enforcement actions is not unknown,[5] presidential control normally manifests itself in two ways—in general support for law enforcement and in structural reorganizations. Historically, certain presidents have been strong advocates of aggressive drug law enforcement (see chapter 2). President Ronald Reagan's war on drugs is only one of many. Equally prominent was Richard Nixon's war on heroin in the 1970s, and the 1920s effort to restrict the use of cocaine and narcotics (Bellis, 1981; Musto, 1987). Two major efforts to de-emphasize drug law enforcement also exist. Franklin Roosevelt's terms saw law enforcement efforts shrink by almost one-half despite added responsibilities in regard to marijuana; President Jimmy Carter was initially a decriminalization advocate and then pro-treatment during his term. In all three cases of law enforcement advocacy, the presidents overseeing these efforts were Republicans; in both cases of de-emphasis, the presidents were Democrats. This variable will be measured as a dummy variable coded 1 when the president is a Republican.

Reorganization can also affect the direction of public policy by lodging responsibility for a program in a supportive or unsupportive organization (see Seidman and Gilmour, 1986). For most of its history, drug control efforts were in the Treasury Department rather than in the Justice Department. In 1968 President Johnson established the Federal Bureau of Narcotics and Dangerous Drugs in the Department of Justice by merging the Federal Bureau of Narcotics with the drug control units of the Food and Drug Administration. This reorganization placed the agency in a department more favorably disposed to law enforcement. In 1973 President Nixon consolidated all drug enforcement units into the Drug Enforcement Administration (DEA), creating for the first time a single agency with jurisdiction over all drug control law enforcement (Rachal, 1982). Dummy variables will be created for both of these reorganizations.

Party competition appears to be a major force in contemporary drug enforcement policy. Senator Joseph Biden mobilized Democrats in an aggressive attack on President Bush's drug policy. As a measure of party competition, a simple dummy variable will be created, coded 1 when the two political parties share control of the presidency and Congress, and coded 0 otherwise. This measure assumes that party competition is relevant only when both parties have a strong institutional base at the national level.

The Court System

In the United States, courts have the power to check bureaucratic agencies by declaring their actions unconstitutional, beyond legislative intent, or in violation of established procedures (Cooper, 1988). For law enforcement agencies, courts have an even greater control. Individuals arrested by law enforcement agencies are brought to court and charged with criminal violations. In the process of trying cases, courts can either ratify agency interpretations of the law or reject them. If used consciously, this power could give the courts control over an agency's policy outputs. The influence of the courts on drug enforcement agencies will be measured by the percentage of cases that the agency wins at the trial court level. This measure includes only those cases where an indictment is brought and omits cases that are dropped before this step.[6]

Citizen-related Forces

Policy implementation takes place within an environment that can either facilitate or restrict policy actions when citizens become active or remain passive. Two environmental forces are especially important in drug control politics. Issue salience varies greatly over time; although drug abuse is frequently mentioned in current public opinion surveys, in other years, virtually no one has cared about drug control (see Maguire and Flanagan, 1991: 150). Peters and Hogwood (1985) found that public opinion historically has stimulated policy activities in a variety of areas. Perhaps the best illustration of this in drug control policy is the 1986 death of basketball player Len Bias from a cocaine overdose. Drug abuse articles in the periodical literature skyrocketed from 18 in 1985 to 113 in 1986. Both Congress and the president almost immediately responded with new policy initiatives. For the salience of drug policy, the number of articles on drug abuse or on marijuana appearing in the periodical literature for each year is the measure.[7]

Second, drug control policy is a discretionary area. Unlike unemployment compensation or social security, drug control policies do not have first call on the nation's resources. Drug control initiatives, in fact, appear to coincide with slack resources. People are concerned about drug abuse when economic concerns wane. When the economy is in recession, efforts are focused on economic issues rather than drug abuse issues. Federal drug law initiatives generally correspond to growth periods in the economy. In the years that major new drug initiatives were adopted since 1910 (1914, 1937, 1951, 1956, 1970, and 1984) the gross national product grew 5.78 percent in real terms compared to 2.82 percent in other years. Economic growth also means that additional tax revenues will be available to budget for drug control.[8] The measure will be the gross national product in constant dollars.

Three other citizen forces merit inclusion—attitudes, immigration, and race. Drug use in the United States clearly ebbs and flows over time (see Musto, 1987). Probably one major success of current drug policy is the antidrug education programs; the percentage of high school students who disapprove of drug use has jumped dramatically since the mid-1970s (Maguire and Flanagan, 1991: 194). The corresponding drop in drug consumption suggests that attitudes toward drugs are a major factor in drug use. Unfortunately, national attitudinal data on drug use are not available for the entire time period of the study (such data exist for 1972 through 1990 and will be used in assessing drug use later in the chapter). As a surrogate, this study uses the percentage of the population who are church adherents. Religious groups, with a few minor exceptions, are opposed to drug usage; as the influence of religious groups grows, one would expect that drug use would drop and there would be less need for enforcement.[9]

Immigration and race have played a major role in the adoption of drug policies in the United States (see chapter 2). Chinese immigrants were the targets of opium laws, Mexican immigrants were the perceived source of marijuana, Puerto Ricans and blacks were used as examples in the 1950s drug law debates, and crack, a drug used primarily by blacks, has been the subject of higher penalties than other forms of cocaine. Two measures will be included in the analysis: the number of immigrants as a percentage of total U.S. population, and the percentage of nonwhite population.[10] Both should be positively related to increased enforcement of drug abuse laws.

Industry Forces

Because the drug production industry is illegal, it cannot participate in the regular policy process. Some historical analysts, however, suggest that the alcohol industry has played a behind-the-scenes role in drug abuse policy. The argument suggests that alcohol producers see illicit drugs as competing with their own product. The alcohol production industry, therefore, should support the passage of strong antidrug legislation and vigorous enforcement. To determine if there is any relationship between the strength of the alcohol production industry and drug policies, the number of alcohol industry workers per 100,000 persons will be included in the analysis.[11]

Bureaucracy and Public Policy

That some bureaucracies influence public policy is beyond doubt (Rourke, 1984; Meier, 1993). The ability of bureaucracies to influence public policy, however, is not constant. According to Francis Rourke (1984), it varies with the agency's political support, expertise, leadership, and vitality. Despite the historical evidence presented in chapter 2, the Drug Enforcement Administration (and its precursors) should be viewed as a weak agency living in the shadow of the federal government's major bureaucratic power brokers. It is far less visible and less than one-third the size of the Federal Bureau of Investigation. The DEA, in fact, does not even control its own policy area. In 1982 the FBI was designated as the lead agency in drug control (Woodiwiss, 1988: 203), and since 1989 leadership has passed to the president's drug czar.

The DEA's weakness is a function of having few of the power resources that Rourke (1984) feels are necessary for policy autonomy. It has not developed a clientele. Drug users, of course, are an inappropriate clientele, and local law enforcement agencies are more likely to identify with and trust the FBI than the DEA. Expertise is generally absent. Unlike the FBI, which invested heavily in crime labs and law enforcement forensics (Poveda, 1990), the DEA's technology has changed little. Undercover agents buy drugs, build cases, and make busts. Vitality has not been especially noticeable. The agency has a reputation for corruption rather than efficiency in law enforcement (Epstein, 1977).

Leadership is one area where the federal drug agency might have developed some policy control. Harry J. Anslinger, commissioner of the Federal Bureau of Narcotics from 1930 to 1962, was considered a preeminent bureaucratic politician (Dickson, 1968), but his activities were confined to mostly international aspects of drug control and overall policy. He presided over a generally declining agency during his tenure. Even Anslinger had little public visibility. In 1935, for example, 2 references to Anslinger appeared in the *New York Times;* in contrast, 37 stories covered his rival, J. Edgar Hoover. Similarly, the Drug Enforcement Administration head, John C. Lawn, appeared in only 5 *New York Times* stories in 1989; drug czar William Bennett appeared in 85.

Because federal drug agencies generally have been weak, this analysis treats the agency as a black box responding to its environment. Such bureaucratic variables as personnel or budgets will be shown to be determined externally. Only leadership visibility will be included in the analysis, and the results for that variable are consistent with the agency's weak position. This measure is a simple count of the number of references to the drug agency head in the *New York Times* for each year.

Modeling Public Policy

A multivariate, interrupted time series model will be constructed to determine the impact of various institutions and environmental forces on drug control policy (see Lewis-Beck, 1986; Lewis-Beck and Alford, 1980). Because the availability of data varies, the length of the time series will also vary with the dependent variable examined.

The strategy of analysis will be to use several independent variables to explain variation in the dependent variables. In addition to those discussed above, a trend variable will be included to eliminate any incremental increase or decrease in policy activities.[12] Such a process will generate a good deal of collinearity, with the result being many coefficients that will be difficult to interpret. To avoid major collinearity problems, each model will be reestimated by removing the insignificant variables from the equation. The reduced models presented should have limited amounts of collinearity and also avoid problems with specification error. These reduced equations will be the focus for the discussion of drug abuse policy.[13]

Findings

Budgets and Personnel

According to Peters (1986) the first step in policy implementation is the attachment of resources to public policy decisions, or, in our terms, creating bureaucratic capacity. Quite clearly public policies can be established and no resources allocated to implement them, thus creating policies that are symbolic (see Kemp, 1981; Appleton, 1985). Drug abuse policy, when it is visible, is quite susceptible to symbolic manipulation. As an illustration, in 1986 President Reagan requested a $2.9 billion increase in funds to combat drug abuse. In his budget document for the next fiscal year, however, $1 billion of these funds was not requested (Moore, 1987: 2956).

Table 3.1 shows the determinants of federal drug agency budgets from 1916 to 1990.[14] Citizen forces and political factors both influence these budgets. As slack resources increase, so do drug control budgets. A billion dollar increase in the GNP is associated with a $45.7 million increase in the drug agency's budget. Both attitudes (church membership) and race play their predicted roles; budgets decrease when church membership increases, and budgets increase when the nonwhite population increases. Congressional control and the funding of drug policies is clearly demonstrated by the significant coefficients for legislation in 1970 and 1984. The first legislation was considered a major step toward consolidating and rationalizing federal drug policies; the latter act was Congress's attempt to wrest drug policy control away from the president. The president's impact comes through reorganization. The DEA creation is associated with a $74.75 million dollar increase in resources for the drug agency.

Several expected relationships did not materialize, and they merit comment. Drug agency budgets were not related to issue salience or to alcohol industry strength. Insignificant impacts are associated with four early congressional actions. Each can be explained. The creation of the Federal Bureau of Narcotics was in response to a scandal involving the head of the Narcotics Division of the Prohibition Unit; no new responsibilities were added. The passage of the Marijuana Tax Act was the result of prior advocacy of state laws; the Federal Bureau of Narcotics argued that it could enforce the law without additional resources (Himmelstein, 1983). The Boggs Act and the Boggs–Daniel Act both were designed to increase penalties for drug violations. They did not expand agency jurisdiction. In fact, the Federal Bureau of Narcotics in 1951 declined authority over amphetamines and barbiturates, which were then assigned to the Food and Drug Administration (Bakalar and Grinspoon, 1985: 96).

Neither bureaucratic leadership nor any partisan variables had an impact on budgeting. The latter finding is unexpected because Republican presidents have been strong advocates of law enforcement approaches to drugs. The former finding is not unexpected because the drug agency has generally been weak and bureau leadership has not been particularly visible.

Table 3.2 shows the determinants of drug agency personnel from 1930 to 1990.[15] Two citizen-related factors appear to influence personnel; there is a negative relationship with church membership and a positive relationship with nonwhite population. Both are as predicted; the drug enforcement agency expands when nonwhite population increases and contracts when church membership increases. A significant relationship between personnel and the alcohol industry exists, but it is negative. Because a negative relationship is unexpected, this finding should be considered an artifact.

Table 3.1

Determinants of Federal Drug Agency Budgets

Dependent variable = federal drug agency budgets in constant dollars (millions)

Independent variables	Full model	Reduced model
Intercept	−27.57	−0.78
Trend	1.19	—
Citizen forces		
Gross national product (billions)	27.76*	45.70*
Drug abuse articles	−0.15	—
Marijuana articles	−0.49	—
Church membership	−4.26*	−3.61*
Immigration rate	4.11	—
% nonwhite population	22.48*	14.20**
Industry forces		
Alcohol industry employment	−0.25	—
Political forces		
Divided government	1.34	—
Republican presidents	6.36	—
Creation of the Drug Enforcement Administration	59.22*	74.75*
Food and Drug Administration merger	15.13	—
Republican members of Congress	−0.60	—
Marijuana Tax Act 1937	0.49	—
Creation of the Federal Bureau of Narcotics	3.49	—
Boggs Act 1951	−6.21	—
Boggs–Daniel Act 1956	−19.24	—
Comprehensive Drug Control Act 1970	33.48*	48.19*
Crime Control Act 1984	55.31*	57.34*
Bureaucratic forces		
Bureau leadership visibility	0.21	—
R-square	.992	.989
Adjusted R-square	.989	.988
Rho	.48	.53
Number of cases	75	75

Notes: Equations are estimated with generalized least squares. A dash means the variable was omitted from the equation.

*p < .05

**p < .10

Table 3.2

Determinants of Drug Agency Personnel

Dependent variable = log of drug agency personnel

Independent variables	Full model	Reduced model
Intercept	2.65	2.94
Trend	−0.0040	—
Citizen forces		
Gross national product (billions)	0.0326	—
Drug abuse articles	0.0000	—
Marijuana articles	−0.0004	—
Church membership	−0.0066*	−0.0103*
Immigration rate	−0.1079	—
% nonwhite population	0.0483*	0.0344*
Industry forces		
Alcohol industry employment	−0.0008*	−0.0013*
Political forces		
Divided government	0.0185	0.0216*
Republican presidents	0.0037	—
Creation of the Drug Enforcement Administration	0.1224*	0.1143*
Food and Drug Administration merger	0.3694*	0.3559*
Republican members of Congress	−0.0019*	−0.0023*
Marijuana Tax Act 1937	−0.0082	—
Creation of the Federal Bureau of Narcotics	−0.0631*	−0.0646*
Boggs Act 1951	0.1626*	0.1677*
Boggs–Daniel Act 1956	0.0084	—
Comprehensive Drug Control Act 1970	0.2626*	0.2690*
Crime Control Act 1984	0.0725*	0.0643*
Bureaucratic forces		
Bureau leadership visibility	−0.0003	—
R-square	.999	.998
Adjusted R-square	.998	.998
Durbin-Watson	1.99	1.82
Number of cases	61	61

Notes: Equations are estimated with ordinary least squares. A dash means the variable was omitted from the equation.

*p < .05

Unlike budgets, personnel levels are significantly related to almost all congressional actions. Since the dependent variable is a log transformation, the coefficients may be interpreted as percentages after a transformation (Tufte, 1974: 125). The creation of the Federal Bureau of Narcotics resulted in a 6.46 percent decline in personnel. This law was passed during an especially weak period in agency history and more likely reflects a general change in government priorities than a specific effort to limit drug agencies. The Boggs Act reverses this trend with a 16.77 percent increase, the Comprehensive Act of 1970 a 26.9 percent increase, and the 1984 law a 6.43 percent increase.[16]

Presidential impacts on agency personnel are also quite strong. The Food and Drug Administration merger increased employment by 35.59 percent (mostly transfers from the FDA), and the DEA creation resulted in an 11.43 percent increase. Partisan factors also play a role. Divided government is associated with approximately a 1.5 percent increase in drug enforcement personnel. Although Republican presidents are not related to enforcement personnel, Republican membership in Congress shows a small negative relationship.

Federal Drug Arrests

Agency budgets and personnel levels are the results of resource decisions made by political institutions. Bureaucratic agencies, especially those with few power resources, have little control over these decisions (Meier, 1993). The agency's policy outputs, however, are under its direct control. The prime policy output of drug control agencies is persons charged with drug violations. Table 3.3 shows the determinants of the federal drug agency enforcement rate from 1930 to 1990.[17]

Perhaps the most striking aspect of Table 3.3 is that all presidential and many congressional variables have little impact on drug enforcement rates. Arrests increased with the Crime Control Act of 1984, and declines in arrests are associated with the Marijuana Tax Act, the creation of the Federal Bureau of Narcotics, and Republican members of Congress. Although these findings might imply that the agency has autonomy relative to these political institutions, that is not the case. The strongest single determinant of enforcement is total personnel. Congress and the president influence drug policy outputs by influencing the number of agency personnel (Table 3.2). The control is indirect, but it remains a control over agency outputs. The courts do not appear to affect agency behavior; although court decisions are negatively related to enforcement, the relationship is not significant.

Bureaucratic implementation also is influenced by citizen/environmental forces. A modest negative trend exists as well as a positive relationship with gross national product. The first reflects the high number of arrests made by the FBN in its early years. Many of these arrests involved physicians who dispensed drugs to addicts. The drug agency conducted a concerted campaign to deter

Table 3.3

Determinants of Federal Drug Enforcement

Dependent variable = federal drug cases per 100,000 persons

Independent variables	Full model	Reduced model
Intercept	−2.8843	2.9192
Trend	−0.2836*	−0.2251**
Citizen forces		
Gross national product (billions)	3.2784*	2.5427*
Drug abuse articles	0.0030	—
Marijuana articles	−0.0337*	−0.0454*
Church membership	0.1566	—
Immigration rate	7.5005*	7.2218*
% nonwhite population	−0.7065**	−0.4256**
Industry forces		
Alcohol industry employment	−0.0020	—
Political forces		
Divided government	−0.1945	—
Republican presidents	0.4862	—
Creation of the Drug Enforcement Administration	1.0026	—
Food and Drug Administration merger	−0.9212	—
Republican members of Congress	−0.0284**	−0.0205*
Marijuana Tax Act 1937	−0.5967*	−0.9515*
Creation of the Federal Bureau of Narcotics	−1.0250**	−1.2546*
Boggs Act 1951	0.9980	—
Boggs–Daniel Act 1956	−0.0565	—
Comprehensive Drug Control Act 1970	0.3055	—
Crime Control Act 1984	1.1275**	1.0767*
Courts	−0.0123	—
Bureaucratic forces		
Bureau leadership visibility	−0.0042	—
Bureau personnel	4.9050	3.9707*
R-square	.950	.937
Adjusted R-square	.922	.925
Durbin-Watson	1.88	1.66
Number of cases	61	61

Notes: Equations are estimated with ordinary least squares. A dash means the variable was omitted from the equation.

*p < .05

**p < .10

physicians from this type of drug practice by making mass arrests; when the Supreme Court upheld this interpretation of the law, many physicians gave up drug treatment practices and subsequent prosecutions dropped dramatically (see Musto, 1987). The positive relationship with the GNP shows that slack resources have an impact separate from agency resources on drug enforcement (perhaps by creating slack resources in agencies that process defendants or perhaps by stimulating demand for drugs).

The more interesting relationships are those for immigration and nonwhite population. The positive relationship with immigration is consistent with the notion that drug enforcement increases with greater immigration. The negative relationship with nonwhite population suggests that the bureaucracy is somehow mediating the impact of drug laws on the minority population. Although only modestly significant, this relationship is consistent with a wealth of literature on urban services that suggests bureaucracy mitigates the forces that would subject minorities to detrimental policy impacts (see Mladenka, 1981). Clearly, the negative relationship would not indicate enforcement targeted at minority populations when such populations increase. Published marijuana articles also have a significant negative relationship. This results because the distribution of marijuana articles peaked during the late 1960s and early 1970s at the same time that attempts were made to restrict federal drug control efforts.

Three congressional control variables have a significant impact—the creation of the Federal Bureau of Narcotics, the Marijuana Tax Act, and the Comprehensive Drug Abuse Prevention and Control Act of 1970. The first two relationships are negative; the last one is positive. All make sense. The creation of the Federal Bureau of Narcotics removed the agency from the protection of the Internal Revenue Bureau and the Prohibition Unit. What remained as the Federal Bureau of Narcotics was a small agency with little power, clearly at the whim of its environment. The Marijuana Tax Act created new authority but no new resources. As a result, any effort to police marijuana could not help but reduce the effort devoted to other drugs. The Comprehensive Drug Control Act consolidated drug policy, giving the DEA authority over all drugs. There is also a negative relationship for Republican members of Congress, suggesting that Democrats, not Republicans, are more likely to be associated with more aggressive enforcement.

Marijuana has played a role in federal drug policies completely out of proportion to its dangers. Because marijuana was a major political issue in the 1960s and 1970s, marijuana enforcement merits separate analysis. Table 3.4 shows the determinants of federal marijuana enforcement.[18] The pattern in Table 3.4 is clearly distinguishable from that in Table 3.3; federal marijuana enforcement, reflecting its political connotations, is influenced by factors different from those driving enforcement for other drugs. Two congressional actions are associated with changes in marijuana enforcement—the Boggs Act and the Boggs–Daniel Act. Both are negatively associated with marijuana enforcement,

Table 3.4

Determinants of Federal Marijuana Enforcement

Dependent variable = federal marijuana cases per 100,000 persons

Independent variables	Full model	Reduced model
Intercept	−7.7824	−5.4128
Trend	0.0155	—
Citizen forces		
Gross national product (billions)	0.0686	—
Drug abuse articles	0.0033	0.0048*
Marijuana articles	−0.0045	−0.0088
Church membership	0.0603*	0.0456*
Immigration rate	−0.4284	—
% nonwhite population	−0.4603*	−0.2821
Industry forces		
Alcohol industry employment	−0.0034	—
Political forces		
Divided government	0.0381	—
Republican presidents	0.1731**	0.2079*
Creation of the Drug Enforcement Administration	−0.5412*	−0.4108*
Food and Drug Administration merger	−0.6626	—
Republican members of Congress	0.0003	—
Boggs Act 1951	−0.9768*	−0.7574*
Boggs–Daniel Act 1956	−0.4416*	−0.2295
Comprehensive Drug Control Act 1970	0.1996	—
Crime Control Act 1984	0.0180	—
Courts	0.0052	—
Bureaucratic forces		
Bureau leadership visibility	−0.0063	—
Bureau personnel	3.8410*	2.6355*
R-square	.936	.926
Adjusted R-square	.899	.910
Durbin-Watson	1.62	1.57
Number of cases	52	52

Notes: Equations are estimated with generalized least squares. A dash means the variable was omitted from the equation.

*p < .05
**p < .10

an easily explained result given that both laws were targeted at other drugs.

In addition to congressional control, evidence of presidential control also exists. Republican presidents are associated with a 0.2079 increase in marijuana enforcement, a result consistent with targeting marijuana under Republican presidents. The creation of the Drug Enforcement Administration reduced marijuana arrests by 0.4108. Of particular interest is the relationship between personnel and marijuana enforcement. Similar to arrests for other drugs, the number of personnel is strongly associated with more marijuana enforcement. This suggests that marijuana enforcement is determined by factors outside the organization (e.g., political considerations) as well as by the availability of officers to investigate cases.

The citizen/environmental forces form a pattern that is somewhat difficult to explain. Marijuana arrests are positively associated with drug abuse articles, yet negatively associated with marijuana articles. Church membership has an unexpected positive relationship, whereas nonwhite population has a negative relationship. The latter is consistent with the finding for all drugs, again suggesting that enforcement of drug laws by federal agents does not increase when minority population increases, even though resources do.

Increasing Penalties

Political institutions may seek to deter drug use in a variety of ways. More enforcement can be perceived as increasing the probability that individuals will be apprehended. Another option is to increase the penalties for those individuals who are convicted. Either might dissuade individuals from using drugs. During legislative debates, much discussion is focused on penalties rather than on arrest rates. Penalties are simple to understand and, at least to legislators, appear likely to deter drug use.

Table 3.5 presents the determinants of drug penalties.[19] The dependent variable is the average sentence (in number of months) for persons convicted of federal drug crimes (marijuana offenses not included). With probation and other factors, the actual time served will deviate from this sentence. Four laws affect federal drug penalties in predictable ways. Drug penalties were increased by the Boggs Act, the Boggs–Daniel Act, and the Crime Control Act. Penalties were reduced and probation was allowed under the Comprehensive Drug Abuse Prevention and Control Act. The empirical findings show that the Boggs Act of 1951 increased the average sentence by 20.27 months; the Boggs–Daniel Act of 1956 added an additional 23.48 months to the average penalty (probation was not permitted under these laws, so actual time served was high). The Comprehensive Drug Abuse Prevention and Control Act of 1970 attempted to rationalize penalties by greatly decreasing them for possession and limiting them for trafficking. The result was a drop in sentence length by 17.75 months (although it remained at a level significantly above the Boggs–Daniel Act).

Table 3.5

Impact of Legislation on Drug Penalties

Dependent variable = average number of months in prison for federal drug violations

Independent variables	Full model	Reduced model
Intercept	258.4550	52.0903
Trend	1.2519	3.3997*
Citizen forces		
Gross national product (billions)	−20.7675**	−36.9040*
Drug abuse articles	−0.0700	—
Marijuana articles	−0.0045	—
Church membership	−2.1098*	−1.8723*
Immigration rate	31.1852	—
% nonwhite population	11.0594*	—
Industry forces		
Alcohol industry employment	−0.4001	—
Political forces		
Divided government	−0.3875	—
Republican presidents	7.0636	—
Creation of the Drug Enforcement Administration	1.7346	−9.7987*
Food and Drug Administration merger	24.7112	—
Republican members of Congress	−0.1143	—
Boggs Act 1951	24.9362*	20.2716*
Boggs–Daniel Act 1956	27.4826*	23.4837*
Comprehensive Drug Control Act 1970	3.0026	−17.7518*
Crime Control Act 1984	21.6635*	16.3966*
Bureaucratic forces		
Bureau leadership visibility	0.4579	—
Bureau personnel	−93.0456	—
R-square	.968	.943
Adjusted R-square	.945	.930
Durbin-Watson	1.84	1.55
Number of cases	46	46

Notes: Equations are estimated with ordinary least squares. A dash means the variable was omitted from the equation.

*p < .05
**p < .10

Finally, the Crime Control Act of 1984 increased penalties by 16.4 months.

The congressional impacts on penalties are the most significant forces; other impacts (all negative) are found for slack resources, church membership, and the creation of the Drug Enforcement Administration. These impacts are relatively modest, however, compared with the direct impacts on congressional legislation.

Table 3.6 replicates the penalty analysis for marijuana offenses. Bonnie and Whitebread (1970) have characterized marijuana as "along for the ride" in legislative policies that govern punishment. They argue that Congress justified the harsh penalties in terms of more dangerous drugs, and that marijuana penalties were increased (or occasionally decreased) with little specific consideration (the exception is the Comprehensive Drug Abuse Prevention and Control Act of 1970). Table 3.6 reveals this along-for-the-ride phenomenon. Marijuana penalties increased by 20.35 months with the Boggs Act, by 19.46 months with the Boggs–Daniel Act, dropped by 19.61 months with the Comprehensive Drug Abuse Prevention and Control Act, and increased by 12.93 months with the 1984 Crime Control Act.

State Enforcement Activities

Federal drug agencies are not the main enforcers of U.S. drug laws. In 1990, federal agencies handled only 19,000 drug cases compared with 1.1 million drug arrests by state and local law enforcement personnel.[20] The two enforcement processes (federal and state) are not unrelated, even though they enforce different laws. In many situations, federal authorities advocated changes in state laws (see chapter 2; see also Himmelstein, 1983, on the Marijuana Tax Act; Bonnie and Whitebread, 1970: 1074, on the Boggs acts); in other situations, state legislative changes created pressure for federal changes (e.g., the Comprehensive Drug Abuse Prevention and Control Act followed state efforts to reduce penalties for marijuana; see Rosenthal, 1977). Federal law enforcement officers also engage in joint law enforcement operations with state agencies. Training and education programs sponsored by the federal government create additional contact between federal and local law enforcement officers. State and local officials currently have an added incentive to enforce drug laws; under federal law, they receive a percentage of the assets seized from drug traffickers.

Local law enforcement agencies essentially have the same policy outputs that federal agencies have—arrests. Data for two arrest series are available. The nationwide arrest rate for drugs (based on 50 state totals) is available from the FBI's *Uniform Crime Reports* from 1945 to 1990.[21] The arrest rate for marijuana is available from the same source for 1965 to 1990.

Because federal drug laws cannot be enforced in state courts, the federal drug law variables will not be used in this analysis of state-level enforcement. Similarly, variables related to the president or federal courts should not affect state enforcement directly. As a result, the model will be reduced to citizen/environ-

Table 3.6

Impact of Legislation on Marijuana Penalties

Dependent variable = average number of months in prison
for federal marijuana violations

Independent variables	Full model	Reduced model
Intercept	305.8660	61.8079
Trend	3.0436*	4.8624*
Citizen forces		
Gross national product (billions)	−36.7062*	−52.2412*
Drug abuse articles	−0.0677	—
Marijuana articles	0.0249	—
Church membership	−2.7317*	−2.6874*
Immigration rate	7.3419	—
% nonwhite population	8.7188	—
Industry forces		
Alcohol industry employment	−0.3261	—
Political forces		
Divided government	−1.0181	—
Republican presidents	5.8991	—
Creation of the Drug Enforcement Administration	1.7982	−9.6222*
Food and Drug Administration merger	27.7567	−12.8075*
Republican members of Congress	0.0314	—
Boggs Act 1951	29.7021*	20.3522*
Boggs–Daniel Act 1956	23.1579*	19.4012*
Comprehensive Drug Control Act 1970	7.2812	−19.6066*
Crime Control Act 1984	21.2891*	12.9280*
Bureaucratic forces		
Bureau leadership visibility	0.1585	—
Bureau personnel	−108.2490*	—
R-square	.941	.917
Adjusted R-square	.895	.899
Durbin-Watson	2.11	1.90
Number of cases	45	45

Notes: Equations are estimated with ordinary least squares. A dash means the variable was omitted from the equation.

*p < .05

mental factors, industry factors, and the federal agency. Because the president might have some indirect influence as a general advocate of drug enforcement, presidential partisanship will be retained. Citizen/environmental forces will include a trend variable, a resources variable (real GNP), a salience variable (number of drug abuse articles), church membership, immigration, and nonwhite population. The impact measures for the federal agency will be the federal enforcement rate for drugs and the bureau leadership variable.[22]

Table 3.7 shows the determinants of state drug arrest rates. Several variables are significant, and the model explains 98 percent of the variation in state arrest rates. The major determinant of state drug arrests is federal activities. An increase of one case in the federal enforcement rate is associated with an increase of 25.9 in the state arrest rate. Bureau leadership also appears to have an influence on state drug arrests. When federal drug administrators become more visible, state drug arrests increase. The encouragement effect is also seen for Republican presidents (also a positive relationship). These findings demonstrate an interesting aspect of federalism. The president and the drug bureau chief have a modest influence on the behavior of federal agencies but a much stronger influence on state agencies. This influence is over and above that of the federal drug arrest rate.

State arrest rates also respond to slack resources and salience. The interesting finding is that drug abuse articles are negatively correlated with state arrest rates. In other words, when drug use becomes more salient, arrests actually drop. One way such a relationship might hold is if salience results in greater pressure on law enforcement officers to limit arrests. In response to such pressure, enforcement might drop. Such a process in the late 1960s generated pressure to reduce harsh marijuana penalties (Rosenthal, 1977).

Two of the most revealing relationships are for immigration and nonwhite population. Total state enforcement of drug laws jumps when immigration and minority population increase. Table 3.7 suggests that state and local law enforcement agencies, not federal agencies, are more likely to enforce drug laws against the powerless. The pattern may also reflect the federal focus on trafficking offenses and the state-local focus on possession offenses.[23] Minorities and immigrants may be less likely to rise in the drug distribution hierarchy.

Table 3.8 presents a similar model for state marijuana arrest rates.[24] The predictive ability of this model is substantially weaker than that for drug arrests, explaining only 88 percent of the variance. Only four variables are significant— federal marijuana enforcement, gross national product, immigration, and nonwhite population. An increase of 1 in the federal marijuana enforcement rate is associated with an increase of 69.72 in the state marijuana arrest rate.

The state and local arrest pattern for marijuana is similar to that for other drugs. Marijuana arrests increase when both immigration and nonwhite population increase. One difference should be noted, however. Neither the president nor bureaucratic leadership has a significant influence on marijuana arrests. We can

Table 3.7

Determinants of State Drug Arrest Rates

Dependent variable = state drug arrests per 100,000 persons

Independent variables	Full model	Reduced model
Intercept	−128.2091	−172.1324
Trend	−13.5203**	−10.1831*
Citizen forces		
Gross national product (billions)	200.6213*	195.2741*
Drug abuse articles	−0.4144**	−0.4406**
Church membership	1.1752	—
Immigration rate	259.5751**	199.0521**
% nonwhite population	28.3318**	21.4913*
Industry forces		
Alcohol industry employment	−1.2040	—
Political forces		
Republican presidents	27.1360**	24.4503*
Bureaucratic forces		
Bureau leadership visibility	2.0609**	2.0093**
Federal drug arrests	26.6404*	25.9418*
R-square	.976	.975
Adjusted R-square	.968	.969
Durbin-Watson	1.65	1.67
Number of cases	42	42

Notes: Equations are estimated with ordinary least squares. A dash means the variable was omitted from the equation.

*p < .05
**p < .10

speculate that marijuana enforcement is enforcement that would occur without any federal stimulus; serious drug enforcement efforts, on the other hand, respond to the exhortations of the president and the chief federal drug law administrator.

The findings in Tables 3.7 and 3.8 underscore the importance of federal drug activities. Federal drug enforcement stimulates state law enforcement activity. Whether as a result of joint activities, federal grants, or serving as a role model, federal drug arrests have an impact far above the number of individuals arrested on federal charges. States following the federal lead provide a 26 to 1 increase in law enforcement effort for serious drug arrests and a 70 to 1 increase for mari-

Table 3.8

Determinants of State Marijuana Arrest Rates

Dependent variable = state marijuana arrests per 100,000 persons

Independent variables	Full model	Reduced model
Intercept	−818.5480	−721.9220
Trend	3.1219	—
Citizen forces		
Gross national product		
(billions)	−231.5109*	−176.0342*
Marijuana articles	−0.3162	—
Church membership	1.8053	—
Immigration rate	263.7490**	238.3500*
% nonwhite population	91.5917*	90.7243*
Industry forces		
Alcohol industry		
employment	−1.3305	—
Political forces		
Republican presidents	−0.6679	—
Bureaucratic forces		
Bureau leadership visibility	0.4190	—
Federal drug arrests	69.5485*	69.7204*
R-square	.893	.883
Adjusted R-square	.815	.860
Durbin-Watson	1.56	1.38
Number of cases	25	25

Notes: Equations are estimated with ordinary least squares. A dash means the variable was omitted from the equation.

   *p < .05
   **p < .10

juana arrests. We need to interpret federal drug policy in this light rather than discount federal activities because they are only a small portion of the total.

Prison Populations

During the enforcement of the Harrison Act, the proportion of the federal prison population incarcerated for drug offenses was a substantial segment of the total inmate population. With the drug war of the 1980s and 1990s, both federal and state prison populations have reached all-time highs. This section of the analysis

examines the impact of drug control policies on federal and state prison populations. The prison population measure is the number of prisoners per 100,000
persons.[25]

The results of the federal prisoners analysis are shown in Table 3.9. The most
important variable is the federal arrest rate; for every federal drug arrest, the
number of federal prisoners increases by 1.08, approximately a one-for-one relationship. Four legislative actions also influence the federal prison rate. The number of prisoners increased with the Marijuana Tax Act of 1937, the creation of
the Federal Bureau of Narcotics, and the Crime Control Act of 1984. The prison
population declined with the adoption of the Comprehensive Drug Abuse Prevention and Control Act of 1970. All relationships are as predicted. We should
also note that federal prison populations increase when slack resources decline
(and economics forces individuals into crime) and decrease with the growth in
church membership.

The impact of drug policies on state prison population is less direct (see Table
3.10). State drug arrest rates are positively associated with state prison populations, but the size of the coefficient is fairly small (0.1078); this relatively small
impact probably results because historically most state drug arrests have been for
possession and recent penalties for possession have not been severe. State prison
population follows the federal pattern of decreasing both with real incomes and
church membership. It also increases with immigration, perhaps reflecting the
relationship between state drug arrests and immigration. The negative relationship with federal drug agency enforcement has no logical explanation.

Policy Outcomes

Funding, personnel, arrests, and perhaps even prison populations are policy outputs. They are actions that political institutions (including the bureaucracy) can
directly affect. What is always an open question is, To what extent can these
outputs affect policy outcomes? Law enforcement agencies do not arrest people
simply for the sake of arresting people; they do so with the idea that arrests or
punishment will serve as a deterrent and, therefore, the undesired behavior will
be reduced. In the case of drug control, the goal is to reduce drug use by
individuals. The general strategy is perceived as taking two steps. First, law
enforcement creates shortages of drugs, thus increasing the street price of drugs
to the consumer. Second, the economic effects of rising prices along with potential legal penalties discourage individuals from buying and using drugs.

Although data on illicit drug prices and use are not as credible as data on
arrest rates or appropriations, efforts have been made to create statistical series
for comparison purposes. The Drug Enforcement Administration, by making
drug purchases and surveying local agencies that also make undercover drug
purchases, estimates a street price for various drugs. Although the DEA could
manipulate this series to make itself look good, it does not appear to do so. The

Table 3.9

Determinants of Federal Prison Population

Dependent variable = federal prisoners per 100,000 persons

Independent variables	Full model	Reduced model
Intercept	32.6732	14.4242
Trend	0.1534	0.5190*
Citizen forces		
Gross national product (billions)	−1.6412	−5.5640*
Drug abuse articles	−0.0307*	—
Church membership	−0.4998*	−0.3747*
Immigration rate	10.7033*	—
% nonwhite population	0.7644	—
Industry forces		
Alcohol industry employment	0.0283	—
Political forces		
Divided government	−0.0253	—
Republican presidents	0.4250	—
Creation of the Drug Enforcement Administration	−0.8381	—
Food and Drug Administration merger	0.0129	—
Republican members of Congress	−0.0592	—
Marijuana Tax Act 1937	3.6267*	3.1939*
Creation of the Federal Bureau of Narcotics	1.6212	2.8938*
Boggs Act 1951	2.3428	—
Boggs–Daniel Act 1956	1.2027	—
Comprehensive Drug Control Act 1970	−0.4654	−2.3602*
Crime Control Act 1984	4.2081*	2.6702*
Bureaucratic forces		
Bureau leadership visibility	0.0312	—
Bureau personnel	−4.7550	—
Federal drug arrest rate	0.8829*	1.0841*
R-square	.842	.812
Adjusted R-square	.757	.786
Durbin-Watson	1.76	0.38†
Number of cases	61	61

Notes: Equations are estimated with ordinary least squares. A dash means the variable was omitted from the equation.

*p < .05

†Rho for generalized least squares estimation.

Table 3.10

Determinants of State Prison Population

Dependent variable = state prisoners per 100,000 persons

Independent variables	Full model	Reduced model
Intercept	434.6341	488.0260
Trend	11.1332*	8.6207*
Citizen forces		
Gross national product (billions)	−58.7407**	−51.6994**
Drug abuse articles	0.1096	—
Church membership	−8.4085*	−7.5968*
Immigration rate	134.5860*	111.8060**
% nonwhite population	1.9789	—
Industry forces		
Alcohol industry employment	1.2254	—
Political forces		
Republican presidents	12.8287	—
Bureaucratic forces		
Bureau leadership visibility	−0.2934	—
Bureau personnel	−125.5990*	−90.5757*
State drug arrest rate	0.1182**	0.1078**
R-square	.957	.947
Adjusted R-square	.941	.938
Rho	.30	.67
Number of cases	42	42

Notes: Equations are estimated with generalized least squares. A dash means the variable was omitted from the equation.

*p < .05
**p < .10

price of drugs in the series has been known to decrease despite increased federal law enforcement. Three price series will be used as the first policy outcome, the estimated street prices for heroin, cocaine, and marijuana.[26] To control for inflation, these prices are adjusted to constant dollars.[27]

Three law enforcement variables should affect the street price of drugs. First, the amount of drugs seized by federal agencies (including the DEA, the Customs

Service, and the Coast Guard) will reduce the supply of drugs entering the United States. If the reduction is sufficient, street prices should rise with scarcity.[28] Data for total state and local seizures are not available. Because federal agencies have the responsibility for interdicting drugs before they reach the United States and give priority to trafficking offenses rather than possession offenses, they seize far more drugs than do local law enforcement agencies.

Second, enforcement activities of federal and state agencies should affect the price of drugs. As the risk of arrest increases, individuals must be compensated by higher prices in order to entice them to traffic in drugs. This risk should, thus, be reflected in the street price of drugs. Although the probability of arrest by state law enforcement officials is greater than that by federal officials, federal arrests are more likely to target traffickers than are state arrests. As a result, it is difficult *a priori* to conclude which should have the greater impact on drug prices.

Table 3.11 shows the determinants of the street price of heroin, cocaine, and marijuana. In all three cases, positive relationships would indicate that agency actions (policy outputs) increase street prices (policy outcomes). The results are disappointing from that viewpoint. Drug seizures and drug arrests have no impact on the price of heroin or cocaine (see also Johnson et al., 1990: 33). For marijuana, federal seizures are associated with increased prices, and state arrests with decreased prices.

Why might law enforcement actions affect marijuana but not heroin or cocaine? The reason is fairly obvious. Marijuana is bulky and has much less value per pound than either cocaine or heroin. As a result, profitable shipments are harder to conceal. Marijuana, therefore, is more difficult to smuggle and less profitable when it is smuggled. The rational drug trafficker would respond to enforcement pressure by leaving the higher-risk, lower-profit traffic to amateurs and concentrating on the lower-risk, higher-profit drugs—heroin and cocaine. Both heroin and cocaine appear to compensate risk sufficiently to entice individuals to smuggle it into the country at the current levels of law enforcement. Changes in the marijuana market (Kleiman, 1989) reveal another reason. As the importation of marijuana has declined, the domestic industry has become more profitable and expanded. Because domestically grown marijuana is approximately four times more potent than imported marijuana, some of the price increase may reflect payments for higher quality (Kleiman, 1989).

Why should federal drug seizures affect marijuana prices when state arrests do not? (The negative relationship for states clearly reflects some other factors because arrests would be unlikely to reduce the price of a good; it probably means that lower prices stimulate increased use, and thus more users are arrested.) One reason might be federal enforcement priorities. According to FBI data, as late as 1982 fully three of every four state drug arrests were for possession rather than sale or trafficking. Federal officials, in contrast, focus on trafficking offenses (78 percent of federal arrests are for trafficking). Because drug

Table 3.11

Determinants of Drug Prices

Dependent variable = DEA estimate of drug prices

Independent variables	Heroin	Cocaine	Marijuana
Intercept	3,055	611.6	3.352
Drugs seized by federal agencies	−305	−3.4	0.034*
Federal drug enforcement rate	−156**	−33.7	−0.008
State drug arrest rate	1	1.3	−0.007*
R-square	.72	.76	.94
Adjusted R-square	.66	.70	.93
Rho	.46	.75	.21
Number of cases	18	18	18

Note: Equations are estimated using generalized least squares.

*$p < .05$
**$p < .10$

traffickers are unlikely to be concerned with policies targeted at users, state arrest rates do not affect supply or, thus, prices.

Although enforcement policies had an impact on some drug prices, the results are disappointing. Enforcement activities had no impact on either heroin or cocaine, both associated with more serious problems, but did have an impact on marijuana, a substance that should really not be the focus of drug policy. In addition, the rise in marijuana prices might have resulted from the shift to more potent domestic marijuana and, thus, reflect changes in drug potency rather than a decrease in supply.

The other major policy outcome is drug use. Estimating the extent of drug use is a major undertaking with political ramifications. This model will employ a data series on drug use that, although biased, is biased in a consistent direction; the series consists of drug use figures for high school seniors. This is the longest existing drug use series, dating back to 1975, and is used in setting drug policy goals.[29] The specific data will be the national percentage of students who said they had tried heroin, cocaine, and marijuana in the past year (Johnston et al., 1989).

This data series has some serious limitations. First, high school students differ dramatically from other population groups. In particular, individuals who drop out of school are more likely to use drugs than students who remain in school. Because the dropout rate has changed only slowly since 1975, this source of bias can be considered constant. High school students are also different from the adult population. Patterns in high school drug use, however, closely mirror the National Institute of Drug Abuse's survey estimates of adult drug use. Any biases appear to be constant over time. The adult surveys are not usable for statistical analysis because they were not taken annually until recently.

Second, the survey question refers to drug use during the past year. Experimentation and even casual drug use is different from drug addiction. Individuals who use drugs once a year cannot be termed addicts under any medical definition of the word. The student surveys also measure drug use in the previous month; unfortunately, these questions produce very small user percentages except for marijuana. Because they are so small, the change of one single respondent can produce a sizable shift in the user percentage. Using this series would probably reveal more about small sample variation than it would about drug use. As a result our findings can be generalized to young, casual users; these individuals might well be more sensitive to efforts to discourage drug use than older individuals who regularly use drugs. Given the weaknesses of this measure, the results should be considered suggestive rather than definitive.

Three law enforcement variables will be used in the analysis. Similar to the assessment of prices, this model will incorporate federal drug seizures, federal drug enforcement, and state drug arrests. All three should produce negative relationships with drug use. Drug prices will also be included in the analysis. If drug demand is elastic, increases in price should reduce demand. If drug demand is inelastic (probably because drug prices are a small portion of total income), then prices will be unrelated to use.

Three other determinants of use will be incorporated in the model of drug usage. Clearly individuals form attitudes about the acceptability of drug use. The drug use survey also includes a question on whether or not students disapprove of drug usage; this variable will be the percentage of students who disapprove of casual use of the drug in question. Drug use might also be the result of drug availability. Some individuals will not use drugs simply because the drugs are not available. Heroin, for example, is difficult to obtain outside major coastal cities; marijuana appears to be available virtually everywhere. The independent variable used will be the percentage of students who state that they could obtain the drug in question if they wanted to do so. Drug use might also reflect the fear of any health consequences. To tap this potential fear, the National Institutes of Health series on accidental drug deaths will be used. Although this series contains data on both illicit and licit drug deaths, it is more comprehensive and more consistent over time than two other series that are based on medical examiner reports and emergency room visits.[30]

Table 3.12 presents the determinants of drug use. Although our prime concern is negative relationships for law enforcement activities, other findings are also of interest. Heroin use is negatively associated with disapproval of heroin and the number of drug deaths and positively related to state and federal enforcement. The negative relationship with deaths is especially important because heroin is the drug most likely to cause accidental overdoses owing to variations in purity. *None of the law enforcement variables has the predicted negative relationship with heroin use.* The positive relationship between federal and state enforcement and heroin use probably results because an increase in users makes the problem more visible, and federal and state law enforcement agencies respond by allocating more resources to heroin than to other drugs.

Cocaine use has somewhat different determinants from heroin use. Student use of cocaine is positively associated with the availability of cocaine, negatively associated with disapproval of use, and negatively associated with price. Enforcement efforts, both arrests and seizures, are unrelated to cocaine use; again we have evidence that law enforcement efforts do not deter casual drug use. Part of the deterrent logic, however, holds. Increases in the price of cocaine reduce cocaine consumption. Unfortunately, law enforcement activities affect so little of the cocaine market that these activities do not influence the price of cocaine (see Table 3.11). The relationship between price and use should also be qualified. These users are the most likely to be dissuaded from use as a result of price increases, because they are (1) casual users and (2) students with limited incomes.

The final column in Table 3.12 examines marijuana use. Four variables affect marijuana use—disapproval of use, the price of the drug, federal enforcement, and state enforcement.[31] One of these impacts, the price of the drug, is in the unexpected direction; that is, as prices increase, use also increases. Because this relationship is barely significant, the appropriate conclusion is probably that cost does not affect marijuana use. For the first time, law enforcement efforts appear to deter drug usage. As federal and state enforcement rates increase, marijuana use declines. Because federal marijuana efforts are targeted at distribution, this might be the result of reductions in supply. The state relationship is likely to be the deterrent effect of arrests (see Table 3.11). However, another possible explanation for these results exists. Similar coefficients would be generated if students were to shift to higher-priced, domestic marijuana when federal and state arrests make imported marijuana more expensive. Such a shift would simply transfer demand from imported marijuana to domestic marijuana. Similar consumption shifts from marijuana to other forms of intoxication (e.g., pills, cocaine, alcohol, etc.) might also occur.

The results of this analysis suggest that deterrence works, but only for marijuana. Enforcement appears to have no influence on experimentation with hard drugs. If marijuana were the nation's major drug problem, these results would be encouraging. Inasmuch as marijuana is not the major drug abuse problem, the results suggest a misallocation of resources.

Table 3.12

Determinants of Drug Use

Dependent variable = percentage of students who used drugs in the previous year

Independent variables	Heroin		Cocaine		Marijuana	
	Full model	Reduced model	Full model	Reduced model	Full model	Reduced model
Intercept	7.727	7.233	34.30	46.56	60.16	71.39
Disapproval of use	−0.086*	−0.082*	−0.367**	−0.581*	−0.372*	−0.395*
Price of drug	−0.000	—	−0.003*	−0.003*	1.415	1.043**
Drug seizures	−0.070	—	−0.038	—	−0.002	—
Federal enforcement	0.091*	0.096*	0.024	—	−3.057**	−3.279*
State arrests	0.004*	0.004*	−0.014	—	−0.019	−0.026*
Drug deaths	−0.168**	−0.106**	−0.940	—	−0.545	—
Drug availability	0.010	—	0.259*	0.183*	0.093	—
R-square	.94	.94	.95	.94	.98	.98
Adjusted R-square	.90	.91	.90	.92	.97	.98
Durbin-Watson	1.72	1.64	1.17	.32†	2.12	2.34
Number of cases	16	16	16	16	15	15

Notes: Equations are estimated with ordinary least squares. A dash means the variable was omitted from the equation.

*p < .05
**p < .10

†Rho for generalized least squares estimation.

Second-Order Consequences

Drug enforcement policies are attractive because drug consumption is related to crime. Whether or not drugs per se cause individuals to commit crimes (without an economic incentive to do so) is the subject of much dispute in the research literature, with most scholars skeptical of the argument that they do (Anglin, 1983; Chaiken and Chaiken, 1990), but a reasonable consensus holds that drug addicts commit crimes to raise money to purchase drugs (Wish and Johnson, 1986; Goldstein, 1989). As a result, decreasing drug usage is perceived as a way to reduce street crime. Two possible theoretical linkages exist between crime and drug enforcement actions.

A deterrence theory would hold that increasing law enforcement activities against drugs would reduce demand for drugs and thus crime (1) by incarcerating individuals who are committing crimes for the purpose of buying drugs, (2) by deterring some individuals from using drugs and committing crimes because the probability of apprehension is increased, and (3) by increasing the street price of drugs (necessary to compensate for risk in distribution) and limiting the amount of drugs an individual can afford. The correlation between drug enforcement activities and crime, therefore, should be negative (see Becker, 1968: 198).

An economic theory of drugs and crime predicts a different result (see Hellman, 1980). Prices for drugs are simply a function of supply and demand. The concept of an addict is an individual who has difficulty in restricting his or her urges for drug consumption; for such an individual, the demand for drugs is inelastic or nearly so. Prices, including the price of being caught, under such circumstances may be irrelevant to the addict. The addict will need either to find drug substitutes for the drug of choice or to increase his or her income to be commensurate with the price of drugs. The result could well be an increase in crime to pay for the increased price of drugs. The correlation between drug enforcement and crime, therefore, will be positive.

Table 3.13 models the impact of drug enforcement policy on major property and violent crimes. The dependent crime variables are the FBI crime rates for all crimes known to police from 1950 to 1990. Each crime variable is predicted, using a trend to eliminate any general increases or decreases in crime rates. Drug enforcement activities are then measured by using the federal and state drug enforcement rates for the previous year. These variables are lagged by one year because individual responses to increased drug enforcement should take some time to materialize. That is, in terms of deterrence, court systems are not instantaneous, nor are price adjustments for risk or perceptions of risk. Similarly, price increases triggering economic behavior changes will probably not be instantaneous but rather occur over a period of time. Because state arrest rates are so much greater than federal rates, state arrests should be more likely to show significant impacts than federal enforcement.

Table 3.13

Impact of Drug Arrests on Violent Crime

Independent variables	Dependent variables = national rates for:					
	Murder	Robbery	Assault	Burglary	Larceny	All violent
Intercept	4.986	19.21	−7.39	127.7	−234.1	19.85
Trend	0.045	3.83*	6.00*	31.39*	70.29*	10.22*
State arrests (lagged)	0.010*	0.31*	0.23*	0.04	0.65	0.63*
Federal cases (lagged)	−0.289	−12.10**	0.51	−10.53	25.78	−15.31
R-square	.91	.97	.98	.93	.97	.99
Adjusted R-square	.90	.97	.98	.93	.97	.98
Rho	.76	.70	.81	.79	.76	.73
Number of cases	41	41	41	41	41	41

Note: Equations are estimated with generalized least squares.

*p < .05
**p < .10

Significant enforcement effects occur only for some of the crime variables. In only one case, the impact of federal drug enforcement on robbery
crimes, does a relationship exist that is consistent with the deterrence hypothesis. Because federal enforcement is targeted primarily at traffickers, the
relationship with robbery is troublesome. Robbery is a user-related crime;
murder is more likely be a dealer-related crime because dealers compete for
distribution territories. This relationship, therefore, should be interpreted with
some skepticism. Four significant relationships are consistent with the economic hypothesis—the impact of state drug arrests on murder rates, on robbery rates, on assault rates, and on rates for all violent crime. As state drug
arrests increase, so too do reported murders, robberies, larceny, and total
violent crimes. This finding is consistent with the notion that drug arrests
trigger compensating behaviors when the drug market adjusts to greater enforcement.[32]

Substantive Conclusions

This chapter examined a wide range of policy outputs and outcomes in drug law enforcement. Substantive conclusions of the study can best be organized by the independent variable under consideration. The study found that drug enforcement efforts are affected by slack resources. When the gross national product increases, federal budgets and personnel allocations to drug law enforcement increase. State drug arrests are also positively related to the gross national product. Salience, as measured by articles about drug abuse and marijuana in popular magazines, is unrelated to drug policy actions. Few relationships exist, and most of those are in the unexpected direction.

Public attitudes toward drugs were measured by church membership. The chapter found that increases in the number of church members are associated with less enforcement of drug laws and more lenient sentencing. The one exception is the positive relationship between church membership and federal marijuana arrests.

The findings in regard to immigrants and nonwhite population are consistent with the historical evidence on the discriminatory intent of drug laws. When nonwhite population increases, the federal government increases resources allocated to drug law enforcement. Federal enforcement of the drug laws, however, is negatively related to nonwhite population. State drug enforcement, rather than federal enforcement, increases when minority population increases. Immigration increases, on the other hand, are associated with both more federal and more state drug law enforcement. The problem identified by historians, therefore, is generally the result of state implementation.

Attempts to find a relationship between the alcohol production industry and drug policy were unsuccessful. None of the predicted relationships is evident. Partisanship produces mixed results. In only one case does party competition appear to make a difference; competition leads to more personnel assigned to the federal drug enforcement agency. Republican presidents have only two impacts; they are positively associated with more federal marijuana enforcement and positively associated with more state drug law enforcement. Congressional Democrats are associated with more personnel assigned to drug law enforcement and more federal drug arrests. Given the large number of possible relationships, these partisan findings should be interpreted as only mixed support for a relationship between partisanship and drug policy.

Presidential reorganization powers are strongly associated with changes in federal drug policies. Reorganizations are able to control both agency policy and some of the consequences of that policy. Congressional laws receive strong support as a control over drug enforcement policy. Such actions appear to work well, although the results of the law are not always as Congress has intended. In total, however, an objective analyst would have to conclude that political institutions, with the exception of the courts, have a great deal of influence on federal drug policy implementation.

Bureaucratic capacity has its predicted impact on agency enforcement. Given that capacity is determined by political institutions, this implies that federal drug enforcement policy is determined less by the bureaucracy and more by national political institutions. The federalism impacts, however, suggest that the national bureaucracy does have an influence that is outside the control of the national political institutions. Federal arrest rates are the major determinant of state arrest rates for both marijuana and other drugs. Bureaucratic leadership has only one significant impact, a positive impact on state drug arrest rates.[33] Federal drug arrest rates have a strong influence on the federal prison population, but state drug arrest rates have only a minor influence on state prison population.

The analysis of policy outcomes and second-order consequences reveals a major shortcoming of U.S. drug abuse policies. State and federal enforcement actions have no impact on the price and use of heroin or cocaine, but do appear to deter the use of marijuana. Such meager success, however, is countered by severely negative second-order consequences. Increases in state drug law enforcement are associated with increases in crime, particularly in murders, robberies, assaults, and all violent crime.

Theoretical Conclusions

Overall the policy theory outlined in chapter 1 showed excellent results; only rarely was it limited to explaining less than 90 percent of the variance. Although time series models generally have high levels of explanation, these results must be considered even more promising than the typical results are. In terms of theoretical clusters, citizen-related forces have several strong impacts, but they would have to be considered passive impacts. Citizen forces seem to be related to being victims of drug law enforcement (nonwhite population, immigration) or avoidance of drugs (church attendance) rather than the active structuring of institutions to influence policy. The impact of industry forces, as expected in an area without a legitimate industry, is nil.

Political institutions are the dominant force in drug abuse policies. Through laws and reorganizations, the major political institutions are able to control a great deal of drug policy implementation. Such a finding is consistent with the literature that suggests political institutions dominate in issue areas that can be framed as noncomplex and salient. Salience, given its lack of impact on drug policies, may well be generated by political institutions rather than having influence over political institutions.

Bureaucracy was a modest player in drug policy. Perhaps the best metaphor for bureaucratic discretion in this area is the water faucet. When the faucet is turned on (that is, when bureaucracy is given resources), the water approaches the top of the basin (enforcement expands dramatically). When the faucet is turned off (when resources are withdrawn), the water level (and enforcement) drops. The political institutions cannot control who is arrested, but they do control the overall volume of arrests.

The findings, especially those regarding policy outcomes, suggest that drug policy in the United States is a failure. Enforcement actions appear to affect only marijuana and at the same time generate some major negative consequences.[34] We might speculate that one reason for this policy failure is the weakness of the federal drug enforcement agency. Without the expertise to challenge the actions of political institutions, it is swept along with the strong political winds generated by the president and Congress. Bureaucracy is unable to play its important role of providing expertise so that drug policy options can be debated. Without such debate, the adoption and resulting enforcement of ill-advised policies are almost a given.

Notes

1. The quality of data varies greatly among the individual measures used in this analysis. My bias is that performing analysis on marginal data is a superior strategy to taking policy actions without any analysis at all.

2. Drug enforcement was initially part of the Internal Revenue Bureau and then a division in the Prohibition Unit of the Treasury Department. The Federal Bureau of Narcotics lasted from 1930 to 1968, when the Federal Bureau of Narcotics and Dangerous Drugs was created in the Justice Department. An additional reorganization transformed this unit into the Drug Enforcement Administration in 1973.

3. In the alcohol chapters, the percentage of Democratic lawmakers is used. If this inconsistency bothers the reader, multiply the slopes in the drug chapters by −1.

4. The creation of the Federal Bureau of Narcotics, although the result of a reorganization, was brought about through congressional legislation rather than executive action. This variable differs somewhat from the others in that it is coded 1 only until 1968, when the Federal Bureau of Narcotics was merged into the Federal Bureau of Narcotics and Dangerous Drugs. Presidents were also involved in the 1937 and 1970 laws, so these impacts may also reflect presidential influence.

5. Perhaps the most prominent example was the Nixon administration's restriction of drug investigations that implicated Nixon campaign contributor Robert Vesco (see Bellis, 1981).

6. Data on court cases at the district level are available from the Administrative Office of the U.S. Courts, *Annual Report* (Washington, DC: U.S. Government Printing Office). In this case the data after 1945 were taken from Maguire and Flanagan, 1991.

7. This measure was created by examining the *Reader's Guide to Periodical Literature* for each year from 1910 to 1990. Drug articles varied somewhat in where they were classified, appearing under narcotics, individual drug names, drug abuse, or drug trafficking. An effort was made to be as inclusive as possible. Marijuana articles are counted separately because marijuana is a relatively harmless drug subjected to fairly heavy penalties. This approach to salience of drug issues has been used by Becker (1963) and Himmelstein (1983). This series shows dramatic changes in salience over time. The number of drug abuse articles ranged from a low of 0 in several years to 113 in 1986 (the Len Bias year).

8. Although data are lacking, one might surmise that consumption of illicit drugs also increases during good economic times. With more money to spend, demand for recreation, including recreational drugs, is likely to increase.

9. Marx stated that religion was the opiate of the masses. In this light one might argue that religion and drugs are substitutes for each other. Church membership data are re-

ported in the U.S. Bureau of the Census, *Historical Statistics of the United States: Colonial Times to 1970* (Washington, DC: U.S. Government Printing Office, 1975), and the annual *Statistical Abstract of the United States* (Washington, DC: U.S. Government Printing Office).

10. The Bureau of the Census provides information on both the number of immigrants per year and the nonwhite U.S. population, which it defines as blacks, Asians, and Native Americans. Data before 1970 can be found in *Historical Statistics of the United States: Colonial Times to 1970,* and data after 1970 can be found in the various issues of the *Statistical Abstract of the United States.* The percentage of nonwhites is used rather than the percentage of blacks, because the census did not report separate figures for blacks for the early part of the twentieth century.

11. The alcohol production industry is capital intensive and thus fairly small. The retail side of the alcohol industry is much larger, yet the conspiracy nature of the alcohol–drugs connection suggests that influence would have to be transmitted behind the scenes by major industrial leaders. The retail side of the industry simply does not produce such individuals. The data can be found in the U.S. Bureau of the Census, *Annual Survey on Manufactures* (Washington, DC: U.S. Government Printing Office).

12. The trend variable is coded 1 in the first year of the analysis and increased by 1 for each year thereafter. When the trend variable picks up the incremental changes from year to year, it more difficult to find significance for other variables. The analysis, therefore, has a conservative bias.

13. Any time series is susceptible to problems related to serial correlation. The statistical impact of serial correlation is that ordinary least squares estimates will be unbiased but not efficient (Lewis-Beck, 1986). Each equation presented was tested for serial correlation. When such correlation was found, the equations were reestimated using generalized least squares. The specific software used was SST (Statistical Software Tools).

14. Data from 1930 to 1990 were taken from the Office of Management and Budget, *Budget of the United States Government* (Washington, DC: U.S. Government Printing Office, annual), for each year. Before 1930, data on appropriations were not listed separately in the budget. Congress, however, did make specific appropriations for narcotics control. These were reported in Schmeckebier, 1929. Because courts do not participate in the budgeting of funds, they were not included in this table or in Table 3.2.

15. This time series is shorter than the budget time series because personnel figures are not available before 1930. Before this year, narcotics enforcement was part of either prohibition enforcement or internal revenue. These agencies did not provide personnel or budget breakdowns for drug control efforts. Budget data date back only to 1916 because Congress made specific drug control appropriations from 1916 to 1930. All data after 1930 are from the annual federal budget.

16. The Boggs Act and the Boggs–Daniel Act can affect personnel but not budgets because budgets are in constant dollars and because we incorporate a measure of overall resources (GNP). Total agency budgets did increase in nominal terms in the 1950s but increased more slowly than overall government growth.

17. These data are from Maguire and Flanagan, 1991. This source provided data for 1945 to 1990. Data prior to 1945 were collected from the annual reports of the U.S. Department of the Treasury to Congress. The actual series runs from 1917 to 1990, but the limitation on one important independent variable (number of personnel) restricts the analysis to 1930–90. This series counts only cases that are referred to the Justice Department for prosecution. Some individuals might be arrested who are not referred. Referrals rather than arrests are used for two reasons. First, reliable data exist because Justice Department figures can be used to corroborate drug agency figures. Drug agency arrest rates are not consistently reported. Second, arrests are less likely to have an impact than are referrals

for prosecution because punishment is possible only if the individual is prosecuted. Federal attorneys may still decline to prosecute if they feel a case is weak.

18. These data are from the same source as the drug arrest data. This series runs from 1938, the first year of enforcement for the Marijuana Tax Act, to 1989, or 52 years.

19. Courts are omitted from this section also because they make the actual decisions on the length of sentences. Data are taken from the annual reports of the Administrative Office of the U.S. Courts.

20. The peak year for state drug arrests was 1989, with nearly 1.4 million drug arrests.

21. Some data exist before 1945, but the coverage of FBI data before then is fairly limited. Even this series is not as reliable as one would like until at least 1960. The level of reporting even at the present time is not universal.

22. I am reasonably confident that federal enforcement influences state arrest rates but that state arrest rates do not affect federal rates. When the two series are examined with lagged responses, federal enforcement from the previous year has a significant impact on state drug arrests for the current year, even controlling for state arrests for the previous year. State drug arrests for the previous year, however, are unrelated to federal drug enforcement for the current year when controlling for federal drug enforcement for the previous year.

23. Data presented later in this chapter reveal that most federal arrests involve trafficking offenses and most state-local arrests involve possession. The state-local pattern has changed recently, but this might have occurred because possession of larger amounts has been designated as "possession with intent to deliver."

24. In this case the Durbin–Watson statistic is borderline. Estimation of this equation with generalized least squares showed the same results.

25. The source of the prison data is the U.S. Bureau of Justice Statistics, *Prisoners in State and Federal Institutions on December 31* (Washington, DC: U.S. Department of Justice, annual). The limited number of data points for some of the independent variables restricts the analysis to 61 years for federal prisoners and 42 years for state prisoners.

26. Data can be found in Maguire and Flanagan, 1991. After 1988 the DEA provides only a range of prices. This change occurred in response to criticism that prices vary by location and by time of year. These price ranges were converted to point estimates by using the midpoint of the range.

27. The failure to control for inflation can produce misleading results; see M. H. Moore, 1990: 125–127.

28. Reuter (1988) argues that interdiction efforts, re futile, that only a minute portion of drug imports is seized. As a result, seizures should have no impact on the price of street drugs because supply will continue to outstrip demand. There is, in fact, some evidence of self-regulation of supply in the recent seizures that have uncovered large storage warehouses. Such warehouses are of use only if large amounts of drugs must be stockpiled rather than put into the distribution pipeline.

29. President Bush's recent drug control plan expressed one goal as a 30 percent reduction in the number of persons who use drugs according to this survey.

30. Data are taken from the National Center for Health Statistics, *Vital Statistics of the United States* (Bethesda, MD: Department of Health and Human Services, annual). The other data series come from the Drug Abuse Warning Network (DAWN), which collects data from selected hospital emergency rooms and medical examiner reports. The DAWN data record the number of times drugs are mentioned (which may or may not be the cause of the visit or death). The DAWN data are difficult to compare from year to year because additional sites are often added. An effort has been made to provide a consistent DAWN series, but that series is fairly short.

31. For a similar finding on disapproval using a different method, see Bachman et al., 1988.

32. This finding should be treated as suggestive. If state drug arrests had been shown to have an impact on price in Table 3.11, then the logic of the economic approach to crime would have greater support. In comparing the reliability of the price series and the crime series, the crime series is probably the better series. It is a substantially longer series, and the determination of crime rates is somewhat more direct than the determination of drug prices. In addition, the price series is not sensitive to location variations in drug prices. State arrests might affect prices in states where large numbers of arrests are made but not have an overall impact on nationwide prices because drug distribution might respond to the risk of apprehension. After completing this analysis, I found a similar argument by Friedman (1991), using a more descriptive look at historical data.

33. Perhaps it is true that a prophet is not without honor except in his own country. Federal drug enforcement leaders appear to be able to influence the actions of state agencies but have little impact on the policy actions at the federal level.

34. Several negative consequences cannot be quantified. It is my impression that drug wars often result in major intrusions on the rights of individuals. The appeals of drug cases that I have read suggest that virtually any violation of criminal procedure will be overlooked if drugs were involved. Others have also noticed this during other periods of peak drug law enforcement (see chapter 2).

4

The State Politics of Drug Abuse[†]

Although the federal government receives the lion's share of publicity in the current war on drugs, that war is largely being fought by state and local governments, not by federal law enforcement agencies. In 1989 the federal government referred only 22,000 drug cases for prosecution, whereas state governments arrested over 1.36 million persons for drug offenses. Even though some of this difference reflects differences in law enforcement priorities (e.g., the federal priority on trafficking offenses), it underscores the vital role of state governments as policymaking entities. Despite this importance, only a single political study of state drug control exists in the literature (Meier, 1992).

This chapter, using the theory outlined in chapter 1, examines state efforts to control drug usage through the passage of legislation and policy implementation. The format of the analysis will be similar to other chapters. After a discussion of the necessary modifications in the theory so that it can be applied to a cross-sectional state analysis, the independent variables will be operationalized. The policy theory will then be tested with measures of state drug laws, state drug enforcement activities, and the policy consequences of state drug activities. An extended analysis of race and drug enforcement at the state level will be included.

Theoretical Modifications

Cross-sectional analysis has some weaknesses that require modification in the policy theory presented in chapter 1. Many drug laws result from political entrepreneurs exploiting a favorable environment to get new legislation passed. The role of Harry Anslinger in passing the Marijuana Tax Act of 1937, the Boggs Act

---

[†]This chapter is a revised, extended, and updated version of an article published in the 1992 *Western Political Quarterly*. Additional independent variables have been added to fit the theoretical framework. Data on the drug treatment bureaucracy, state arrest rates, and the impact of drug enforcement on crime have been updated. The materials found in Tables 4.5, 4.6, and 4.8 were not examined in that article.

of 1951, and the Boggs–Daniel Act of 1956 is well known (see chapter 2). The activities of libertarian Republicans in passing marijuana decriminalization statutes in the 1970s are also documented (see chapter 2). Recent federal drug entrepreneurs have included William Bennett and Joseph Biden. Cross-sectional analysis generally does not reveal political entrepreneurs because the role of such individuals can usually be discovered only with in-depth case studies. Similarly the political environments that are exploited by entrepreneurs are often national trends in public opinion and other factors that will be relatively constant across states. The role of political entrepreneurs, in this chapter, will be a residual hypothesis. That is, if political entrepreneurs are a major determinant of the adoption of state drug laws, then political factors that can be measured will explain little of the variation in state drug laws. This relationship should hold only for laws; the implementation of those laws should reflect political and bureaucratic factors that can be measured.

The other set of variables that needs to be modified, as it does in all illicit drug chapters, is that of industry. The drug industry is illegal and, therefore, tapping its presence is difficult. Even if the presence could be openly established, the industry would not be able to participate in the policy process along with legitimate industries. The only industry forces examined in this chapter, therefore, will be for the alcohol industries. The remaining variables—citizen forces, political forces, and bureaucratic influences—can be measured and will be included in the model. The nature of state-level data is such that laws, implementation, and policy outcomes can all be assessed.

Independent Variables

Since the initial attempts at empirical policy analysis using state-level data (see Dawson and Robinson, 1963; Dye, 1966), our models have grown more sophisticated. Yet the general approach has changed little. Policy is seen as resulting from the interaction of political institutions (parties, legislatures, governors, bureaucracies, etc.), subject to constraints imposed by the social, economic, and political environments (Dye, 1966; Hofferbert, 1969; Lowery and Gray, 1990). This analysis focuses specifically on drug control policies, but the general approach is consistent with these past efforts.

Citizen Forces/the Policy Environment

Policy issues are not equally salient. Some issues are so salient that they must be addressed in nearly every legislative session (e.g., taxes). Other issues reach the legislative agenda only periodically; drug abuse is such an issue. The ebb and flow of drug issues imply that a relevant environmental variable is the visibility of drug usage.[1] A state with highly visible drug markets or with escalating drug-related crime is more likely to perceive the need to address its drug policies. A state with marijuana as the only available illicit drug will see less need to act. The hypothesis is that, when visible drug use (and thus salience) increases in a state, then that state will be more likely to pass strong drug control policies and to support aggressive implementation of those policies.

The amount of drug usage is difficult to measure. Because drug consumption, at least for drugs other than marijuana, is generally an urban phenomenon, the percentage of the population living in urban areas can be used as a surrogate, although it is a fairly indirect measure of use. A second indicator of use attempts to measure it more directly by looking at some consequences of drug use. As drug usage increases, a state should see more of the harmful effects of drug use: more individuals will seek drug treatment, more individuals will acquire drug-related diseases, and law enforcement officers will seize more drugs. Five indicators are used. The first three are the numbers of drug abuse treatment admissions per 100,000 persons for 1979, 1985, and 1987. The fourth indicator is the hepatitis B rate per 100,000 persons; hepatitis B can be transmitted by using contaminated needles to inject drugs (see Johnson et al., 1990: 50). The fifth indicator is a per capita measure of drug seizures by the Drug Enforcement Administration; the drugs include heroin, cocaine, marijuana, and pills (amphetamines and barbiturates).[2] These indicators were factor analyzed, with a single factor explaining 48 percent of the variance. States that score high on this measure will be considered to have greater drug usage.

Chapter 3 argued that drug wars are fought when the nation has slack resources. Historically, drug legislation was passed in times when the economy was booming. At the state level, therefore, states with ample financial resources should be more likely to devote a greater effort toward drug control. The measure of state potential resources will be per capita income in that state.[3]

Chapter 3 also showed that drug use is strongly correlated with attitudes toward the use of drugs. At the state level, good surveys on attitudes toward drugs do not exist; therefore, surrogates are needed. The first surrogate is the percentage of the state population that belongs to churches. Ties to religion are expected to discourage individuals from using drugs. The second measure of attitudes attempts to tap individuals who have had negative experiences with drugs. Substance abuse is a policy area with a wide variety of voluntary self-help organizations composed of persons with negative drug experiences. Although most of these organizations are visible because they are active in alcohol treatment (e.g., Alcoholics Anonymous), they also participate in drug rehabilitation efforts. Self-help groups have a vested interest in drug control policies because the policies generate potential members. Self-help organizations benefit if individuals are made aware of their drug problems by law enforcement agencies, but they do not benefit if these individuals are removed from their reach (that is, placed in prison). The measure used is the number of Alcoholics Anonymous, Al-Anon, Alateen, and National Council on Alcoholism chapters per 100,000 persons.[4] Self-help organizations will generally favor treatment and education approaches over law enforcement approaches. Among law enforcement policies, however, self-help groups are more likely to favor vigorous enforcement of drug laws (contacts that make people aware of their problem) but oppose harsh penalties because they believe that treatment is superior to punishment as a solution to drug abuse.

A final citizen/environmental variable that must be considered is race. Historians have documented the racial biases in drug control policies (Helmer, 1975). Our first drug laws, aimed at prohibiting opium smoking (but not consumption by other means), were passed after an influx of Chinese immigrants in the nineteenth century (Morgan, 1978; Hamowy, 1987a: 13). Restrictive state marijuana laws during the 1930s were justified by contentions that marijuana-intoxicated blacks and Mexicans were responsible for the bulk of violent crime (Musto, 1987). Harsh federal penalties were adopted during the 1950s after federal law enforcement officials argued that drug use by blacks and Puerto Ricans had increased dramatically (King, 1972). When drug use by white middle-class young people became common in the late 1960s and early 1970s, the federal government and many state governments relaxed their drug laws (Rosenthal, 1977).

Some evidence exists that race plays a role in the current enforcement of drug laws. Surveys by the National Institute on Drug Abuse (1988) show that the proportions of whites (37 percent) and blacks (36 percent) who have ever used illicit drugs are approximately equal, as are the proportions of whites (7.0 percent) and blacks (7.8 percent) who used drugs in the past month. Arrest statistics collected by the Federal Bureau of Investigation (1990), however, reveal that blacks, who constitute only 12.4 percent of the population, account for 40.7 percent of all persons arrested for drug offenses. Chapter 3 revealed that drug arrests for all 50 states increased when minority population increased. Some authors attribute these differences to racial discrimination in enforcement, arguing that blacks are more likely to be stopped without probable cause and searched for drugs (Helmer, 1975; Kolb, 1962: 156–158). The historical evidence as well as the current arrest data, then, suggest that states with larger minority populations will pass stronger drug control laws and implement the laws more aggressively. The race measures are straightforward; for each state, measures of the percentage of black population and the percentage of Hispanic population will be used.[5]

Political Forces

The politics of drugs differs from the politics of most other policy areas. No one supports drug abuse; virtually everyone is opposed. Neither political party currently advocates liberalization of drug control polices. A reading of several case studies involving the decriminalization of marijuana and the passage of federal drug control laws (Anderson, 1981; Himmelstein, 1983; Bonnie and Whitebread,

1974; see chapter 2) reveals a politics dominated by one or more entrepreneurs seeking to shape drug policy for political gain (e.g., Congressman Hale Boggs during the 1950s; Senator Joseph Biden, today).

Despite bipartisan support for the current drug war, the major political parties have advocated two different approaches to the problem. The Republican party is more closely associated with law enforcement approaches to drug abuse than is the Democratic party. (Contrast the national debate between President Bush and Senator Biden; see Biskupic, 1989.) The Democrats' preference for treatment rather than law enforcement can be tied to their more liberal political ideology. Still, individuals who seek to modify the predominant law enforcement approach to drug abuse are taking a major political risk because law enforcement advocates may label them as soft on drugs. Challenges to the law enforcement approach to drug abuse are likely to occur only when the possible benefits of such action greatly outweigh the costs. As a result, Democrats might be more likely to make this effort when they have a real chance of becoming the majority party or of losing majority party status. In other words, when party competition intensifies, alternatives to the law enforcement approach to drugs might find favor. The political hypotheses, therefore, are that states with competitive parties, more liberal orientations, and even more Democratic policymakers will be less likely to adopt and to support aggressive implementation of law enforcement–oriented drug control policies.

Political forces will be measured by three variables—Democratic partisanship, party competition, and liberal voters. Democratic partisanship is simply the Democratic percentage of the vote in state elections for 1980–86. Party competition is the Ranney party competition index constructed by Bibby and colleagues (1990). Liberal voters were operationalized as the percentage of the 1972 vote cast for George McGovern. The McGovern election is used because it occurred when drugs were a salient political issue, and the two candidates took contrasting stands on the dangers of drug use.

Industry/Interest Group Forces

One major difference between drug control policies and other regulatory policies is that the industry producing the product (illicit drugs) has no political standing. Even in areas that regulate products with potential harms (alcohol or tobacco, for example), the production industry is perceived as a legitimate political interest with the right to petition governments for favorable public policies (see chapter 7). In drug abuse control the production industry is illegal, and attempts by the industry to influence public policy, at least in the United States, would likely be rejected out of hand. Except for the small and marginally effective National Organization for the Reform of Marijuana Laws (NORML), the interests of illicit drug consumers are also absent from legitimate politics.

Just because traditional producer and consumer groups are not found in drug control politics does not mean that organized interests have no stake in drug control policies. An industry with a potential interest in drug abuse policy is the alcohol industry. Historians and journalists have intimated that the infamous Marijuana Tax Act of 1937 was adopted at the urging of distillers and brewers in order to eliminate marijuana as a competitive intoxicant (Sloman, 1979: 202; Hamowy, 1987a; Grinspoon, 1971: 16). A report by the U.S. Public Health Service, in fact, attributed the perceived rise in drug addiction in the 1920s to prohibition (Bonnie and Whitebread, 1974: 55). Although the quantitative historical study found no evidence of the involvement of the alcohol industries, this chapter will attempt to link those industries with contemporary drug policies. If states with large alcohol industries have stronger drug control laws and more aggressive enforcement of drug laws, then some circumstantial evidence linking the alcohol industries to drug policies will be established.

Alcohol producers will be measured by the number of licensed commercial alcohol producers per 1 million persons.[6] Tavern owners, who represent the retail side of the alcohol industries, will be measured by the number of establishments selling for on-premises and off-premises consumption per 100,000 persons.[7]

Bureaucratic Forces

That bureaucratic agencies are major players in the policy process has been established in a wide variety of contexts (Rourke, 1984; Meier, 1993; Scholz and Wei, 1986; Wood, 1988; Mladenka, 1981). Agencies frequently participate in the formulation of public policies by lobbying policymakers. Federal drug agencies have a long history of influencing the actions of other policymakers. Congress passed the Marijuana Tax Act in response to pressure from the Treasury Department (which housed the Federal Bureau of Narcotics; see Himmelstein, 1983). The Federal Bureau of Narcotics in the 1950s skillfully shaped the agenda of the Kefauver hearings on organized crime and eventually persuaded Congress to pass two laws (the Boggs Act of 1951 and the Boggs–Daniel Act of 1956) that greatly increased penalties for violating federal drug laws (Kolb, 1962).

Bureaucracies also implement policy decisions made by legislatures and chief executives. In the implementation process they must interpret policy objectives, adapt the policy to changing circumstances in the real world, and integrate the policy with other policies delegated to the agency. During implementation agencies can use their political support, expertise, vitality, and leadership skills to remake public policy (Rourke, 1984; Mladenka, 1981).

State governments face bureaucratic pressures from two sources. First, law enforcement agencies can be expected to press for stronger laws and more aggressive enforcement. Second, state governments also face bureaucratic pressures from the federal drug enforcement agencies. The general structure of state controlled-substance laws is similar to the federal law because federal agencies helped draft the Uniform State Controlled Substance Act (the law also requires local law enforcement officials to cooperate with federal drug agents). Federal law enforcement officials also lobbied for state laws that restricted marijuana in the 1930s (see Himmelstein, 1983) and laws that increased penalties in the 1950s (Bonnie and Whitebread, 1974). When he was drug czar, one of William Bennett's activities was to lobby for stronger state laws. In addition to lobbying and urging new legislation, federal drug agencies can encourage states to be more aggressive in enforcing laws by undertaking joint operations with local officers. Both local and federal law enforcement agencies, therefore, should support strict drug laws and aggressive enforcement. The state law enforcement bureaucracy measure is the number of law enforcement persons employed by state and local government per 100,000 persons.[8] The federal law enforcement measure is the number of cases referred to federal courts for marijuana or for other drugs per 100,000 persons in the state.[9]

The interests of law enforcement agencies in drug control policies are fairly obvious. Not so obvious is the interest of another bureaucracy, the treatment bureaucracy (see Sharp, 1992). Drug control laws generate clientele for treatment agencies; as a result, the temptation exists for these agencies to support drug control policies that generate more demand for their services. Drug treatment bureaucracies may support efforts to notify individuals that they have drug problems but oppose policies that put these individuals beyond their reach. Specifically, these agencies might support aggressive implementation of drug laws because drug arrests may cause individuals to seek help. They will probably oppose harsh drug penalties because they perceive that treatment, not punishment, is the appropriate method for combating drug abuse. The drug treatment bureaucracy measure is the state treatment capacity for drug abuse (e.g., number of beds per 100,000 persons).[10]

Findings

This chapter uses data from the 50 U.S. states to examine drug control policies. Drug control policies will be divided into two categories—those concerning marijuana and those for other drugs (e.g., heroin, cocaine, amphetamines, and barbiturates). Dating back to the Marijuana Tax Act of 1937 and the classic cult movie *Reefer Madness* in 1936, U.S. policies have paid far more attention to marijuana than its dangers merit. Other nations that have adopted restrictive marijuana laws have generally done so at the urging of U.S. officials participating in international drug conferences. The analysis will also be divided into policy formulation (or the adoption of laws) and policy implementation (the arrest of offenders).

Marijuana Laws

Despite the effort to encourage uniform state drug legislation, state drug control laws vary, especially in the level of punishment for different infractions. The greatest variation in state drug laws concerns the treatment of marijuana. Some states follow the federal example and include it in the same category as heroin, cocaine, and other dangerous drugs. Other states classify marijuana as a separate drug for purposes of law enforcement.

To provide an overview of state marijuana policy, nine aspects of state marijuana laws were examined. These items are both the maximum fine and the maximum jail term for possession of small amounts of marijuana, the maximum fine and the maximum jail term for cultivating small amounts of marijuana, the maximum fine and the maximum jail term for sale of small amounts of marijuana, the maximum fine and the maximum penalty for sale of large amounts of marijuana, and whether or not the state has a conditional discharge law (permitting an individual to be placed on probation with the record expunged if no further offenses occur).[11] These nine variables were factor analyzed, and the process produced three significant factors. The first factor, designated marijuana fines, has positive scores for states that have large fines for marijuana offenses. The second factor, designated marijuana jail terms, has positive loadings for longer jail terms for marijuana offenses. The third factor, termed light marijuana penalties, is composed of policies of small fines and short jail terms.[12] A fourth marijuana policy exists that should be included in the analysis. Eleven states have essentially decriminalized the possession of small amounts of marijuana; in those states possession of marijuana is subject to a small fine but not a jail term. A dummy variable is included for those states that have decriminalized marijuana.[13]

Table 4.1 shows the impact of the various policy forces on the adoption of marijuana laws (insignificant variables were deleted from the analysis). Immediately noticeable is the modest level of explanation ranging from 17 percent to 42 percent. Several environmental forces have an impact on various marijuana policies. As expected, legislators respond to how serious the drug problem is. In states with higher drug consumption, marijuana is less likely to be decriminalized, fines for marijuana offenses are likely to be higher, and jail terms for marijuana are likely to be longer.[14]

Several other citizen/environmental forces are associated with marijuana laws. Income is negatively associated with stiff jail penalities. Church membership is correlated with criminalization of marijuana and large fines for violations. In contrast Hispanic population is associated with decriminalization and lower fines. Black population is also related to decriminalization but to heavier penalties (negatively correlated with light penalties). Finally self-help groups are associated with decriminalization but also longer jail terms.[15] None of these relationships is especially strong.

Political forces have modest impacts on marijuana laws. Democratic majorities are associated with decriminalization and lower fines, but also longer jail terms. Party competition is related to decriminalization and greater jail terms, and liberal voters are correlated with lower penalties for marijuana offenses. The

Table 4.1

Determinants of State Marijuana Laws

Independent variables	Dependent variables = marijuana laws that involve:			
	Decriminalization	Fines	Jail	Light penalties
Citizen forces				
Demand for drugs	−0.194*	0.33*	0.19**	—
Income (thousands)	—	—	−0.16**	—
Church membership	−0.008**	0.02**	—	—
% urban population	—	—	—	—
% Hispanic population	0.017*	−0.04**	—	—
% black population	0.012**	—	—	−0.02**
Self-help groups	0.017**	—	0.04**	—
Political forces				
Democratic partisanship	0.008**	−0.02	0.03**	—
Party competition	0.010**	—	0.03**	—
Liberal voters	—	—	—	0.12**
Industry forces				
Alcohol producers	—	—	—	—
Bars per capita	—	—	0.03**	—
Bureaucratic forces				
Drug treatment capacity	0.003*	—	—	0.05*
Police employment	−0.002**	—	—	−0.08*
Federal marijuana arrests	—	0.38*	—	—
R-square	.42	.35	.17	.31
Adjusted R-square	.29	.28	.06	.25
F	3.20	4.82	1.50	5.11

Note: A dash means the variable was omitted from the equation.

$*p < .05$
$**p < .10$

lack of a clear pattern among these relationships may be due to marijuana policies being a mixture of permissive policies adopted during the 1970s and restrictive policies adopted in the late 1980s and 1990s.

Alcohol producers are unrelated to marijuana policies, and taverns are associated with longer jail terms for marijuana offenses. The most interesting influences on marijuana laws are the bureaucratic forces, even though these are legislative rather than bureaucratic policies. Drug treatment capacity is positively associated with decriminalization and light penalties. Police employment has only two significant relationships; it is negatively correlated with light marijuana penalties and decriminalization (as expected). The federal government's enforcement effort also appears to play a role. Federal marijuana arrest rates are higher in states that have high fines rather than jail terms. This relationship implies that federal law enforcement officers are modifying the impact of state laws by increasing marijuana enforcement in states with moderate penalties.[16]

Controlled-Substance Laws

A preliminary examination of state controlled-substance laws revealed that they generally cluster into four groups. First, some states stress the use of fines as a deterrent to drug crimes. A measure was created by factor analyzing the state's maximum fine for possession, the maximum fine for a first-offense sale, and the maximum fine for a second-offense sale.[17] A single factor accounted for 65.4 percent of the variation in these items. Second, some states target users.[18] A user-targeted measure was created by a factor analysis of whether or not the use (versus possession) of drugs was illegal, the maximum fine for possession, the minimum jail term for possession, the maximum jail term for possession, and the minimum jail term for a first-offense sale.[19] A single significant factor accounted for 40.3 percent of the variation in these items. Third, states can try to target individuals who traffic in drugs. A dealer measure was created by a factor analysis of the maximum jail term for possession, the maximum jail term for a first-offense sale, the minimum jail term for a second-offense sale, and the maximum jail term for a second-offense sale. A single significant factor was able to explain 53.9 percent of the variation in these items. Finally, some states have laws that allow stronger penalties if certain drugs are involved. A measure was created that was simply the sum of whether or not the state could invoke stronger penalties if the offense involved either cocaine or heroin.

The policy model in Table 4.2 is very weak, accounting for only 9–24 percent of the variation in controlled-substance policies. The few relationships found are generally consistent with the hypothesis. Competitive party systems produce weak drug legislation, as do states with more liberal voters. Stronger drug legislation is produced in states with larger police employment and a larger drug-treatment bureaucracy. Examining the individual relationships for controlled-substance laws and marijuana laws, however, should not detract from the main finding: the policy model does not explain a great deal of variation in drug control laws. These results are consistent with the notion that changes in drug policy have been triggered by individual political entrepreneurs who have been able to take advantage of a favorable political environment to strengthen drug laws. Because controlled-substance laws are generally of a more recent vintage than marijuana laws, they are more likely to be the result of political entrepreneurs. The lower overall level of explanation for controlled-substance laws is consistent with that argument.[20]

Table 4.2

Determinants of State Controlled-Substance Laws

	Dependent variable = drug laws that focus on:			
Independent variables	Fines	Users	Dealers	Cocaine and heroin
Citizen forces				
Demand for drugs	—	−0.41*	—	—
Income (thousands)	—	—	—	—
Church membership	—	−0.02**	—	−0.02**
% urban population	—	0.02*	—	—
% Hispanic population	—	0.03**	—	−0.02**
% black population	—	—	—	—
Self-help groups	—	—	—	—
Political forces				
Democrats	—	—	—	—
Party competition	−0.03*	—	—	−0.02*
Liberal voters	—	−0.03**	−0.04*	—
Industry forces				
Alcohol producers	—	—	—	—
Bars per capita	—	—	—	—
Bureaucratic forces				
Drug treatment	0.01*	—	—	—
Police employment	—	—	0.01**	0.01*
Federal drug arrests	−0.05**	—	—	—
R-square	.19	.24	.09	.22
Adjusted R-square	.13	.15	.05	.15
F	3.50	2.77	2.24	3.23

Notes: All coefficients are standardized regression coefficients. A dash means the variable was omitted from the equation.

*$p < .05$
**$p < .10$

Policy Implementation

The distinction between passing laws and enforcing them is well established in the literature (Appleton, 1985; Sabatier and Mazmanian, 1981). Drug laws are implemented by law enforcement agencies making arrests. The precise measure of enforcement will be the number of drug arrests per 100,000 persons.[21] Because law enforcement officers have a great deal of discretion in making arrests, several different arrest rates will be examined. Measures include arrest rates for all drugs, for cocaine and heroin, for marijuana, for possession of drugs, and for sale of drugs. Federal statistics combine arrest totals for heroin and cocaine despite the different effects of the two drugs.

Policies adopted by legislatures can be altered in the administrative process by bureaucracies that possess discretion (Rourke, 1984; Wood, 1988). Few administrative agencies have as much discretion as law enforcement agencies. By not enforcing a law, a bureaucracy can render a legislative action null and void. State morality laws are prominent examples of laws that are rarely if ever enforced (Nice, 1988; Gusfield, 1963). Similarly, agencies can rigidly enforce laws, going beyond what was intended by legislatures. Early enforcement of safety laws by the Occupational Safety and Health Administration is an example (see Scholz and Wei, 1986); federal enforcement of the Harrison Act is another (see chapter 2).

As drug policy moves from the legislative arena dominated by entrepreneurs to the bureaucratic arena controlled by more stable forces, the ability of the policy model to explain state-to-state variation should improve. Table 4.3 shows the determinants of five state-level drug arrest rates. What is immediately apparent from the table is that the level of explained variation for implementation is substantially higher, 53–81 percent, than it was for legislative policies.

The results clearly show law enforcement agencies adapting implementation policies to conditions in the policy environment. Arrest rates for all drugs, for serious drugs (opiates and cocaine), for marijuana, for sale of drugs, and for possession of drugs are all positively related to the measure of drug use. Although this might imply that arrests are easier to make when drug use is more visible, we must also consider the resources required in making arrests. A consensus in the literature suggests that drug arrest rates are highly correlated with police resources allocated to drug crimes (Johnson et al., 1990: 36; Kleiman and Smith, 1990: 71). The relationships in Table 4.3, therefore, probably indicate that law enforcement agencies devote more resources to drug offenses when drug usage increases. Similarly, slack resources, measured as income, should permit more law enforcement resources to be transferred to drug control; in fact, income is positively correlated with all five arrest measures.[22]

Attitudinal factors also play a role in drug policy. When church membership increases within a state, so do arrest rates for serious drugs, marijuana, and sale of drugs. The positive relationships suggest an advocacy of greater enforcement rather than churches encouraging their members not to use drugs (see chapter 3). Self-help groups are associated only with greater possession arrests, but individuals arrested for possession might be the most amenable to treatment.

Race also plays a role in enforcement policies. States with more black residents have higher arrest rates for all drugs, serious drugs, sale of drugs, and possession of drugs. States with more Hispanic residents have higher overall

Table 4.3

Determinants of Drug Arrest Rates I

Independent variables	Dependent variable = arrest rate for:				
	All drugs	Opiates and cocaine	Marijuana	Sales	Possession
Citizen forces					
Demand for drugs	41.01**	38.76*	16.36*	16.52**	19.82**
Income (thousands)	61.85*	36.75*	5.81**	13.56*	18.08
Church membership	—	2.98*	1.78*	1.03**	—
% urban population	−1.97**	—	—	—	1.81*
% Hispanic population	—	—	—	1.54**	3.61*
% black population	10.66*	6.39*	—	4.39*	2.69*
Self-help groups	—	—	—	—	3.77**
Political forces					
Democrats	—	—	—	—	—
Party competition	—	—	−0.68**	—	−2.58*
Liberal voters	—	−3.78**	−3.89*	—	−7.37*
Industry forces					
Alcohol producers	131.76*	131.76*	32.44*	27.08**	153.64*
Bars per capita	—	—	—	—	—
Bureaucratic forces					
Drug treatment capacity	—	—	—	—	—
Police employment	—	—	—	—	—
Federal drug arrests	—	8.50*	−6.30*	—	—
Federal marijuana arrests	29.99*	—	16.74*	—	—
R-square	.69	.81	.53	.71	.81
Adjusted R-square	.65	.79	.44	.66	.77
F	16.17	25.81	5.74	17.17	19.31

Notes: All coefficients are unstandardized regression coefficients. A dash means the variable was omitted from the equation.

*p < .05
**p < .10

drug arrest rates for both sale of drugs and possession of drugs. All six relationships are consistent with the notion that law enforcement agencies are more likely to arrest minorities for drug violations. This higher arrest rate might result from either racial targeting of enforcement or more contact between police and minorities.

Political forces have a greater impact on policy implementation than they do in establishing legislative policies, but the impact is still fairly small. Competitive party systems are associated with lower arrest rates for marijuana and for possession charges; competition appears to matter, but only for the relatively minor aspects of drug policy. Liberal voters are similarly associated with lower serious drug arrest rates, lower marijuana arrest rates, and lower possession arrest rates. Party competition and liberalism, thus, appear to reduce enforcement in regard to casual users. Democratic partisanship has no impact on drug arrests.

Implementation measures show consistent impacts for industry. States with more alcohol producers have higher arrest rates for all five drug arrest measures. Tavern owners have no impact on any of these measures. Although some historical literature asserts that alcohol producers have had a behind-the-scenes influence on drug policy in the United States, this is the first empirical confirmation of that influence in this study (see also Meier, 1992).

Two of the bureaucratic forces—the treatment bureaucracy and the law enforcement bureaucracy—have no direct independent effect on drug arrest rates.[23] The impact that law enforcement agencies have on drug implementation policies is either uniform across states or works through other variables (e.g., race). Federalism, however, does show a bureaucratic impact. Federal drug arrests for serious drugs are associated with greater state arrests for serious drugs and fewer state arrests for marijuana. Federal arrests for marijuana are positively associated with more state arrests for marijuana and, because of this influence on marijuana arrest rates, for all drugs. Both sets of relationships are consistent with the notion that the federal bureaucracy is able to influence the drug enforcement patterns of state agencies.

Examining Table 4.3 from the perspective of the dependent variables reinforces the contention that states stress different priorities in drug law enforcement. Arrest rates for heroin and cocaine, marijuana, sales, and possession have somewhat different determinants. State variation on these dependent variables is substantial. In 1987–88, 57.3 percent of drug law arrests in the average state were for marijuana offenses (indicating the days of *Reefer Madness* are still with us), but the range was from 16 percent to 81 percent. Similarly in the average state only 25.5 percent of all drug arrests were for the sale of drugs, with a range of 5 percent to 58 percent.

This targeting of arrests plus the relationships between race and drug arrests in Table 4.3 suggest that further investigation of enforcement priorities would be informative. Four measures are presented in Table 4.4—the drug arrest rate for juveniles, the drug arrest rate for persons who are black, the percentage of arrests for serious drugs (heroin or cocaine), and the percentage of arrests for marijuana. Juvenile arrest rates are of interest not only because the protection of young people plays a major role in legislative debates over drug laws (see Himmelstein, 1983) but also because individuals may be easier to treat if drug problems are found early.

Table 4.4

Determinants of Drug Arrests II

	Dependent variable = arrest rate for:			
Independent variables	% juveniles	% blacks	% cocaine or heroin	% marijuana
Citizen forces				
Demand for drugs	4.58*	—	3.59*	—
Income (thousands)	1.75**	17.11*	—	−1.84**
Church membership	0.16**	—	—	0.33*
% urban population	0.18*	1.12*	0.47*	−0.28*
% Hispanic population	—	—	—	—
% black population	0.26**	9.62*	0.58**	−0.87*
Self-help groups	—	—	—	—
Political forces				
Democrats	—	—	—	—
Party competition	—	—	—	—
Liberal votes	—	—	—	−0.74*
Industry forces				
Alcohol producers	—	—	—	—
Bars per capita	−0.07*	—	—	—
Bureaucratic forces				
Drug treatment	—	—	—	—
Police employment	0.09*	—	—	—
Federal drug arrests	—	—	—	—
Marijuana arrests	—	—	—	—
R-square	.75	.76	.65	.65
Adjusted R-square	.71	.74	.63	.61
F	18.13	47.33	28.31	16.02

Note: A dash means the variable was omitted from the equation.

*p < .05
**p < .10

The juvenile drug arrest rate does not appear to be unique. The juvenile arrest rate is positively associated with drug use, income, church membership, urbanism, percentage of black population, and police employment; it is negatively related to the tavern measure. Because these findings are relatively similar to those for all arrests, they imply that juvenile drug arrests are simply a by-product of drug arrests in general, that no special effort is made to target juveniles.[24]

The drug arrest rate for blacks allows us another look at the racial dimension of drug control policy. The findings are not surprising. The percentage of blacks arrested for drugs is a function of black population and urbanism (blacks are more likely to live in urban areas). The positive relationship for income suggests that racial discrimination in drug arrests increases when more slack resources are available for drug policy.

The percentage of the arrests for cocaine or heroin and the percentage for marijuana can be analyzed simultaneously because one represents a focus on more serious drugs and the other a focus on less serious drugs.[25] The results are consistent with this interpretation. In urban states with higher drug use, the focus is on serious drugs and away from marijuana. Black population is associated with more charges for serious drugs and fewer for marijuana. This may be the result of either discrimination (blacks being charged with more serious crimes) or of drug preferences (crack generally is consumed by blacks rather than by whites). The targeting of marijuana also drops in states with more liberal voters and with greater incomes, and increases in states with more church membership. Two drug wars appear to be going on at the state level. One war is focused on hard drugs and is related to high drug usage in urban areas; blacks bear the brunt of this war. The second war is on marijuana in poor, rural, conservative states (fewer liberal voters and more church members) and is enforced against whites. The latter pattern is striking in its consistency with the status politics that Gusfield (1963) describes for prohibition.

The black arrest rate in Table 4.4 is somewhat misleading in that it is the number of black persons arrested per 100,000 persons, a measure that does not control for the number of black persons in the state's population. Perhaps a more accurate assessment of race and drugs can be obtained by calculating a separate arrest rate for black persons and for all other persons. Table 4.5 presents this information for all 50 states. The drug arrest rate for blacks in that table is the number of blacks arrested for drug offenses per 100,000 black persons in the state. This figure can be directly compared with the drug arrest rate for nonblacks (meaning Caucasians and Asians, including Hispanics and Native Americans) in the third column, which is the number of arrests of nonblacks per 100,000 nonblacks in the state population.[26] The race differences in arrest rates are dramatic. Only in Alaska is the arrest rate for blacks lower than it is for nonblacks. The last column in Table 4.5 shows the ratio of black to nonblack arrest rates. This ratio climbs as high as 15.17 for Ohio, which means that the arrest rate of blacks for drug offenses is 15 times greater than the arrest rate for nonblacks (recall that the drug usage of blacks and whites is relatively equal).

The figures in Table 4.5 suggest that an analysis of state drug arrests by race would be valuable. Table 4.6 presents this analysis. The pattern of relationships for blacks and nonblacks is distinctly different with a few modest overlaps. Black drug arrest rates are positively associated with income, church membership, urbanism, alcohol producers, larger treatment bureaucracies, and federal drug arrests. Nonblack drug arrests are positively associated with use of drugs, income, black population, alcohol producers, and federal marijuana arrests; non-black arrest rates are negatively associated with urbanism and federal drug arrests.

Several of these findings underscore the potential for racism in drug law enforcement. First, black drug arrest rates are not associated with drug use; with other arrest measures, enforcement has consistently increased when use has increased, but the relationship does not exist for blacks. This lack of relationship suggests that factors other than drug use play a role in black drug arrests. Second, federal drug arrests for serious drugs appear to stimulate state arrests of blacks but reduce state arrests of nonblacks. This implies that the federal drug enforcement agencies may be inadvertently encouraging state agencies to target black persons for drug enforcement. Third, the drug treatment bureaucracy is positively associated with more arrests of black persons. If this results from advocacy of drug laws, it is a distressing finding, because blacks are less likely than whites to gain access to treatment.

The final column of Table 4.6 reveals the determinants of the ratio of black to nonblack drug arrests. These relationships underscore those found concerning race and drugs. The ratio of black to nonblack drug arrests increases as drug use *decreases,* increases in more urban states, increases in states with competitive party systems, increases with federal drug enforcement, and decreases with federal marijuana enforcement. The federalism relationships are consistent with an enforcement strategy that relies on joint federal–state law enforcement whereby the federal government prosecutes the major traffickers and tosses the small fish back to the state to prosecute.

This assessment of race and drugs has reconfirmed the long-standing link between drug law enforcement and race. The patterns found here should not be surprising. The 1980s saw a variety of laws passed with clear racial dimensions. Many laws, including the federal law, provide stiffer punishments for violations involving crack than for those involving cocaine powder (Marshall, 1992). Chemically, crack and cocaine are the same thing; the differences are that crack can be smoked, and black cocaine users prefer crack to powder. The high arrest rates for blacks have a devastating impact on the economics of the black community. One study found that three-fourths of the decrease in employment among young black dropouts could be accounted for by incarceration rates (see Marshall, 1992).

Linking Legislation to Enforcement

Thus far we have examined the policy process in drug control as if policy formulation and policy implementation were two completely separate phenomena. Quite clearly they are not separate, because much legislation is passed in order to influence the implementation process (see Sabatier and Mazmanian, 1981). To determine if states that adopted different marijuana or controlled-substance laws also had differences in implementation, the equations in Table 4.3

Table 4.5

Drug Arrest Rates by Race

State	All persons	Drug arrest rate for: Blacks	Nonblacks	Ratio of blacks to nonblacks
Alabama	333.76	809.36	187.67	4.31
Alaska	1,060.70	272.71	1,094.39	0.25
Arizona	404.58	1,720.74	363.87	4.73
Arkansas	272.50	555.44	219.01	2.54
California	957.57	3,680.56	739.97	4.97
Colorado	253.31	1,430.13	204.28	7.00
Connecticut	624.96	2,675.26	439.38	6.09
Delaware	330.74	1,222.16	149.45	8.18
Florida	597.09	2,335.87	323.39	7.22
Georgia	667.84	1,630.67	311.73	5.23
Hawaii	339.65	544.09	334.41	1.63
Idaho	198.04	460.44	197.25	2.33
Illinois	313.55	1,267.66	146.50	8.65
Indiana	169.35	659.83	127.28	5.18
Iowa	119.59	863.12	106.73	8.09
Kansas	225.52	902.28	183.85	4.91
Kentucky	321.00	786.59	285.42	2.76
Louisiana	430.11	887.95	226.34	3.92
Maine	175.64	460.91	174.49	2.64
Maryland	690.05	1,710.10	351.84	4.86
Massachusetts	489.81	3,120.36	351.36	8.88
Michigan	343.39	1,402.78	172.37	8.14
Minnesota	149.44	885.73	132.87	6.67

Mississippi	271.56	412.12	193.86	2.13
Missouri	375.32	2,084.01	170.58	12.22
Montana	136.20	626.20	134.73	4.65
Nebraska	274.87	2,107.95	202.46	10.41
Nevada	157.88	184.01	156.04	1.18
New Hampshire	231.51	663.14	228.90	2.90
New Jersey	751.80	3,112.52	386.51	8.05
New Mexico	364.81	1,399.31	343.70	4.07
New York	762.73	2,394.86	454.16	5.27
North Carolina	391.10	992.08	221.60	4.48
North Dakota	95.39	180.66	94.87	1.90
Ohio	335.30	2,032.98	134.01	15.17
Oklahoma	305.17	1,239.19	230.53	5.38
Oregon	394.17	3,017.88	351.51	8.59
Pennsylvania	228.05	1,174.59	132.14	8.89
Rhode Island	341.57	2,131.57	268.93	7.93
South Carolina	449.14	793.84	302.81	2.62
South Dakota	106.90	234.31	106.26	2.20
Tennessee	206.34	266.39	194.90	1.37
Texas	397.00	1,201.52	288.34	4.17
Utah	226.26	1,278.57	218.84	5.84
Vermont	111.03	531.49	109.77	4.84
Virginia	312.13	908.10	174.15	5.21
Washington	285.30	994.01	262.62	3.78
West Virginia	93.43	708.98	73.74	9.61
Wisconsin	199.57	1,034.42	155.63	6.65
Wyoming	145.16	398.93	143.11	2.79

Source: Author's calculations from FBI data.

Table 4.6

Determinants of Drug Arrest Rates by Race

Independent variables	Dependent variable = drug arrest rate for:		Ratio
	Blacks	Nonblacks	
Citizen forces			
Demand for drugs	—	47.69*	−1.277*
Income (thousands)	94.48**	47.91*	—
Church membership	21.50*	—	—
% urban population	13.41*	−2.99*	0.078*
% Hispanic population	—	—	—
% black population	—	3.75**	—
Self-help groups	—	—	—
Political forces			
Democrats	—	—	—
Party competition	—	—	0.056*
Liberal votes	—	—	—
Industry forces			
Alcohol producers	824.51*	106.57*	—
Bars per capita	—	—	—
Bureaucratic forces			
Drug treatment	1.84**	—	—
Police employment	—	—	—
Federal drug arrests	39.39**	−16.87**	0.376**
Federal marijuana arrests	—	57.48*	−0.962*
R-square	0.66	0.55	0.38
Adjusted R-square	0.61	0.47	0.31
F	13.67	7.24	5.39

Note: A dash means the variable was omitted from the equation.

*p < .05
**p < .10

and 4.4 were taken as the base level of explanation. Then each legislative policy examined in Tables 4.1 and 4.2 was tested as an independent variable to see if it significantly improved the model. If the legislation variable was not a significant predictor of implementation, it was not included in the final equation. Two laws had no significant impacts on any implementation measure: (1) the decriminalization of marijuana, and (2) special provisions that increased penalties if cocaine or heroin were involved.

The results for other laws are listed in Table 4.7. Although the impacts are modest, the pattern is informative. Marijuana laws generally have more impact on policy implementation than do laws dealing with other drugs. States with long jail terms for marijuana offenses have lower arrest rates for marijuana, a lower percentage of arrests for serious drugs, and a lower percentage of arrests for marijuana. These relationships might seem counterintuitive, but they are not. What is happening is that law enforcement personnel are mediating the harsh impact of drug laws. When marijuana is penalized too harshly, police enforce marijuana laws (and perhaps other drug laws as well) less often, particularly when only small amounts are involved.

Light penalties for marijuana and fines have similar results. Law enforcement officers should feel little restraint in making a marijuana arrest if they know that the action will be punished but not severely. Light punishments for marijuana violations are associated with more drug arrests, more arrests for marijuana, and more arrests for possession. States with higher fines for marijuana offenses are also associated with more marijuana arrests. Again these findings support the idea that law enforcement officers moderate the impact of marijuana laws.

Controlled-substance laws have less impact on implementation. States that rely on heavy fines for drug offenses have lower arrest rates for sales and lower arrest rates of blacks. States targeting users have more drug arrests (obviously because they are arresting users). States that target dealers have more arrests for possession (perhaps to get users to turn in their sources).

Examining the impact of legislation on implementation can also be viewed from the implementation's perspective. If an increase of five percentage points in the adjusted R-square is taken as evidence that legislation has affected implementation, then legislative policy actions have influenced the marijuana arrest rate (11 percent) and the percentage of arrests for marijuana offenses (5.6 percent). The direction of these influences, however, suggests that legislatures seeking to influence implementation need to anticipate the decisions made by implementation agencies. In this case, greater law enforcement occurs when laws are less stringent. The bottom line, however, is that state drug laws have little impact on the implementation vigor of law enforcement agencies. What impact they do have may not be in the direction intended.

Policy Outcomes

Drug arrests are not an end in and of themselves. Something must be done with the individuals who are arrested—either referral to the criminal justice system or placement in drug treatment. Two fairly obvious policy outcomes that are likely to be affected by drug policies are the state's prison population and its drug treatment population. Table 4.8 shows the relationships between drug policies and these two policy outcomes. In addition to the independent variables used in previous analyses, this table will include the state drug arrest rate as a measure of policy implementation.[27]

Table 4.7

The Impact of Laws on Arrest Rates

Independent variables (targets of arrests)	Before adusted R-square	Dependent variable = severity and focus of laws						After adjusted R-square
		Marijuana			Controlled Substances			
		Jail	Light	Fines	Fine	User	Dealer	
All drugs	.6929	—	0.16**	—	—	0.14**	—	.7246
Heroin and cocaine	.8114	—	—	—	—	—	—	.8114
Marijuana	.5281	−0.15**	0.33*	0.26*	—	—	—	.6381
Sales	.7056	—	—	—	−0.22*	—	—	.7498
Possession	.8129	—	0.15**	—	—	—	0.12**	.8323
Juveniles	.7513	—	—	—	—	—	—	.7513
Blacks	.7553	—	—	—	−0.17*	—	—	.7835
% heroin and cocaine	.6487	−0.12**	—	—	—	—	—	.6632
% marijuana	.6455	−0.24*	—	—	—	—	—	.7019

Notes: Each equation controls for all significant variables in Tables 4.3 and 4.4. Coefficients are standardized regression coefficients. A dash means the variable was omitted from the equation.

*p < .05
**p < .10

The interesting relationships for the prison population equation are for the bureaucratic forces. The strongest individual relationship (standardized coefficients not shown) is for state drug arrests. Every state drug arrest increases prison population in that state by 0.37, or about one inmate for every three arrests, all other things being equal. The reason the coefficient is less than 1.0 should be obvious: states spend a great deal of effort on relatively minor drug offenses (possession of drugs and marijuana), and arrested individuals are often given probation rather than jail time. The coefficient is large enough, however, to

Table 4.8

Impact of Drug Enforcement on Prisons and Treatment

Independent variables	Dependent variable = rates per 100,000 persons	
	State prisoners	Drug treatment
Citizen forces		
Demand for drugs	—	37.58*
Income (thousands)	−0.27*	—
Church membership	−4.09*	—
% urban population	1.78*	—
% Hispanic population	—	—
% black population	—	—
Self-help groups	—	—
Political forces		
Democrats	—	−0.66*
Party competition	—	—
Liberal votes	—	—
Industry forces		
Alcohol producers	−92.97*	—
Bars per capita	—	—
Bureaucratic forces		
Drug treatment	−0.29**	NA
Police employment	0.84	—
Federal drug arrests	−10.04*	—
Federal marijuana arrests	—	−8.16*
State drug arrests	0.37*	0.18*
R-square	.67	.72
Adjusted R-square	.60	.69
F	10.26	28.35

Note: A dash means the variable was omitted from the equation.
NA = not appropriate.

*p < .05
**p < .10

conclude that some of the recent state problems with prison overcrowding result from the war on drugs.[28]

Prison populations are also associated with larger law enforcement bureaucracies and smaller treatment bureaucracies. Both relationships suggest that each bureaucracy is pursuing its self-interest. Individuals who are incarcerated cannot in most cases be available to treatment agencies. More police mean more arrests.

The negative relationship for federal arrests can be interpreted only after one recognizes that the positive influence of federal drug activities on state prison populations operates through state drug arrests. Controlling for state drug arrests, we can see that federal drug arrests could actually reduce state prison populations because the federal government prosecutes and incarcerates individuals who might otherwise be in state prisons.

Drug policy also has a direct impact on the number of individuals who are in drug treatment. Treatment clientele increases most rapidly with the increase in drug usage (as one would expect). The relationships for bureaucracy are not as strong, but two are present. Every state drug arrest is associated with an additional 0.18 persons in drug treatment, all other things being equal. A vigorous enforcement of state drug laws does indeed increase the demand for treatment services (although not all that demand is likely to be voluntary). The negative relationship with federal marijuana arrest rates has no obvious explanation (although individuals arrested by the federal government are unlikely to be available for treatment in state or private facilities).[29]

Second-order Consequences

Drug control laws are frequently justified by the relationship between drug use and street crime. Although little research concludes that taking drugs "causes" an individual to be violent or to commit crimes that he or she would not otherwise commit (see Anglin, 1983),[30] substantial evidence exists that drug users commit crimes to finance drug purchases (Wish and Johnson, 1986; Goldstein, 1989; Tonry and Wilson, 1990). Decreasing drug usage, therefore, might have the positive second-order consequence of reducing street crime.

Good data on drug use at the state level simply do not exist. As a result, we are left with attempting to determine if drug law enforcement efforts have an impact on other crimes. We are concerned with law enforcement rather than the actual laws, because laws might be implemented in a fashion different from the intent of the law (see the implementation of marijuana laws in Table 4.7).

Law enforcement is intended to reduce both the supply of drugs and the demand for drugs (see M.H. Moore, 1990; Kleiman and Smith, 1990). Two theoretical perspectives, however, provide contrasting expectations for the relationship between arrests for drugs and arrests for other crimes. First, deterrence theory uses assumptions similar to rational choice to argue that law enforcement actions discourage individuals from using drugs because the cost of using drugs increases (as an illustration see Becker, 1968: 198). Three costs should be considered. Two are fairly obvious—the penalties if arrested and the out-of-pocket costs of buying drugs (which rise when supply is reduced); both costs should reduce the demand for drugs. The third cost is the increase in search time required to find a drug dealer willing to sell. Because fewer people will be willing to supply drugs if drug arrests increase, the user will have to spend more time seeking out reliable suppliers.[31] Search costs, according to Kleiman and Smith (1990: 78), may be the most significant cost in discouraging drug use (i.e., demand), especially for casual users. Considering all these factors, if individuals decide that the costs of using drugs exceed the benefits, they will refrain from drug use. In addition to users who are deterred, other users will be jailed and, thus, unable to purchase drugs in these markets. Under the deterrence theory, fewer individuals will be in the drug market (demand will drop), and that means that fewer individuals will need to steal to support their habit. The relationship between drug law enforcement and crime, therefore, should be negative.

An economic view of crime predicts a different outcome. This view agrees that enforcement increases the cost of drugs by incorporating a higher risk factor. But, the argument contends, the concept of an addict is an individual whose short-term demand for drugs is inelastic or nearly so (Hellman, 1980: 155; but see M.H. Moore, 1990: 113–114). Essentially, this position holds that reductions in the supply of drugs or increases in price will have only modest impacts on the demand for drugs. When drug prices increase, drug addicts must simply increase their income by a commensurate amount or shift to an alternative drug (probably alcohol). The result should be more street crime to generate more income to pay the higher drug prices if users do not shift to other drugs. If users shift to alternative drugs and those drugs are more directly linked to violence (e.g., alcohol), crime should also increase. In addition, as Mark Moore (1990: 135) and Hellman (1980: 138) argue, compared with legal markets, illegal markets will supply smaller amounts of drugs at higher prices and will generate more violence and corruption. Moore contends that aggressive enforcement will only exacerbate these effects. Arresting dealers in particular will generate more violence when various competitors seek to control the temporarily vacant market by driving out other potential drug dealers (Kleiman and Smith, 1990: 71; see also Hunt, 1990: 191). The relationship between drug law enforcement and crime, therefore, should be positive.

To assess the impact of drug law enforcement on crime, a fairly simple model will be used. Numerous factors influence the level of crime within a state. Rather than build an elaborate model, this study will simply use the level of crime in the past to predict the current level of crime. This approach should account for state variations in crime determinants by incorporating them into the prior crime level. To this equation, the drug enforcement rates are added. This test is fairly stringent because the drug enforcement rate will be forced to explain changes in the level of crime. The FBI crime rate for the number of crimes known to police will be used as the measure of crime. Six crime rates are included in the analysis— murder, all violent crime, robbery, assault, burglary, and larceny.[32] Current (1990) crime rates will be predicted using 1980 rates. To this equation, state and federal drug arrest rates will be added.[33] The results are presented in Table 4.9.

The models of crime in Table 4.9 predict reasonably well, explaining from 61

Table 4.9

Impact of Drug Enforcement on Crime Rates

Independent variables	Murder	All violent crime	Robbery	Assault	Burglary	Larceny
		Dependent variables = 1990 crime rate for:				
Crime rate for 1980	0.2568*	1.074*	0.832*	1.229*	0.474*	0.682*
State drug arrests	0.0023**	0.152**	0.101*	0.094**	0.082	0.004
Federal drug arrests	−0.09127	−4.460	−0.791	−1.761	26.792*	37.206*
R-square	.82	.83	.85	.79	.61	.74
Adjusted R-square	.80	.82	.84	.78	.58	.73
F	67.83	75.58	88.04	57.74	23.78	44.50

*$p < .05$

**$p < .10$

percent to 85 percent of the variation. Previous levels of crime, of course, are the major determinants of current levels of crime. Six drug enforcement coefficients are statistically significant. State drug arrests are positively related to state murder rates, all violent crime rates, robbery rates, and assault rates. Federal drug enforcement is positively related to burglary and larceny rates. All six relationships are consistent with the economic view of crime and inconsistent with the deterrence view. These findings suggest, therefore, that one second-order consequence of increasing the rate of drug law enforcement may be a commensurate increase in the rate of other serious crimes.

The magnitude of the increase in crime associated with greater drug law enforcement is not readily apparent from Table 4.9. It is well within the range of experience for a state to double its effort in drug law enforcement; for the federal government to double its enforcement in a single state would be relatively easy. If all other things were to remain equal, a state that doubles its drug law arrest rate would be likely to see a 11.4 percent increase in murders, 9.9 percent increase in violent crime, a 22.6 percent increase in robbery, and a 9.8 percent increase in assaults. Again if all other things were to remain equal, a doubling of federal drug law enforcement in a state would be associated with a 15.6 percent increase in burglaries and a 7.7 percent increase in larcenies.

Substantive Conclusion

This chapter underscores the crucial difference between the passage of laws and the implementation of laws. The passage of drug laws may well get the lion's share of media attention, but the real action in drug policy is in implementation. Both laws and implementation increase as drug usage increases suggesting again that states act because they perceive problems. The impact of drug demand on laws is relatively modest, but its impact on implementation is one of the strongest. Urbanism, the other demand measure, is only weakly related to drug control policies and implementation.

Slack resources, measured as income, affect state drug policy implementation just as they do federal activities (see chapter 3). Increases in income are associated with increases in a variety of arrests for drug offenses. Citizen attitudes, measured by church membership and self-help groups, have a modest impact on drug policies. The existence of more self-help groups is not related to many policy actions, but greater church memberships are correlated with more vigorous enforcement of drug laws.

Race again plays a key role in drug control policies. Relationships between race and drug law adoptions are somewhat mixed, but the relationships for policy implementation are strong. For eight different measures of drug policy implementation, a higher percentage of black population is associated with more vigorous enforcement. A higher percentage of Hispanic population is associated with more vigorous enforcement in two cases. All 10 relationships are consistent with the hypothesis that the enforcement of drug control laws will fall heaviest on minorities.

Although not as strong as citizen forces, political forces also influence drug policy. Party competition generates somewhat weaker drug control laws and in a few cases less vigorous enforcement. Liberal political attitudes are also associated with more lenient drug control laws and less vigorous enforcement. Industry forces were limited to the alcohol industries, but some circumstantial evidence was found that these industries have an influence on drug laws. That influence is through the production industry rather than the retail side of alcohol. In seven cases, states with a larger alcohol production industry are associated with higher levels of drug arrests.

Bureaucratic forces have only modest impacts. The drug treatment bureaucracy is not a major player. It is associated with decriminalization of marijuana, lighter penalties for marijuana, and the use of fines for drug violations. Police employment is associated with stronger marijuana laws and stronger controlled-substance laws; it is associated with only one implementation measure—more arrests of juveniles for drug violations.

Federalism continues to have a very specific but significant impact. The federal government's implementation actions are directly related to state implementation actions. When the federal government increases its marijuana arrests, state agencies increase marijuana arrests and all drug arrests. When the federal government increases its arrests for dangerous drugs, state governments increase their heroin and cocaine arrests and decrease their marijuana arrests.

Theoretical Conclusion

The major theoretical finding in this chapter is that laws and implementation are two different phenomena. The models had little success in explaining the adoption of laws but did very well in explaining policy implementation. Laws, in turn, were shown to have almost no impact at all on how drug policy is implemented. The lack of relationships for the adoption of laws was taken as support for the notion that the politics of drug laws is dominated by entrepreneurs. The predictive ability of the model for implementation, as well as the lack of relationship between laws and implementation, suggests that the real politics of drug control is in how the policies are implemented.

The implementation of drug control policy in turn affects some policy outcomes. Although data on drug use are not available, a variety of other impact measures are. An increase in the enforcement of state drug laws is associated with a large increase in state prison population and a smaller increase in drug treatment admissions. The enforcement of drug control laws is also associated with an increase in crime. Enforcement rather than laws per se is what transforms a market from legal to illegal. Resulting violence and crime should be expected.

Comparing the results of this chapter with my earlier attempt to explain drug control laws (Meier, 1992) reveals some interesting changes in drug policy from the mid-1980s to the 1989–90 time period. First, the relative influence of the treatment bureaucracy has declined. Earlier a large treatment bureaucracy was associated with four marijuana laws, three controlled-substance laws, and one implementation measure. That influence has been reduced by at least one-half. Similarly, the influence of liberal voters has also dropped. Earlier, liberals were a major force for more lenient drug laws and less enforcement; some of these relationships still exist but at a weaker level. At the same time, the alcohol production industry has become more strongly associated with higher arrest rates (seven cases rather than only four). Other differences are that laws now have less impact on policy implementation than they did in the earlier period, and the second-order consequences of drug policy are clearer.

These changes suggest a transition in drug control policies at the state level. The influence of federalism and law enforcement has remained relatively constant, whereas the influence of the treatment bureaucracy and liberal population has declined. The implication of these findings is that the law enforcement coalition is gaining hegemony over drug control policies at the state level.

Notes

1. The literature on public policy often shows that states are more likely to act when they perceive they have serious problems; see Lowery and Gray, 1990: 19; Thompson and Scicchitano, 1987; and Dye, 1988.

2. The percentage of urban population is from the 1980 *U.S. Census of Population.* Drug abuse admissions are from the National Institute on Drug Abuse, *National Drug and Alcoholism Treatment Unit Survey* (Rockville, MD: NIDA, annual). Admissions for more than one year were used because they vary greatly from year to year. Data for hepatitis B cases are taken from the Center for Disease Control, *Morbidity and Mortality Weekly Report.* The number used is the average from 1986 through 1988. DEA drug seizures were provided to the author by the DEA for 1988. Because four different drugs were seized, the variable measure standardizes the four drug measures and sums them. The factor analysis produced the following loadings:

Independent variable	Loading
Drug abuse admissions 1979	.84
Drug abuse admissions 1985	.78
Drug abuse admissions 1987	.77
Hepatitis B case rate	.57
Drug seizures	.42

One indicator of the validity of the factor measure is that it is positively correlated with the U.S. Senate's (1990) measure of cocaine consumption. The Senate measure is not usable in this analysis because it is based on drug testing of individuals who are arrested. Since one of the dependent variables used in this analysis is arrest rates, the cocaine use variable would bias the results if it were used.

3. Income is for 1986 and was taken from the *Statistical Abstract of the United States* (Washington, DC: U.S. Government Printing Office, 1988).

4. Data were provided directly to the author by Alcoholics Anonymous.

5. Data are for 1980 and were taken directly from the *U.S. Census of Population.*

6. The production of distilled spirits, beer, and wine is a small, highly concentrated industry. As a result, figures for each state are not presented by the federal government to avoid identifying individual firms. This eliminates the possibility of using employment or production measures. The number of firms licensed to produce alcoholic beverages in each state, however, is available from the federal Bureau of Alcohol, Tobacco, and Fire- arms, *Annual Report* (Washington, DC: Bureau of Alcohol, Tobacco, and Firearms, 1988). This measure has a limitation. It treats all firms as equal despite variations in size. A large brewing plant associated with a major brewer is counted the same as a small winery with limited production.

7. Data for establishments selling for on-premises and off-premises consumption were taken from the Distilled Spirits Council of the United States, *Annual Statistical Review, 1984–85* (Washington, DC: Distilled Spirits Council, 1985).

8. The data on law enforcement personnel were taken from U.S. Bureau of the Census, *Government Employment* (Washington, DC: U.S. Government Printing Office, 1989. Data are for October of 1987.

9. The data are from the Administrative Office of the U.S. Courts, *Annual Report* (Washington, DC: U.S. Government Printing Office). The measure is an average for 1986–88. These data are actually the number of cases taken to federal court rather than the total number of arrests. Some federal arrests result in no action taken. Data on federal arrests are not available by state.

10. Treatment capacity data are from the National Institute on Drug Abuse, *National Drug and Alcoholism Treatment Unit Survey 1989 Final Report* (Rockville, MD: NIDA, 1989).

11. The data were collected by the National Organization for the Reform of Marijuana Laws (NORML) and were published in the Office of Justice Programs, 1988: 112–115. The conditional discharge variable is a dummy variable. The fine variables are the actual dollar amount permitted, and the jail variables are the jail term in months. States vary in what they consider a large or a small amount. In coding, the smallest amount recognized in law was taken as a small amount. Similarly, a "large" amount is the largest amount specified in law.

12. The factor analysis produced the following loadings:

Variable	Factor 1	Factor 2	Factor 3
Jail term for possession	.09	.21	−.80
Fine for possession	.95	−.11	−.08
Jail term for cultivation	.12	.85	.04
Fine for cultivation	.97	.17	−.02
Jail term for small sale	.05	.93	−.00
Fine for small sale	.97	.15	−.04
Jail term for large sale	−.05	.84	−.45
Fine for large sale	.08	.01	−.57
Conditional discharge law	−.22	−.38	−.44

The three factors account for 75.4 percent of the variance in the individual items. State scores for each factor can be obtained from the author.

13. Data are from NORML; see note 12. Each state defines for itself how much a small amount is. The supreme court for the state of Alaska established the most liberal law by declaring that laws governing possession in private violate the Constitution of the state of Alaska. Alaska repealed this policy in a 1990 referenda vote. Three other states have limited the scope of their decriminalization statute in recent years.

14. A logit analysis was done for decriminalization, because a dummy variable does not technically meet the assumptions of regression. The analysis found that marijuana decriminalization is negatively associated with drug use and positively associated with treatment capacity and with alcohol producers. The model correctly predicted 88 percent of the cases for a 45 percent proportionate reduction in error.

15. This finding is unexpected, but in light of the low level of significance should probably not be given much credence.

16. Alternatively, the federal enforcement agencies might feel that states with stringent laws can handle their own drug problems but that states with lax laws need extra federal enforcement.

17. All data on drug law penalties were taken from Gwen A. Holden et al., *A Guide to State Controlled Substances Acts* (Washington, DC: National Criminal Justice Association, February 1988).

18. The factor loadings for each of the three variables are listed below:

Drug Fines Factor

Variable	Loading
Fine for possession	.35
Fine for sale, first offense	.96
Fine for sale, second offense	.96

Drug User Factor

Variable	Loading
Use is illegal	.34
Fine for possession	.45
Minimum jail for possession	.87
Maximum jail for possession	.69
Minimum jail for sale, first offense	.68

Drug Dealer Factor

Variable	Loading
Maximum jail for possession	.69
Maximum jail for sale, first offense	.72
Minimum jail for sale, second offense	.61
Maximum jail for sale, second offense	.89

Scores for individual states can be obtained directly from the author.

19. Because virtually all drug users either sell or give drugs to friends or other close associates, first-offense sale laws affect drug users as much as they affect drug dealers.

20. The model here performs less well than in Meier, 1992, for several reasons. The models here are estimated with ordinary least squares. The models in Meier, 1992, were estimated with iterative weighted least squares, and the dependent variable was subjected to two different transformations. The technique and the transformation were efforts to increase the explanatory power of the model. Without such efforts, the conclusion that state drug laws are fairly idiosyncratic is pretty obvious.

21. Data for drug arrests were sent to the author by the Federal Bureau of Investigation. Drug arrest data are not reported by state in the *Uniform Crime Reports,* although the FBI gathers these data. The actual measure is the average for 1989 and 1990. The FBI did not report data for Georgia for 1990, so the measures for Georgia will be for 1989 only.

22. Income could also be an indirect measure of drug use.

23. The finding that drug arrest rates are not a function of the total number of law enforcement personnel suggests that law enforcement agencies make conscious decisions about the amount of resources they are willing to commit to drug control problems. Two states with the same relative level of law enforcement personnel are likely to invest different proportions of these resources in drug enforcement. This finding also means that legislatures cannot increase drug enforcement merely by providing additional resources to law enforcement agencies. Such resources must be directly earmarked for drug control, or agency discretion might be used to transfer them to other priorities.

24. The correlation between overall state drug arrest rates and state drug arrest rates for juveniles is 0.74.

25. The sum of these percentages does not equal 100 because arrests for "dangerous drugs," mostly amphetamines and barbiturates, are also included in the arrest data.

26. Hispanics are classified as white by the FBI. The number of Asians and Native Americans arrested for drug violations is relatively small.

27. The prisoner data are from U.S. Bureau of Justice Statistics, *Prisoners in 1989*

(Washington, DC: Bureau of Justice Statics, 1990). The treatment data are from the same source as treatment capacity data; see note 10 above.

28. The current impact of a 0.37 increase per arrest is more than three times the historical impact reported in chapter 3. This difference reflects the recent escalation of penalties for drug crimes.

29. Adding the treatment slope to the incarceration slope suggests that 45 percent of drug arrests result in neither incarceration nor a treatment admission.

30. Generalizing about the impact of drugs on crime is difficult because drugs affect different individuals differently. The drugs that have been associated with violent behavior are alcohol, barbiturates, and cocaine, with alcohol by far the most serious. These impacts, however, are not universal, suggesting that the relationship between these drugs and violence is mediated by individual attributes (e.g., personality). For drugs other than those just mentioned, there is virtually a complete lack of evidence showing any direct linkage to violence (see Anglin, 1983).

31. This argument assumes no rise in prices such that dealers earn monopoly rents. Such conditions would attract new sellers until profits are reduced to a level commensurate with the level of risk.

32. Murder really cannot be used to finance a drug habit except in unusual circumstances (individuals who kill for a profit and use the proceeds to buy drugs). Murder rates are more likely to result from efforts by individuals to gain control over the drug market. When rival groups seek control over the local market, drug-related murders are common. Drug arrests affect the competition over drug markets because arrests disrupt these markets. By taking suppliers and dealers off the streets, enforcement opens opportunities for other individuals to seek a larger market share.

33. When drug use was added to these equations (both the use measure used in this analysis and the cocaine use measure created by the U.S. Senate), the relationships between enforcement and crime remained. In many cases drug use as measured here was not related to these crime rates.

5

A Historical Review of Public Policies Regarding Alcohol

In the United States alcohol and politics have a binge–purge relationship that predates the American Revolution. A substantial portion of the American public has always liked its alcohol and has vigorously opposed efforts to limit access to it. Others, concerned about the ill effects of alcohol on morals and health, have sought limitations on and even prohibition of alcohol to protect society from these deleterious consequences. The salience of this battle has ebbed and flowed with the rise and fall of other issues. This chapter uses a historical approach to examine the twentieth-century politics of alcohol policies. Although such policies have their roots in nineteenth-century political struggles (see Aaron and Musto, 1981; Lender and Martin, 1987; Gusfield, 1963; Blocker, 1989), little is lost by beginning the study in 1900. The twentieth-century era of alcohol politics can be divided into five time periods: 1900–19, the triumph of prohibition; 1920–32, the enforcement of prohibition laws; 1932–33, the repeal of prohibition; 1934–70, taxes and treatment; and 1970 to the present, neotemperance concerns with the consequences of alcohol.

Modifications of the Theory

The theoretical approach used in this analysis requires little modification for use in this chapter. The most difficult variables to measure will be the bureaucratic ones, because alcohol enforcement policies were grouped with a variety of other functions in a single agency. Less attention will also be paid to policy outcomes, but that area is more amenable to quantitative analysis.

The Triumph of Prohibition

The nineteenth century saw several vigorous temperance movements achieve some short-term success (see Aaron and Musto, 1981). After the Civil War, the Women's Christian Temperance Union (WCTU) and the Prohibition party composed the organized core of a new prohibition movement. Support for prohibition was strong among Protestant churches, especially rural fundamentalist sects. Despite public support for temperance, Prohibition party candidates rarely won, because Protestant voters were unwilling to abandon their ties to the Republican party. Perceived massive support yet little electoral success presented the prohibition movement with two options. One option was to broaden the appeal of the prohibition movement in an attempt to form a coalition with other reform-oriented groups. The Prohibition party adopted this strategy and became a general reform party advocating, among other things, a federal income tax, women's suffrage, black voting rights, railroad regulation, free schools, business regulation, and inflationary monetary policy (Gusfield, 1963: 94; Aaron and Musto, 1981: 146). The WCTU also advocated prison reform, laws against rape and prostitution, and the Americanization of immigrants. The broader political coalition strategy failed; in 1892 at its peak the Prohibition party polled only 2.3 percent of the vote for president.

The second option was to seek a bipartisan solution by creating a single-issue group devoted only to prohibition. The Anti-Saloon League, founded in Ohio in 1893, performed that role.[1] Central to the league's strategy was the role of the saloon in American life. The saloon was a unique, multifunctional urban institution of the time. Often owned by major brewers, saloons offered a variety of incentives (e.g., free lunches, credit) to entice drinking to excess (Timberlake, 1963). The saloon also was a key element in the urban political machines of the day, serving as gathering places for machine regulars, as locations to recruit voters, and as election day polling places (Lender and Martin, 1987: 104). Because local governments were the major regulator of alcohol and the saloon,[2] much effort went into local political activities. In areas where saloons did not control local politicians, the saloons often ignored local regulations with impunity. Saloons were also associated with other urban social ills, such as illegal gambling and prostitution (Burnham, 1968: 53). Gusfield (1963) argues that the saloon, as an institution, distinctly drew the social boundaries between middle-class, Protestant, rural Americans and immigrant, working-class, Catholic, urban Americans.[3]

The Anti-Saloon league pioneered many of the tactics of the modern pressure group; indeed the league might be best described as the National Rifle Association of the prohibition movement (see Odegard, 1928). Under the astute leadership of Wayne B. Wheeler and Howard Hyde Russell, the league's tactic was to provide the swing vote to influence the outcome of close elections. The league would support a candidate of any party if that candidate supported league proposals. Operating at the state and local levels, the league sponsored legislation and then worked to elect individuals who supported the legislation and to defeat those who did not. The league generally picked only races that it had a chance of winning; rarely did it support Prohibition party candidates unless neither major candidate was acceptable (Kerr, 1985: 95).

The success of the league's strategy depended heavily on a competitive party system. In one-party areas and eras, the balance-of-power tactic would be unlikely to produce results. In rural areas with a majority supporting prohibition, the league made effective use of referenda establishing prohibition rather than using the swing vote strategy.

Under Wheeler, the league retained close ties with Protestant churches, billing itself as the Church in Action. Fully three-fifths of the paid staff of the league were members of the clergy (Blocker, 1989: 102).[4] The skillful use of public relations and the careful selection of elections built a powerhouse reputation for the league.[5] Their first major victory in 1905 was the defeat of Ohio Republican governor Myron Herrick, who opposed the league's local option law, during an election when other Republicans won easily (Blocker, 1989: 96).

The league followed a pragmatic, piecemeal strategy on the local level. If liquor establishments were licensed locally, the league worked to elect anti-license politicians at the local level and sought local option (Blocker, 1989: 104). Their strategy was to dry up communities, then counties, and then move to prohibition on the state level.

Opposition to the Anti-Saloon League was provided by the alcohol industries. In 1919 the nation had 177,790 saloons, 1,217 legal breweries, and 507 legal distilleries. Sales of alcoholic beverages totaled $916 million in 1915, making it the fifth largest industry in the nation (Chidsey, 1969: 59).

The Anti-Saloon League, by all accounts, was a successful organization. In 1919 it had 300,000 regular contributors and a budget of $2.5 million. Prominent businessmen such as John D. Rockefeller and S. S. Kresge were heavy contributors. Corporations with a potential to benefit from prohibition (e.g., soft drink manufacturers) were also rumored to be large contributors (Thornton, 1991: 52). Industrialists in general supported prohibition, perceiving it as a way to provide for a sober, more productive work force (Rumbarger, 1989).

Public relations efforts touted the league's successes, at times even exaggerating them (Blocker, 1989: 105). In 1906 only 3 states were dry. Six more states went dry by 1909 (though the league was active in only two of them). Nine more accepted prohibition in 1913, and a total of 23 did by 1916. Many states, especially in the West and South, adopted prohibition through the use of state referenda elections.[6] Although an impressive accomplishment, it should not be overstated. According to Merz (1931: 20–22), only one-half of the 26 states that adopted prohibition before 1920 were bone dry. Most permitted the sale of beer and wine and also permitted local residents to order distilled spirits through the mail.

In 1913 the Anti-Saloon League abandoned its state-by-state strategy and sought a national prohibition amendment to the Constitution. Blocker (1989: 112–113) cites three reasons for this decision. First, previous prohibition movements had achieved success at the state level and lost their gains when anti-prohibition forces made a comeback. The liquor industry at this time had mounted a counteroffensive against the league by advocating stricter regulation of the industry. The industry was successful in reversing prohibition successes in Ohio and other states (Kerr, 1985: 141).[7] Rather than defend state-level gains one state at a time, the decision was made to move the conflict to the national level. Second, the league's predominant position in the prohibition movement was being challenged by former Prohibition party members who were seeking support from the same church base as the league. The league needed to remain at the cutting edge of the movement to retain members and support. Third, national prohibition had always been a long-term goal of the league; in 1913 the league was able to get Congress to pass the Webb–Kenyon Act, which prohibited the transportation of liquor into states that had adopted prohibition. A constitutional amendment, therefore, appeared feasible and would protect these prohibition gains from future changes in political majorities. A change in public opinion concerning alcohol was perceived as quite likely, given the rapid increase in immigration and the linkage of immigrants to urban, wet areas (Kyvig, 1979: 7).[8]

A proposed prohibition amendment passed the House of Representatives in 1914 but failed in the Senate. The league returned to its electoral strategy, and the 1916 congressional elections were perceived as a landslide victory for the dry forces. In 1917 the Senate approved the prohibition amendment (drafted by the Anti-Saloon League) by a vote of 65 to 20, and the House approved by a vote of 282 to 128. Voting on the amendment was bipartisan, with majorities from both parties voting in favor.[9] The amendment was rapidly ratified by the legislatures in the required three-fourths of the states in approximately 13 months. The effective date of the amendment was January 17, 1920.

A constitutional amendment was only the first step in the national prohibition process. Congress still had to implement the amendment by passing enforcement legislation. Intoxicated by their success, the Anti-Saloon League sought strict enforcement. The Volstead Act, drafted with substantial input from Wayne Wheeler, established a rigid enforcement law (Kerr, 1985: 223). Exceptions for wine or beer were not allowed; the Volstead Act defined an intoxicating beverage as anything with over 0.5 percent alcohol.[10] To permit the Anti-Saloon League to influence prohibition enforcement, enforcement personnel (placed in the Treasury Department) were exempted from civil service regulations (Schmeckebier, 1929: 8).[11] John Kramer and Roy Haynes, the first two heads of the prohibition agency, were perceived as approved by Wheeler and the league (Lender and Martin, 1987: 149). Not waiting for the prohibition amendment to take place, President Wilson prohibited brewing beer stronger than 3.2 percent alcohol as a wartime prohibition policy to run until the end of World War I. Congress later extended this limitation and other wartime distilling restrictions (e.g., no foodstuffs could be used for distilling) until the start of Prohibition (Lender and Martin, 1987: 130).

The passage of the prohibition amendment resulted from the convergence of a wide variety of forces. First, the demands of industrialization ran counter to traditional American drinking patterns. Whereas before workers could, with few ill effects, eliminate the drudgery of the workplace by consuming liquor, the rise of mechanized manufacturing made such practices dangerous. Business leaders supported prohibition as a way to achieve a safer, more productive work force (Rumbarger, 1989; Burnham, 1968: 54; Kyvig, 1985a: 9). Second, the U.S. entry into World War I made the need for sacrifices more apparent. Raw materials used in the production of beer and spirits were needed for the war effort. In addition, the strong association of beer with Germany made prohibition a patriotic policy (Blocker, 1989: 118).

Third, social class and social status clearly played a role. Gusfield (1963) argues that prohibition was a way for rural, Protestant, middle-class Americans to reassert the primacy of their values over urban, Catholic, immigrant Americans. State legislatures, as well as the U.S. Congress, were malapportioned at this time, providing far more representation to rural voters than their numbers warranted.[12] Although evidence from statewide referenda suggests that prohibition probably had the support of a majority of the people (Kyvig, 1985a: 11; but see Blocker, 1976: 238), its support was likely much stronger in state legislatures (Gusfield, 1963: 117). Fourth, a fear of radicalism, especially among labor, was associated with the increase in liquor consumption. Some industrialists saw the saloon as the focal point for labor agitation (Rumbarger, 1989: 117). Prohibition was enacted just prior to the major red scare of 1919–20 (Murray, 1955).

Fifth, prohibition forces were simply better organized than their opponents. The brewing industry let the distilled spirits industry fight the prohibition battle by itself (Blocker, 1989: 115). Brewers felt certain that beer would be exempt from national prohibition just as it was from many state laws. The market for beer had been expanding for several years at the expense of distilled spirits (Kerr, 1985: 21).[13] Immigrants and urban workers, the other major beneficiaries, had no organizations to press for their interests in opposing prohibition. Sixth, the progressive movement provided a strong precedent for the use of laws to correct moral failings. Law was perceived as an instrument for doing good, and the reforms adopted by the progressive movement meant that prohibition could be presented as a similar type of reform (Timberlake, 1963; Kyvig, 1985a: 10; Rumbarger, 1989: 109–22). Gusfield (1963: 102), in fact, finds a positive correlation between state support for Populist candidates in the 1892 and 1894 elections and state adoption of prohibition in the 1906–19 period.

Seventh, the passage of the federal income tax eliminated a major barrier to the ban of alcoholic beverages. In 1910 the United States government was financed almost exclusively by sin taxes and the import tariff. Alcohol taxes alone raised $208.6 million, or 31 percent of the total federal budget of $675 million (tobacco taxes raised an additional $58.1 million in the same year). The adoption of the federal income tax provided the federal government with an alternative source of revenue (see Table 5.1). By 1917 individual and corporate income taxes totaled $387.3 million (Bureau of the Census, 1975: 1107). Eighth, public

Table 5.1

Alcohol Taxes and the Federal Budget (in millions of dollars), 1910–20

Fiscal year	Total revenues	Alcohol taxes	% alcohol
1910	675.5	208.6	30.9
1911	701.8	219.6	31.3
1912	692.6	219.7	31.7
1913	714.5	230.1	32.2
1914	725.1	226.2	31.2
1915	683.4	233.9	34.2
1916	761.4	247.5	32.5
1917	1,100.5	284.0	25.8
1918	3,645.2	443.8	12.2
1919	5,130.0	488.1	9.4
1920	6,648.9	139.8	2.1

Source: Bureau of the Census, 1975.

support was perceived as favorable toward prohibition. Part of this perception was generated by the active role of the WCTU and its ability to convince legislators that *all* women supported prohibition. In addition to the WCTU's public advocacy, most school children had been exposed to temperance education (a policy goal of the WCTU) as part of their primary school education.[14]

Enforcing Prohibition

"All laws will be violated"—Andrew J. Volstead (Kerr, 1985: 233).

Transforming a market for a legal good into an illegal one creates a market with distinctive characteristics, and prohibition was no exception. First, demand will drop; but if some demand remains, sources of supply will arise to service that demand. Al Capone claimed that he was only supplying a public demand. By the late 1920s, 1 million gallons of Canadian liquor a year were being smuggled into the United States (Kyvig, 1979: 12). Demand for sacramental wine increased by

800,000 gallons in the first two years of Prohibition (Zimring and Hawkins, 1992: 67). Additional alcohol was diverted illegally from industrial uses (before denaturing), and substantial amounts (perhaps 20 million gallons) of pre-Prohibition liquor were stolen from bonded warehouses. An illegal (i.e., non-tax-paying) alcohol production industry existed prior to Prohibition (from 1876 to 1919, 66,794 stills were seized by federal authorities) and would expand to produce even more moonshine during it (Merz, 1931: 54). Individuals could also legally distill or brew their own alcoholic beverages as long as none was offered for sale.

Second, in illegal markets prices rise to compensate entrepreneurs for the increased risk involved. Because beer was relatively inexpensive and bulky to hide, bootleggers focused on the distilled spirits market (Blocker, 1989: 120).[15] Kyvig (1985a: 12) estimates the cost of a cocktail rose from 15 cents during World War I to 75 cents or more during Prohibition. Individuals who drank, particularly those who drank distilled spirits, paid a premium for the privilege.

Third, illegal markets generate violence. An illegal market does not have access to the court system to enforce contracts or agreements with competitors concerning distribution networks. Force is used as a substitute, resulting in numerous deaths, an estimated 1,000 in New York City alone during the 1920s (Nelli, 1985: 127). Major gang wars were fought to establish market control in numerous cities. Although most of the fatalities were persons involved in illegal activity, some were innocent bystanders.

Fourth, law enforcement officers will get little help from citizens in solving crimes. Unlike most property crimes or violent crimes, the "victim" in prohibition is a willing customer who has no incentive to cooperate with the police. Fifth, because illegal markets tend to be highly profitable and the pay of law enforcement officers relatively low in comparison, inevitably entrepreneurs will seek to reduce their risks by bribing police officers. Whether the illegal good is alcohol, drugs, prostitution, or gambling, such markets increase corruption in law enforcement. The first two federal agents were arrested for corruption only 33 days after the Volstead Act took effect (Merz, 1931: 57). Sixth, with the great pressure to generate arrests and the unwillingness of citizens to assist, law enforcement officers will adopt highly questionable tactics involving searches, entrapment, and so forth.

The Prohibition Unit

Enforcement of the Volstead Act was assigned to the Treasury Department, which in turn created the Prohibition Unit in the Bureau of Internal Revenue.[16] The absence of civil service hiring and the influence of the Anti-Saloon League and politicians in the selection of employees meant that the Prohibition Unit would be unlikely to develop the bureaucratic expertise necessary to become an effective agency. These restrictions were exacerbated by the agency's lack of resources. Only 1,500 agents were initially allocated to the Prohibition Unit (growing to about 3,200 at its peak), to be spread throughout the country across thousands of miles of border (Aaron and Musto, 1981: 158). Modest appropriations meant low pay and low skill levels (Department of the Treasury, 1920: 1502). A federal grand jury characterized Prohibition Unit personnel as follows: "Almost without exception the agents are not men of the type of intelligence and character qualified to be charged with this difficult and important duty" (quoted in Schmeckebier, 1929: 45).

Table 5.2 shows that prohibition agents had little trouble finding people to arrest. From fiscal year 1922 through fiscal year 1933, never fewer than 42,000 persons per year were arrested for prohibition violations. The official agency figures in Table 5.2, however, are about 10 percent higher than those reported by the U.S. Court system, as shown in Table 5.3.[17] Court data show that the agency was generally successful in prosecuting cases, attaining guilty pleas or verdicts in more than 80 percent of all cases and winning two of every three cases that went to trial. The influx of cases threatened to overwhelm the federal court system; alcohol cases constituted about two-thirds of all federal criminal cases between 1921 and 1933. Prosecutors used plea bargains with relatively light penalties to handle the influx of cases. The average sentence for a prohibition violation in 1928 was a fine of $102.94 and a jail term of about 35 days (see Schmeckebier, 1929: 78). Such modest penalties could hardly have deterred resolute bootleggers.

Federal enforcement of prohibition was to be assisted by concurrent enforcement by state law enforcement agencies. Every state but Maryland adopted some form of state prohibition enforcement law; many went beyond the federal law in terms of enforcement and penalties (Merz, 1931: 202). State enforcement, however, could not be termed enthusiastic. Chidsey (1969) found that states were quite willing to pass tough laws but much less willing to pay for enforcing those laws. In 1927, only 18 of 48 states appropriated funds to enforce prohibition (Burnham, 1968: 58). Several states allocated less than $1,000 to that effort (Lender and Martin, 1987: 154).[18] In its 1926 annual report, the Prohibition Unit specifically criticized state governments for their lack of assistance (Department of the Treasury, 1926: 140). As more problems of prohibition enforcement arose (see below), states refused to cooperate with the federal government. New York repealed its enforcement law in 1923 in the process marking Governor Al Smith as the leading wet politician of the decade. In the previous two years, however, the New York law produced approximately 7,000 arrests but only 20 convictions and jail sentences. Over 6,000 arrests in Philadelphia produced only 212 convictions (Merz, 1931: 205, 145). Even during the later years of Prohibition, annual reports of the Prohibition Unit from 1930 to 1933 claimed only between 7,600 and 11,980 state convictions a year with federal assistance. The contribution of state enforcement must be considered modest. The limits of federalism, therefore, restricted the overall enforcement of prohibition.

Table 5.2

Prohibition Enforcement Activities, 1920–33

Fiscal year	Budget (thousands of $)	Arrests	Prosecutions	Convictions	% convicted
1920	2,200	10,548	5,095	4,315	84.7
1921	6,350	34,175	21,297	17,962	84.3
1922	6,750	42,223	28,743	22,749	79.1
1923	8,500	66,936	42,730	34,069	79.7
1924	8,250	68,161	46,609	37,181	79.8
1925	10,012	62,747	47,925	39,072	81.5
1926	9,670	58,391	52,989	41,154	77.7
1927	11,993	64,986	50,250	36,546	72.7
1928	11,991	75,307	70,034	58,813	84.0
1929	12,401	66,878	75,308	56,546	75.1
1930	NR	68,178	72,673	54,085	74.4
1931	9,623	63,117	59,805	51,360	85.9
1932	NR	73,883	70,252	61,383	87.4
1933	9,124	98,159	60,044	52,797	87.9

Sources: Schmeckebier, 1929: 79; Merz, 1931: 329–333; and annual reports of the Department of the Treasury and the Department of Justice.

NR = not reported.

Although most state governments provided little assistance, the federal court system was generally supportive of prohibition efforts. Several cases were filed challenging the Eighteenth Amendment or the Volstead Act by opponents of prohibition. Individual cases alleged that the Eighteenth Amendment conflicted with other parts of the Constitution or that the method of ratification was incorrect. New York adopted a law in 1920 setting the legal limit for beer at 2.75 percent alcohol, a direct challenge to the Volstead Act's 0.5 percent (Kyvig, 1979: 56). These cases were consolidated in *National Prohibition Cases* (253 U.S. 350, 1920); the Supreme Court unanimously upheld the constitutionality of

Table 5.3

Prohibition Enforcement Activities in Federal Court, 1920–33

Year	Total cases	Number dismissed	Number acquitted	Alcohol cases, number pled guilty	Number convicted	% convicted[a]	% trial wins[b]
1920	5,095	655	125	4,108	207	84.69	62.35
1921	21,297	2,570	765	16,652	1,310	84.34	63.13
1922	29,418	5,212	1,225	20,767	2,214	78.12	64.38
1923	43,654	7,475	1,814	31,248	3,117	78.72	63.21
1924	47,338	9,726	1,812	34,066	3,546	76.52	66.18
1925	48,738	7,824	1,838	35,418	3,654	80.17	66.53
1926	49,356	10,373	1,330	34,767	2,886	76.29	68.45
1927	41,749	8,363	979	29,537	2,870	77.62	74.56
1928	59,784	8,419	1,459	46,384	3,522	83.48	70.71
1929	57,823	8,096	1,502	44,763	3,462	83.40	69.74
1930	54,266	6,954	1,550	41,654	4,108	84.33	72.61
1931	62,915	7,480	1,397	50,100	3,938	85.89	73.81
1932	70,766	7,366	1,272	58,284	3,844	87.79	75.14
1933	60,365	6,244	931	50,841	2,700	88.18	74.36

Sources: Annual reports of the Department of the Treasury and the Department of Justice.

[a] Includes all plea bargains.
[b] Percentage of trials won by the prosecution.

the amendment and the way it was ratified. The Supreme Court later held that individuals could be prosecuted under both state and federal laws for the same prohibition violations (*U.S.* v. *Lanza,* 260 U.S. 377, 1922), that Congress could proscribe the medicinal use of beer (*Everard's Breweries* v. *Day,* 256 U.S. 545, 1924), and that wiretapping was not an illegal search under the Fourth Amendment (*Olmstead* v. *U.S.,* 277 U.S. 438, 1925).

The expected corruption appeared both in the Prohibition Unit and among local police. Schmeckebier (1929: 51–52) documents that from January 1920 to

February 1, 1926, 752 prohibition agents were discharged for delinquency or misconduct (approximately 1 in 12 employees). During this period 141 agents were convicted of taking bribes, participating in the bootlegging process, or committing some other criminal offense. The Wickersham Commission (1931: 17; see below) reported that the number of employees dismissed for cause reached 1,600 by 1930 and that the amount of corruption might have been significantly higher. Although such exhaustive documentation does not exist for state and local law enforcement officers, the toll of prohibition in all likelihood had a similar impact on them (see, for example, Merz, 1931: 159–161; Nelli, 1985: 127; Solomon, 1985: 84).

Along with corruption came abuse of power when prohibition agents were pressured to make arrests. Examining the decisions of the U.S. Seventh Circuit Court of Appeals, Solomon (1985) documents a wide assortment of creative enforcement techniques that violated the spirit if not the letter of the Bill of Rights. In Indiana local police illegally seized evidence and turned it over to the federal officials. Because federal officials played no role in the illegal seizure, they were permitted to use this evidence in court (see *Fowler* v. *U.S.,* 289 F. 47 [7th Cir., 1923]). Random searches without warrants appeared to be common (Woodiwiss, 1988: 22). Entrapment, especially in gathering evidence against public officials, was a standard operating procedure (see *O'Brien* v. *U.S.,* 51 F. 2d 674 [7th Cir., 1934]). Allegations of excessive use of force were made, and on occasion federal officers killed individuals who were not involved in bootlegging or any other illegal activity (Kyvig, 1979: 74; Schmeckebier, 1929: 53). The *Chicago Tribune* on November 11, 1928, listed 23 civilian deaths for which prohibition agents were indicted by local grand juries. The federal government transferred all 23 cases to federal court and dismissed the charges (Woodiwiss, 1988: 19).

A variety of other evidence also suggests that the Prohibition Unit was not considered an effective agency. Poorly performing agencies are often reorganized in the belief that changes in structure will improve performance (Seidman and Gilmour, 1986). While in the Treasury Department, the unit was reorganized in 1922, in 1925, and again in 1927, when Congress required that the separate Bureau of Prohibition be created. The Bureau of Prohibition in turn was reorganized in 1929 and then reorganized again and transferred to the Department of Justice in 1930. Reorganizations of field units were also common (Merz, 1931: 125–127).

The Treasury Department was never a particularly hospitable home for prohibition enforcement. The department's skepticism about prohibition was reflected in its 1920 annual report: "The activities of the prohibition unit cannot be expected to suppress entirely the persistent attempts at various evasions of the law . . . " The priority placed on prohibition by the Treasury Department is perhaps best illustrated by the department's annual reports. In a document that regularly exceeded 800 pages, prohibition was often discussed in a total of 5–10 pages.

A Midpolicy Reassessment

By the mid- to late 1920s criticism of prohibition had become fairly common. Although prohibition had not been a partisan issue, the Republican party held control over the presidency during Prohibition. In 1928 the Democratic party nominated Alfred Smith, the nation's most prominent wet politician, to run against Herbert Hoover. Hoover's position that the amendment had to be enforced established a clear-cut choice between the two candidates on the basis of prohibition. Hoover, however, also had the advantage of eight years of prosperity under Republican presidents. Hoover's landslide victory is important for two reasons. First, it started the realignment of the Democratic party by building a coalition of labor, urban areas, Catholics, immigrants, and minorities; this coalition would form the basis for the Democratic governing coalition from 1932 to 1968. Second, Hoover appointed the National Commission on Law Observance and Enforcement (known generally as the Wickersham Commission, after its chair George Wickersham) to study the enforcement of prohibition.

The Wickersham Commission provided government documentation for the limitations of prohibition. Its report included examples of corruption in the Prohibition Unit and evidence that illegal alcohol was reasonably available in major cities. Even though the commission did not endorse the Volstead Act, its conclusions were taken as an indicator by Hoover that prohibition was working.

In response to administrative problems with prohibition, Congress in 1927 placed the agency under the personnel rules of the Civil Service Commission. Congress, however, did not follow the general practice of automatically extending civil service protection to current employees of the Prohibition Unit; rather, exams were to be given to fill all positions. The low quality of the prohibition enforcement personnel was confirmed in January 1928, when the commissioner of prohibition revealed that almost three-fourths of all existing employees had failed to pass the civil service exam (Schmeckebier, 1929: 57).

After the Wickersham report, the Anti-Saloon League was able to achieve one additional legislative success. If prohibition was not completely successful, then perhaps the penalties in the law were not sufficient. In 1929 Congress passed the Jones Act, amending the Volstead Act to impose a five-year jail term and a $10,000 fine for first-time violators of the law. Lender and Martin (1987: 163) interpret this act as breaking prohibition away from its general public support by providing for harsh punishments and raising the specter of a police state.

Table 5.4 shows that in 1930 after passage of the Jones Act the average jail term for prohibition violations doubled. The proportion of convicted persons who were sentenced to prison increased from 32.3 percent in 1926 to 72.8 percent in 1932. The average jail term, however, never exceeded six months.

Table 5.4

Prohibition Penalties and Agency Efficiency, 1922–33

Year	Personnel[a]	Arrests	Penalty[b]	Penalty[c]	% sentenced to jail	Arrest rate[d]
1922	1,950	42,223	—	—	—	21.7
1923	1,913	66,936	—	—	—	35.0
1924	1,892	68,161	—	—	—	36.0
1925	2,137	62,747	41.9	—	—	29.4
1926	2,102	58,391	43.3	134	32.3	29.0
1927	2,403	64,986	44.7	138	32.4	27.0
1928	2,517	75,307	34.9	130	26.8	29.9
1929	2,635	66,878	48.0	142	33.8	25.4
1930	2,668	68,173	95.6	231	41.4	25.6
1931	2,679	63,117	131.3	224	58.6	23.6
1932	3,188	73,883	129.6	178	72.8	23.2
1933	—	98,158	118.2	164	72.1	—

Sources: Calculated from annual reports of the Department of Treasury and Department of Justice.

[a] Personnel involved in prohibition enforcement are estimated from 1922 to 1929.

[b] Average number of days spent in prison when calculated with the total number of persons convicted.

[c] Average number of days spent in prison when calculated with only the number of persons sentenced to prison.

[d] Number of arrests per prohibition employee.

Dash = Data not available.

Table 5.4 also suggests that prohibition enforcement had an electoral component. Arrests jumped during presidential election years and then dropped in subsequent years. The only exception to this pattern was the large increase in arrests in 1933, which was not corroborated by the court data in Table 5.3. Because these are fiscal year data, however, many election year arrests would have shown up in the following fiscal year.

The perception of prohibition as a failure has generally blinded individuals to the successes of the law. Although America did not go "bone dry," the consumption of alcoholic beverages dropped substantially. By examining indirect evidence such as hospital admission rates for alcoholism, arrest rates for drunkenness, cirrhosis of the liver rates, and national death rates, historians have concluded that per capita alcohol consumption dropped to three-fourths of a gallon in 1921–22, the lowest level in history (Warburton, 1932: 259; Burnham, 1968; Miron and Zwiebel, 1991a: 242; Blocker, 1989: 119; Feldman, 1930; Aaron and Musto, 1981: 165). Even consumption rates of 1.1 gallons per capita, during the latter part of Prohibition after bootleggers were able to develop good distribution systems, were still substantially below pre-Prohibition levels (about 1.7 gallons). The largest drop in consumption occurred among working-class persons, who were less able to afford the premium prices of illegal alcohol (Burnham, 1968: 63).

The Repeal of Prohibition

Passing a constitutional amendment has always been a significant event in American politics; repealing one was an unprecedented event. The amending process was designed to prevent simple majorities from running roughshod over the rights of minorities. Requiring a two-thirds vote of both houses of Congress as well as ratification by state legislatures (or conventions) in three-fourths of the states, the amendment process can be frustrated by a simple majority in single houses of 13 state legislatures. Prohibition advocates felt reasonably secure that the process would protect their policy, whereas prohibition opponents perceived a near impossible task. The repeal of prohibition required the decline of the advocacy coalition supporting prohibition, the rise of the coalition supporting repeal, and a series of catalytic events that made such changes possible.

Decline of the Prohibition Coalition

Sabatier (1988) argues that policy issues are determined by competition between loose advocacy coalitions on both sides of an issue. Such coalitions are composed of interest groups, elected officials, bureaucrats, media, interested academics, and other participants in the policy process. Sabatier's advocacy coalition framework provides a good structure for explaining the reasons why the prohibition amendment was repealed.

The Anti-Saloon League

The core of the prohibition advocacy coalition was the Anti-Saloon League. With the passage of prohibition, the league continued to operate as a pressure group, making sure that individuals supporting prohibition and its goals were elected to Congress. With the establishment of national prohibition, the state and local activities of the league were permitted to atrophy because national prohibition prevented action at the state level.

A general law of interest groups is that group leaders tend to have more extreme views on policy issues than group members or the population at large (Luttbeg and Zeigler, 1966; Franke and Dobson, 1985; Sabatier and McLaughlin, 1988; 1990). Extreme views are the natural result of the investment necessary to rise to a leadership position in an organization. Only those people who feel strongly about an issue will devote the effort necessary to take an active role in an organization. Because group leadership interacts with itself more than with any other set of individuals, group leaders may perceive that extreme positions are common and be encouraged to be even more vigorous in their advocacy.

The Anti-Saloon League in the early 1920s was racked by a struggle for leadership. The moderates, led by Ernest Cherrington, wanted to stress education with the idea that the league should use its propaganda facilities to educate persons away from drink. Wayne Wheeler led the more extreme faction of the league, advocating continued use of pressure tactics with emphasis on electing legislators interested in stringent enforcement (Kerr, 1985: 11). Wheeler's faction won, and the league began to take positions that were extreme even for the prohibition movement.[19] The Jones Act (see above) was one such result. The league also opposed legislation that would prevent police entry into private homes without a search warrant and supported the poisoning of industrial alcohol perceiving that the resulting fatalities would be a warning to drinkers (Blocker, 1989: 125).

When Wheeler died in 1927, he was replaced by a Methodist bishop, James Cannon. Cannon was an extreme advocate of prohibition but lacked the political skills and graces of Wheeler. During the 1928 election campaign Cannon attacked Alfred Smith with a vengeance. Claiming that Smith would invite the pope to reside in the White House, Cannon attempted to persuade southern Democrats to abandon Smith for Hoover (Lender and Martin, 1987: 162). Such tactics alienated league members who were Catholics or immigrants. Cannon's position was further weakened in 1929 when a series of charges were brought against him by Senator Carter Glass of Virginia (Cannon was perceived as a possible Senate candidate from Virginia; Kyvig, 1979: 136). Charges included securities fraud, hoarding flour during World War I, misuse of campaign funds, and adultery. From 1930 to 1933 Cannon defended himself before a Senate committee, in federal court, and in front of a Methodist church special committee. Stripped of effective leadership, by 1932 the Anti-Saloon League was a shadow of its former self.

The Women's Christian Temperance Union

The Women's Christian Temperance Union had similar problems. With the adoption of prohibition, the WCTU became less tolerant of other positions and less interested in issues other than prohibition. Rehabilitation of alcoholics was criticized as a waste of time. WCTU President Ella Boole was a rigid and self-righteous defender of prohibition and prohibition enforcement. Her strident speeches and her claims to represent all American women alienated a number of people and were instrumental in the formation of antiprohibition groups (Lender and Martin, 1987: 160–161). Under Boole's leadership, or perhaps because of it, the WCTU union suffered a decline in members (Lender, 1985: 182).

The Republican Party

The Republican party was the final major member of the prohibition coalition in the 1920s. Prohibition was initially a nonpartisan issue, with voting support from a majority of Democrats and Republicans serving in Congress. The Republican party inherited prohibition by default because it controlled the White House after 1920, and the Democrats nominated Alfred Smith in 1928. Despite the national party's support for prohibition, the party itself was not unified. In 1930 Republican state party platforms in Connecticut, New Jersey, New York, Washington, and Wisconsin endorsed repeal, and two other state platforms pledged support to antiprohibition referenda that also passed (Kyvig, 1979: 142). The 1932 Republican national platform, however, rejected repeal and adopted instead a plank supporting vigorous law enforcement (Kyvig, 1979: 154).

The Repeal Coalition

The Association Against the Prohibition Amendment

The focal point for opposition to prohibition was the Association Against the Prohibition Amendment (AAPA). Founded in 1918 by William Stayton to oppose the passage of prohibition, the AAPA stressed the imposition of federal power on state governments with some libertarian concerns about using law to reform people. The AAPA was originally designed to be a mass membership organization; it grew rapidly to 100,000 members in 1921 and claimed more than 400,000 members by 1922 and close to three-quarters of a million in 1926 (Kyvig, 1979: 46).[20] The initial goal of the AAPA was to become a counterweight to the Anti-Saloon League and to seek to influence election results. It had little success in this vein; many candidates that it endorsed in 1922 and 1924 repudiated that endorsement (Kyvig, 1979: 48).

Stayton then changed tactics and converted the AAPA into an elite organization. By recruiting prominent business and professional members, the AAPA gained stature (separating itself from the general saloon patrons) and a source of financial support. Members recruited included John Raskob of General Motors, Pierre and Irenee du Pont, Marshall Field, Senator James Wadsworth, and others of similar backgrounds. As an illustration of the elite nature of the AAPA, the members of its board of directors in the early 1930s owned or managed businesses with over 2 million employees and assets of $40 billion (Chidsey, 1969: 128). The disastrous election of 1928 motivated such individuals to become more aggressive in directing the activities of the AAPA. Wadsworth hosted a meeting of 12 members, who agreed to reorganize the AAPA and make an executive committee (rather than Stayton) the governing body of the organization (Kyvig, 1979: 91). Pierre du Pont was named to chair the executive committee. With elite control, the financial status of the organization was secure. Its budget in 1933 roughly matched that of the Anti-Saloon League's at its peak ($2.5 million).

Much of the AAPA's effort was then directed into public relations. A research division was established that drafted critiques of prohibition; the studies emphasized the corruption in enforcement, the deaths related to prohibition enforcement, the loss of tax revenues to government, the flood of illegal liquor, the effect on courts and prisons, and the benefits of a Canadian system of liquor regulation (Kyvig, 1979: 106–109). The argument that alcohol taxes could be used to make a substantial cut in income taxes was probably the most appealing to the AAPA's elite membership. The AAPA goal was to influence the media and through them politicians and public opinion. By 1930 several important newspapers such as the *New York Times,* the *Washington Post,* and the *New York Herald-Tribune,* as well as the Hearst papers, supported the repeal of prohibition (Kyvig, 1979: 117).

Table 5.5 shows the fruits of the AAPA media effort. Although the AAPA was not the only organization publicizing prohibition, articles on alcohol and prohibition hit their all-time high in 1930. Indeed, after a brief flurry of articles in 1933, media coverage of alcohol dropped to pre-Prohibition levels.

Women's Organization for National Prohibition Reform

The WONPR was founded by Pauline Morton Sabin in response to a speech by Ella Boole of the WCTU. Sabin, a Republican political activist, recruited a group of upper-class women as the core of the organization in 1929 (Kyvig, 1979: 121). The WONPR was a mass membership organization with Sabin as the leading recruiter and publicist.[21] Her concern was the violence, corruption, and alcoholic excesses produced by prohibition. In less than one year 100,000 women had joined the organization; by April 1932 membership was 600,000 with branches in four states. Although the WONPR contributed a great deal of publicity to the prohibition battle, its main contribution was as a counterweight to the WCTU. As the sole women's organization involved in temperance activities, the WCTU claimed to speak for all women portraying them as advocates of prohibition. Sabin and the WONPR undercut the legitimacy of the WCTU, especially after the WONPR membership exceeded that of the WCTU (Kyvig, 1979: 126).

Table 5.5

The Salience of Alcohol: Articles in Periodicals, 1910–40

Year	Number of articles
1910	20
1911	35
1912	8
1913	14
1914	50
1915	81
1916	96
1917	78
1918	40
1919	87
1920	69
1921	50
1922	64
1923	92
1924	67
1925	107
1926	155
1927	92
1928	112
1929	147
1930	214
1931	124
1932	135
1933	170
1934	67
1935	32
1936	41
1937	42
1938	36
1939	27
1940	29

Source: Calculated from *Reader's Guide to Periodical Literature.*

Voluntary Committee of Lawyers

A group of antiprohibition lawyers founded the Voluntary Committee of Lawyers to mobilize support in the legal community for repeal. Through its efforts, bar associations in New York, Philadelphia, Boston, Detroit, Washington, D.C., St. Louis, San Francisco, and Portland, as well as state bar associations in New Jersey, Nevada, and Virginia, adopted resolutions in favor of returning liquor regulation to the states (Kyvig, 1979: 129). The American Bar Association in 1930 polled its members and announced a two-to-one majority for repeal. Other nationally prominent groups that went on record against prohibition were the American Legion and the American Federation of Labor (Kyvig, 1979: 135, 58). The AFL actively worked for repeal or modification of the Volstead Act to permit the sale of beer.

The Democratic Party

After his nomination for president in 1928, Alfred Smith appointed John Raskob, a prominent businessman and member of the AAPA, as chair of the Democratic National Committee. Raskob might well have been purged from this position after the disastrous election of 1928, but he was credited with raising substantial sums of money from business, so that for the first time since 1912 the Democrats had more campaign contributions than the Republicans (Kyvig, 1979: 142). Raskob contributed large sums of his own money to hire and retain a professional staff for the national Democratic party. Although his identification with Al Smith (also a candidate for the nomination in 1932) meant that Franklin Roosevelt would replace Raskob in 1932, Raskob had incurred substantial support from Democratic leaders that proved helpful to the wet cause.

At the 1932 convention, a vigorous platform debate, instigated by Raskob and a perceived support for repeal, led Franklin Roosevelt to release his delegates on the prohibition issue to vote as they pleased. The wet platform plank passed by nearly a 4.5 to 1 vote. Of all the likely Democratic nominees, Roosevelt was perceived as the least wet. The ambivalence of Roosevelt for repeal led many of the repeal groups to avoid endorsing him, thus suffering a repeat of 1928. Of the major prohibition groups, only the Women's Organization for National Prohibition Reform endorsed Roosevelt (Kyvig, 1979: 160–162).

Public Opinion

Although scientific public opinion polls did not exist during this period, some evidence suggests that public support for prohibition was declining. Elite opposition to prohibition always found enthusiastic advocates such as Clarence Darrow, H. L. Mencken, and Walter Lippmann. Late in the debate such individuals as William Randolph Hearst and John D. Rockefeller, Jr., joined the repeal forces. As early as 1926, mass opinion on prohibition also appeared to move toward repeal. Eight state referenda were held in 1926. In New York, Illinois, Wisconsin, Montana, and Nevada prorepeal measures were passed. In three states, California, Missouri, and Colorado, voters rejected the repeal of state enforcement laws. While these results were mixed, they indicated less than complete support for prohibition in several disparate states (Kyvig, 1979: 68).

Public opinion appeared to shift further in 1928 with four more states passing antiprohibition referenda. In an early 1930 *Literary Digest* poll, 30.5 percent of respondents supported prohibition (down 8 percent from 1922), 29.1 percent favored modification to permit wine and beer, and 40.4 percent favored repeal (up from 20.6 in 1922) (Kyvig, 1979: 117).[22] In 1932 a similar *Literary Digest* poll found that 73.5 percent of the respondents favored repeal. Probably many events contributed to this ground swell of support for repeal, among them prohibition itself. Prohibition, for all its faults, had eliminated some of the worst abuses of alcohol by making it more expensive. Without constant reminders of the evils of alcohol, the public could look more favorably on legal alcohol (see Lender, 1985: 184; Blocker, 1989: 125).

Catalytic Events and the Repeal of Prohibition

Given the long organizational struggle, the swiftness of events leading to repeal was startling. Because prohibition was identified as a partisan issue, the election of 1932 was seen in part as a referendum on prohibition. Prohibition, however, was unlikely to have been a major influence on the election results because the depression made the economy the most salient election issue of the day. President Hoover simply had no chance of winning the 1932 election. Had he endorsed repeal and had Roosevelt supported prohibition, Roosevelt in all likelihood would still have won in a landslide. Similar results occurred in congressional races. The Democratic party won large majorities in both houses; even larger than the Democratic margins were the reported wet majorities among the new Congress.

The importance of the *perception* of the election as a prohibition referendum is illustrated by how quickly the repeal amendment passed. Repeal was passed not by the new Congress but rather by the lame-duck Congress meeting shortly after the election. Several attempts were made to pass a repeal amendment early in the session, but these came to naught until Democratic Senator Joseph Robinson, one of the foremost dry leaders and Senate majority leader, endorsed repeal and put his political skills to work (Kyvig, 1979: 171). On February 16, 1933, the Senate approved the Twenty-first Amendment by a vote of 63 to 23; on February 20, 1933, the House approved it 289 to 121. Both Democrats and Republicans supported repeal, but a larger percentage of Democrats voted in favor.

Proponents of repeal were concerned that the rural-dominated state legislatures would reject the repeal amendment. To avoid such a roadblock, for the first and only time in history, Congress specified that the amendment would be ratified by conventions held in the states for the express purpose of considering the amendment. Because such a procedure had never been undertaken, the Voluntary Committee of Lawyers made a major contribution to repeal by drafting a model state law that would set up a ratifying convention. The plan provided for pledged delegates to the convention so that the election itself would be as close as possible to a direct referendum on prohibition. Thirty-nine state legislatures acted within four months to establish conventions (Kyvig, 1979: 174).

Some 21 million Americans voted in convention delegate elections. The results were generally landslides for the repeal slate, with 72.9 percent of all votes cast for repeal delegations (Kyvig, 1979: 178). Conventions met and rapidly considered the amendment, so that by December 5, 1933, the necessary three-fourths of the states had ratified the Twenty-first Amendment. Prohibition was over.

During the ratification debate President Roosevelt not only endorsed the repeal effort but also requested modification of the Volstead Act to permit the sale of beer with less than 3.2 percent alcohol. Congress quickly passed the proposed change. Eight months before the passage of the Twenty-first Amendment, beer became available in those states that did not expressly prohibit it.

The reasons for repeal are numerous. As argued above, the advocacy coalition for repeal gradually gained strength relative to the dry coalition. Strategic action by the dry coalition during this time period might have been able to save prohibition. The wet coalition might well have accepted some compromise changes in prohibition before the election of 1932 (for example, exempting beer and wine), but the dry coalition's extremist positions prevented such a compromise. Equally relevant was the Great Depression and its impact on party fortunes. Prohibition had often been cited as the reason for the prosperity of the 1920s. With the depression, that argument lacked persuasiveness. The massive Democratic landslide of 1932 swept many wet politicians into office. A great many changes in a wide variety of areas were anticipated. Although most repeal action was completed before Roosevelt and the new Congress took office, the anticipation that they would act in all likelihood motivated the lame-duck Congress to pass the repeal amendment. Had there been no Great Depression, the conditions for party realignment would not have existed. Without the Democratic landslide of 1932, prohibition in some form might have survived.

Taxes and Treatment

Federal Tax Policies

With the passage of the Twenty-first Amendment to the Constitution an industry was recreated without any existing regulatory structure to handle it. One option, of course, was to let the free market regulate alcohol; but pre-Prohibition problems with no federal regulation and weak local regulation did not make that a viable option. At the federal level, presidential advisors actually discussed creating a government monopoly over the wholesale liquor trade with strict regulation of the retail sector. Adding the regulation of this industry on top of all the other New Deal responsibilities, however, was perceived as too much for the federal government (see Kyvig, 1979: 189).

Instead the federal government initially decided to treat the alcohol industry just like every other industry. Under the National Industrial Recovery Act (NIRA), the federal government permitted industries to meet and establish industry rules, prices, and production quotas. To assist the industry in this regard, the Federal Alcohol Control Administration (FACA) was created in the National Recovery Administration. Headed by Joseph Choate, the FACA encouraged industry self-regulation with codes governing advertising, pricing, production quotas, relationships between wholesalers and retailers, and restrictions on shipment into dry areas. The FACA period is important because it introduced the industries to self-regulation (Baron, 1962: 325). The brewing industry in particular appeared to have learned that it could head off troublesome government interventions by voluntarily policing itself. The FACA code also prohibited the tied saloon, and alcohol producers were able to convince the federal government and later the state governments that price posting was a way to eliminate the tied saloon (Blocker, 1989: 134).[23]

The National Industrial Recovery Act was declared unconstitutional in 1935, and the Federal Alcohol Control Administration was swept away with the NIRA. Perhaps because state regulation was well established by 1935, the federal government made no effort to reestablish a federal regulatory presence. Rather, the federal government concerned itself with the tax revenues that it could raise. As Table 5.6 shows, although alcohol tax revenues have never approached pre-Prohibition levels (compared with overall federal taxes), they have provided significant revenue for the federal government. In 1935 alcohol taxes totaled 11.1 percent of total federal revenues. Alcohol taxes rose to $5.81 billion by 1990, but that figure represents only 0.5 percent of all federal tax revenues.

Federal tax policy on alcohol follows a fairly interesting pattern. The New Deal and World War II created large demands for government revenue, and federal alcohol taxes were raised frequently. Distilled spirits taxes jumped from $2.00 a proof gallon in 1934 to $9.00 a proof gallon in 1944. Beer tax rates jumped from $5.00 a barrel in 1934 to $8.00 a barrel in 1944 (wine taxes produce little revenue). The 1944 tax increase was considered temporary and was scheduled to decrease after the end of the war; a series of legislative actions continued this tax until 1951, when the distilled spirits tax jumped to $10.50 per proof gallon and the beer tax to $9.00 per barrel. Again the taxes were passed with the provision that they were temporary until the end of the Korean War. Congress, faced with rising deficits and the need to raise taxes, again extended these taxes until they were raised in 1985 and again in 1991. Current tax rates are $13.50 per proof gallon of distilled spirits and $18.00 per barrel of beer. Wine taxes vary depending on alcoholic content.

Table 5.7 shows the distilled spirits tax and the beer tax for selected years in

Table 5.6

Federal and State Alcohol Tax Revenues, 1920–90

Year	Federal taxes (millions of $)	Per capita	State taxes (millions of $)	Per capita
1920	140	1.31	NA	NA
1925	26	0.22	NA	NA
1930	11	0.09	NA	NA
1935	411	3.23	231	1.82
1940	624	4.72	474	3.59
1945	2,309	16.50	998	7.13
1950	2,219	14.57	1,230	8.08
1955	2,743	16.53	1,433	8.64
1960	3,194	17.68	1,778	9.84
1965	3,773	19.42	2,187	11.26
1970	4,746	23.15	3,168	15.45
1975	5,351	24.78	4,092	18.95
1980	5,700	25.03	5,243	23.02
1985	5,400	22.57	5,784	24.17
1990	5,810	23.36	6,098	24.52

Sources: State figures are from U.S. Bureau of the Census, *Government Finances* (Washington, DC: U.S. Government Printing Office, various years). Federal figures are from Office of Management and Budget, *Budget of the United States Government* (Washington, DC: U.S. Government Printing Office, various years).

NA = not appropriate.

both current dollars and constant dollars. The striking pattern of Table 5.7 is that since the end of World War II federal alcohol taxes have declined dramatically in real terms. Current federal distilled spirits taxes are only about 20 percent of what they were in real terms in 1944. Although alcohol remains a highly taxed

Table 5.7

Federal Tax Rates for Distilled Spirits and Beer, 1934–90

Year	Distilled spirits[a]		Beer[b]	
	Current $	Constant $	Current $	Constant $
1934	2.00	15.75	5.00	39.38
1938	2.25	17.03	5.00	37.85
1940	3.00	22.71	6.00	45.42
1941	4.00	28.17	6.00	42.25
1942	6.00	37.62	7.00	43.90
1944	9.00	51.39	8.00	45.68
1951	10.50	40.49	9.00	34.70
1985	12.50	11.62	9.00	8.36
1990	12.50	9.56	9.00	6.89

Source: U.S. Department of the Treasury, annual reports.

[a] Taxes per proof gallon.
[b] Taxes per barrel.

product (approximately one-fourth of the price of distilled spirits is federal taxes), the failure of federal alcohol tax rates to keep up with inflation has meant that the real purchase price of distilled spirits has dropped significantly since the end of Prohibition.

Another pattern in Table 5.7 is not readily apparent. Beer has been taxed at a lower rate (relative to alcohol content) than distilled spirits. This has always been a concern to the distilled spirits industry, especially when the distilled spirits' share of the alcohol market ceased to grow in the late 1980s. At one time the distilled spirits industry conducted a fairly visible, but unsuccessful, publicity effort to tax all alcohol products on their actual alcohol content (thus increasing the tax on beer by about three times). In 1991 such efforts proved to be partly successful. That year distilled spirits taxes were increased by about 8 percent, whereas federal beer taxes were doubled and wine taxes increased fivefold. Although distilled spirits still had a relative tax disadvantage, the difference had narrowed greatly.

The Federal Alcohol Administration Act of 1935 created a unit in the Department of the Treasury to collect federal tax revenues and maintain some minor

Table 5.8

Enforcement of the Alcohol Tax Laws after Prohibition, 1934–44

Year	Number of cases
1934	20,656
1935	20,802
1936	28,863
1937	26,784
1938	23,512
1939	24,768
1940	21,956
1941	22,451
1942	17,414
1943	6,855
1944	6,774

Source: Administrative Office of the U.S. Courts, *Annual Report* (various years).

regulatory functions (see Harrison and Laine, 1936: 36–41). The federal tax rate was set at $2.00 per proof gallon of distilled spirits; foreign spirits were charged a $5.00 per gallon import fee in addition to the federal tax. This rate was almost double the tax rate before Prohibition. As a result, bootleggers who could provide low-cost distilled spirits still had a market for their product. Federal tax collections, therefore, were disappointing relative to expectations; an estimated 50–60 percent of all distilled spirits was supplied by bootleggers (Harrison and Laine, 1936: 203).

The high taxes and lack of compliance meant that the alcohol tax unit had law enforcement responsibilities not unlike those of the old Prohibition Unit. Some 1,400 agents were initially assigned law enforcement duties. Table 5.8 shows that prosecutions for violating the federal alcohol tax laws exceeded 20,000 cases a year for the first eight years after Prohibition. Although these numbers were down substantially from the annual average of 60,000 cases during Prohibition, they do reflect an active illegal alcohol industry.

The trends in federal alcohol taxation, however, had major implications for the law enforcement activities of the alcohol tax unit (now the Bureau of Alcohol, Tobacco, and Firearms in the Department of the Treasury). As federal taxes dropped in real terms, so did the price of distilled spirits and thus the incentive to

manufacture alcohol illegally. This trend coupled with a second factor, the popularity of marijuana in the 1960s, sounded the death knell for most of the bootlegging industry. Marijuana was more profitable and easier to grow (it is not a lot of
fun lugging 50-pound sacks of sugar up and down mountains to moonshine
stills). Although illegal alcohol is still available in some areas of the country, the
relative decline of the industry is probably reflected by the federal arrest statistics. By the 1990s, fewer than a dozen cases a year of alcohol tax violations are
being prosecuted in federal courts.

The concern with taxes means that prohibition never again became a serious
federal issue. Perhaps the most likely time for a return to prohibition would have
been World War II. Legislation was introduced in 1941 to create dry zones
around U.S. military bases, but the legislation was opposed by the War Department and failed (Baron, 1962: 333). Beer, in fact, was seen as crucial to the war
effort. A federal order in 1943 required that brewers set aside 15 percent of their
production for the armed forces. Brewery workers were given draft deferments
when the industry was declared crucial to the war effort (Baron, 1962: 334).

The War Production Board in October 1942 did halt the production of distilled spirits, but then incorporated spirits manufacturers into the war effort.
Mechanized warfare requires vast quantities of industrial alcohol. Distillers were
provided with funds to retool their plants and profitable contracts to convert their
production to industrial alcohol (Baron, 1962: 335). After the war, these plants
converted back to the production of distilled spirits. Prohibition, at least at the
federal level, was not a viable policy option during the war.

State Regulatory Policies

The Twenty-first Amendment grants to state governments the right to regulate
the sale of alcoholic beverages. Because prohibition eliminated the corrupt local
regulation of alcohol, states did not face the political opposition that would have
occurred had they tried to centralize control over alcohol in earlier periods. Both
the distilled spirits industry and the beer industry learned from the prohibition
experience that an unregulated industry created major political liabilities. Some
type of state regulatory structure was a given.

John D. Rockefeller, Jr., played a significant role in setting the regulatory
policy agenda. In January 1933 he sponsored a study to provide guidelines for
state regulation of alcoholic beverages. The report, issued in October, recommended that state governments create a state monopoly for the retail sale of
distilled spirits, fortified wines, and strong beer. As an alternative, the report,
Toward Liquor Control, suggested a state licensing board to replace local liquor
regulatory authorities; individuals desiring to sell alcoholic beverages either for
off-premises consumption or for on-premises consumption had to acquire a state
license. Under both systems state agencies were to regulate prices, advertising,
time of sales, number and location of outlets, and other aspects of the industry

(Blocker, 1989: 135). Both systems would provide the alcohol industries with a stable legal environment to conduct business. Even a monopoly system has little effect on distillers and brewers because it takes over control of the wholesale and retail distribution industry, not the production industry. Producers generally supported the Rockefeller report recommendations.

State governments faced a series of decisions in reregulating the alcohol industries. First, should the state exercise full control over the industries or should it delegate or share powers with local governments? Although most states opted for full control, many states permitted local governments to participate in the regulatory process by setting local hours of operation or granting individual licenses. No state gave local governments full control over the regulation of alcoholic beverages (see Harrison and Laine, 1936).

Second, should the state repeal its own prohibition laws? Many states had already repealed their laws or never actually adopted a prohibition statute before the expiration of federal prohibition. A state, however, could elect to remain dry; and eight states did so (Alabama, Georgia, Kansas, Mississippi, North Carolina, North Dakota, Oklahoma, and Tennessee). Except for Alabama and Kansas, these states permitted the sale of at least 3.2 beer (Harrison and Laine, 1936: 43). The politics of remaining dry was fairly obvious. All dry states except for North Dakota were southern or border states with large Protestant fundamentalist populations. Gradually these dry states joined their wet neighbors. Kansas (1948), Oklahoma (1957), and Mississippi (1966) were the last states to repeal their prohibition laws.

Third, should the state adopt a monopoly control system or a license system? Fifteen of the states adopted a monopoly system, and 25 adopted a licensing system. Of the 8 dry states, 3 eventually adopted a monopoly system, bringing the current total to 18. These broad general systems, however, mask a great deal of variation among the states in liquor control. States were more or less permissive in regulating hours of operation, advertising, number of establishments, and the rules for establishments that served beer and distilled spirits (see chapter 7). Some states initially prohibited the sale of liquor by the drink. Beer was usually regulated in a more permissive manner than distilled spirits. Maryland adopted an interesting system based on licensing, but several counties in the state were permitted to exert monopoly control through a county dispensary system (see Harrison and Laine, 1936).

The politics of adopting alcohol regulation systems has not been studied. Kyvig (1979: 187) suggests that monopoly systems were generally created in states that were close to the Canadian border and, therefore, could observe the Canadian monopoly systems at work, or they were in states with strong support for prohibition (states where one-third or more of the voters cast ballots against repeal in 1933). The latter situation suggests that monopoly systems were a method of establishing tighter control over the alcohol industries. Given the state's role in operating a monopoly, however, there are cross-pressures in such a system. Liquor store revenues are part of the tax collections of a state; states facing revenue shortages (a chronic situation, it seems) might be tempted to increase sales so as to increase revenues (see, for example, the state of New Hampshire, chapter 7). Whatever the reason for initially adopting a regulatory structure, states appear to be happy with their choices. Not a single monopoly control state has changed to a license system or vice versa.[24]

Fourth, should states permit local governments to become dry at their option? Local option, of course, was the procedure that the prohibition movement used to build the foundation for nationwide prohibition. Local option elections have a long tradition, and 28 states initially permitted them (Harrison and Laine, 1936). At the present time 38 states allow local option (Distilled Spirits Council, 1991). For a few decades, the liquor industry perceived local option elections as a threat that could lead to prohibition. The Distilled Spirits Council, for example, annually reported the results of such elections. The pattern of local dry areas, however, appears to have stabilized, with few areas switching from dry to wet or wet to dry in recent years.

Related to all these policies are state alcohol tax policies. Because monopoly states also receive revenue from the profits of their operations, actual alcohol tax rates have to take into consideration these revenues (otherwise a state can have low official taxes but high prices which become a de facto tax). Table 5.6 also shows state ⸱lcohol tax revenues. These revenues have increased steadily and now exceed total federal alcohol taxes. The $6.1 billion collected by the states in 1990 was approximately 2.2 percent of all state tax revenues. Politically, alcohol taxes, along with tobacco taxes, appear to be a relatively easy tax to raise in years when states need a modest amount of additional revenue.

Federal Treatment Concerns

Federal alcohol policy from the 1940s until the 1980s is an interesting example of a self-help group providing the stimulus for an advocacy coalition that was successful in defining the federal alcohol agenda. Beginning with Alcoholics Anonymous (AA), an advocacy coalition formed around the core belief that alcoholism is a disease. The logic of alcoholism as a disease suggests that policy should be treatment oriented rather than coercive and that control over policy should move from law enforcement and morality to medicine.

Alcoholics Anonymous was founded by William Wilson and Dr. Robert Smith in 1939. Both individuals had problems with alcohol and were able to achieve sobriety through the group self-help approach that came to characterize AA. AA teaches individuals that they lack physical control over alcohol and that they should seek to avoid alcohol "one day at a time." Using group counseling and interaction as well as the acceptance of some higher power (which might be no more than AA itself), AA has claimed high success rates in sobriety.[25] Favorable publicity resulted in rapid growth; AA had fewer than 100 members in 1939 but in excess of 100,000 by 1951 (Blocker, 1989: 141) and 583,995 by 1983 (Mann et al., 1991: 363).

The success of Alcoholics Anonymous spawned a variety of other self-help groups that attempted to apply the same type of treatment to other problems. At the same time a resurgence of research on alcohol problems was occurring. During Prohibition many of the problems of drunkenness and alcoholism were hidden from view. As a result, little scholarly work was conducted in the area (Blocker, 1989: 145). With repeal and the resurgence of problems, psychiatrists involved in treatment funded a review of the scholarly literature by E. M. Jellinek at Yale University. Jellinek had no formal training in alcoholism and its problems, but in his literature review and subsequent writing he was successful in defining alcoholism as a disease. Despite an absence of empirical support for the alcoholism-as-disease concept, acceptance of this concept implied that scientific treatment rather than moral concerns should be the approach in dealing with alcohol-related problems. Coercive mechanisms, whether prohibition or incarceration, were painted as primitive and ineffective (Blocker, 1989: 146).

Jellinek was subsequently hired by the Laboratory of Applied Physiology at Yale University to head its Section on Alcohol Studies. The section published the *Quarterly Journal of Studies on Alcohol* (now the *Journal of Studies on Alcohol*) to publicize the scholarly literature on alcoholism and its treatment. The section also opened treatment clinics in 1944 in New Haven and Hartford, using group therapy and individual counseling; such clinics became known as Yale plan clinics. Finally, the section sponsored a summer school program for social workers, ministers, teachers, counselors, and other individuals involved in alcoholism treatment (Blocker, 1989: 147).

One individual, Marty Mann, who attended the summer program and had previously participated in AA, created a publicity organization, the National Committee for Education on Alcoholism (NCEA; later the National Council on Alcoholism). NCEA generated an information campaign that argued alcoholism is a disease and that with the right treatment alcoholics can be rehabilitated (Blocker, 1989: 148).

The alcoholism-as-disease advocacy coalition was joined by a variety of other interests. The alcohol production industry was supportive because the disease concept suggested that physiological problems, not alcohol itself, were the key to alcoholism. Churches could join the coalition and address their traditional concerns with individuals and alcohol, yet avoid the political thicket of prohibition politics. Several major ecumenical organizations endorsed the disease concept of alcoholism (Blocker, 1989: 149). Other organizations to support this position were the American Medical Association and the major health insurance organizations. The advocacy and the resulting publicity were reflected in public opinion. According to Blocker (1989: 150) public opinion surveys in the late 1940s found that only about one-fifth of the population accepted the position that alcoholism is an illness; by the early 1960s the proportion was two-thirds.

Accepting the idea that alcoholism is a disease implies the advocacy of specific policy options. First, government should provide treatment for alcoholics just as it does for individuals who suffer from other diseases. Graduates of the Yale program had established state alcoholism programs in 12 states by 1949; by 1973 every state had a program (Blocker, 1989: 151). Federal funding for these programs became available during the Great Society programs of the 1960s and was institutionalized in 1970 with the creation of the National Institute on Alcohol Abuse and Alcoholism (NIAAA) in the National Institutes of Health.

Second, the advocacy coalition encouraged states and the federal government to eliminate the criminal punishment aspects of alcoholism. They sponsored the Uniform State Law on Alcoholism and Intoxication and tried to get states to eliminate criminal sanctions for public drunkenness. Table 5.9 shows how successful this movement was. In 1950 the arrest rate for public drunkenness was 2,183.6 per 100,000 persons; by 1965 that rate had dropped by one-half, and by 1990 the arrest rate was only 370.3. Similar though not as dramatic drops in arrests were recorded for disorderly conduct and vagrancy, both crimes associated with public intoxication.

Third, treatment of individuals was necessary even if they did not necessarily recognize it. The NCEA was instrumental in setting up employee assistance programs in major corporations that provided treatment for workers; the first such program interestingly enough was at Du Pont. Such programs were hardly voluntary on the part of the employee who risked losing a job, but treatment was the goal even if coerced (Blocker, 1989: 152).

Fourth, alcoholism as a disease removes alcohol from the political agenda (Watts, 1982: 1235). Because the problem is alcoholics rather than alcohol, what is needed is personal controls for the small number of alcoholics, not political controls on alcohol. This emphasis on personal control means alcohol is no longer a political issue.

The alcoholism-as-disease advocacy coalition was successful in establishing many of these policies and providing an institutional basis of support for them. From 1933 through the early 1960s most alcoholism treatment was conducted by private organizations, many with religious affiliations. The advocacy coalition was then able to secure public funding for treatment and create public organizations to do so (Weisner, 1983: 119).[26]

What the movement did not do, however, was establish an empirical base of support for their underlying claim. That alcoholism is a disease was an assumption. Criticism, although not always direct, came from those who saw the deleterious second-order consequences of alcoholism—high death rates, more accidents, traffic fatalities, and so on. Whether designed as punishment or coercion to force individuals into treatment, many of the policies adopted in response to these critics were more reminiscent of prohibition concerns than of the treatment orientation of the postwar era.

Table 5.9

Arrest Rates (per 100,000 persons) for Alcohol-related Problems, 1950–90

Year	DUI	Liquor law violations[a]	Drunkenness	Disorderly conduct	Vagrancy
1950	169.9	69.0	2183.6	556.0	297.8
1955	207.7	76.0	2282.9	597.0	205.7
1960	169.1	97.8	1298.2	437.1	140.8
1965	180.1	133.7	1144.7	425.2	89.8
1970	279.4	146.7	997.8	388.9	66.7
1975	507.1	149.0	656.3	353.0	33.1
1980	626.3	205.5	504.2	347.9	14.1
1985	740.4	230.1	411.1	287.4	14.7
1990	718.3	285.3	370.3	299.6	16.1

Source: Federal Bureau of Investigation, *Uniform Crime Reports* (annual).

[a] Includes sales to minors, failure to pay taxes, violation of license requirements, operating during illegal hours, and so on.

Neotemperance Concerns

The policy consensus on alcohol was disrupted in the 1970s and 1980s by a series of events. In 1960 the National Institute of Mental Health funded a five-year grant to create the Cooperative Commission on the Study of Alcoholism. The commission's report in 1967, *Alcohol Problems,* reraised a series of alcohol policy questions. Alcohol consumption had been increasing in the United States, and with the increase came a variety of social problems. Table 5.10 shows the rise in alcohol consumption in the United States and the seemingly parallel rise in rates of cirrhosis of the liver deaths and traffic fatalities (50 percent of which involve alcohol). Although the post-1965 trends for consumption, cirrhosis, and traffic fatalities demonstrate that other factors also influence cirrhosis rates and traffic fatalities, evidence available in the 1960s suggested major problems that appeared to be caused by alcohol consumption.

Addressing these problems, the commission made several recommendations.

Table 5.10

Trends in Alcohol Consumption, Cirrhosis, and Traffic Fatalities, 1950–90

Year	Alcohol consumption[a]	Cirrhosis rate[b]	Traffic fatalities[c]
1950	2.0689	9.2	23.1
1955	2.0109	10.2	23.4
1960	2.0462	11.3	21.3
1965	2.1978	12.8	25.4
1970	2.5636	15.5	26.9
1975	2.7688	14.8	21.3
1980	3.0834	13.5	23.5
1985	2.9490	11.2	19.2
1990	2.7600	10.6	19.0

Sources: Alcohol consumption: U.S. Bureau of the Census, *Statistical Abstract of the United States* (various years); cirrhosis rate: National Center for Health Statistics, *Vital Statistics of the United States* (various years); traffic fatalities: National Safety Council, *Accident Facts* (Chicago: National Safety Council, various years).

[a] In gallons of pure alcohol per capita.
[b] Number of deaths from cirrhosis per 100,000 persons.
[c] Number of traffic deaths per 100,000 persons.

First, it noted that with the decline in temperance organizations, new organizations were needed to encourage individuals to drink responsibly. Second, the disease concept of alcoholism was questioned, and a multidisciplinary approach to alcoholism was encouraged. Third, the commission supported the creation of an alcoholism unit in the National Institute of Mental Health. This unit eventually becomes the NIAAA (see Blocker, 1989: 156).

Although the commission recommended a federal agency focused on alcohol, credit for the creation of the NIAAA should go to Senator Harold Hughes of Iowa. Hughes, himself a recovering alcoholic, used his Senate Subcommittee on Alcoholism and Narcotics to publicize the need for a federal agency with a series of hearings in 1969 and 1970. Hughes, with the active support of the alcoholism-as-disease advocacy coalition, authored and lobbied for the passage of the Comprehensive Alcohol Abuse and Alcoholism Prevention, Treatment and Rehabilitation Act of 1970. The act created the NIAA and increased federal funding for alcohol-related research (Pike, 1988; Smithers, 1988).

Starting with the Cooperative Commission, many scholars and policymakers began suggesting that current alcohol policies (or the lack of policies) were not working. Consumption was increasing, and alcohol-related problems were also increasing. Alcohol consumption's linkage to various diseases, declines in worker productivity, and increases in accidents (both on and off the job) implied that current alcohol policies were imposing significant costs on the nation as a whole. The National Council on Alcoholism contended that alcohol took 97,500 lives a year, added $15 billion annually in health care costs, and in 1983 reduced economic productivity by $117 billion (Farhi, 1990). Within this setting, neotemperance interests found a flourishing soil to sow proposals for more coercive alcohol policies (see Watts, 1982: 1236).

The alcoholism-as-disease approach was gradually replaced by the "new public health" approach to alcohol policies (Beauchamp, 1980: 153). This approach sought to use public policy to focus on the ill effects of alcohol consumption and to construct an environment in which social controls prevent or limit alcohol-related problems. Alcohol policy was to be preventative, similar to public health polices that focused on disease prevention. The new public health approach allowed the NIAAA to be aggressive in defining its policy turf to include all areas related to alcohol and its consumption.

Drunk Driving

Each year some 1.5 million persons are arrested for drunk driving; estimates are that a person who is intoxicated has 1 chance in 2,000 of being arrested (Ross, 1982), implying 3 billion episodes of drunk driving per year. Fully 24 percent of the population admits to driving after drinking too much (*Public Opinion,* 1989: 32). Alcohol is implicated in approximately one-half of more than 40,000 traffic fatalities per year. Most alcohol-related fatalities, however, involve only one car; a drunk driver usually kills himself and/or people riding with him. As a result, alcohol-related fatalities involving persons who are not intoxicated are fairly rare. Rare or not, however, they do inspire outrage. Mothers Against Drunk Driving (MADD) was able to capitalize on one of these fatalities. Nothing is more likely to gain public sympathy than an alcohol-related accident where a child is killed by a driver with previous convictions for drunk driving. More than any other single person, Candy Lightner, the mother of such a child and founder of MADD, set the agenda for alcohol policies of the 1980s. Before 1980, drunk driving penalties were relatively light and often not enforced. The rise in salience of alcohol problems during the 1980s is shown by the increased media coverage. The number of periodical articles on alcohol and alcohol-related problems jumped from an average of 26.8 per year in the 1970s to 64.9 per year in the 1980s.

MADD and a similar organization, Remove Intoxicated Drivers (RID), were assisted in their organizational efforts by grants from the National Highway Traffic Safety Administration (NHTSA) (Jacobs, 1989: xv). In the late 1980s MADD grew to 300 local chapters; RID had 150. MADD and its associated groups (Students Against Drunk Driving, Business Against Drunk Driving) launched state-level legislative campaigns to strengthen the laws against driving while intoxicated. An agenda of proposals was established by the 1983 report of the President's Commission on Drunk Driving. Some proposals were for incremental changes of existing policy—larger fines, longer jail terms, mandatory jail terms, and so on. Some were for innovations such as administrative per se laws that allow a police officer to seize a license on the spot from a drunk driver or random sobriety checkpoints.[27] In 1986 MADD endorsed a constitutional amendment that would provide a right to financial compensation for the victims of drunk drivers. Much of the agenda was highly coercive rather than reflective of the treatment and education orientation of the consensus years.[28]

Little opposition to MADD surfaced. No one supports drunk driving. Major brewers even contributed funds to MADD. The federal government encouraged the effort by providing $125 million in extra highway safety funds for fiscal years 1983–85 to those states that strengthened their drunk driving laws. Most state governments created an anti-drunk-driving unit in their transportation agency (Jacobs, 1989: 197). Drunk driving became a motherhood issue, with a wide variety of changes adopted in virtually every state. Many of these changes were adopted with little consideration of their likely effectiveness. The deterrence literature suggests that increasing the severity of punishment will have little impact on behavior; rather, the most effective deterrent is increasing the probability of punishment, which means greater levels of enforcement (see chapter 7). The levels necessary to have an impact on behavior, however, might well exceed what the public will tolerate. Arrest rates for driving under the influence (DUI) skyrocketed from 169.1 per 100,000 persons in 1960 (see Table 5.9) to an all-time high of 803.6 in 1983. After 1983, arrests for driving under the influence gradually dropped, perhaps because enforcement personnel were being reallocated to the drug war or perhaps because the arrest level had reached the point that it saturated the ability of law enforcement agencies and the courts to deal with it. An assessment of the politics of this movement and the effectiveness of the policies is found in chapter 7.

The Minimum Drinking Age

A second related issue is the drinking age. Most states lowered the drinking age to 18 during the late 1960s and 1970s in response to the political mobilization of youth related to the Vietnam War and domestic social issues. In 1982 only 14 states prohibited the sale of all alcoholic beverages to persons under the age of 21 (O'Malley and Wagenaar, 1991: 478). The increase in traffic fatalities noted above also played a role in setting the drinking age issue on the agenda. An estimated 5,000–10,000 traffic fatalities involved drinking and people between the ages of 16 and 21. Whether or not a higher drinking age reduces traffic fatalities or merely transfers them to higher age groups (see Asch and Levy, 1987; O'Malley and Wagenaar, 1991), many state legislators believed the former to be the case. A dozen states raised their drinking age back to 21 before 1984. MADD was also active in this movement at the state level.

In 1984 the federal government took action that essentially preempted state policy in this area. In 1983 the President's Commission on Drunk Driving recommended that the federal government take away 100 percent of federal highway funds from those states with a minimum drinking age under 21. With limited data, the National Transportation Safety Board in 1982 concluded that higher age limits save lives.[29] Despite opposition from student groups, restaurant owners, the retail alcohol industry, the Distilled Spirits Council, and conservatives (for states' rights reasons), the federal government adopted a de facto national drinking age. A rider to a bill promoting the use of child safety seats was amended with a provision that would have reduced total state highway funds by 5 percent in 1987 and 10 percent in 1988 if the state did not raise its minimum drinking age to 21.

Federal highway funds are a major source of revenue for highway construction in the states. As a result, states rapidly complied with the federal law. A few states showed some brief resistance, and one, South Dakota, even went to court to challenge the federal government's right to put such strings on highway aid. In the end, however, the incentive of federal funds overwhelmed any opposition, and all states adopted a minimum drinking age of 21.

Diversion Programs

The institutions engaged in alcohol treatment have also become more coercive. A large treatment bureaucracy needs a continuing supply of clientele to maintain itself. To procure this supply, Weisner (1983: 121) documents that treatment agencies have moved away from the chronic alcoholic to treat individuals with less extensive alcohol problems (see also Levine, 1984: 50). One source of clientele has been individuals diverted from the criminal justice system. A first offender (often for DUI but sometimes for felonies) will be given the option of jail time or treatment. By the mid-1980s the largest source of treatment clientele was the criminal justice system (Weisner: 1983, 126). Treatment was no longer voluntary, but rather mandated.[30]

Labeling Programs

One notable exception to the change to coercive alcohol policies during the 1980s was the adoption of an information policy for alcoholic beverages. Health groups had long advocated that alcoholic beverage containers have health warnings similar to those on cigarette packages. Senator Strom Thurmond of South Carolina had introduced such legislation every year since 1981. The measure was supported by a coalition of health care and consumer groups and opposed by the alcoholic beverage industries.

The measure was surprisingly adopted in 1988 as an amendment to that year's antidrug bill. Although the Distilled Spirits Council and other representatives of industry made brief public statements of opposition, they let it be known that they would accept warning labels. Parallel legislation was being discussed by state legislatures, so the industries might have seen federal labeling as a way to preempt what could have been more stringent labeling by some states. At the very least federal legislation avoided the necessity of addressing the issue in 50 state legislatures.

Contemporary alcohol politics sees a divided industry besieged by an aggressive advocacy coalition built on health issues. President Bush's surgeon general, Antonia Novello, led an effort to equate the dangers of alcohol with those of illicit drugs. The Bureau of Alcohol, Tobacco, and Firearms has started to police advertising, forcing Coors to drop its "Won't Slow You Down" campaign, Heileman to withdraw its Powermaster malt liquor, and red wine producers to eliminate health claims (Moore, 1992: 8).[31] President Clinton has proposed higher alcohol taxes as part of his deficit reduction plan. Other members of the current new public health advocacy coalition include safety groups (the National Safety Council), the NIAAA, citizen groups such as MADD, and key members of Congress (Strom Thurmond and John Conyers).

The alcohol industries appear divided. Major brewers are sponsoring separate campaigns against drunk driving. The 1991 tax fight furthered such divisions when beer and wine taxes were doubled but distilled spirits taxes increased by only 8 percent (Moore, 1992). The alcohol industries have formidable economic and political resources but appear to lack the ability to act in concert.

The health advocacy coalition appears to be winning the public opinion battle. The proportion of adults who say they drink peaked at about 71 percent in 1978 and dropped to 63 percent by 1988 (*Public Opinion,* 1989: 30). Exposure to alcohol-related problems is high; 56 percent of the population claims to have been closely associated with an alcoholic (*Public Opinion*, 1989: 33). An overwhelming majority of the American public supports warning labels on alcoholic beverages (67 percent v. 16 percent) or forcing producers to contribute 10 percent of revenues to charity (58 percent v. 25 percent), and plurality supports a ban of beer and wine advertising on television (48 percent) and a ban on all advertising in print (42 percent, see *National Journal*, 1989: 3124).

With a variety of factors in addition to the new public health movement contributing to these trends, alcohol consumption and some of its negative consequences have declined. The percentage of high school seniors who regularly consume alcohol peaked in 1979 and then dropped (O'Malley and Wagenaar, 1991: 482). Total alcohol consumption per capita dropped from 3.1 gallons in 1982 to 2.76 gallons in 1990. In 1990, 57 percent of high school seniors reported drinking alcohol during the last month; in 1980 that figure was 72 percent

(Taylor, 1991b). Alcohol involvement in traffic fatalities dropped from 50 percent in 1980 to 43 percent in 1984. A major national roadside test for alcohol levels in 1986 found that 3.1 percent of late-night, weekend drivers had blood alcohol concentration levels of 0.10 percent or more compared with 4.9 percent of these drivers in 1973 (Lund and Wolfe, 1991: 293). The Center for Disease Control's Behavioral Risk Factor Surveillance System found that the proportion of adults who admit driving after drinking too much dropped from 3.6 percent in 1986 to 2.9 percent in 1990.

Substantive Conclusion

Alcohol policies in the twentieth century are divisible into five general eras: the battle for prohibition, the enforcement of prohibition, the repeal of prohibition, the era of taxes and treatment, and neotemperance concerns with the ill effects of alcohol. Few public policies have seen the range of government activities that those pertaining to alcohol have. Alcohol has been banned, permitted to operate virtually without government controls, subjected to government monopoly, and regulated through a licensing system. From this wide array of public policies, several lessons are evident.

First, establishing a bureaucratic capacity to implement any public policy is extremely important. The Prohibition Unit was unable to do this; by the time the agency became more effective in its job, public opinion had turned against prohibition. The current fight against drunk driving may well be similar. Law enforcement agencies do not have the resources to eliminate drunk driving. Placing more emphasis in this area means lower levels of resources devoted to other areas of law enforcement.

Second, creation of illegal markets by government fiat will generate predictable ramifications. Someone will create a black market for the good. That market will be associated with higher prices, lower quality, and higher levels of violence. Enforcement directed against that market will generate corruption in law enforcement. A rational public policy should contrast the benefits of a prohibition with the costs associated with it.

Third, much of government perceives the alcohol industries as a source of tax revenue. In addition to specific alcohol taxes, the industry also pays all the taxes associated with any other industry (income taxes, social security taxes, etc.). The tax contribution of the alcohol industries is no where near as large as it was earlier in this century. Continual fiscal crises at the federal and state levels, however, suggest that governments will be hesitant to agitate these industries with consumer-driven reforms. Those reforms that have been adopted (such as drunk driving laws) tend to be in areas where the industry has only a peripheral interest or where the federal government has forced the issue (e.g., the drinking age).

Fourth, even policy failures sometimes have positive consequences. Prohibition was considered a failure by the political system in 1933, yet in many ways prohibition produced some positive consequences. Alcohol consumption, especially among the working classes, dropped. Many of the problems associated with alcohol consumption were also reduced.

A Theoretical Recapitulation

This chapter illustrated the utility of our general theory of public policy for describing a policy history of alcohol. Citizen forces were found at numerous points in the process. The battle over prohibition pitted two major citizen coalitions against each other. The dry coalition reflected the middle-class reform nature of prohibition with support from rural populations and from fundamentalist Protestants. The wet coalition included urban dwellers, immigrants, and Catholics. The repeal of prohibition featured the same citizen forces but also included an elite repeal movement as reflected in the membership of the Association Against the Prohibition Amendment and the Women's Organization for National Prohibition Reform. Later in alcohol politics, self-help groups become extremely important when Alcoholics Anonymous played a major role in defining alcoholism as a disease. The 1980s saw the development of yet another influential citizen group, Mothers Against Drunk Driving. Of all the citizen influences, race was the only one that did not play a clear-cut role. Although some historians present a role for race in alcohol politics, most literature does not.

Political forces play a crucial role at key points in the history of alcohol policies. Party competition made possible the Anti-Saloon League's strategy of using the swing vote to pressure for change. Partisan values were extremely important in the repeal of prohibition, but for the most part, alcohol issues are not partisan issues. Discounting the role of political institutions, however, is not wise, because virtually all the policy changes (prohibition, repeal, taxes, treatment, drunk driving reforms) must be ratified by political institutions.

Bureaucratic forces were the most difficult to tap in this chapter. In part this reflects the inability of the Prohibition Unit to develop the institutional capacity to be an effective organization. NIAAA, however, did develop this capacity and provided a focal point for treatment policies. Federalism was especially noticeable in terms of bureaucracy. The unwillingness of state and local law enforcement agencies to enforce prohibition laws left the national agency with an impossible task. Influence from the other direction of federalism was revealed by the federal government's effort to convince states to raise their drinking age in the 1980s. Finally, some evidence of bureaucratic competition exists. The health care bureaucracy was successful for a period of time in defining alcohol as a treatment issue rather than a law enforcement issue. With the new public health movement, however, law enforcement issues have returned to the political agenda.

Industry forces are often the counterpoint for citizen forces. The lack of unity in the alcohol industries, for example, is cited as one reason prohibition was possible. After Prohibition, banning the tied saloon meant that the retail side of the industries was likely to have policy goals different from those of the production side. The alcohol production industry appears to have learned a lesson from prohibition and frequently participates in efforts to limit the negative consequences of alcohol.

Policy implementation and its effects on policy enforcement were also clearly evident. The Prohibition Unit's enforcement of the law was marked by corruption and abuse of citizens. When treatment became the dominant alcohol policy, state agencies reduced the level of law enforcement activities. When drunk driving became a salient issue, implementation activities increased with higher arrest rates for driving while intoxicated.

Policy outcomes have played a key role in the alcohol policy process. If alcohol consumption were the sole measure, prohibition would have to be considered a success in that it reduced alcohol consumption but a failure in that it did not eliminate drinking completely. Debates over the policy outcomes framed the debate over prohibition repeal. The results of alcohol consumption set the neotemperance issues of the 1970s and 1980s back on the agenda. Some evidence suggests that the 21-year-old drinking age reduces traffic fatalities. However, the research on drunk driving policies does not provide much consistent evidence (see chapter 7).

Notes

1. Rumbarger (1989: 156) argues that the Anti-Saloon League was just a vehicle for upper-class industrialists' interests. Had they not used the Anti-Saloon League, these interests would have used some other organization. Rumbarger (1989: 158) states: "Despite the attention it has received, the League was but one such agency, and whatever hegemony it attained over others within the coalition was as much shadow as substance. The League itself was never in a position to dictate the course of antisaloon politics; the larger exigencies of America's economic order ultimately set that agenda." For a contrary view not based on conspiracy theories, see Kerr, 1985: 7.

2. The federal government's primary concern was collecting alcohol taxes.

3. Merz (1931: 5) feels that brewers could have avoided prohibition by giving up the saloon or by reforming it.

4. The league also stressed its adoption of business practices, portraying itself as part of the modern scientific management movement. The numerousness of the clergy members employed, however, suggests that the organization used internal normative appeals rather than the more traditional monetary appeals of business to retain employees.

5. Odegard (1928: 74) reports that at its peak production the league was producing 40 tons of literature a month. Kerr (1985: 151) estimates 10 tons of literature a day.

6. According to Kerr's (1985: 124) history of the Anti-Saloon League, most of the southern victories in referenda were the result of church organizations, not activities on the part of the league.

7. Liquor interests were able to overcome the rural biases of state legislatures by relying on popular votes in state referenda. Ohio is a key state because it is the home of the Anti-Saloon League.

8. For a good description of the changes in organization, fund raising, and strategy to undertake a national campaign, see Kerr, 1985: 144–150.

9. One interesting proposed amendment in the Senate would have made illegal the use and purchase of alcoholic beverages; this amendment failed by a vote of 62 to 4 (Merz, 1931: 31). While the use and purchase loophole protected ordinary consumers from punishment, it also reflected the unwillingness of Congress to go to extremes at this time.

10. The law allowed an exemption for farmers to possess sweet cider which would eventually become hard cider. This exception shows clearly the rural bias in the prohibition coalition (see Merz, 1931: 49).

11. Wheeler thought that he could trade patronage for congressional support for the agency (Kerr, 1985: 229).

12. The role of race is subject to some dispute. Gusfield (1963: 105) argues that race is a primary factor in prohibition in the South. Higham (1963) discusses the relationship between prohibition and Klan activities in the South. Blocker (1989) finds that prohibitionists used the argument that alcohol would generate more black assaults on white women but that antiprohibitionists argued that prohibition would invite the federal government in to address other morality questions, including those involving race. In the nineteenth century, prohibition advocates were also often abolitionists.

13. Blocker argues that the increase in beer consumption during this time period lulled the brewers into thinking that they would be exempted from prohibition (see also Kerr, 1985: 15).

14. Mary Hunt of the WCTU was a key person in temperance education. Not only was the WCTU able to bring about national and state legislation requiring instruction in temperance hygiene in elementary and secondary schools, it was also able to gain monopoly control over the selection of textbooks. Hunt, herself, was an author of a leading text and owned a major publishing firm (Rumbarger, 1989: 98).

15. Note how the impact of prohibition on beer, which resulted in illegal shipments of more profitable distilled spirits, was similar to the 1980s' impact on marijuana and the shift to smuggling cocaine.

16. Wheeler specifically argued for placement in the Treasury rather than in Justice (Kerr, 1985: 223). The Prohibition Unit had responsibility for apprehending bootleggers and other violators of the law, regulating the production and access to industrial alcohol, controlling the bonded warehouses where existing liquor was stored for future medicinal uses, issuing permits to physicians to prescribe alcohol, and enforcing the nation's narcotic laws. Only about one-half of the resources of the Prohibition Unit were allocated to the enforcement of prohibition.

17. Several circumstances can account for these discrepancies. First, arrests might not translate into prosecutions, or a prosecution might not result in a conviction until the following year. Second, prosecutors dismissed a portion of the cases given to them by the Prohibition Unit. Third, the definitions used by both the agency and the courts varied somewhat from year to year.

18. Merz (1931: 205–206) estimates total state prohibition enforcement expenditures of $548,629 in 1923 and $689,855 in 1927. Federal prohibition expenditures for those years were $8.5 million and $12.0 million, respectively.

19. The league also suffered a funding crisis as the result of two factors. First, with the adoption of prohibition many sources of funds began to contribute money to other organizations. Second, church contributions in particular would more likely be made for moral education and temperance persuasion but less likely for the encouragement of law enforcement.

20. Kyvig argues that these claims overestimate the size of AAPA membership.

21. Even though the WONPR was a mass membership organization, it was a relatively elite organization. Women who belonged were generally activists in political and social causes and were middle-class and upper-class. Sabin, herself, was the daughter of the Morton Salt Company founder.

22. I know that political scientists should take *Literary Digest* polls with a grain of salt. Kyvig argues that with 4.8 million responses this poll should be given some credence. This position was later endorsed by President Alf Landon in 1937.

23. Blocker notes that the larger brewers saw the tied saloon as a way for small brewers to keep the major brewers from entering their market, because a tied saloon served only one brand of beer. Although the large brewers owned many saloons before prohibition, they felt that they were better off in a market without tied saloons.

24. There have been some modest changes in some of the monopoly states. During the 1980s West Virginia permitted private stores to sell wine, and Iowa permitted private sales of wine and distilled spirits.

25. Actual data are scarce because AA is not operated as a strict medical enterprise. However, large numbers of individuals claim that AA has made a difference.

26. For a discussion of a later attempt to build an advocacy coalition around teenage drinking, see Chauncey, 1980.

27. The U.S. Supreme Court upheld random sobriety checkpoints in *Michigan* v. *Sitz* (No. 88–1897, 1990).

28. MADD also conducts significant public education activities in the schools (Jacobs, 1989: 167).

29. The NHTSA currently contends that the 21-year-old drinking age saves about 1,000 lives a year or reduces the traffic fatalities between the ages of 16 and 20 by about 13 percent (Taylor, 1991b).

30. Weisner (1983: 129) contends that these changes have produced a more middle-class clientele for alcohol treatment agencies, implying that less treatment is available for lower-class persons with alcohol-related problems.

31. Subsequently wine producers have been allowed to put removable tags on the necks of wine bottles that would present this information concerning red wine.

6

One for the Road:
A Quantitative Historical Analysis
of U.S. Alcohol Policies

Few public policies in the United States have varied as much as policies toward alcohol. Our nation has left the alcohol industry to the free market, has extended government regulation over the market, has operated government monopolies at the state level, and has banned all or some alcoholic beverages. Historically alcohol policies give the analyst access to the greatest range of policies within a single arena. The objective of this chapter is to evaluate these policies and provide guidelines for other drug policy efforts.

The analysis takes five parts. First, the public policy theory will be modified to the quantitative historical approach. Second, the measures for individual forces affecting alcohol policy as independent variables will be discussed. Third, federal and state tax policies will be examined in light of the model. Fourth, state and federal enforcement of alcohol beverage laws and regulations will be analyzed. Fifth, the impact of state and federal alcohol policies on several policy outcomes will be assessed, including consumption of alcohol, prison population, health consequences, and crime.

Theoretical Modifications

Most dependent variables in this chapter concern policy implementation efforts. The passage of prohibition laws is a topic more amenable to nonquantitative historical analysis (see chapter 5) or, if sufficient variation exists, cross-sectional analysis (see chapter 7). Enforcement is a crucial question in alcohol policies because compliance with prohibition policies and, until recently, tax policies has been erratic (see Merz, 1931). Understanding alcohol politics in the United States, therefore, is primarily a function of understanding how laws are enforced and what impact enforcement has on individual citizens.

Several modifications of the policy theory will be made in this chapter. Citizen forces can be tapped with a variety of surrogates measuring policy attitudes held by the general public. Industry forces can be quantified and incorporated into the models. Although political forces are limited to partisan influences, good measures of such political forces exist. Bureaucratic variables are a weakness of this approach. The absence of a single law enforcement agency with readily available data limits the analysis, but measures of bureaucratic competitors and federalism can be included. Individual enforcement policies—tax rates, arrest rates, prohibition, and so on—form the core of the theory. These can be examined both as dependent and as independent variables.

A Policy Model

Citizen-related Forces

Alcohol politics has aggressive citizen movements that seek to restrict or free up access to alcohol. Alcohol policies are rarely complex, even though the ramifications of a policy might well be (see Gormley, 1986); the prevalence of alcohol in American society means virtually everyone is an expert on the topic. Alcohol policies, however, vary greatly in salience. Prohibition was a major political issue in the early twentieth century and played a key role in the 1928 and 1932 presidential elections. For many years during the 1950s and 1960s few alcohol-related issues were on the political agenda. Only with the rise of the new public health concerns in the 1970s and 1980s did issues such as drunk driving increase the salience of alcohol policies. The measure of alcohol policy salience is the number of articles appearing in the periodical literature on alcohol and alcohol abuse.[1] Alcohol policies should become more restrictive as the salience of alcohol increases.

The second citizen variable is a demand measure or actually a demand capacity measure. Alcohol consumption increases as real incomes increase (see Dye, 1966: 220; Schweitzer, Intriligator, and Salehi, 1983: 117). To tap the increased demand that results from changes in real income, mean real per capita income is included in the analysis.[2] This measure might also reflect the social-class dimensions of alcohol policies (see Gusfield, 1963). As income increases, alcohol policies should become less restrictive.

Gusfield (1963) and others have presented prohibition as resulting from the competition between rural, Protestant drys and urban, Catholic, immigrant wets. Attitudes toward alcohol are perceived to covary with a wide range of demographic factors. As a result, demographic surrogates for policy attitudes are possible. As surrogates for the dry coalition, this chapter uses the percentage of the population that belongs to Baptist churches and the percentage of the population residing on farms.[3] As surrogates for the wet coalition, the measures will be the percentage of Catholic population and the immigration rate (total immigration for a given year expressed as a percentage of the total population). As rural population and Baptist membership increase, alcohol policies should become more restrictive. As Catholic population and immigration increase, the policies should be less restrictive.

Race plays a prominent role in drug policy, and alcohol is a drug. Policies are often adopted owing to fear of others (see chapter 2). Gusfield (1963) portrays the dry coalition as reacting to the threat of others to its values. Race could well mobilize this coalition, as could increased immigration. For race and immigration, therefore, hypotheses exist in both directions. If these individuals play a key role in the wet coalition, then increases in immigration and nonwhite population should be correlated with less restrictive alcohol policies. If the dry coalition is mobilized by fears of race or immigration, then increases in nonwhite population and immigration should be associated with more restrictive alcohol policies.[4]

The Alcohol Industries

Unlike the illicit drug industry, legitimate alcohol industries exist, even if they have not been popular at times. Given the controversy over the saloon and its role in the adoption of prohibition (see chapter 5), any analysis has to distinguish between the production industry and the retail sales industry. As a measure of the economic strength of the alcohol production industry, the number of individuals employed in the manufacture of distilled spirits, wine, and beer per 100,000 persons will be used. Even though alcohol is thought to involve industries that produce jobs, few jobs are actually in the production industry; most are in retail. As a measure of the strength of the retail sales industry, retail alcohol sales per capita will be used. If the alcohol industries are able to influence policy, we would expect that as alcohol employment and retail sales increase, alcohol policies will become less restrictive.[5]

Political Forces

When public policies become salient, elected officials have the incentive to participate in policy formation. Salience implies that policy action will have electoral consequences; as a result, any investment needed to participate effectively in the policy process is likely to be rewarded with electoral benefits. Two political forces will be examined—elected executives and legislators. Courts will not be included in this analysis, because court decisions on alcohol-related policies have been too infrequent (for a not especially successful attempt in drug policy, see chapter 3).

Legislative Controls on Policy

In alcohol policies legislators have generally used two of their four major powers to control policy implementation—legislation and budgeting. Oversight hearings and legislative vetoes have not played an appreciable role in the politics of alcohol policy. The major legislative action is, of course, prohibition. Similar to drug prohibition, the federal prohibition act banned the sale of alcoholic beverages. Operationalizing prohibition, however, is not as easy as it appears. At the federal level prohibition officially began in 1920 and ended in 1933, but wartime legislation had greatly limited the sale of alcoholic beverages before 1920. States also enacted prohibition laws both before the federal government did and after federal prohibition ended. Two measures of prohibition will be used in this study. The first taps federal prohibition only and is measured with a dummy variable coded 1 for the years 1920 through 1932. The second measure attempts to incorporate state activities; it is the number of states that were officially dry.[6]

The use of budget controls to limit policy implementation is readily apparent from the funding pattern for the Prohibition Unit during Prohibition (see chapter 5). Never was the unit given sufficient funds to implement the policy. Unfortunately for any quantitative assessment of alcohol policies, the federal alcohol enforcement agencies have often been imbedded within other law enforcement agencies or had multiple tasks, so that budgeting data are not available. Without budgeting data, one option is to retreat a step and attempt to measure political attitudes of legislators.

The best surrogate for Congress's predisposition to use government powers to intervene in alcohol policy is partisanship. Although prohibition was not initially a partisan policy, it became one during enforcement (see chapter 5). Republicans advocated greater law enforcement while Democrats advocated repeal or, failing that, less law enforcement. Democrats have also been associated with the expansion of government programs, especially during the 1960s; the growth in health-related funding devoted to alcohol treatment should reflect this partisan bias. The measure used will be the percentage of Congress that is controlled by the Democratic party (both Houses weighted equally). This Democrat measure should be negatively correlated with law enforcement policies and positively correlated with treatment-oriented policies.[7]

Elected Executives

Elected executives, the president and state governors, influence policy implementation by appointing bureaucrats with values similar to their own, by exercising executive authority, by advocating increases in resources, by reorganizing an agency, and by stressing the importance of a policy area (see Meier, 1993). Some of these actions have discrete, measurable indicators, but others do not. As a result, partisanship will again be used as a surrogate for executive predispositions to act. Two variables will be used. For the analysis of national policy, the measure will be a dummy variable coded 1 if the president was a Democrat and 0 if a Republican. For state policies, the number of governors who are Democrats will be the measure. Democrats should be associated with less law enforcement and more treatment-oriented policies.

Party Competition

Party competition plays a historical role in alcohol policies. The Anti-Saloon League used an electoral balancing strategy that required competitive elections to be effective. The total vote provided by the Anti-Saloon League was too small to influence elections unless the elections were relatively close (see chapter 5). The measure of party competition used here is the folded scale of party competition based on the national level (see Bibby et al., 1990). It is essentially the percentage of the majority party in Congress subtracted from 50 percent. The absolute value of that number is subtracted from 100 to generate a measure of competitiveness. Although early prohibition policy suggests that party competition will be associated with restrictive alcohol policies, the salience of the issue suggests that competition is also a method for wets to influence the government. Even though the hypothesis concerning party competition is somewhat ambiguous, its importance in the historical literature suggests that it must be included in the analysis here.

Bureaucracy

Bureaucracies have played a role in the setting of alcohol-related policies. Although the historical evidence does not show influence as great as that of the drug control agencies, the influence has been there. The law enforcement agencies and their impact is problematic in measurement terms. Clearly the Prohibition Unit influenced the path of alcohol policies with its corrupt and generally ineffective implementation of the law. The absence of good measures of the relative effort of these agencies, however, prevents them from being used in the analysis. Although something might be lost in the explanatory process by excluding alcohol law enforcement agencies, they were generally not major players in the policy process. The Prohibition Unit was abolished, and the alcohol functions of the Bureau of Alcohol, Tobacco, and Firearms are currently limited to routine tax collection. Arrest rates and tax collections can be interpreted as bureaucratic activities; however, the analysis here will demonstrate that these activities are externally determined.

The one portion of the bureaucracy that is measurable is the treatment bureaucracy. As a surrogate for those agencies with an interest in the treatment of alcohol-related problems, total government health care employment per 100,000 persons will be used. Health care agencies provide a wide variety of public health services, and only a portion of these are concerned with alcohol and alcohol treatment. The agencies, however, provide a sympathetic bureaucratic locale for policies that are treatment-oriented. To fund such policies or to avoid the problems of alcohol, such agencies would also be likely to support greater taxation of alcohol.[8]

Modeling Public Policy

Similar to chapter 3, a multivariate interrupted time series model will be constructed to determine the impact of institutions and environmental forces on alcohol policies (see Lewis-Beck, 1986). Because the availability of data varies, the length of the time series will also vary. Data for almost all independent variables exist for 1901 through 1990. The time series for most dependent variables is generally shorter.

The strategy of analysis will be to use models with indicators of all the independent variables to explain policy and its outcomes. In addition to the independent variables discussed above, a trend variable will be included in all models to eliminate any incremental increase or decrease in policy activities.[9] The modeling process with all independent variables will generate a great deal of collinearity, with the result being unstable regression coefficients (see Berry and Feldman, 1987). To avoid collinearity problems, all models will be reestimated by removing insignificant variables from the equation. The objective is to create a reasonably parsimonious explanation of the alcohol policy process. The discussion in this chapter will be based on the reduced models only.

Autocorrelation problems are inherent in time series models. For each equation, estimates of autocorrelation will be made. The general rule of thumb is that ordinary least squares is a superior estimation technique unless the autocorrelation exceeds 0.3 (Johnston, 1972: 262; Hanushek and Jackson, 1977: 173). When autocorrelation was found, the equations were reestimated using a maximum likelihood correction if the equation contained a lagged dependent variable and the Prais–Winston correction if it did not (see Johnston, 1972: 313).

Findings

Taxation Policy

With the end of Prohibition, federal alcohol policies became focused on using alcohol as a tax source. While alcohol taxes provide approximately $6 billion annually to both federal and state governments, their relative contribution has dropped as government has grown. The total dollar volume of alcohol taxes, however, is not trivial. Tax rates will be measured in dollars per capita for both the federal and the state governments (summed for all 50 states). For the federal government, 75 years of data are available (1916–90), and for state governments 57 years of data from the post-Prohibition period exist (1934–90).[10]

The model of federal tax rates performs exceptionally well, explaining 99 percent of the variation in rates (see Table 6.1). The significant declining trend

Table 6.1

Historical Determinants of Alcohol Taxes

	Dependent variables					
	Per capita federal tax rate		Per capita state tax rate		Per capita federal and state tax rate	
Independent variables	Full model	Reduced model	Full model	Reduced model	Full model	Reduced model
Intercept	24.211	8.111	−12.389	−8.055	66.897	30.759
Trend	−0.418*	−0.306*	0.478*	0.419*	−0.225	−0.245**
Citizen forces						
Income (thousands)	0.671*	0.697*	−0.967*	−0.549*	−1.032*	−1.029*
Articles	−0.004	—	0.005	—	‑ 0.038**	0.044*
% Baptist population	4.246**	4.091*	−3.407*	—	−1.721	—
% Catholic population	−0.283	—	−0.074	−0.543*	−0.318	—
Immigration rate	−1.831**	—	1.552	—	16.638*	16.301*
% nonwhite population	−0.520	—	0.747**	—	0.002	—
% farm population	−0.626*	−0.543*	−0.139	—	−1.482*	−1.140*
Alcohol industries						
Employment	0.095*	0.092*	0.042*	0.012*	0.088**	0.109*
Retail sales	NA	NA	0.031*	0.024*	0.090*	0.091*
Political forces						
Democratic Congress	−0.053**	−0.048*	NA	NA	−0.291*	−0.145*
Democratic president	−0.113	—	NA	NA	−0.150	—
Party competition	0.002	—	0.037*	0.015*	−0.090	—
Democratic governors	NA	NA	0.005	—	0.005	—
Bureaucratic forces						
Health care employment	0.064*	0.038*	0.044*	0.043*	0.143*	0.154*
R-square	.99	.99	.99	.99	.99	.99
Adjusted R-square	.99	.99	.99	.99	.99	.99
Rho	.54	.63	.51	.45	NA	NA
Durbin–Watson	NA	NA	NA	NA	1.71	1.56
Number of cases	75	75	57	57	57	57

Notes: State and federal equations are estimated via generalized least squares. The combined equation is estimated with ordinary least squares. A dash means the variable was omitted from the equation.

NA = not appropriate.

*p < .05
**p < .10

reflects the slow rise in alcohol taxes relative to population growth; as noted in the previous chapter, federal alcohol tax revenues have not kept pace with inflation. Three citizen-related forces are associated with federal tax rates. Federal alcohol taxes increase as incomes increase (likely reflecting increased consumption) and as Baptist membership increases; both are in the hypothesized direction. Alcohol taxes decrease as the farm population increases. Although this last relationship contradicts the hypothesis, rural populations were given favorable treatment during Prohibition (on the hard cider issue), suggesting that rural populations may have had multiple goals.

The positive relationship with the alcohol industries shows that, as the industries become more powerful, their tax burden increases. This finding suggests that the industries are unable to control taxation issues involving alcohol, a finding that the industries would probably endorse. Although the industries have consistently opposed tax increases, federal tax rates have increased since 1916.

The one political force that is significant, congressional Democrats, is consistent with our hypothesis. When Democrats become more numerous in Congress, the federal tax rate on alcohol declines. The only government advocate for tax increases appears to be the health bureaucracy, perhaps because it sees taxes as a way to increase prices and reduce consumption.

State tax rates follow a different pattern from federal rates, although the level of explanation is similar (99 percent). State tax rates started much lower than the federal rate but have more consistently increased, as reflected in the positive trend variable. State taxes are inversely related to income, unlike federal taxes. Higher state taxes are associated with smaller Catholic populations, larger alcohol industries (both retail and production), more party competition, and a larger health care bureaucracy. These findings suggest that state taxes are the result of competition, with advocates of higher taxes able to overcome the alcohol industries unless those industries can pick up support from the general population (e.g., Catholics).

The final equation models the combined state and federal tax rates. The predictive level of the equation remains high (99 percent), and the pattern appears to be a combination of patterns from the state and federal equations. Two new relationships emerge that merit discussion. First, salience has an impact, albeit a small one. Since many articles published on alcohol deal with its negative consequences, the positive relationship between articles and taxes should not be surprising. The strong positive relationship between tax rates and immigration supports our argument that taxes could be targeted at immigrants (racial targeting appears to be absent from tax policy).

Per capita taxes are only one way to measure alcohol taxation and perhaps not even the best way. Taxes are important because they are directly reflected in the cost of alcoholic beverages; their relative impact is a function of the tax rate, the mix of alcoholic beverages consumed, and the income of the consumers. To provide a tax measure that includes such elements, the per capita tax measures in

Table 6.1 were divided by per capita consumption figures to get the effective tax rate per gallon of alcohol, all forms.[11] This figure was converted into constant dollars to provide for a relative cost of alcohol taxes given the inflation over the century. The results of the analysis of these new dependent variables are shown in Table 6.2.

One striking finding in Table 6.2 is that political and bureaucratic forces have almost no impact on these tax rates. A single political variable is significant: Democratic presidents are associated with higher real alcohol tax rates. Again industries are shown to be a nonfactor in taxation policy. Larger alcohol industries, both production and retail sales, are associated with higher, not lower, alcohol taxes—evidence that is inconsistent with the notion that industries can dominate these policies.

Citizen forces predominate. In all three cases higher taxes are associated with higher incomes, with larger Baptist populations, and with smaller nonwhite populations. Generally these forces, as well as the negative relationship for immigration and federal taxes and the positive relationship for farm population and state taxes, reflect the interests of the individual groups. Only two relationships are in the unexpected direction—the percentage of Catholic population and state taxes, and the percentage of farm population and federal taxes (the latter might reflect a stronger influence of rural populations in states which were more malapportioned for much of the period of this study).

Federal Enforcement Policies

Federal law enforcement efforts did not end with the repeal of prohibition. Total federal alcohol arrests dropped by about two-thirds, but several thousand persons per year were arrested for federal alcohol violations, most involving tax evasion. Most individuals arrested for federal alcohol offenses are not part of the legal alcohol industries, but those industries are also subject to those laws and occasionally are prosecuted for violations. The measure of federal alcohol enforcement is the number of cases brought to federal court per 100,000 persons. Cases initiated in federal court are a better measure than arrests in that a consistent set of court data is available, and arrest data, when they exist, often include some cases that are without merit and thus unlikely to have any impact on compliance with the law.[12] The data series is available from 1920 to 1990, or for 71 years.

To the independent variables included in the previous model, a dummy variable for federal prohibition is added. The resulting model explains 97 percent of the variation in federal court cases with only eight variables (see Table 6.3). Although federal prohibition is the single strongest determinant of alcohol-related cases, several citizen and political forces are also linked to them. Alcohol cases decrease with increases in income, the percentage of Catholic population, and immigration. The linkage with income at first glance might seem counterintuitive, but it is not. As incomes rise, people are more able to afford legal

Table 6.2

Historical Determinants of Alcohol Taxes

	Dependent variables = tax rate per gallon					
	Federal tax rate		State tax rate		State and federal tax rate	
Independent variables	Full model	Reduced model	Full model	Reduced model	Full model	Reduced model
Intercept	23.502	22.041	-35.249	-28.427	36.785	42.994
Trend	-0.466	-0.529*	-0.475*	0.376*	-1.392*	-1.365*
Citizen forces						
Income (thousands)	1.128	1.116**	0.925*	0.700*	2.138*	2.321*
Articles	0.008	—	-0.002	—	0.036	—
% Baptist population	10.157**	12.627*	8.707*	7.838*	11.988	21.479*
% Catholic population	0.018	—	1.161*	0.892*	1.498	—
Immigration rate	-6.967*	-8.196*	0.756	—	13.277	—
% nonwhite population	-2.851	-4.276*	-1.589*	-0.969*	-3.777	-5.766*
% farm population	-0.375	-0.543*	0.839*	0.603*	-0.457	—
Alcohol industries						
Employment	0.183*	0.186*	0.088*	0.060**	0.151	0.096**
Retail sales	NA	NA	0.011	0.012**	0.060*	0.048*
Political forces						
Democratic Congress	0.001	—	NA	NA	-0.005	—
Democratic president	1.598	1.632**	NA	NA	0.061	—
Party competition	-0.002	—	0.007	—	0.042	—
Democratic governors	NA	NA	-0.009	—	0.004	—
Bureaucratic forces						
Health care employment	-0.058	—	0.034	—	-0.028	—
R-square	.95	.95	.96	.96	.98	.97
Adjusted R-square	.94	.95	.94	.95	.97	.97
Rho	.57	.61	NA	.39	.30	.40
Durbin–Watson	NA	NA	1.42	NA	NA	NA
Number of cases	75	75	57	57	57	57

Notes: All equations are estimated with generalized least squares except the full model for state taxes. A dash means the variable was omitted from the equation.

NA = not appropriate.

*p < .05
**p < .10

Table 6.3

Federal Prosecutions for Liquor Law Violations

Independent variables	Dependent variable = cases per 100,000 persons	
	Full model	Reduced model
Intercept	37.091	8.083
Trend	0.327	0.185**
Citizen forces		
Income (thousands)	−0.965**	−1.621*
Articles	0.026	—
% Baptist population	−3.112	—
% Catholic population	−1.231**	−1.312*
Immigration rate	−13.332*	−17.934*
% nonwhite population	−2.646	—
% farm population	−0.057	—
Alcohol industries		
Employment	−0.180*	−0.181*
Political forces		
Democratic Congress	0.491*	0.478*
Democratic president	−0.997	—
Party competition	0.134*	0.157*
Bureaucratic forces		
Health care employment	0.020	—
Policy		
Prohibition	26.275*	28.906*
R-square	.98	.97
Adjusted R-square	.97	.97
Durbin–Watson	1.64	1.46
Number of cases	71	71

Notes: Equations are estimated with ordinary least squares. A dash means the variable was omitted from the equation.

*p < .05
**p < .10

alcohol, and therefore the purchase of illegal alcohol becomes less attractive.

Enforcement of federal alcohol laws declines with the increase in the economic strength of the alcohol industries. Enforcement increases with party competition (see chapter 5 on the election cycle in prohibition enforcement) and with Democratic majorities in Congress. The relationship with Democrats is interesting in that it holds only because the prohibition measure absorbs much of the increase in enforcement that occurs when more Republicans are elected to Congress.

Impact on Consumption of Alcohol

The new public health movement advocates increased taxes on alcohol to reduce consumption (see chapter 5). Such advocacy is hardly new; Benjamin Rush, a physician and signer of the Declaration of Independence, made the same argument in Congress in 1791 (Stoil, 1987: 35). The logic supporting high alcohol taxes is that because taxes constitute a large portion of the cost of alcoholic beverages, they will be immediately reflected in price and thus affect demand. Evidence on the ability of taxes to affect apparent alcohol consumption has been mixed. Some studies have found that demand for alcohol is price elastic (Cook, 1981; Ornstein and Hanssens, 1985), whereas others have found no impacts (Schweitzer, Intriligator, and Salehi, 1983: 120) or that high taxes convince individuals to drink cheaper forms of alcoholic beverages (Johnson and Meier, 1990). Our dependent variable is per capita consumption of alcoholic beverages in gallons of alcohol to take into consideration the varying alcoholic content of distilled spirits, beer, and wine. These consumption figures are based on federal tax data and do not include consumption of illegal alcohol.[13] Because the analysis is concerned with the impact of tax and enforcement policies, the time period is limited by the availability of both tax data and enforcement data (71 years for federal policies and 57 years for state policies and state and federal policies combined).

Table 6.4 presents the determinants of per capita alcohol consumption using federal policies, state policies, and both federal and state policies. In all cases, the models work well, accounting for at least 97 percent of the variance in per capita consumption. Since our major concern is the impact of tax and enforcement policies on alcohol consumption, the bulk of the discussion of Table 6.4 will focus on these policy variables. First, prohibition clearly had a fairly consistent impact in all three equations. The prohibition measure is the number of dry states. Each additional dry state reduced mean alcohol consumption by 0.010 to 0.022 gallons, all other things being equal. This means that federal prohibition (48 states) reduced consumption by 1.06 gallons per capita, or about 40 percent from the pre-Prohibition levels of 2.5 gallons. This finding is consistent with other literature on the impact of prohibition (see chapter 5; Miron and Zwiebel, 1991a).

Table 6.4

The Impact of Policies on Alcohol Consumption

Dependent variable = per capita consumption in gallons

Independent variables	Federal policies Full model	Federal policies Reduced model	State policies Full model	State policies Reduced model	State and federal policies Full model	State and federal policies Reduced model
Intercept	4.339	−2.136	−0.246	−0.065	1.006	−0.070
Trend	−0.011	−0.023*	−0.007	−0.018*	−0.012	0.017*
Citizen forces						
Income (thousands)	0.072**	0.014*	−0.027	—	−0.015	—
Articles	−0.002	—	0.001	—	0.001	—
% Baptist population	−0.166	—	−0.103	—	−0.106	—
% Catholic population	−0.115*	—	0.026	—	−0.019	—
Immigration rate	0.110	0.248**	0.215	—	0.359	—
% nonwhite population	0.059	0.216*	−0.006	—	−0.035	—
% farm population	−0.077*	—	−0.022	—	−0.039	−0.023**
Alcohol industries						
Employment	0.003	0.012*	0.013*	0.012*	0.014*	0.010*
Retail sales	NA	NA	0.006*	0.005*	0.006*	0.006*
Political forces						
Democratic Congress	−0.010	—	NA	NA	0.000	—
Democratic president	−0.006	—	NA	NA	−0.007	—
Party competition	−0.005*	—	0.002	—	1.447	—
Democratic governors	NA	NA	0.001	—	0.001	—
Bureaucratic forces						
Health care employment	0.003	—	0.007*	0.005*	0.006*	—
Policies						
Federal tax rate	0.002	—	NA	NA	NA	NA
State tax rate	NA	NA	−0.025**	−0.026*	NA	NA
Federal and state taxes	NA	NA	NA	NA	−0.014*	−0.015*
Federal enforcement	0.000	—	NA	NA	−0.004	—
Prohibition	−0.026*	−0.022*	−0.020*	−0.015*	−0.015	−0.010**
R-square	.99	.97	.98	.98	.99	.98
Adjusted R-square	.98	.96	.98	.98	.99	.98
Rho	.39	.53	NA	.34	NA	.42
Durbin–Watson	NA	NA	1.61	NA	1.89	NA
Number of cases	71	80	57	57	57	57

Notes: All equations with rho are estimated with generalized least squares. A dash means the variable was omitted from the equation.

NA = not appropriate.

*p < .05

**p < .10

The impacts of other policies are not so promising. In the first equation for federal policies, federal taxes and federal enforcement are unrelated to consumption. State taxes and combined state and federal taxes, however, are associated with lower consumption in the second and third equations. These findings are not consistent with the notion that law enforcement can reduce consumption, but they are consistent with the position that taxation rates, particularly state taxation rates, can reduce consumption. State taxes affect consumption, but federal taxes do not because they started at extremely high rates after World War II and have dropped relative to increases in real income since that time. State taxes have increased faster than federal taxes have declined in recent years, and this increase might be sufficient to persuade some individuals to consume less alcohol.

The citizen forces show that consumption of alcoholic beverages is positively related to immigration, income, and the percentage of nonwhite population (in different equations) and negatively related to the percentage of farm population. All these relationships are consistent with the values that these surrogate measures represent. The health care bureaucracy is associated with less consumption, but only in the second equation covering 1934–90. Also of interest is the positive relationship between the strength of the alcohol industries, particularly the retail industry, and the consumption of alcohol. Although the relationship is not especially strong, perhaps the Anti-Saloon League had a point.

Federal policies have frequently been charged with favoring one type of alcoholic beverage over another. The distilled spirits industry has long argued that, on the basis of alcohol content, beer and wine are taxed less than distilled spirits, a situation that was partly but not totally corrected by the 1991 tax increases (see chapter 5). Prohibition probably had its greatest impact on beer rather than on distilled spirits.

The equations showing the impact of federal and state policies on the consumption of beer, wine, and distilled spirits are shown in Table 6.5. Here, too, the relationships of concern are those for public policy. Prohibition again is a major influence with a strong reduction in the consumption of beer, wine, and distilled spirits. The size of the coefficient is largest for beer consumption and relatively similar for distilled spirits and wine. Combined federal and state tax rates are negatively related to consumption of all forms of alcoholic beverages. Federal enforcement has a negative impact on beer and wine consumption, but no impact on distilled spirits, which should be the focus of the policy. This suggests that prohibition enforcement was able to limit beer consumption but not the consumption of distilled spirits. Such evidence is consistent with historians' claims about social class and prohibition (see chapter 5).

State Enforcement

State governments also enforce a variety of alcohol-related laws. Some of these laws are similar to the federal law on taxation, but most deal with the conse-

Table 6.5

Impacts on the Consumption of Beer, Wine, and Spirits, 1934–90

| | Dependent variable = per capita consumption of: | | | | | |
| | Beer | | Wine | | Distilled spirits | |
Independent variables	Full model	Reduced model	Full model	Reduced model	Full model	Reduced model
Intercept	78.298	47.617	−9.652	−8.348	−3.603	−0.973
Trend	0.190	—	0.040*	0.046*	−0.064**	−0.021*
Citizen forces						
Income (thousands)	−0.946*	−0.650*	0.036	—	0.060	—
Articles	0.006	0.002*	−0.001	—	0.003	—
% Baptist population	−7.834*	−6.111*	0.673*	—	0.444	—
% Catholic population	−1.034*	—	−0.019	—	0.172*	0.111*
Immigration rate	5.264	9.909*	−0.641	—	0.410	—
% nonwhite population	−0.094	—	0.065	0.150*	−0.098	−0.130**
% farm population	−1.492*	−0.966*	0.120*	0.057*	0.039	0.059*
Alcohol industries						
Employment	0.209*	0.232*	0.008	0.012*	0.008	0.011*
Retail Industry	0.066*	0.074*	0.002**	0.002*	0.008*	0.007*
Political forces						
Democratic Congress	0.026	—	0.019*	0.024*	−0.007	—
Democratic president	0.167	—	−0.008	—	−0.032	—
Party competition	−0.020	—	0.013*	0.018*	0.002	—
Democratic governors	0.006	—	0.003*	0.005*	0.000	—
Bureaucratic forces						
Health care employment	0.005*	0.058*	−0.000	—	0.010*	0.010*
Policies						
Federal and state tax	−0.105**	−0.178*	−0.013*	−0.009*	−0.019**	−0.015*
Federal enforcement	−0.107	−0.157*	−0.022*	−0.014*	0.008	—
Prohibition	−0.015	−0.302*	−0.020**	−0.023*	−0.032	−0.021**
R-square	.98	.97	.99	.99	.95	.94
Adjusted R-square	.97	.97	.99	.99	.93	.93
Rho	NA	NA	NA	NA	NA	NA
Durbin–Watson	2.06	1.47	1.76	1.62	1.77	1.41
Number of cases	57	57	57	57	57	57

Note: A dash means the variable was omitted from the equation.

NA = not appropriate.

*p < .05

**p < .10

quences of drinking alcoholic beverages. Six different measures of state enforcement will be examined; all are for arrests—driving under the influence, liquor law violations (sales to minors, failure to pay taxes, violating license requirements, etc.), drunkenness, disorderly conduct, vagrancy, and the sum total of all alcohol-related arrests. To the independent variables used in previous analysis, the per capita consumption of alcoholic beverages will be added.[14] Arrests for alcohol-related crimes should reflect the level of alcohol-related problems, which in turn should be associated with the consumption of alcoholic beverages.

Tables 6.6 and 6.7 show the model's results for the six state enforcement variables. The striking relationship is for alcohol consumption. State arrest rates for alcohol-related crimes are unrelated to alcohol consumption, suggesting that forces other than alcohol consumption influence the arrest of individuals for alcohol-related offenses (e.g., political pressures). Other state and federal policies also have little impact on state arrest rates. Prohibition never matters, although it is only fair to note that this post-1934 measure has limited variation and excludes the time period of prohibition's major impact. Taxation rates are positively related to arrests for all liquor laws and negatively related to DUI arrests. The former might be the result of high taxes encouraging bootlegging, but then this should show up in the liquor violations equation (which it does not). The negative relationship between taxes and arrests for driving under the influence might reflect the reduced consumption when taxes increase; but given the lack of relationship to consumption, this relationship must be confirmed with state-level data before that conclusion can be accepted (see chapter 7).

For drug laws federal enforcement is a major determinant of state drug enforcement rates. This impact of federalism does not appear for alcohol policies because federal and state officials enforce laws that are targeted at different crimes. The federal government wants to collect federal taxes; state governments focus on the consequences of consuming alcohol. Federal enforcement has dropped precipitously in recent years, just as state enforcement, especially for DUI, has increased.

One political force merits mention. Arrests for driving under the influence increase when party competition increases, suggesting that arrest rates are politically determined. The citizen forces reinforce this. Dry religious groups are associated with more arrests for DUI, drunkenness, disorderly conduct, and all alcohol-related arrests. Wet religious groups are associated with fewer arrests for drunkenness, disorderly conduct, vagrancy, liquor law violations, and all alcohol-related arrests. Increases in income are also associated with fewer arrests.

Enforcement of state alcohol laws is the best place to see the conflict within the alcohol industries. The production industry is concerned about selling alcoholic beverages and continuing to operate without controls. It is quite willing to endorse vigorous enforcement of laws regarding driving under the influence or other state laws. The retail industry, on the other hand, bears the brunt of this enforcement, whether it be for underage drinking or by arrests of individuals

Table 6.6

Determinants of State Alcohol Enforcement

	Dependent variables					
	All alcohol-related arrests		DUI violations		Liquor law violations	
Independent variables	Full model	Reduced model	Full model	Reduced model	Full model	Reduced model
Intercept	−3191	−5161	−864	524	635	−6
Trend	297.6*	112.2*	3.25	−15.60*	10.93*	7.84*
Citizen forces						
Income (thousands)	−405.4*	−222.0*	−17.03	—	−9.29	—
Articles	−0.3	—	0.21	—	−0.08	—
% Baptist population	1708.0**	829.9*	370.68*	270.03*	−110.79*	—
% Catholic population	−326.3*	−286.4*	−13.79	—	−13.15**	−9.55*
Immigration rate	−1021.3	—	−82.09	—	−11.27	—
% nonwhite population	69.7	—	0.33	—	−0.67	—
% farm population	250.0	—	28.71	—	−11.61**	—
Alcohol industries						
Employment	64.0*	56.3*	−0.82	—	−0.70	−0.92**
Retail sales	1.2	—	0.61	—	−0.05	−0.20*
Political forces						
Party competition	−4.5	—	1.89**	2.52*	−0.30	—
Democratic governors	−5.3	—	0.34	—	−0.19	—
Bureaucratic forces						
Health care employment	−4.9	—	0.20	—	−0.59	−0.63*
Policies						
Federal and state tax	114.5*	40.7*	−11.21**	−22.17*	−0.46	—
Federal enforcement	262.2	—	−10.68	−10.64*	−1.87	—
Prohibition	−94.3	—	14.38	—	2.89	—
Alcohol consumption	1257.2**	—	42.20	—	−34.34	—
R-square	.97	.96	.99	.99	.99	.98
Adjusted R-square	.95	.96	.96	.99	.98	.98
Rho	NA	NA	NA	NA	.31	.51
Durbin–Watson	2.28	2.17	2.01	1.57	NA	NA
Number of cases	42	42	45	45	48	48

Note: A dash means the variable was omitted from the equation.
NA = not appropriate.
*$p < .05$
**$p < .10$

Table 6.7

Determinants of State Alcohol Enforcement—Status Crimes

| | Dependent variables | | | | | |
| | Drunkenness | | Disorderly conduct | | Vagrancy | |
Independent variables	Full model	Reduced model	Full model	Reduced model	Full model	Reduced model
Intercept	16,068	12,364	1,350	−728	786	1,341
Trend	−86.50**	−93.60*	7.19	—	−9.81	−10.55*
Citizen forces						
Income (thousands)	65.87	—	−45.77	−21.06*	−10.48	−15.22*
Articles	1.41	—	−0.19	—	0.65	0.72**
% Baptist population	680.42	520.38**	76.33	284.91*	3.55	—
% Catholic population	−276.87*	−238.20*	−53.24	−25.49*	−15.54**	−13.43*
Immigration rate	−266.34	—	150.38	—	−4.57	—
% nonwhite population	−149.33	—	−0.24	—	−14.59	—
% farm population	−128.15	−87.24**	−26.48	—	1.40	—
Alcohol industries						
Employment	10.26	—	5.96	8.19*	0.94	—
Retail sales	−6.37*	−9.22*	−1.00	—	−0.93*	−1.09*
Political forces						
Party competition	−1.61	—	−0.55	—	−0.91*	−0.90*
Democratic governors	1.07	—	0.18	—	−0.01	—
Bureaucratic forces						
Health care employment	−1.40	—	−0.11	—	1.28	1.44*
Policies						
Federal and state tax	−6.69	—	6.69	—	−1.89	—
Federal arrests	−200.01*	−140.23*	−12.85	—	−1.51	—
Prohibition	−49.20	—	−8.66	—	14.25	—
Alcohol consumption	−219.76	—	66.85	—	−18.62	—
R-square	.98	.98	.88	.85	.97	.97
Adjusted R-square	.97	.97	.80	.84	.96	.95
Rho	NA	NA	NA	NA	NA	NA
Durbin–Watson	2.49	2.04	2.04	1.66	1.80	1.75
Number of cases	46	46	46	46	46	46

Note: A dash means the variable was omitted from the equation.

NA = not appropriate.

*p < .05

**p < .10

who drink in public. The production industry is associated with more arrests for all liquor laws, more arrests for disorderly conduct, and fewer arrests for liquor violations (although the latter is barely significant). The retail industry is negatively associated with arrests for liquor violations, drunkenness, and vagrancy.

The Impact on Corrections

One criticism of prohibition was that alcohol-related crimes were swamping the federal courts and, in turn, the federal prisons (see chapter 5). The analysis in chapter 3 showed that one consequence of drug laws was a major increase in the number of federal and state prisoners. Table 6.8 shows the analysis for federal and state prison populations (standardized to prisoners per 100,000 persons). The equations explain 80 percent of the variation in federal prison rates from 1926 to 1990 and 98 percent of state prison rates from 1934 to 1990.[15]

The suprising findings in Table 6.8 are the strong *negative* relationships between alcohol consumption and the number of both state and federal prisoners; increases in alcohol consumption are associated with fewer prisoners, not more. Neither did prohibition negatively impact the prison system; all other things being equal, the more states that prohibited alcoholic beverages, the fewer prisoners. This relationship is especially strong for state prisons. Two policies do have the expected relationship with prison population. First, for each additional federal arrest for alcohol violations, the number of prisoners increases by 0.114; the increase is less than 1 because the penalties for violating federal alcohol laws are relatively modest. Second, higher federal alcohol taxes are also associated with increases in the federal prison population. Higher alcohol taxes, of course, make bootlegging a more attractive crime, so the expected relationship is positive.

Some of the other relationships in Table 6.8 merit comment. Both alcohol industry employment and health care employment are negatively related to prison population. One would expect the latter, given the health care bureaucracy's emphasis on treatment (the negative relationship may also indicate a state's endorsement of treatment rather than incarceration). Increases in both the Catholic and Baptist populations are associated with fewer prisoners. As suggested in chapter 3, this relationship likely exists because attachment to religious groups is one of the social constraints on individuals and makes them less likely to commit crimes. No evidence from this table indicates any racial impacts, although there are positive relationships between state prison populations and both increased immigration and rural population. These relationships, however, are unlikely to have any relationship with alcohol policies, since state alcohol policies appear to have little impact on state prison populations.

Policy Outcomes: The Health Question

A driving force behind the new public health movement in regard to alcohol has been a concern with the health ramifications of alcohol consumption (see chapter 5). Clinical and epidemiological studies have linked alcohol consumption to

Table 6.8

Impact of Policies on Jail Population

Independent variables	Dependent variable = prisoners per 100,000 persons			
	Federal prisoners		State prisoners	
	Full model	Reduced model	Full model	Reduced model
Intercept	31.512	42.342	−25.25	−18.57
Trend	1.061*	0.990*	15.51*	12.45*
Citizen forces				
Income (thousands)	−0.048	—	−7.63*	−4.11*
Articles	−0.033*	−0.036*	0.00	—
% Baptist population	−2.379	—	−48.39*	−48.00*
% Catholic population	−1.897*	−2.393*	−16.42*	−11.59*
Immigration rate	4.591	—	41.48	108.35*
% nonwhite population	0.051	—	−1.68	—
% farm population	0.106	—	4.64**	4.58*
Alcohol industries				
Employment	−0.112**	−0.138*	−0.07	−0.63*
Political forces				
Democratic Congress	−0.150**	−0.187*	NA	NA
Democratic president	−0.476	—	NA	NA
Party competition	−0.120*	−0.141*	−0.44*	—
Democratic governors	NA	NA	−0.09	—
Bureaucratic forces				
Health care employment	−0.107*	−0.109*	−0.71*	−0.82*
Policies				
Federal tax rate	0.162	0.143**	NA	NA
Federal and state taxes	NA	NA	0.56	—
Federal enforcement	0.117	0.114*	−0.01	—
Prohibition	−0.204**	−0.222*	−2.09	−1.69*
Alcohol consumption	−5.338*	−5.076*	−72.62*	−48.90*
R-square	.81	.80	.99	.98
Adjusted R-square	.74	.76	.98	.97
Rho	.29	.30	.32	.45
Number of cases	65	65	57	57

Note: A dash means the variable was omitted from the equation.
NA = not appropriate.
*$p < .05$
**$p < .10$

numerous health risks, including more accidents and greater mortality. Because several policies have affected the consumption of alcohol, these policies should also influence the health risks of alcohol, although probably indirectly. Three alcohol-related health risks will be examined—deaths from cirrhosis of the liver, deaths from suicide, and deaths from automobile traffic accidents. Alcohol consumption is related to a greater risk of death from all three causes (see NIAAA, 1990: 22, 164, 168).

Cirrhosis Deaths

Alcohol consumption, especially heavy alcohol consumption for long periods of time, is directly related to deaths from cirrhosis of the liver (Popham, Schmidt, and de Lint, 1978: 259). Cirrhosis deaths are a good indicator of public policy impact because the causal linkage between alcohol and cirrhosis is strong (80 percent of cirrhosis deaths are related to alcohol; Schmidt and de Lint, 1973) and also because persons who stop drinking have an immediate impact on the health of their liver (Terris, 1967: 2076; Cook, 1981: 276). Even though data for the number of cirrhosis deaths per 100,000 persons in the United States are available for the entire century, limits on federal alcohol enforcement data restrict the analysis to the years 1920–90.

Table 6.9 shows the results of the policy impact analysis for cirrhosis deaths. Only four variables remain in the reduced model (and explain 93 percent of the variance), and only three of those are significant—a time trend,[16] wet religious groups, and alcohol consumption.[17] Cirrhosis death rates are positively associated with the percentage of Catholic population and alcohol consumption and are negatively related to time. Prohibition is not related to cirrhosis deaths only because its impact on cirrhosis is through alcohol consumption; some, if not all, of the impact of the Catholic population might also be the result of unmeasured consumption. The degree of impact for alcohol consumption is fairly large. A one-gallon reduction in annual consumption is associated with a drop of 1.66 in the cirrhosis rate, or approximately 15 percent of the average rate for this century.[18]

Reestimating the cirrhosis equation for the time period 1934–90 allows an assessment of state and federal tax rates. The second equation in Table 6.9 shows that the impact of alcohol consumption on cirrhosis deaths is twice as great from 1934 to the present as it is from 1920 to the present (perhaps because the amount of illegal alcohol consumed is less). A one-gallon reduction in consumption is associated with a drop of 2.6 in the cirrhosis death rate, or approximately 24 percent of the twentieth-century average. For cirrhosis of the liver, then, public policies are able to affect alcohol consumption, and consumption in turn affects cirrhosis death rates.

Suicide

Alcohol is a depressant; as a result, alcohol consumption is also implicated in approximately 20–36 percent of all suicides (Roizen, 1982; Colliver and Malin,

Table 6.9

Impact of Policies on Cirrhosis Death Rates

	Dependent variable = cirrhosis deaths per 100,000 persons			
	1920–90		1934–90	
Independent variables	Full model	Reduced model	Full model	Reduced model
Intercept	19.034	–4.498	–0.648	–2.683
Trend	–0.378*	–0.055**	–0.473*	–0.288*
Citizen forces				
Income (thousands)	0.161	—	0.654*	—
Articles	–0.006	—	–0.016	—
% Baptist population	–1.289	—	0.922	—
% Catholic population	0.816*	0.747*	1.059*	1.049*
Immigration rate	–2.663*	—	–1.472	—
% nonwhite population	–0.505	—	–0.266	—
% farm population	–0.368*	—	0.038	—
Alcohol industries				
Employment	0.054*	—	0.058	—
Retail sales	NA	NA	–0.013	—
Bureaucratic forces				
Health care employment	0.066*	—	0.069*	0.034*
Policies				
Federal tax rate	0.017	—	NA	NA
Federal and state taxes	NA	NA	0.067	—
Federal enforcement	0.055*	0.017	0.087	—
Prohibition	0.047	—	0.193	—
Alcohol consumption	2.102*	1.660*	3.626	2.596*
R-square	.96	.93	.95	.93
Adjusted R-square	.95	.93	.93	.92
Rho	.33	.76	NA	.62
Durbin–Watson	NA	NA	1.42	NA
Number of cases	71	71	57	57

Note: A dash means the variable was omitted from the equation.
NA = not appropriate.

*p < .05
**p < .10

1986). Limitations on the independent variables again restrict the analysis of suicides to the 1920–90 period.[19] The first equation in Table 6.10 shows that public policies are associated with suicide rates in two ways. First, increases in alcohol consumption are positively associated with increases in suicide rates. Second, an increase in federal alcohol enforcement has a separate positive impact on suicides. Although the reason for this latter relationship is not known, it might be the result of pressures created by a large number of arrests during Prohibition. For example, the second set of equations in Table 6.10, which are limited to the post-Prohibition period, do not show a significant linkage between enforcement and suicide. The positive relationship to health care employment is in all likelihood a case of reverse causality; more suicides can be used to justify more mental health care funds (see also Table 6.9).

Traffic Fatalities

Until recently approximately one-half of all traffic fatalities were linked to alcohol. Despite this obvious relationship, attempts to relate alcohol consumption to traffic fatalities at the aggregate level have not been especially successful. Traffic fatalities are measured in traffic deaths per 100,000 persons. The equation in Table 6.11 is estimated for the years 1920–90 as a result of the availability of data for the independent variables.[20]

The analysis of traffic fatalities is able to explain only 74 percent of the variation. This low level of explanation is probably the result of missing variables, such as the increase in highway speeds associated with muscle cars of the 1960s and the absence of variables measuring improved vehicles and roads (see Meier and Morgan, 1982). Alcohol consumption is unrelated to traffic fatalities in the reduced model; it has a weak positive relationship in the full model. Two less-direct influences are related. Prohibition is associated with a significant decline in the number of traffic fatalities, perhaps owing to the decline in alcohol consumption. Federal enforcement, however, is positively related to traffic fatalities, although no obvious reason for this relationship exists. The citizen variables reflect the often-found relationships between traffic fatalities and income and urban areas.

Alcohol and Crime

Alcohol is one drug consistently associated with violent crime (Fagan, 1990). Unlike the situation with illicit drugs, where it is the illegality that motivates crime, with alcohol, crime is directly linked to the consumption. Because alcohol was banned during Prohibition, it is also interesting to see if the perceived rise in crime since then (particularly murders) can be tapped by our statistical models. Finally, enforcement of drug laws is related to crime (see chapters 3 and 4); a fair empirical question is whether or not crime is also related to enforcement of alcohol laws.

Table 6.10

Impact of Policies on Suicide Death Rates

| | Dependent variable = suicides per 100,000 persons | | | |
| | 1920–90 | | 1934–90 | |
Independent variables	Full model	Reduced model	Full model	Reduced model
Intercept	14.494	17.628	–57.176	–13.943
Trend	0.208*	0.222*	0.068	—
Citizen forces				
Income (thousands)	–0.922*	–0.982*	–0.570*	–0.351*
Articles	–0.003	—	–0.001	—
% Baptist population	–4.948*	–4.766*	–1.538	—
% Catholic population	0.424*	0.384*	0.386*	0.644*
Immigration rate	–2.110*	–1.331**	0.753	—
% nonwhite population	0.274	—	0.555*	0.297**
% farm population	–0.004	—	0.387*	0.593*
Alcohol industries				
Employment	0.010	—	–0.032	—
Retail sales	NA	NA	–0.004	—
Bureaucratic forces				
Health care employment	0.035*	0.033*	0.034*	0.040*
Policies				
Federal tax rate	0.021	—	NA	NA
Federal and state taxes	NA	NA	0.072*	—
Federal enforcement	0.085*	0.065*	0.073	—
Prohibition	–0.002	—	–0.005	—
Alcohol consumption	0.920**	1.378*	1.382**	0.545**
R-square	.92	.93	.95	.94
Adjusted R-square	.90	.92	.94	.93
Rho	NA	.35	NA	NA
Durbin–Watson	1.46	NA	2.21	1.73
Number of cases	71	71	57	57

Note: A dash means the variable was omitted from the equation.
NA = not appropriate.

*p < .05
**p < .10

Table 6.11

The Impact of Alcohol Policies on Traffic Fatalities, 1920–90

Independent variables	Dependent variable = fatalities per 100,000 persons	
	Full model	Reduced model
Intercept	70.820	68.828
Trend	−0.066	—
Citizen forces		
Income (thousands)	−1.064	−0.550**
Articles	−0.004	—
% Baptist population	−13.484*	−8.641*
% Catholic population	1.003	—
Immigration rate	−4.304	—
% nonwhite population	−1.421	—
% farm population	−1.188**	−1.130*
Alcohol industries		
Employment	0.020	—
Bureaucratic forces		
Health care employment	0.031	—
Policies		
Federal tax rate	−0.005	—
Federal enforcement	0.246*	0.227*
Prohibition	−0.289*	−0.305*
Alcohol consumption	0.817	—
R-square	.76	.74
Adjusted R-square	.70	.72
Rho	.34	.50
Number of cases	71	71

Note: A dash means the variable was omitted from the equation.

*p < .05
**p < .10

Many factors cause crime. Modeling crime rates, therefore, would be difficult with the variables that have been used in previous tables. As a result, a different strategy will be used here. Crime will be predicted by the level of crime in the previous year, a trend variable, alcohol consumption, prohibition, and enforcement. Most of the explanation for crime in any one year will be the level of crime in the previous year (which will act as a surrogate for the various causes of crime). The alcohol factors, therefore, will be subjected to a fairly rigorous test. Explaining significant relationships for any variable when a lagged measure of the dependent variable is in the equation is difficult.[21]

Models with lagged dependent variables create some autocorrelation problems that cannot be measured or solved by the common detection and correction methods (see Johnston, 1972: 313). The models, however, can be estimated with a maximum likelihood technique that estimates a level of autocorrelation and incorporates it directly into the model. When such methods are necessary, an autoregressive term will be reported. For all models, the accepted approach for estimating the degree of autocorrelation will be reported.[22]

Table 6.12 shows the alcohol–crime relationships for six crimes—murder, all violent crime, assault, robbery, burglary, and larceny. The equation for murder merits extended discussion. Murder rates are, of course, related to murder rates the previous year (poverty, family problems, youth violence, etc., tend to persist), alcohol consumption, and prohibition. A one-gallon increase in alcohol consumption is associated with a 0.756 increase in murders per 100,000 persons. Although this figure is only about 8 percent of current murder rates, that is a fairly substantial estimate, given the lagged equation format. The expected increase in crime during Prohibition also appears. Each additional dry state is associated with a 0.043 increase in the murder rate. For federal prohibition with 48 states, this increase is about 2.1 murders per 100,000 persons (about 20 percent of current rates).

The other relationships between alcohol and crime can be discussed in a summary manner. Alcohol consumption is positively related to the rates for all violent crimes, for robbery, and for burglary; the absence of a relationship for assault is interesting given alcohol's role in interpersonal violence. Prohibition is actually associated with a drop in robbery and burglary, whereas federal enforcement is associated with only a drop in larceny. Although it might be the case that prohibition attracted individuals to bootlegging who might otherwise have made a living by theft, such a conclusion would be pure speculation at this point.

Alcohol consumption and prohibition might also be associated with other forms of crime, such as gambling, prostitution, and sex offenses (see NIAAA, 1990: 172–174). Such crimes, however, are not reported with any degree of accuracy. The data that are available are the arrest rates for such crimes. The relationship between alcohol and arrest rates is indeterminate. On the one hand, consumption of alcohol might make some individuals more likely to commit such crimes, thus creating a positive relationship. On the other hand, the con-

Table 6.12

Impact of Alcohol and Policies on Crime Rates

Independent variables	Dependent variables = crime rate for:					
	Murder	All violent crimes	Assault	Robbery	Burglary	Larceny
Intercept	1.277	−198.5	0.107	−435.2	−3926	973
Trend	—	2.68*	—	—	—	—
Crime in previous year	0.858*	0.78*	1.047*	0.60*	0.45*	0.68*
Alcohol consumption	0.756*	40.72**	—	63.14*	450.11*	—
Federal enforcement	—	—	—	—	—	−236.30*
Prohibition	0.043*	—	—	−6.82*	−67.88*	—
Autoregressive term	0.330*	—	—	0.59*	0.69*	0.75*
R-square	.95	.99	.99	.98	.99	.99
Adjusted R-square	.94	.99	.99	.98	.99	.99
Estimated rho	−.03	.01	.07	.13	.07	−.08
Autocorrelation t-test	0.70	0.72	0.05	1.76	0.74	0.88
Number of cases	71	45	48	44	44	44

Notes: Equations for murder, violent crime, and assualt are estimated with ordinary least squares. Other equations are estimated by maximum likelihood estimation with first-order autocorrelation. Autocorrelation t is the significance of any residual autocorrelation in the equation estimated. A dash means the variable was omitted from the equation.

*p < .05
**p < .10

sumption of alcohol might increase other crimes and move law enforcement personnel to those crimes, thus limiting resources available for these crimes. Arrests for these offenses are highly discretionary and often reflect the relative amount of resources that police departments invest in these areas. Table 6.13 estimates the crime models for four arrest rates—prostitution, gambling, sex offenses (other than sexual assault), and crimes against the family.

Table 6.13

Impact of Alcohol and Policies on Arrest Rates

Independent variables	Dependent variables = arrest rate for:			
	Prostitution	Gambling	Sex offenses	Family crimes
Intercept	132.8	723.9	151.2	147.0
Trend	—	—	0.53*	—
Arrests in previous year	0.56*	0.46*	0.49*	0.23**
Alcohol consumption	15.47*	−29.27*	−11.67*	−16.38*
Federal enforcement	—	—	—	—
Prohibition	3.15*	12.56*	2.84*	1.59*
Autoregressive term	—	—	—	—
R-square	.79	.97	.78	.95
Adjusted R-square	.77	.97	.76	.95
Estimated rho	−.06	−.18	−.06	.06
Autocorrelation t-test	0.55	1.72	0.57	0.57
Number of cases	41	41	41	41

Note: A dash means the variable was omitted from the equation.

*$p < .05$
**$p < .10$

The results of this analysis show two distinct patterns. First, prohibition is associated with increased arrest rates for all four status crimes. Whether this occurs because prohibition created a general climate of lawlessness and more people committed these offenses or because more aggressive law enforcement agencies made more arrests for all crimes cannot be determined from the data at hand. Alcohol consumption is positively associated with prostitution arrests but negatively associated with gambling, sex offenses, and family crime arrests. The last three of these relationships suggest that the increase in alcohol consumption transfers law enforcement personnel to violent crimes, but again such a conclusion is speculation only. The analysis presented in Table 6.13 should be considered only the first step in attempting to untangle the relationships between alcohol policies and consumption and discretionary arrest patterns.

Substantive Conclusions

The chapter has generated a variety of substantive conclusions concerning alcohol policies; the conclusions can be summarized best by recapitulating the findings by independent variable. Income, a measure of potential consumer demand for alcohol as well as middle-class interests, performed modestly well. Income is positively related to effective tax rates and positively related to alcohol consumption in the equation for federal policies. It is negatively related to per capita alcohol taxes, beer consumption, federal enforcement, several state enforcement measures, and state prison rates. These findings suggest that middle-class populations are able to dampen enthusiasm for enforcement efforts. Salience continued its rather dismal showing. It is positively related to combined state and federal taxes per capita, beer consumption, and vagrancy arrests, and negatively related to federal prison population. Either salience per se has little to do with alcohol policies, or the measure used here did not accurately tap the concept.

Among citizen forces, religious variables have major impacts, for the most part in the direction predicted. Baptist population is positively associated with all effective tax rates and with four state enforcement variables. It is negatively related to beer consumption, suicides, and automobile deaths. Catholic population is negatively related to federal enforcement, five measures of state enforcement, and state and federal prison population; it is positively related to distilled spirits consumption, cirrhosis deaths, suicides, and effective state tax rates (only the last impact was not expected). The religious measures, therefore, do a good job of summarizing the varying expectations of wet and dry coalitions.

Other citizen forces performed less well but not poorly. Immigration is negatively associated with effective federal tax rates, federal enforcement, and suicides, and positively associated with consumption of alcohol of all types, consumption of beer, and state prison population. Nonwhite population is negatively associated with all effective tax rates and has mixed relationships with consumption. Farm population has mixed relationships with several variables. The overall citizen findings suggest, however, that policies reflect the relative balance of citizenship forces. There was little evidence in alcohol policies of targeting nonwhites or immigrants.

The most interesting findings are for industry, revealing that the alcohol industries clearly do not dominate alcohol politics and that at times the industries are divided. Alcohol industry size is consistently related to higher tax rates. One should not feel sorry about the government imposition of taxes on the industries, however, because industry size also is associated with greater consumption. The one area of policy influence in the expected direction is the negative relationship between the production industry and federal enforcement and between the retail industry and state enforcement. The divided nature of the industries is best illustrated by state enforcement where the production industry is associated with greater rather than lower levels of enforcement.

Political institutions generally register the results of the citizen and interest group forces. There are a few independent relationships between partisanship and alcohol policies but not enough to declare that a pattern exists. Party competition, however, does appear to affect some alcohol policies; specifically, increases in party competition produce higher state taxes (per capita), greater federal enforcement yet lower prison populations, and greater state enforcement of DUI laws. The health care bureaucracy is associated with several dependent variables, but the pattern of results is such that it is unclear if the bureaucracy has been a force in policymaking or if the bureaucracy has grown as the result of changes in policy.

Alcohol policies, unlike drug policies, have a major impact on the general public. Prohibition, despite its lack of enforcement, illustrates that major changes in government policy can make a difference. During Prohibition federal alcohol enforcement increased; six different assessments showed that alcohol consumption declined during Prohibition. Prohibition also was associated with declines in automobile fatalities and in the number of state and federal prisoners (calling into question the claim that prohibition adversely affected the corrections system).

State alcohol tax rates are negatively associated with the consumption of alcoholic beverages; indeed high state taxes are associated with less consumption of beer, wine, and distilled spirits. Federal taxes have little impact. Federal enforcement also has an impact on policy outcomes. Greater federal enforcement is associated with declines in the consumption of beer and wine; it is also associated with an increase in federal prisoners and has an unexplained positive impact on suicides and automobile deaths.

Because many policies affect the level of alcohol consumption, these policies also have a variety of indirect consequences. Declines in alcohol consumption are associated with declines in the death rates from cirrhosis of the liver and suicide. Alcohol consumption is negatively related to prison populations.

Alcohol policies also have some negative second-order consequences in regard to crime. Transforming a market from a legal to an illegal one generates violence. Prohibition was associated with a significant increase in the murder rate and a general increase in arrests for status crimes (e.g., prostitution, gambling). However, it was also associated with declines in the robbery and larceny rates. Federal enforcement is associated with a decline in the larceny rate. Alcohol consumption (as noted, partly determined by public policies) is in turn associated with increases in the murder rate, violent crime, robbery, burglary, and prostitution, but with declines in arrests for other status crimes.

Theoretical Conclusions

The historical analysis of alcohol policies shows that they are much different from drug control policies. Drug control policies have been dominated by political institutions, but alcohol policies have seen political institutions as relatively passive, as ratifying the results of the competition between citizen and industry groups. This finding should not be taken to downplay the role of politics in the policymaking process. That a political system is sensitive to the demands of the public is a positive contribution to public policy, even if the political system makes few additional independent contributions.

The match between the industries and citizens, which, according to the relative resources of each, should result in victories by the industries, is not that clear-cut. The industries have lost as much as they have won. They have never achieved significance in predicting any policies without citizen groups who support the same position also generating significant relationships. In other words, the alcohol industries are able to win only in coalitions with others or in environments that are generally supportive of alcoholic beverages. Such a description is not one of a political powerhouse. The industries are also divided, particularly on the enforcement of state laws that affect one of the industries less than the other.

Federalism influences are notable in their absence. The implementation activities of the federal bureaucracy have no impact on the activities of state and local bureaucracies. Interaction between the two bureaucracies is fairly rare, because state and local bureaucracies enforce a set of laws that rarely overlap federal concerns.

One interesting theoretical finding is that state enforcement of alcohol laws is unrelated to the consumption of alcoholic beverages. In general, law enforcement responds to the crime problems in society; that is, as crime increases, so do arrest rates. The absence of a relationship between alcohol consumption and state alcohol-related arrest rates suggests that these arrest rates are driven by other, more political forces. In fact, the arrest rates are related to a variety of political forces in the state's environment. Although this chapter did not assess the efficacy of such policies, such a set of relationships would suggest that arrests have little impact on the level of alcohol-related problems (see chapter 7).

The impact of government policies on their environments is complex and often indirect. Alcohol policies in many cases have achieved some of their objectives; prohibition and high state taxes have been associated with lower levels of alcohol consumption. Lower levels of consumption, in turn, result in improved levels of health and, in a few instances, lower levels of crime. Government policies are not without second-order consequences, however. Prohibition was associated with higher murder rates and higher arrest levels for status crimes.

Notes

1. This measure is a count of the number of articles appearing in the *Reader's Guide to Periodical Literature* for every year from 1901 to 1990. An effort was made to be comprehensive. The subject listings varied over time with the ebb and flow of terms or

designations. For example, in the early years many listings were found under "drunkenness"; during the 1930s the term *liquor problems* was common. The measure ranges from a low of 3 in 1904 to a high of 214 in 1930. The post-Prohibition high was 83 in 1987.

2. Data on income, percentage of Baptists, percentage of Catholics, immigration, percentage of nonwhites, and percentage of farm population were taken from the U.S. Bureau of the Census, *Historical Statistics of the United States: Colonial Times to 1970* (Washington, DC: U.S. Government Printing Office, 1975) and the annual updates from the *Statistical Abstract of the United States* (Washington, DC: U.S. Government Printing Office, annual). Data on all these variables were available from 1901 to 1990.

3. Annual data on individual churches for the entire century are difficult to obtain. Baptists were used because data were available. Baptists were prominent in the dry coalition, although it was hardly the only church active on prohibition issues. The definition of farm population was changed in 1974. For all years after 1974 I made estimates of farm population on the basis of the definition used before 1974.

4. This chapter does not have a variable for self-help groups because data on membership are not available over time.

5. Data on alcohol employment are from the U.S. Bureau of the Census, *Annual Survey of Manufactures* (Washington, DC: U.S. Government Printing Office, annual). Retail sales data are from the U.S. Bureau of Labor Statistics, *Consumer Expenditure Survey: Results from 1990* (and other years). Production data exist for the entire century; sales data exist for 1933–90. One measure of the alcohol industries that is used in the cross-sectional chapter but is not used here is the tourism industry. Because the retail sales figures will include sales in hotels as well as sales in restaurants, using data on hotel receipts and eating and drinking establishment receipts seemed redundant.

6. I determined the number of dry states. For dry states before federal prohibition, see Gusfield, 1963; after prohibition, see the Distilled Spirits Council of the United States, 1991.

7. All political data are taken from the *Statistical Abstract of the United States* (various years).

8. The data are from U.S. Bureau of the Census, *Public Employment in 1990* (and other years) (Washington, DC: U.S. Government Printing Office, annual). The figures are total federal, state, and local health employees.

9. This measure is a simple counter coded as 1 in 1901 and increasing by 1 for each year thereafter.

10. State taxes are from U.S. Bureau of the Census, *Government Finances* (Washington, DC: U.S. Government Printing Office, annual). Federal taxes are from the Office of Management and Budget, *Budget of the United States Government* (Washington, DC: U.S. Government Printing Office, annual). During Prohibition federal tax revenues dropped to almost nothing. The tax was collected on medicinal alcohol during that time period, and those payments were counted as beverage alcohol taxes here.

11. Gallons of alcohol consumed were estimated by assuming that distilled spirits contain 45 percent alcohol; wine, 11 percent; and beer, 4.5 percent. This assumption is the same as that used by the various government agencies and interest groups to estimate alcohol consumption. The price series is the Consumer Price Index, with the 1982–83 period set equal to 1.00.

12. Data on court cases are taken from the Administrative Office of the U.S. Courts, *Annual Report* (various years) (Washington, DC: U.S. Government Printing Office).

13. All alcoholic consumption data are from the *Historical Statistics of the United States, Colonial Times to 1970* and the *Statistical Abstract of the United States*. Data on beer consumption exist from 1901 to 1990, and data on wine and distilled spirits consumption are available from 1911 to the present.

14. State arrests usually result from the consumption of alcoholic beverages. Increasing arrests should not reduce consumption because the policies are not targeted at consumption per se, but rather at the ill effects of consumption in public places. All dependent variables are from the Federal Bureau of Investigation, *Uniform Crime Reports* (Washington, DC: U.S. Department of Justice Statistics, annual).

15. The availability of the federal and state tax measure limits the analysis to 57 years. State prisoner data exist from 1926 to 1990. The source of the prison data is U.S. Bureau of Justice Statistics, *Prisoners in State and Federal Institutions on December 31* (annual).

16. The trend variable picks up a lot of environmental forces that affect cirrhosis rates, including changes in diet, improvements in medical care, greater access to treatment facilities, and growth in Alcoholics Anonymous membership (see Smart and Mann, 1991).

17. Enforcement is not significant, but its inclusion in the equation improves the fit of the regression line significantly.

18. The cirrhosis data are from the National Center for Health Statistics, *Vital Statistics of the United States* (Bethesda, MD: Department of Health and Human Services, annual). The consumption–cirrhosis relationship is very robust. If one estimates cirrhosis rates as a function of the previous year's cirrhosis rates, alcohol consumption, and prohibition, alcohol consumption still has a significant impact. Using a simple interrupted time series for federal prohibition suggests that it had a reduction of 4.19 in the cirrhosis death rate.

19. Suicide deaths can be found in the National Center for Health Statistics, *Vital Statistics of the United States* (annual).

20. Automobile accident data are from the National Safety Council, *Accident Facts* (Chicago: National Safety Council, annual).

21. Data are from the Federal Bureau of Investigation, *Uniform Crime Reports* (annual). The series on murder rates that predates FBI data collection was taken from *Historical Statistics of the United States: From Colonial Times to 1970.*

22. For models with lagged dependent variables, the appropriate method of estimating autocorrelation is to take the residuals from the ordinary least squares model, lag these residuals, and regress them on all the independent variables as well as the residuals. If the relationship between the residuals and the lagged residuals is significant, then autocorrelation exists (Hanushek and Jackson, 1977: 169–174; Johnston, 1972: 313). Tables 6.12 and 6.13 include the estimated autocorrelation following the line "estimated rho," with the t-test below it giving the significance test for this degree of autocorrelation. If this autocorrelation test was significant after the ordinary least squares run, an autoregressive term was included in the equation, estimated by maximum-likelihood techniques (Trends module in SPSS has such a program). For the equations estimated in this manner, an autoregressive term will appear in the table (it will show the autocorrelation estimate that was included). The estimated rho in these equations will be for the residuals of the maximum likelihood estimates.

7

Dealing with the Devil: State Regulation of Alcohol[†]

Alcohol is one of the most widely used legal drugs in the United States. Fully three-fifths of the U.S. adult population currently drink alcohol, and nearly 90 percent admit having done so in the past (National Institute on Drug Abuse, 1988). In 1990 Americans of all ages spent $26.4 billion on alcoholic beverages in their various forms (Bureau of Labor Statistics, 1991).

Alcohol consumption is a political issue because excessive use of alcohol imposes major costs on society. Estimates of the number of Americans with drinking problems range from 5.75 million to 18 million (see Coakley and Johnson, 1978). More than 1.4 million persons a year are treated for alcohol abuse and dependence (NIAAA, 1990: 22). The National Highway Traffic Safety Administration (1988) concluded that 52 percent of traffic fatalities in 1986 (25,300 deaths) involved alcohol. Alcohol is also implicated in 50 percent of accidental deaths from falls (Haberman and Baden, 1978), approximately 50 percent of fire deaths (NIAAA, 1990: 167), and 38 percent of drownings (NIAAA, 1990: 167). Owing to accidents and greater health risks, the mortality rate for persons with alcohol problems is two to six times higher than the average for all persons (Schmidt and de Lint, 1973). In addition to 97,500 premature deaths per year (Fahri, 1990), the costs of alcohol include lost productivity from excessive absenteeism and accidents, increased health care expenditures (1.1 million hospital admissions per year; NIAAA, 1990: 20), and increased burdens

---

[†]This chapter is an updated, expanded, and extended version of Meier and Johnson, 1990. All the dependent variables except for drunk driving laws have been updated. Several new dependent variables have been added. The independent variables in that article were adapted to fit the theory used in this book. Special thanks go to Cathy M. Johnson for her contribution to the original article. Her insights deserve credit for the findings here; I retain the blame for the changes I have made. In the update several relationships changed; that should be a lesson to those who seek to replicate their own work.

on the criminal justice system. The National Council on Alcoholism (Farhi, 1990) estimated that alcohol problems cost American society about 3.87 percent of the gross national product (the equivalent of $202 billion in 1989).

This chapter presents a systematic overview of contemporary U.S. state public policies toward alcohol. First, the policy theory introduced in chapter 1 is modified for the cross-sectional study. Second, the political forces likely to affect alcohol policies are operationalized. Third, public policies designed to regulate the sale and use of alcohol are measured. These measures are divided into two parts—regulations that restrict the sale of alcoholic beverages, and those that seek to limit a major negative impact of alcohol, drunk driving. Fourth, the effectiveness of public policies is assessed by investigating whether or not alcohol regulatory policies can reduce alcohol consumption or alcohol-related mortality rates and whether or not drunk driving laws can reduce fatal automobile accidents. Finally, some second-order consequences of alcohol and alcohol policies are examined.

Theoretical Modifications

A state cross-sectional examination of alcohol policies requires two modifications to our theory. First, highly salient policies generate political entrepreneurs who exploit the salient environment and attempt to pass whatever policy ideas exist at that time. Quantitatively measuring the impact of policy entrepreneurs is difficult if not impossible. Lacking such measures, the second best alternative is to hypothesize that the existence of policy entrepreneurs will reduce the predictive ability of the policy model because the model incorporates fairly long-term political forces. Highly salient policies are the most amenable to entrepreneurship, in this case policies affecting drunk driving. States have adopted many reforms over the last decade, when drunk driving has become a highly visible issue through the efforts of MADD and other groups. Other alcohol policies such as sales regulation, taxes, or the number of outlets should be more predictable with the policy model because they have not been subject to the same entrepreneurial forces.

Second, federalism variables will be missing from this chapter. The primary way to measure the impact of the federal government on individual states is through its implementation activities. Virtually all other federal policies from advocacy of minimum drinking ages to tax rates are essentially constants at any single time point, so that a state cross-sectional analysis cannot incorporate them. Unfortunately, federal implementation activities in regard to alcohol have virtually disappeared. Although the federal government once aggressively enforced federal alcohol laws, by 1990 the total number of federal alcohol prosecutions was fewer than a dozen per year nationwide. Federalism impacts, therefore, will not be included in the analysis.

Measurement

Independent Variables

Citizen Forces

Four citizen forces are likely to affect alcohol policies—pressures for consumption, attitudes (religious affiliation), race, and self-help groups. The two measures of consumption pressures are per capita income and percentage of the state population living in urban areas. Higher levels of alcohol consumption are associated with increases in both income and urbanism (see Gliksman and Rush, 1986: 11; Hutcheson and Taylor, 1973: 419; Weinstein, 1982: 741).[1] Income provides the discretionary funds necessary to purchase alcohol (see Popham, Schmidt, and de Lint, 1978: 251; Room, 1978: 285), and urbanism provides the relative anonymity to consume without the admonition of neighbors (Dye, 1966: 220; Wilson, 1983: 23–44). Income and urbanism should be negatively associated with restrictive alcohol policies.

A major restraint on an individual's consumption of any drug is that individual's approval or disapproval of consumption (see chapter 3). Attitudes toward alcohol in this country have been continually shaped by the positions of several churches (Makowsky and Whitehead, 1991: 555). The temperance movements of the nineteenth century and the Anti-Saloon League of the early twentieth century are just two examples (Gusfield, 1963). Anticonsumption groups have long had ties to conservative Protestant religions (Hutcheson and Taylor, 1973; Miller, 1958; Meyer, 1960). Our measure of religious groups supporting restrictions on the sale and consumption of alcohol is the percentage of state residents who belong to Protestant churches that have traditionally opposed alcohol consumption.[2] Dry religious forces, however, must share the political landscape with religious groups that permit drinking, at least in moderation (Fairbanks, 1977). Our measure of wet religious forces includes the percentage of state population who belong to all churches not classified as dry.[3] States with more dry religious members should adopt more restrictive policies, and states with more wet religious members should adopt less restrictive policies.

Race has been an integral part of this analysis of drug policies. Although little evidence in either the historical or the quantitative chapter has tied race or racism to alcohol laws, two measures of race will be included in this state analysis for comparison purposes. The two measures are the percentage of black population and the percentage of Hispanic population.[4]

Since the 1940s a new reformist–citizen force exists in alcohol policy—self-help groups. Groups that organize to help provide treatment, although sharing many characteristics with religious groups, are more likely to view alcoholism as a disease rather than as a moral failing (see chapter 5; Aaron and Musto, 1981: 142). Some evidence suggests that these groups are successful in reducing overall alcohol consumption and its ill effects (Mann et al., 1991: 361). Our measure of self-help groups is the number of Alcoholics Anonymous, Al-Anon, Alateen, and National Council on Alcoholism chapters per 100,000 persons.[5] Our hypothesis concerning self-help groups is somewhat complex. Such groups should support restrictive laws and enforcement so that people are informed of their alcohol problems but oppose stringent punishment in favor of treatment.

Political Forces

Three political system forces are included in the analysis. The first, conservative public opinion, is a mass political force. The Wright, Erikson, and MacIver (1985) political conservatism scale aggregates public opinion polls to measure the electorate's conservatism.[6] The second, party competition, is measured by the competitiveness of state legislatures from 1980 through 1986 (Bibby et al., 1990). A perfectly competitive state has a score of 100. The third, Democratic partisanship, is the percentage of Democrats in the state legislature from 1980 to 1986.

For party competition the hypothesis is straightforward. Party competition has long been associated with sensitivity to public pressures, particularly to non-industry groups (Bibby et al., 1990). The hypothesis is that party competition will be associated with less restrictive alcohol regulation. Our hypotheses concerning the other two political forces are less specific. In general, conservative public opinion might be associated either with restrictive policies on alcohol, because conservatives view alcohol in much the same way as dry religious groups do, or with support for less regulation, which is consistent with the conservative philosophy of smaller government. Similarly, the Democratic party faces cross-pressures on alcohol policy issues. On the one hand, the Democratic party draws much of its strength from urban areas and Catholic voters. These forces should discourage stringent regulation of alcohol. On the other hand, Democrats in southern states draw their support from conservative Protestants, who are likely to be members of dry denominations. Although these two variables do not provide consistent hypotheses, the conflicting predictions make both forces an interesting political study.

Industry/Interest Group Forces

In virtually all regulatory policies, the regulated industry is a major force (Noll and Owen, 1983; Meier, 1985). Two different industry groups are likely to participate in alcohol policy debates. The first is the firms producing and selling the goods in question. Two industries, alcohol production and retail alcohol sales, are used in the analysis. For alcohol producers, the number of firms on the Bureau of Alcohol, Tobacco, and Firearms list of licensed producers per 1 million persons is used.[7]

Alcohol producers may well have interests different from those of the individuals who sell alcohol to consumers (see chapter 5). The actions of the Anti-Saloon League suggest that retail sales outlets are considered a problem distinct from the question of drinking (see Aaron and Musto, 1981: 137). The second producer industry measure is the number of establishments for on-premises and off-premises consumption per 100,000 persons in the state population.[8] The hypothesis is that producer industry groups will be negatively related to restrictive alcohol policies.

A second industry group concerned with alcohol policies includes those industries that consume alcohol in conjunction with other products. The major consumption industries are tourism and conventions. Indirect measures of these industries can be calculated as each state's per capita revenues for the hotel industry and for eating and drinking establishments.[9] Because the consumption industry has a major financial interest in selling alcohol, a large consumption industry should be associated with less restrictive alcohol policies.

Bureaucratic Forces

Two bureaucracies compete for control over alcohol policies. The law enforcement agency, of course, is charged with enforcing various alcohol laws. How important such laws are to the law enforcement bureaucracy, however, is unclear because alcohol crimes are likely to be assigned a low priority by law enforcement personnel. The indicator of the law enforcement bureaucracy is the number of law enforcement personnel per 1,000 persons. Competing for policy influence is the treatment bureaucracy, probably advocating policies that are less punishment oriented. This does not mean the treatment bureaucracy will not favor strict laws and enforcement, however, because such actions generate clientele. The measure is the number of alcohol treatment beds per 1,000 persons.[10]

Alcohol Policy Options

With the demise of federal prohibition, most public policy decisions affecting alcohol were returned to state governments. Some states continued prohibition for as many as 30 years after its repeal at the federal level. Other states established control over the industry by creating a state monopoly to sell alcoholic beverages (either at wholesale or at retail levels). Still other states licensed private businesses to distribute and sell alcohol. Regardless of the general approach, all states established elaborate regulatory policies that defined how and when alcohol may be sold or consumed. This section describes the current variation in state alcohol policies.

Alcohol Sales Regulations

State governments can regulate alcohol (separately from regulating drunk driving) in four different ways. First, they can pass laws or regulations limiting the sale or conditions of sale for alcoholic beverages (see Popham, Schmidt, and de Lint, 1978: 242). States vary substantially in how permissive they are in allowing the sale and advertisement of alcohol. Although all states now permit the sale of alcohol, some virtually prohibit advertising and greatly limit where and when alcohol may be sold.

Fourteen state policies were examined to measure this element of alcohol policy. States vary in their restrictions on (1) advertising alcohol in newspapers, (2) advertising on billboards, (3) advertising in a liquor store, (4) advertising in the windows of liquor stores, (5) using novelties (e.g., bottle openers, hats, etc.) to encourage purchases, (6) using discount coupons for alcohol, (7) using mail-in rebates on liquor prices, (8) permitting contests by alcoholic beverage manufacturers, (9) permitting establishments for on-premises consumption to have taste testings, (10) allowing establishments for off-premises consumption to have taste testings, (11) limiting the number of hours a liquor store may be open on Sunday, (12) limiting the number of hours a bar may be open on Sunday, (13) limiting liquor store hours on election day, and (14) restricting liquor store hours on a regular weekday.[11] The 14 items were factor analyzed and produced a single dimension that ordered states from most restrictive to least restrictive.[12] This measure, termed strictness of alcohol regulation, is the first dependent variable. Although past research on sales restrictions, especially advertising, is mixed, sales restrictions might lead to reduced consumption (see Smart, 1988; Makowsky and Whitehead, 1991).[13]

A second option available to states is to pass on the responsibility for regulation to local governments by permitting local option. In these states local jurisdictions can prohibit the sale of alcoholic beverages. Most states permit local option, and in 15 states portions of the state have opted to go dry. The specific measure used is the percentage of the state's population who live in localities that are dry by local option.[14]

A third policy option for state governments is to use the state's taxing powers to increase the cost of alcohol (Terris, 1967). Federal and state taxes constitute about 45 percent of the cost of distilled spirits and 25 percent of the cost of all alcoholic beverages (Pogue and Sgontz, 1989: 240). Because the three basic forms of alcoholic beverages involve differences in tax rates and packaging volumes, a tax rate was calculated on the basis of alcoholic content of beverages.[15] States with high alcohol tax rates expect that overall consumption of alcohol will be reduced.

A fourth policy option is to limit the number of retail sales outlets available. State governments or, by delegation, local governments license retail outlets. Access to alcoholic beverages can be restricted by limiting the number of retail outlets (see Rush, Gliksman, and Brook, 1986: 5; Bonnie, 1985: 139). The measure is the number of alcohol licenses for both on-premises consumption and off-premises consumption establishments per 100,000 persons (Distilled Spirits Council of the United States, 1985).[16]

A fifth policy option for state governments, although one not discussed frequently, is to accept alcoholism as a disease and to focus policy responses on treatment rather than regulation. Such a policy assumes that alcohol-related problems are a function of individual problems rather than ineffective regulatory policy. Our measure of treatment policy is the number of alcoholism treatment beds in the state per 1,000 persons.[17]

Alcohol Sales Regulations Not Examined

Two major alcohol sales policies will not be examined in this chapter. One policy is the decision to sell alcoholic beverages through a state monopoly rather than by licensing private organizations to do so. Monopoly systems, as noted in chapter 5, vary a great deal in what they cover; many permit private sale of beer and/or wine, and others do not. Although the decision to sell alcoholic beverages through a state monopoly is a significant policy decision that may well affect other policies (e.g., number of sales outlets), these policies, with the exception of a recent change in Iowa (Wagenaar and Holder, 1991), were adopted 60 years ago. Such policies, therefore, should reflect the politics of the 1930s, not the politics of the 1990s.[18]

The second alcohol policy not examined is the minimum drinking age. An increase in the minimum drinking age is associated with a modest decline in alcohol consumption by young persons (O'Malley and Wagenaar, 1991: 481–482) and a substantial decline in traffic fatalities among young drivers (O'Malley and Wagenaar, 1991; Bonnie, 1985; but see Asch and Levy, 1987). With the federal government's pressure to adopt a minimum drinking age of 21, there is no longer any variation among the states. Uniform policies simply cannot be analyzed in a cross-sectional state analysis.

Drunk Driving Laws

Policies against drunk driving, although perceived as being related to policies of alcohol regulation, have a separate purpose. Rather than restricting access to alcohol, they are intended to punish individuals who abuse alcohol by driving under the influence (DUI). In recent years drunk driving has become a highly salient political issue resulting in a flurry of legislation passed. These reforms fall into four different categories.

Some reforms address the question of proof and seek to make it easier for law enforcement officers to prove that an individual was driving while intoxicated. Six proposals fall into this category: defining intoxication as a blood alcohol level above 0.10 percent, prohibiting open containers in a motor vehicle, prohibiting consumption in a motor vehicle, allowing law enforcement officers to test for intoxication without first making an arrest, allowing the refusal to take a blood-alcohol test to be admitted as evidence in court, and providing automatic license suspensions for repeat offenders. An additive scale of these laws was constructed with a potential range of 0 to 6.[19]

A second alternative is restitution: requiring the drunk driver to compensate any victims. Three proposals have been discussed: passing dram shop laws that hold people who serve alcohol responsible for damages caused by others who drink there, requiring the presentation of a victim impact statement at the trial of a drunk driver, and requiring the drunk driver to make restitution to any victims as part of the penalty. An additive scale ranging from 0 to 3 was created for the restitution measure.

The third alternative in drunk driving laws is to simplify the procedures used to convict drunk drivers.[20] Three procedural reforms are considered. The first, the administrative per se law, permits a law enforcement officer to suspend a driver's license on the spot without going through the courts. The second change is to permit preconviction actions to be taken, temporarily limiting the individual's ability to drive. The third is to eliminate plea bargaining so that the driver cannot plead guilty to a lesser offense. An additive scale ranging from 0 to 3 was created for the procedure measures.

The final alternative, but the one most frequently discussed in the media, is increasing the penalties for drunk driving. Seven items are included: (1) requiring a minimum jail term for a DUI conviction, (2) requiring a minimum fine for DUI, (3) requiring community service, (4) requiring mandatory suspension of the driver's license, (5) requiring mandatory education classes for the driver, (6) permitting impoundment of the vehicle as a penalty, and (7) making it a felony to cause a death while driving under the influence. An additive scale ranging from 0 to 7 was created for the penalties measure.

The Politics of Alcohol Policies

As noted above, state governments have several options in regard to the sale of alcohol. They can limit access by regulating sales, transfer control to local governments, use taxing powers, or invest in alcohol treatment facilities. All states regulate alcoholic beverages including restrictions on advertising, promotions, and hours of operation. The states range in strictness from Utah, a state that places major limits on the sale of alcohol, to Nevada, a state with almost a free market in alcoholic beverages.

Alcohol Regulation

Restrictions on Alcohol Sales

The determinants of alcohol sales regulation are shown in the first column of Table 7.1 Many variables had no significant impact on sales regulation and, therefore, were deleted from the model. Only two forces are associated with stricter regulation of alcohol sales—dry religious groups and urbanism. The first is to be expected. The latter is not. Urban states may have more visible alcohol

Table 7.1

Determinants of State Alcohol Policies

Independent variables	Dependent variables				
	Regulation	Dry areas	Taxes	Outlets	Treatment
Citizen forces					
Income (thousands)	—	—	—	—	—
% urban population	0.0083**	–0.09**	—	–1.280*	–0.0027**
Wet religious groups	—	—	—	1.787*	—
Dry religious groups	0.0165**	0.44*	—	–1.623*	–0.0043**
% Hispanic population	—	—	—	–1.598**	—
% black population	—	—	—	—	—
Self-help groups	—	—	—	—	—
Political forces					
Democratic					
partisanship	–0.0129**	0.16*	0.0065**	—	–0.0042*
Party competition	—	—	0.0069**	—	—
Conservatism	—	–33.99**	1.5682*	—	—
Industry forces					
Alcohol producers	—	—	—	—	0.1272**
Bars per capita	–0.0061*	—	—	—	—
Eating establishment					
receipts	—	—	—	—	—
Hotel receipts	–0.0006*	—	—	0.026*	–0.0001*
Bureaucratic forces					
Alcohol treatment	–0.0018**	—	—	—	NA
Police employment	—	—	–0.0021*	0.446*	0.0016**
R-square	.44	.50	.40	.69	.38
Adjusted R-square	.36	.46	.34	.65	.30
F	5.60	11.40	7.39	15.91	4.43

Notes: All coefficients are unstandardized regression coefficients. A dash means the variable was omitted from the equation.

NA = not appropriate.

*p < .05
**p < .10

problems and thus be more likely to place limits on the sale of alcoholic beverages. Urbanism does permit greater contact, which is conducive to organizing citizen groups (Meier, 1987). The relationship is fairly weak, however, and probably should not be given too much credence.

Four forces are associated with more lenient alcohol sales regulation. A larger industry (retail sales outlets and hotel receipts) is associated with weaker regulation of alcohol sales as predicted. One bureaucratic force, the alcohol treatment bureaucracy, is negatively associated with sales regulation, as is partisanship. A state with more Democratic legislators is likely to have more lenient alcohol sales regulation.

Dry Population

One option for state governments is to permit local governments to ban the sale of alcoholic beverages. Although the practice of local governments voting to go dry has stabilized over the past 20 years, areas that have voted to prohibit the sale of alcohol remain in several states. The second column of Table 7.1 shows the determinants of local dry population.

By far the most significant influence on dry population is dry religious forces; as predicted, states with larger dry religious forces are associated with a greater percentage of officially dry population. Other forces affecting dry population are partisanship, conservatism, and urbanism. The dry population results show the cross-pressured response of the Democratic party to the forces of moralism. Although supporting few restrictions on sales (see above), Democrats are also willing to let local governments ban alcohol. Such policy positions allow the party to respond to both parts of its constituency.[21] Rural states, consistent with our predictions, have larger dry populations. States with more conservative voters are associated with smaller dry populations, a finding supporting the small-government view of conservatives.

Alcohol Taxes

A state's third policy option is to use alcoholic beverages as a revenue source. Although high tax rates could be defended as an effort to limit consumption (Room, 1978: 284; Pogue and Sgontz, 1989; Coate and Grossman, 1988; Ornstein and Hanssens, 1985: 207), some studies show that alcohol taxes have little impact on consumption at their current rates (Johnson and Meier, 1990). All three political forces have significant impacts on the overall level of alcohol taxes.[22] Higher alcohol taxes are associated with competitive party systems, Democratic majorities, and conservative public opinion. These three relationships suggest that two different types of states have high alcohol taxes: states with competitive party systems and southern states. The remaining significant relationship is for police employment. Why law enforcement agencies would support lower taxes is unclear. Two processes might be involved. The relationship might reflect a law enforcement preference for limiting enforcement of alcohol violations; low taxes would take away the incentive to bootleg alcohol. The other option is that the relationship is spurious; states with low overall tax rates tend to have higher alcohol taxes. Since law enforcement bureaucracies must have revenue to support them, their relationship to alcohol taxes is negative.[23]

Retail Sales Outlets

State and local governments can regulate access to alcohol by limiting the number of retail sales outlets that can sell alcoholic beverages. The fourth column of Table 7.1 shows that the number of sales outlets reflects primarily the impact of citizen forces. Three forces are associated with fewer liquor outlets—dry religious groups, urbanism, and Hispanic population. The urbanism measure is not as predicted, but could reflect the closer urban distances that enable fewer retail outlets to serve more people. In opposition to these forces limiting the number of outlets are wet religious groups, the tourism industry (hotel receipts), and police employment. The two former relationships are as predicted by the theory. The law enforcement relationship was not expected.

Treatment Capacity

The final option in alcohol policy is different from the previous ones. Sales regulation, permitting local option, high taxes, and limiting the number of outlets are designed to dissuade individual consumption by using the state's regulatory powers. States can also invest in facilities to treat alcoholics, thus interpreting alcohol-related problems as a health problem rather than a regulatory problem (see chapter 5). Treatment is clearly an alcohol issue that is distinctly different from restrictive policies, and the results of our model underscore these differences (see Table 7.1, fifth column).

Two interesting coalitions appear in the regression equation. Positively related to treatment are larger law enforcement bureaucracies and larger alcohol production industries. The larger law enforcement bureaucracy probably reflects the states' orientation toward positive government (i.e., a large bureaucracy in general). The positive relationship with the production industry is interesting because alcohol producers, much more so than the retailers, have a vested interest in reducing the salience of alcohol abuse. The industry's interest is the long-term ability to sell alcohol, not the maximization of short-term profits. Two ways to reduce the salience of alcohol are to promote moderate consumption and to support treatment.[24]

Negative relationships were found between treatment capacity and urbanism, dry religious groups, Democrats, and tourism (hotel receipts). This suggests an interesting coalition because treatment orientation is associated with rural states with few dry religious groups, governed by Republicans, and without a large tourism industry. How all these forces might support treatment is unclear.

Policies on Drunk Driving

Policies on drunk driving are distinctly separate from those regulating the sale of alcoholic beverages. Except for a small negative correlation between dry population and drunk driving policies that ease burdens of proof, alcohol regulation policies are unrelated to policies for drunk driving. This pattern is not unexpected. Drunk driving policies are more salient than alcohol regulation and are passed by legislatures in the glare of publicity. Interest groups have traditionally had less success in influencing policy outcomes when regulatory issues become salient (Berry, 1979; Gormley, 1986). As a result, the political models that perform fairly well for policies affecting the sale of alcoholic beverages should be less efficacious in predicting drunk driving policies.

Easing the Burden of Proof

One proposal to improve enforcement of drunk driving laws is to ease the burden of proof on law enforcement officers. That drunk driving laws are distinctly different from alcohol regulation laws is perhaps best illustrated by the burden of proof that drunk driving laws require of law enforcement officers. The model is able to explain only 8 percent of the total variation (see Table 7.2). Only two variables are significant, and those only marginally so. Burden of proof reforms were adopted by states with a large alcohol production industry and a Republican governing coalition. The predictive ability of the equation is so low, however, that one could conclude the adoption of such laws is random with respect to the measured political forces.

Restitution

The ability of our model to explain variations in drunk driving laws that require restitution is only slightly better than it is for easing the burden of proof (Table 7.2, column 2). A state is more likely to have drunk driving laws that emphasize restitution if the state has a large wet religious population, a large Hispanic population, a large alcohol treatment bureaucracy, and a small tourism industry (eating establishment receipts).[25] The relationships, however, are modest at best and able to explain only 26 percent of the variation in restitution laws.

Easing Procedures

Similar to other aspects of drunk driving laws, legal procedures that make it easier to convict drunk drivers are relatively independent of the forces that affect alcohol regulation (see Table 7.2). The model explains only 21 percent of the variance with significant relationships for income, the alcohol treatment bureaucracy, and the law enforcement bureaucracy. The negative relationship for median income merits some comment. Laws easing procedures eliminate the use of legal tactics to prevent a drunk driving conviction. Such tactics are the refuge of individuals who can afford the legal expertise to use them.[26] That such procedures are adopted in poorer states is entirely consistent with who benefits from the use of complex legal procedures in drunk driving cases.

Table 7.2

Determinants of State Drunk Driving Laws

Independent variables	Dependent variables			
	Proof	Restitution	Procedures	Punishment
Citizen forces				
Income (thousands)	—	—	−0.0003*	—
% urban population	—	—	—	0.0130**
Wet religious groups	—	0.017*	—	—
Dry religious groups	—	—	—	—
% Hispanic population	—	0.023**	—	—
% black population	—	—	—	−0.0356**
Self-help groups	—	—	—	−0.0396**
Political forces				
Democratic partisanship	−0.015**	—	—	—
Party competition	—	—	—	—
Conservatism	—	—	—	—
Industry forces				
Alcohol producers	0.535**	—	—	—
Bars per capita	—	—	—	−0.0054**
Eating establishment receipts	—	−0.002*	—	—
Hotel receipts	—	—	—	—
Bureaucratic forces				
Alcohol treatment	—	0.002*	0.0020**	—
Police employment	—	—	0.0092*	—
R-square	.08	.26	.21	.24
Adjusted R-square	.04	.20	.16	.17
F	2.13	4.02	4.04	3.53

Note: A dash means the variable was omitted from the equation.

*p < .05
**p < .10

The two bureaucratic forces provide an interesting pattern. The relationship between law enforcement bureaucracy and simplified procedures is obvious because law enforcement personnel are the prime beneficiary of the reduced procedural requirements. The support by the treatment bureaucracy could well be related to a desire for more clientele. The treatment bureaucracy is interested in people being aware of their problems so that they seek help. It has no real interest in permitting individuals to avoid the sanctions of law unless those penalties are so strong that the treatment bureaucracy cannot gain access to offenders (e.g., because of lengthy jail terms).

Stronger Penalties

The adoption of stronger penalties is also weakly associated with the forces that affect alcohol regulation. Stronger penalties are associated with urbanism, and weaker penalties are associated with black population, self-help groups, and retail sales outlets. The negative relationships are all as predicted, but the urban relationship probably reflects the visibility of drunk driving in urban areas, where greater population density results in more cases of abuse. The model is able to explain 24 percent of the variance.

Overall, drunk driving laws are explained weakly by our model, a model that works much better for policies involving alcohol regulation. One explanation for this finding is that drunk driving legislation, unlike alcohol regulation, is not a morality issue. To be viewed as a morality issue in American politics, an issue must have not only a moral component but also some controversy. Laws against murder, for example, have a moral component; but they are not controversial. As a result, discussions of such laws find agreement among all concerned rather than divisions on religious or other moral grounds. Drunk driving laws are similar. No one favors drunk driving. All participants in the debate oppose drunk driving; as a result, the goals of legislation are not controversial.

The politics of drunk driving, therefore, should also be different from that of alcohol regulation policies. Legislators could well perceive drunk driving legislation as a policy area without costs; that is, most drunk driving laws will not alienate any constituents. The politics of regulatory policy under such circumstances are likely to revolve around individual political entrepreneurs who see drunk driving legislation as a painless way to make a political reputation (Wilson, 1980: 370). Because these laws have no built-in opposition, their adoption will be as idiosyncratic as the rise of individual entrepreneurs. The result will be a low level of explanation using traditional models of policy.

The lack of a coherent organized focus for opposition might also give rise to another policy characteristic. Without opposition little debate will focus on the consequences or the effectiveness of public policy. Policy proposals will be quickly adopted from whatever list is available with little consideration of which policies might be more or less effective in fighting the problem. This suggests that drunk driving laws will have less of an impact on drunk driving than is intended by advocates of such legislation.

Drunk driving laws in both regards are similar to current controlled-substance laws. Both were adopted or changed during periods of high salience. Opposition was rare. Neither area is explained well by political forces. Controlled-substance laws also have had little impact on policy implementation.

Policy Implementation: Enforcing the Laws

Alcohol laws, similar to all other laws, must be implemented. Alcohol laws are implemented by law enforcement agencies who arrest violators. In many cases, persons are arrested as a consequence of a negative occurrence (e.g., an accident and a breath test, a phone call to police during a domestic dispute, etc.). The determinants of alcohol policy implementation are shown in Table 7.3. The level of explanation exceeds that for drunk driving laws but generally falls short of that for alcohol policies.

Arrests for Driving Under the Influence

Arrest rates for driving under the influence are determined mostly by citizen forces. The percentages of both black population and Hispanic population are significant but in different directions. As a result of the divergence in direction, the conclusion is neither that racism is involved nor that minority populations influence DUI enforcement. A more likely situation is that black and Hispanic populations are collinear with other factors that actually influence DUI enforcement.

The other relationships are consistent with the hypotheses. DUI enforcement decreases when wet religious groups become larger but increases when self-help groups increase in size. Self-help groups benefit when more individuals are made aware of their problems. One of the strongest relationships is for alcohol producers. Again the positive relationship is consistent with the producers' recent campaigns to limit drunk driving and thus protect their long-term economic stake in the industry.[27] Drunk driving arrests also decrease with competitive parties. Since no one supports drunk driving, such laws should be enforced in all situations. Only with highly competitive parties would the interests in less enforcement get the attention of political elites.

Other Alcohol-related Arrests

The results for three other measures of enforcement also appear in Table 7.3. Liquor law violations concern the operation of the retail industry (selling to minors, operating illegal hours, etc.). Minor offenses are arrests for drunkenness, disorderly conduct, and vagrancy, all charges used to jail a public drunk for a short period of time. The "all alcohol" column is the arrest rate for all alcohol-related offenses (including DUI). Although citizen forces dominate these equations, other factors also influence enforcement.

Dry religious groups are associated with stronger enforcement for all alcohol arrests and arrests for minor alcohol offenses. Their citizen allies on enforcement appear to be self-help groups with positive relationships for liquor law violations and all alcohol arrests. Five industry relationships are significant, and four of those are positive. The relationship for producers might reflect their interest in lower salience for alcohol, but the majority of the relationships suggest that the industry is consistently beaten on enforcement issues.

Political forces play a role in enforcement but mostly for minor offenses. The relationships probably reflect other political forces that are present in states with competitive parties yet Democratic majorities. One bureaucratic factor is significant; states with more law enforcement personnel have more arrests for liquor

Table 7.3

Determinants of Alcohol Law Enforcement

	Dependent variables = arrest rate for:			
Independent variables	DUI	Liquor law violations	All alcohol	Minor offenses
Citizen forces				
Income (thousands)	—	—	—	—
% urban population	—	—	—	3.70**
Wet religious groups	−9.74*	—	—	—
Dry religious groups	—	—	35.68*	21.88*
% Hispanic population	13.85*	—	22.26*	—
% black population	−10.07*	−13.01*	—	—
Self-help groups	15.54*	9.64**	26.69*	—
Political forces				
Democratic partisanship	—	—	—	8.34**
Party competition	−3.63**	—	—	8.99**
Conservatism	—	1459.09*	—	—
Industry forces				
Alcohol producers	178.07*	—	409.44*	—
Bars per capita	—	—	2.79**	1.43**
Eating establishment receipts	—	−0.45**	—	—
Hotel receipts	—	—	0.21**	—
Bureaucratic forces				
Alcohol treatment	—	—	—	—
Police employment	—	2.25*	—	—
R-square	.59	.43	.41	.36
Adjusted R-square	.54	.37	.32	.29
F	10.52	6.70	4.91	5.05

Note: A dash means the variable was omitted from the equation.

*p < .05
**p < .10

law violations. The level of explanation is moderate for the four measures of implementation ranging from .36 for minor offenses to .59 for DUI arrests.

The Relationship between Laws and Enforcement

For public policies to have more than symbolic impact, the laws must influence the implementation behavior of the bureaucracy. Given its highly salient nature and its entrepreneurial base, drunk driving laws are especially susceptible to symbolic politics. Law enforcement agencies have enforcement responsibility for a wide variety of laws. Quite clearly major urban police forces are likely to give higher priority to violent felonies than they are to drunk driving enforcement. For many police departments, drunk driving enforcement is a by-product of other actions. That is, law enforcement agencies might not target drunk driving per se but simply take action during their routine patrols or during accident investigations. In such cases, drunk driving enforcement is something that law enforcement agencies do whenever they have nothing else to do.

To determine if drunk driving laws influence implementation, the equations for arrest rates for DUI and for all alcohol-related offenses are taken from Table 7.3. To these equations, the four measures of drunk driving laws are added. If laws affect implementation, then they should have a positive, significant impact on implementation, controlling for the other factors that affect implementation. The results are in Table 7.4.

The regression equations show that drunk driving laws have no influence on the number of arrests for DUI. Easing the standards of proof, requiring restitution, easing the administrative procedures of the arrest, and increasing punishment are unrelated to DUI arrest rates. Neither are the laws related to overall alcohol offense arrests. A slight negative relationship between easier standards of proof and arrests for all alcohol offenses exists, but the relationship should be positive, not negative.

The Impact of Public Policies

Policy Outcomes

The public policies examined in this chapter all have the goal of altering some aspects of behavior. Alcohol sales regulation policies seek, in part, to limit the consumption of alcoholic beverages or at least to limit the ill effects of consumption (see Loeb, 1978). Drunk driving legislation seeks to limit the number of individuals who drive while intoxicated. How effective these policies are in achieving their policy goals is rarely discussed. This section examines the impact of these policies on four outcomes—the consumption of alcoholic beverages, the incidence of heavy drinking, the rate of drunk driving, and the incarcerated population.

Alcohol consumption figures were derived from data provided by the Advisory Commission on Intergovernmental Relations (1990). The data are in proof gallons of alcohol consumed. Heavy drinking will be estimated by death rates from cirrhosis of the liver and suicides. Death rates from cirrhosis of the liver have frequently been used to measure the ill effects of alcohol consumption (Cook, 1981). An estimated 20–36 percent of all suicides are alcohol related. The death rates from cirrhosis and suicide are for 1988.[28]

Table 7.4

The Influence of Drunk Driving Laws on Enforcement

	Dependent variables = arrest rate for:	
Independent variables	DUI	All alcohol offenses
Citizen forces		
Wet religious groups	−9.36*	—
Dry religious groups	—	33.89*
% Hispanic population	13.54*	20.50*
% black population	−10.72*	—
Self-help groups	14.44*	32.12*
Political forces		
Party competition	−3.78**	—
Industry forces		
Alcohol producers	188.06*	471.18*
Bars per capita	—	2.65**
Hotel receipts	—	0.19
Drunk driving laws focused on		
Proof	−3.78	−87.97**
Restitution	−0.51	−74.90
Easing procedures	7.60	94.64
Punishment	−17.39	25.81
R-square	.60	.47
Adjusted R-square	.50	.33
F	5.94	3.41

Note: A dash means the variable was omitted from the equation.

*$p < .05$
**$p < .10$

Drunk driving is more difficult to measure. Although many states collect data on the number of traffic fatalities where alcohol is involved, these data are highly unreliable because of variations in state reporting requirements (see Saffer and Grossman, 1987: 408). A common, accepted measure of drunk driving is night-time fatalities, since a high proportion of nighttime fatalities are alcohol related (Asch and Levy, 1987: 183; O'Malley and Wagenaar, 1991: 487). The specific measure is the number of nighttime traffic fatalities per 100,000 persons averaged for 1989 and 1990.[29] Finally, because alcohol is associated with a wide variety of crimes, one might also expect that alcohol policies might influence the size of the state prison population.[30]

Consumption of Alcohol

Data on per capita alcohol sales have two sources of error as measures of consumption. First, some states, through pricing policies, industry promotion, or location, encourage out-of-state individuals to purchase alcoholic beverages. Such policies inflate the sales figures of these states and reduce the figures for nearby states. Two states in particular pursue policies that encourage the sale of alcoholic beverages to out-of-state persons—Nevada and New Hampshire. Nevada, with its extensive tourism industry based on gambling and its lenient alcohol regulations, encourages visitors to consume alcoholic beverages. New Hampshire, by keeping alcoholic beverage taxes and thus prices modest and by locating state-owned liquor stores near state boundaries, encourages individuals from neighboring states to purchase alcohol in New Hampshire. This source of measurement error can be controlled for by including a dummy variable for these states. The second source of error, the consumption of home brews and illegally produced alcohol, cannot be eliminated since reliable data on it do not exist.[31]

Table 7.5 models per capita alcohol consumption (in proof gallons) as a function of citizen forces that affect consumption (dry religious groups and percentage of black population), industry forces (eating establishment receipts, hotel receipts), states that encourage consumption (the Nevada–New Hampshire phenomenon), and the five alcohol regulatory policies—sales regulation, dry population, alcohol tax rates, liquor outlets, and treatment facilities.[32] The citizen and industry influences are the independent variables from prior models that were related to alcohol consumption. The model explains 88 percent of the variation in per capita alcohol consumption, although much of this explanation is a function of nonpolicy variables. None of the five alcohol policies has any impact on the level of alcoholic beverage consumption.[33] Although the coefficients for sales regulation, dry population, and alcohol taxes are negative as expected, none is significant.[34]

The lack of findings in Table 7.5 is especially interesting, because Meier and Johnson (1990) using 1985 data found a significant relationship between sales regulation and lower levels of consumption. The second column of Table 7.5 shows that 1985 sales regulation policies still have a negative impact on 1988 alcohol consumption. Why is the updated measure no longer significant? An examination of the individual items of the factor analysis reveals that several states made changes in alcohol sales regulation policies. Although the number of states that made changes was not large, those that did change often made major changes. Most changes involved states passing more lenient regulation, but some states became more restrictive. These shifts eliminated the impact of alcohol sales regulation on the level of consumption. As more time passes and the residual effect of these older regulations declines, the relationship between the 1985 measure and alcohol consumption should also drop to zero.

Table 7.5

The Influence of Alcohol Policies on Alcohol Consumption

	Dependent variables = per capita alcohol consumption	
Independent variables	Policies	1985 sales measure
Citizen forces		
Dry religious groups	−0.0168*	−0.0154*
% black population	0.0096*	0.0089*
Industry forces		
Eating establishment receipts	0.0007*	0.0006*
Hotel receipts	0.0001	0.0001
Nevada–New Hampshire	1.5008*	1.5227*
Alcohol policies		
Sales regulation	−0.0257	—
Dry population	−0.0003	—
Alcohol taxes	−0.1066	—
Licensed sellers	−0.0002	—
Treatment capacity	0.0190	—
Sales regulation 1985	—	−0.0640**
R-square	.88	.88
R-square without policies	.88	.88
Adjusted R-square	.85	.87
F	28.72	53.74

Note: A dash means the variable was omitted from the equation.

$*p < .05$
$**p < .10$

Heavy Drinking

Alcohol consumption patterns are not equally distributed; Room (1978: 278) estimated that 10 percent of the U.S. population consumes 60 percent of all alcoholic beverages. The research literature on alcoholism provides ambiguous results in regard to the nature of heavy drinking. Some studies argue that heavy drinkers are merely a given percentage of the overall drinking population, so that efforts to reduce alcohol consumption in general will reduce it for heavy drinkers (Popham, Schmidt, and de Lint, 1978: 259). Other studies suggest that heavy drinkers are more difficult to reach than moderate drinkers and that the illness of alcoholism will produce heavy drinking regardless of restraints on consumption

(Room, 1978: 281). Despite this research controversy, the consensus is that cirrhosis death rates are a good indicator of heavy drinking behavior (Popham, Schmidt, and de Lint, 1978: 250; Smart and Mann, 1991: 233). Cirrhosis rates dropped during Prohibition in the United States (see chapter 6), and cirrhosis is fairly sensitive to alcohol consumption at the individual level (Terris, 1967: 2076; Cook, 1981: 276).

Our measure in this analysis is the death rate per 100,000 persons from cirrhosis of the liver in 1988. Included in the model are those independent variables from previous analyses that were significantly related to cirrhosis rates (urbanism and the New Hampshire–Nevada dummy). To control for historical patterns, health care delivery, and a variety of long-term influences, the cirrhosis rate for 1980 was incorporated as a dependent variable. This permits our analysis to focus on change in the cirrhosis rate rather than overall levels. Second, per capita alcoholic beverage consumption is added to the model along with the five alcohol regulation policies and the arrest rate for alcohol offenses (see Table 7.6).

Table 7.6 shows the impact of the five public policies and one implementation measure on the death rate from cirrhosis of liver. Sales regulation, alcohol tax rates, treatment capacity, dry population, and the alcohol arrest rate do not affect the cirrhosis rate.[35] One policy measure that does affect the cirrhosis rate is the number of retail sales outlets. As the number of retail sales outlets increases, so too does the cirrhosis of the liver rate. Even though the strongest influence on the 1988 cirrhosis rate is the 1980 cirrhosis rate and alcohol consumption, state policies can have some influence on the incidence of heavy drinking and thus the cirrhosis rate.

The second part of Table 7.6 examines the impact of alcohol policies on 1988 suicide rates. The equation is similar to that for cirrhosis; it uses all significant independent variables introduced in earlier analyses, the alcohol policy measures, and the 1980 suicide rate. Although this equation does not find a significant positive impact for alcohol consumption, it does find two alcohol policies that are negatively related to the suicide rate. As alcohol taxes increase, the suicide rate drops. If alcohol taxes were related to reduced consumption, one would be tempted to conclude that taxes affect demand. Perhaps the relationship reflects the difficulty of access by marginal consumers. These individuals would not be able to purchase alcohol, but their absence would not affect total consumption appreciably. More significant, as treatment capacity increases, the suicide rate in the state drops. This suggests that treatment can address an ill effect of alcohol consumption.[36]

Traffic Fatalities

Some individuals who have consumed alcohol experience death from cirrhosis or suicide; except for the costs that these deaths impose on families and co-workers, there are few externalities to such deaths. Drunk driving policies are salient

Table 7.6

The Influence of Alcohol Policies on Cirrhosis and Suicide Rates, 1988

	Dependent variables			
	Cirrhosis rate		Suicide rate	
Independent variables	Full model	Reduced model	Full model	Reduced model
Citizen forces				
Income (thousands)	—	—	−0.396*	−0.337*
% urban population	0.012	—	0.011	—
Wet religious groups	—	—	0.036**	0.020**
% Hispanic population	—	—	0.036	0.053**
Nevada–New Hampshire	−2.477**	−2.798*	−0.260	—
Alcohol policies				
Sales regulation	−0.151	—	−0.321	—
Dry population	0.037**	—	0.007	—
Alcohol taxes	1.508**	—	−1.057	−1.368**
Licensed sellers	−0.006**	−0.009*	−0.006	—
Treatment capacity	0.606	—	−1.482**	−1.641*
Implementation				
Alcohol arrest rate	−0.000	—	0.000	—
Alcohol consumption	2.215*	2.435*	0.440	—
Cirrhosis rate 1980	0.600*	0.572*	NA	NA
Suicide rate 1980	NA	NA	1.055*	1.021*
R-square	.82	.80	.91	.90
R-square without policies	.74	.72	.89	.88
Adjusted R-square	.78	.78	.87	.88
F	18.16	45.32	26.63	62.12

Notes: A dash means the variable was omitted from the equation.
NA = not appropriate.

*$p < .05$
**$p < .10$

precisely because drunk driving has negative externalities. Although most drunk driving fatalities involve single-car accidents, a portion involve nondrinking individuals in other vehicles or as pedestrians (see Asch and Levy, 1987). The image of innocent children killed by drunk drivers has been perhaps the most effective weapon of MADD and other advocacy groups in strengthening drunk driving laws (see chapter 5).

To predict the nighttime fatality rate (our measure of drunk driving), we include two of the original independent variables found to be related to the nighttime fatality rate plus the five alcohol policy measures, the DUI arrest rate, and alcohol consumption. In addition, the states' daytime traffic fatality rate is included. The inclusion of the daytime fatality rate means that the model will focus on the differences between the daytime and the nighttime fatality rates. This should control for such factors as the relative danger of state highways, variation in weather patterns, and other factors that influence state-by-state variation in fatalities.

The first two columns of Table 7.7 show the relative efficacy of various alcohol policies. Although daytime traffic fatalities are the best predictor of nighttime fatalities, two alcohol policies are also related to our surrogate for drunk driving. Stronger regulation of alcohol sales is associated with a drop in nighttime traffic fatalities, and a higher DUI arrest rate is also associated with fewer nighttime traffic fatalities.[37]

Alcohol policies (other than the DUI arrest rate) are not directly targeted at drunk driving. To determine if drunk driving laws have any influence on nighttime fatalities, the four drunk driving laws were added to the equation in the third column of Table 7.7. The results are unambiguous. None of the drunk driving laws is significantly related to the number of nighttime traffic fatalities. This suggests that passing additional drunk driving laws will have no impact on nighttime fatalities. Enforcing the laws that are currently on the books appears to be a more promising option.[38]

The lack of relationship between drunk driving laws and nighttime fatalities should not be surprising. In a comprehensive review of studies, Ross (1982) found that increasing the severity or swiftness of punishment has no impact on drunk driving. Increasing the certainty of punishment has a modest short-term deterrent effect. A DUI arrest guarantees punishment, either from the judicial system or one's insurance company.[39]

An Alternative Look at Drunk Driving and Heavy Drinking

Examining the rates of traffic fatalities and cirrhosis is an indirect method of examining the extent of drunk driving and heavy drinking. An alternative way of measuring these phenomena is through survey research. The Center for Disease Control (CDC) has sponsored the Behavioral Risk Factor Surveillance System for several years. Essentially the Behavioral Risk system surveys individuals about behaviors that could create risks to their health. The advantage of the Behavioral Risk system survey is that each state takes its own survey. Although not all states participate, most do. In 1990 the survey contained two questions relevant to this research.[40] It asked individuals if they had driven in the past year after drinking too much and if they had had more than five drinks in an evening during the same time period. The latter is termed binge drinking and is CDC's

Table 7.7

The Influence of Alcohol Policies on Traffic Fatalities

Independent variables	Dependent variable: nighttime fatality rate		
	Full model[a]	Reduced model[a]	Reduced model[b]
Citizen forces			
% urban population	0.013*	0.016*	0.018*
Nevada–New Hampshire	−1.755*	—	—
Alcohol policies			
Sales regulation	−0.180**	−0.236*	−0.244*
Dry population	−0.008	—	—
Alcohol taxes	0.019	—	—
Licensed sellers	0.001	—	—
Treatment capacity	−0.623	—	—
Implementation			
DUI arrest rate	−0.001**	−0.001*	−0.001*
Alcohol consumption	0.578**	—	—
Daytime fatality rate	0.585*	0.584	0.591*
Drunk driving policies			
Proof			−0.044
Restitution			0.035
Easing procedures			−0.139
Punishment			−0.060
R-square	.96	.95	.95
R-square without policies	.94	.94	.95
Adjusted R-square	.95	.95	.94
F	87.39	218.62	105.78

Note: A dash means the variable was omitted from the equation.

[a] Full model and reduced model without the drunk driving policies factored in.
[b] Reduced model with the drunk driving policies factored in.

*p < .05
**p < .10

method of assessing heavy drinking. For both questions, the percentage of males between the ages of 18 and 34 who admitted to the behavior was used. This sex and age cohort is the most likely to drive after consuming alcoholic beverages (see Lund and Wolfe, 1991: 297).

Surveys of behavior, particularly behavior that is illegal (e.g., driving while intoxicated), have problems of validity and reliability. Many individuals are hesitant to report this behavior or may overestimate their tolerance for alcohol. These problems, however, should not covary across the states but rather be fairly constant. Even so, analysis of the Behavioral Risk survey data should be interpreted with caution. The strategy of analysis is similar to that of the previous section. First the measure is predicted by the independent variables for the policy model, and then policy measures are added to the model to see if they affect the behavior in question.

Table 7.8 shows the resulting equations for the persons who say they drive after having too much to drink. The initial independent variables are interesting in that such behavior occurs more when wet religious groups become larger and occurs less when the number of law enforcement personnel increases. One, but only one, of the policy measures is significantly related to this measure of drunk driving—the number of retail liquor store outlets. As the number of outlets increases, so do self-reported instances of drunk driving. Unfortunately, the model does not show significant relationships for sales regulation and DUI arrests, unlike the fatalities model.

The model for binge drinking is also shown in Table 7.8. As one would expect, binge drinking is positively related to per capita alcohol consumption. Given the relatively skewed distribution of alcohol consumption, one would expect overall average consumption to be associated with the proportion of heavy drinkers. Once again, retail liquor outlets are a significant positive influence on binge drinking. As the number of outlets increases (and thus the convenience of alcohol), the amount of reported binge drinking also increases.

Prison Population

Given the consistent association of alcohol with violence and criminal activities, expecting an association between alcohol consumption and the prison population is rational. Similarly effective alcohol policies might reduce consumption or reduce the access to alcohol for individuals likely to engage in crime and thus reduce the prison population. Counter to these expectations are the findings in chapter 6, which showed a decline in state prison populations when alcohol consumption increased.

Table 7.9 shows the model for state prisoners. Although the positive correlation between law enforcement personnel and the prison population is inherently interesting, the purpose of this analysis is to assess alcohol policies. Unfortunately, only one alcohol policy is related to the size of state prison populations. As the number of retail outlets increases, so too does the prison population. None of the other factors, in particular alcohol consumption and the alcohol crimes arrest rate, is related to the size of the prison population. In sum the relationship between alcohol consumption and the prison population can probably be ignored in alcohol policies.

Table 7.8

The Influence of Alcohol Policies on Reported Drunk Driving and Binge Drinking

	Dependent variables = percentage of population who say they:			
	Drink and drive		Binge drink	
Independent variables	Full model	Reduced model	Full model	Reduced model
Citizen forces				
Dry religious groups	—	—	0.032	0.007
Wet religious groups	0.048	0.042	0.232**	0.216**
% Hispanic population	0.113	0.130*	—	—
Industry forces				
Hotel receipts	—	—	0.008	0.007
Bureaucracy forces				
Police employment	−0.023	−0.026**	−0.044	−0.043**
Alcohol policies				
Sales regulation	−0.212	—	−0.223	—
Dry population	−0.025	—	−0.001	—
Alcohol taxes	−0.332	—	−1.304	—
Licensed sellers	0.025*	0.027*	0.038**	0.041**
Treatment capacity	−1.708	—	−0.208	—
Implementation				
DUI arrest rate	0.001	—	0.002	—
Alcohol consumption	−0.478	—	4.937**	4.756**
R-square	.42	.41	.52	.51
R-square without policies	.28	.28	.45	.45
Adjusted R-square	.25	.35	.35	.43
F	2.40	6.68	3.10	6.44

Note: A dash means the variable was omitted from the equation.

$*p < .05$

$**p < .10$

Second-order Consequences—Crime

The final policy outcome of interest is a second-order consequence—crime. Similar to the analysis for drug law enforcement, this chapter examines the relationship among alcohol consumption, the level of alcohol enforcement, and

Table 7.9

The Influence of Alcohol Policies on the Prison Population

Independent variables	Dependent variable = prison population per 1,000 persons	
	Full model	Reduced model
Citizen forces		
Income (thousands)	0.1385**	0.1328**
Wet religious groups	−0.0347*	−0.0360*
% black population	0.0454*	0.0433*
Bureaucratic forces		
Police employment	0.0083*	0.0086*
Alcohol policies		
Sales regulation	−0.0484	—
Dry population	−0.0025	—
Alcohol taxes	−0.0406	—
Licensed sellers	0.0027	0.0034**
Treatment capacity	0.3149	—
Implementation		
Alcohol arrest rate	0.0001	—
Alcohol consumption	−0.1195	—
R-square	.57	.56
R-square without policies	.54	.54
Adjusted R-square	.44	.51
F	4.52	11.14

Note: A dash means the variable was omitted from the equation.

*$p < .05$
**$p < .10$

state crime rates. The model is fairly simple. Crime rates for 1990 are predicted as a result of crime rates for 1980, the state alcohol arrest rate, and the per capita consumption of alcohol in the state.[41]

The result of the crime analysis is shown in Table 7.10. Similar to the historical analysis, alcohol consumption is negatively associated with crime rates when previous crime rates are controlled. The negative relationship holds for all six measures of crime. On the basis of this evidence and previous results in this chapter, one would be hard pressed to argue that controls over alcohol will have a positive impact on the level of crime. Three of the relationships for alcohol arrests are significant—two that show a deterrent effect (murder and robbery)

Table 7.10

Impact of Alcohol Enforcement on Crime Rates

	Dependent variables = 1990 crime rates for:					
Independent variables	Murder	Violent crime	Robbery	Assault	Burglary	Larceny
Crime rate for 1980	0.7917*	1.074*	0.925*	1.355*	0.628*	0.795*
State alcohol arrests	−0.0007**	−0.016	−0.025**	0.004**	−0.008	0.028
Alcohol consumption[a]	−0.4061*	−29.213*	−8.409**	−16.352*	−44.068**	−63.487**
R-square	.82	.84	.85	.80	.57	.73
Adjusted R-square	.81	.83	.84	.78	.54	.73
F	71.00	80.74	86.04	60.57	20.53	41.50

Note: A dash means the variable was omitted from the equation.

[a] Logged, and the coefficient was adjusted to be an increase of 10 percent in alcohol consumption.

*$p < .05$
**$p < .10$

and one that does not (assault). The weak nature of the relationships, however, suggests that the reader should be skeptical about these findings.

Substantive Conclusions

This chapter investigated the politics of drugs when the drug in question is legal and regulated. Alcohol policies vary in salience and in their pattern of development. Regulations involving sales have a long history of discussion and development, while drunk driving legislation in recent years has become entrepreneurial. The substantive conclusions of this chapter can best be recapped by examining the independent variables.

Citizen forces have a great deal of influence on alcohol policies. Demand for alcohol was measured with income and urbanism. Neither measure worked especially well; in fact, urbanism seems to be associated with restrictions on alcohol rather than more lenient regulation. This pattern suggests that, when problems become more visible, state governments are more likely to take action.

Attitudes toward alcohol, measured by religious affiliation, did fairly well. Dry religious groups are associated with more stringent sales regulation, a greater dry population, fewer retail sales outlets, a smaller treatment capacity, and greater enforcement of alcohol laws. Wet population is positively associated with retail outlets and negatively associated with DUI enforcement.

Race has few significant relationships, and those do not follow a consistent pattern. The obvious conclusion is that race is not a factor in alcohol policies. Self-help groups are associated with greater enforcement of alcohol laws but lower levels of punishment. This pattern is consistent with informing individuals about their problems but not removing them from the potential access of self-help groups.

Political forces have strong impacts on selected policies but are totally absent from others. Drunk driving laws in particular are unaffected by political forces. The Democratic party is cross-pressured on the alcohol issue, and accordingly the relationships found are mixed. Democrats are associated with more lenient sales regulation, a greater dry population, higher taxes, a smaller treatment capacity, and greater enforcement of minor laws. Party competition is linked with higher alcohol taxes, a lower DUI arrest rate, and greater enforcement of minor alcohol-related crimes. Conservative ideology is associated with higher taxes, a smaller dry population, and more enforcement of liquor laws.

The alcohol industry is not a dominant force in alcohol politics. Some evidence, in fact, suggests a divided industry, with the production side willing to endorse restraints on the retail side to protect its own long-run viability. Alcohol producers are associated with a greater treatment capacity, more enforcement of DUI and general alcohol laws, and with drunk driving laws that ease the burden of proof. The retail side of the industry has been successful in reducing sales regulation, increasing the number of outlets, and opposing drunk driving laws affecting restitution and stronger penalties, but is generally associated with higher levels of enforcement.

The results for bureaucratic forces are mixed. The treatment bureaucracy is almost a total nonfactor in alcohol policies. The law enforcement bureaucracy has a mixed impact. In some cases it influences policies so that they are favorable to the bureaucracy. In other cases, strong relationships exist, but they appear to be spurious.

Alcohol policies including drunk driving laws are unrelated to policy implementation. None of the policies appears to influence the consumption of alcoholic beverages. This does not mean that the policies or enforcement do not have any impact; in some cases they do. The number of retail liquor sales outlets is negatively associated with the cirrhosis rate and positively associated with the prison population. Alcohol tax rates are inversely related to the suicide rate. Both strict alcohol sales regulation and arrests for driving under the influence are associated with declines in nighttime traffic fatalities. Treatment capacity is negatively correlated with suicide deaths.

Theoretical Conclusions

Alcohol policies vary in salience. When policies become highly salient, as drunk driving policy did in the 1980s, politics become entrepreneurial. Explaining the outcomes of entrepreneurial politics with citizen, political, interest group, and bureaucratic forces is difficult. As would be expected, this chapter found better predictions for alcohol regulation policies that have developed over a longer period of time than for drunk driving policies that underwent rapid change in the 1980s. Entrepreneurial policies, because they have little opposition, tend to be poorly designed. They frequently do not work. This chapter provided evidence that drunk driving policies have no impact on the level of drunk driving in the states. More relevant is the enforcement of DUI laws by the bureaucracy.

Notes

1. The consumption of alcohol is positively associated with income (0.55) and urbanism (0.29). Data are from the *Statistical Abstract of the United States* (Washington, DC: Government Printing Office, annual). Income is for 1986, and urbanism is for 1980.

2. Data on church membership are taken from Bernard Quinn et al., *Churches and Church Membership in the United States* (Atlanta: Glenmary Research Center, 1980). The dry religious forces include people who are either Protestant fundamentalists or members of antidrink religions. The following churches were classified as Protestant fundamentalist: Church of God, Mormons, Church of Christ, Church of the Nazarene, Mennonites, Conservative Baptist Association, Missouri Synod Lutherans, Pentecostal Free Will Baptists, Pentecostal Holiness Church, the Salvation Army, Seventh-Day Adventists, southern Baptists, and Wisconsin Synod Lutherans. Nonfundamentalist churches classified as antidrink include all other Baptists, Methodists, and Presbyterians.

3. See previous note. The largest proportion of these individuals is Catholic, although the measure includes a fair number of liberal Protestants.

4. Both measures are for 1980 and from the *U.S. Census of Population.*

5. An alternative measure was tried, Mann and colleagues' (1991: 363) measure of Alcoholics Anonymous members per 1,000 persons, but it was not as successful as the organization's measure. This suggests that AA's impact is a result of its structure, not its membership size.

6. Holbrook-Provow and Poe (1987) examine this measure and conclude that it is similar to several other ideology measures that use either policy or elite voting as their base. Data for this measure were added for Alaska and Hawaii by estimating values based on other measures of ideology.

7. Procuring data on industrial production for alcohol by state is difficult because the industry is fairly small and highly concentrated. As a result, the federal government does not release some data in its *U.S. Census of Manufacturing* to avoid identifying individual firms. The flaw in this measure is that all firms are counted equally. A small winery will have the same impact on the measure as a brewery for a national beer company. Without data from individual firms or states, however, this flaw cannot be corrected.

8. The source is the Distilled Spirits Council of the United States, 1985.

9. These measures are for 1986. They were taken from the U.S. censuses on service industries and retail trade, respectively.

10. Law enforcement data for 1987 are from the U.S. Bureau of the Census, *Government Employment* (Washington, DC: U.S. Government Printing Office, 1987). Treatment data are from the National Institute on Drug Abuse, *National Drug and Alcoholism Treatment Unit Survey 1989 Final Report* (Rockville, MD: NIDA, 1989).

11. All data are from the Distilled Spirits Council of the United States (1991), which annually publishes a summary of state laws. For newspaper and billboard ads, a state was assigned a score of 1 to 4 with the following meaning: 1 = no restrictions; 2 = restrictions equal to those of the Federal Alcoholic Administrative (FAA) regulations; 3 = restrictions stronger than those of the FAA; 4 = a ban on advertising. For inside ads, window advertising, and novelties, a three-point scale was used, with 1 = no restrictions; 3 = a ban on such activities; and 2 = some intermediate regulation. Coupons, refunds, contests, and taste-tests were dummy variables, coded 1 if the practice was permitted. The hours variables were the actual number of hours that liquor stores must be closed. This regulation measure correlates only at .62 with the one examined by Meier and Johnson (1990), which was for 1985. Although only a few states altered their alcohol regulation from 1985 to 1991, those that did made substantial changes. The inclusion of an additional indicator also explains some of the low correlation.

12. The first factor accounted for 26.7 percent of the variance in these measures with an eigenvalue of 3.73 (in 1985, policies grouped more strongly). Each item loaded on this factor in a direction consistent with the notion that a single underlying dimension of alcohol regulation exists. Restrictions on advertising and novelties loaded positively; use of coupons, refunds, contests, and taste-tests loaded negatively; and the number of hours closed loaded positively. Changing this measure to a two-factor or a three-factor solution had no impact on the results of the analysis.

13. Smart's (1988) review of advertising studies, for example, leaves him skeptical that advertising has any influence on consumption levels.

14. The measure is taken directly from reports of the Distilled Spirits Council of the United States, 1985.

15. Proof gallons of distilled spirits, wine gallons of wine, and barrels of beer were all transformed into gallons of pure alcohol. A wine gallon is a regular gallon of liquid. A proof gallon is a gallon of liquid that is 100 proof, or 50 percent alcohol. The conversion figures used were provided by the Distilled Spirits Council. Total state taxes raised from all alcohol-related taxes (including license taxes and monopoly liquor store profits) were then divided by total consumption to get the effective alcohol tax rate. The tax data for 1990 were taken from U.S. Bureau of the Census, *Government Finances.* Consumption figures were from the Advisory Commission on Intergovernmental Relations, 1990.

16. Although this policy variable is different from the bars variable in that it includes both by-the-drink establishments and package stores, the measures are closely enough related that they will not be used in the same equation.

17. See note 10 for data source. This is the treatment bureaucracy measure.

18. Just for sport, a logit analysis of state liquor monopoly policies was conducted with the independent variables introduced in this chapter. Monopoly policies were negatively associated with wet religious groups, Hispanic population, Democratic majorities, and self-help groups, and positively associated with bars per capita.

19. All data on drunk driving laws were taken from the National Commission Against Drunk Driving, *Progress Report on Recommendations Proposed by the Presidential Commission on Drunk Driving* (Washington, DC: National Commission Against Drunk Driving, December 1987). The grouping of the measures is mine, not the National Commission's. The Cronbach's alpha reliability coefficients for these scales are 0.83 for easing the burden of proof, 0.80 for restitution, 0.89 for procedural changes, and 0.81 for stronger penalties.

20. This differs from the proof dimension in that it changes procedures but does not affect the level of proof required.

21. Different state parties probably respond to different parts of this constituency. Southern Democrats probably respond to dry forces, and northern Democrats respond to wet forces. This permits individual state parties to respond to the more numerous group in crafting policies on alcohol.

22. The alcohol tax variable was somewhat skewed, so the dependent variable was subjected to a log transformation. The influence of purely political variables probably reflects the constant need of states to raise revenues.

23. The simple relationship between police employment and the logged alcohol tax rate is −0.51.

24. Several brewers are currently running television advertisements to discourage excessive drinking. Anheuser-Busch's "Know When to Say When" campaign is the most prominent example. Miller operates the "Think When You Drink" campaign.

25. The argument can be made that wet forces, be they industry or individuals, have an interest in the availability of alcohol but no interest in promoting the abuse of alcohol. Wet religious groups are also a measure of religious strength, which might well favor restitution. Retail sellers of alcohol, although not interested in promoting alcohol abuse, do have an interest in not being held liable for such abuse. Hence, specific provisions such as dram shop laws might engender opposition from this segment of the industry.

26. As is often noted, possession of a lawyer is nine-tenths of the law.

27. Alternatively, it might also suggest that producers cannot control the policy area.

28. The data are from the National Center for Health Statistics, *Vital Statistics of the United States* (Bethesda, MD: Department of Health and Human Services, 1988).

29. Nighttime fatalities are defined as those that occur between 6:00 P.M. and 6:00 A.M. The data were provided directly to the author by the Fatal Accident Reporting Service in the U.S. Department of Transportation.

30. The state prison data are from U.S. Bureau of Justice Statistics, *Prisoners in 1989* (Washington, D.C.: U.S. Bureau of Justice Statistics, 1990).

31. The number of stills seized by federal authorities has dropped dramatically in recent years. This suggests that illegal alcoholic beverages are becoming less of a problem. See chapter 6.

32. The strategy is to predict the policy measure with the independent variables used in Tables 7.1 through 7.4. Those variables found to be significant will be retained in the model as controls. To this equation, the policy variables will then be added.

33. In contrast see the arguments on alcohol taxes presented by Terris (1967: 2087), Pogue and Sgontz (1989), Ornstein and Hanssens (1985), and Coate and Grossman (1988). Mann and colleagues (1991: 362) also find no impact for treatment, as was the case for Meier and Johnson (1990: 420).

34. Examination of the equations for distilled spirits, wine, and beer showed results that were fairly similar to these results. This finding for taxes contradicts that of Cook (1981: 256) on alcohol taxes, but he does not control for a variety of the variables included in our model. In addition, his use of a quasi-experimental time series makes his findings difficult to compare with these.

35. Bonnie (1985: 132), in a statement similar to that of Gusfield (1963) on prohibition, contends that sales restrictions and advertising bans are important because they constitute a public endorsement of the public health perspective on alcohol and alcohol-related problems.

36. Meier and Johnson (1990) using earlier data also found cirrhosis was affected by treatment capacity. They also found that sales regulation affected alcohol consumption so that sales regulation had an indirect impact on the cirrhosis rate. For all these variables, the current study uses more recent data.

37. This study contributes to the mixed findings on the number of retail sales outlets. See Bonnie, 1985: 139–140, for a review of these studies.

38. Meier and Johnson (1990) found that per se laws had an impact on nighttime traffic fatalities. That relationship disappears when one includes the DUI arrest rate in the model. The actual influence is the arrest rate, not the per se law.

39. Zador and colleagues (1989) have found evidence that administrative per se laws reduce alcohol involvement in fatal crashes, but similar to Meier and Johnson, 1990, that study did not control for DUI arrest rates.

40. See Center for Disease Control, *Weekly Morbidity and Mortality Report* 40, no. SS–4 (1991).

41. The crime data are from the Federal Bureau of Investigation, *Uniform Crime Reports* (annual).

8

The Politics of Sin

This study of the politics of drug policy had two major objectives—one theoretical and one substantive. The theoretical objective was to unify the study of public policy within political science by using a single theory to guide a descriptive historical study, a quantitative historical study, and a quantitative cross-sectional analysis. Policies affecting both alcohol and illicit drugs were examined in this manner. The substantive objective was to compile some generalizations about the politics of drug policy and to evaluate the effectiveness of those policies. How well these objectives have been met can be gleaned from the theoretical and substantive conclusion sections at the end of each chapter. Little value would accrue from repeating those findings; rather, this chapter will address some more general issues that have not been adequately discussed in previous chapters.

Theoretical Conclusions

The attempt to use a single theory of public policy to examine two different morality policies, each in three different ways, was a qualified success. The theory generated quantitative historical tests that achieved high levels of explanation when compared with studies of a similar style. The cross-sectional analysis resulted in reasonable levels of explanation and the ability to probe interesting policy impacts. The theory was able to structure the historical case studies to provide theoretically informed analyses. The three approaches often varied in their ability to address certain questions; but, in combination, each was able to compensate for the weaknesses of the other approaches.

Two conclusions are relevant. First, all three political science approaches to public policy are doing the same thing. The lack of communication between the state policy scholars, the descriptive historical scholars, and the quantitative historical scholars, therefore, is lamentable. Just as methods should not determine results, neither should methods limit one's audience. Multimethod policy studies that bridge the gap between policy approaches are possible; we need to overcome the limits of our graduate training and become methodologically flexible students of public policy.

Second, our policy theories are more flexible than we give them credit for being. Theoretical complexity is often traded off for methodological complexity. The result is that quantitative scholars shy away from the mind-numbing complexity provided by the more elaborate policy theories, and theoretical scholars view quantitative research as being obtuse while making obvious points. The theory used in this study was only moderately complex. At the same time it was similar to a variety of theories currently in use in a variety of public policy studies. More complex theories simply need more talented scholars, but they clearly can be operationalized.

The general theoretical success of this project should be tempered by a variety of qualifications. The effort was a first attempt; others should be able to use my effort as a guide to make additional progress. Perhaps the greatest empirical limitation of the study was the failure to make all the relationships among variables consistent across the studies. One of the disappointments of quantitative research is that relationships do not always conform to one's theoretical expectations. Nothing is more frustrating than to see a relationship conform to the theory in one test and then be inconsistent with the theory in the next test. The lack of consistent relationships between the quantitative historical studies and the cross-sectional quantitative studies may well be a function of measurement. Indicators are rarely optimal and often are a great distance from the concept they are intended to measure. Solving these measurement problems offers a great deal of promise for progress in empirical tests of public policy theories.

A second general weakness of this effort was the inability to find some relationships that were strongly suggested by theory. Few concepts were more disappointing than salience. The role of salience in mobilizing the public to participate in morality politics has been well-developed theoretically. As issues become salient, public forces should be more influential, political forces should also increase in influence, and industry and bureaucracy forces should decline in power. Measures of salience in the empirical chapters, however, were rarely related to any policy decisions, be they policy adoptions or policy implementations. One problem might be the use of periodicals as a measure of issue salience. Although such indicators have been used in a variety of historical studies, they have never been subjected to rigorous statistical tests, as in this book. Other possibilities are that more precise measures of salience are needed or that the content of articles must be assessed. Alternatively, the theory might be adjusted. Some have argued that public opinion on morality issues is fairly easy for politicians to manipulate (Jensen, Gerber, and Babcock, 1991). If salience is simply the public's response to the stimuli offered by political elites, then its lack of impact is understandable.

Comparing the relative impact of different political institutions was handicapped by the weak quantitative measures available for bureaucracy and bureaucratic influence. Just as bureaucracy is the least understood political institution, it is also the one that generates the fewest quantitative indicators. Despite the poor measures which generally tapped bureaucratic capacity only, the studies demonstrated numerous bureaucratic influences on public policy. Bureaucratic capacity, however, is not a one-dimensional concept. Rourke's (1984) seminal work suggests that expertise, clientele support, leadership, and cohesion are all elements in the power setting of a bureaucracy. This analysis attempted a weak measure of leadership in the illicit drug chapters but was unable to measure the other dimensions of bureaucratic power. Such dimensions can be measured (see Grady, 1989) and should provide valuable explanation in other studies of public policy.

Another weakness of the empirical chapters was the inability to come to grips with the notion of policy entrepreneurs. Policy entrepreneurs are relatively easy to find and discuss in descriptive public policy studies; however, measuring them in quantitative studies may well be impossible. The present effort, using entrepreneurs as a residual category, is less than desirable. This specification requires that no other relevant concepts are omitted from the models, a position that would be hard to defend. I remain at a loss concerning other methods of incorporating the concept of policy entrepreneurs into quantitative policy studies; I leave this to the reader to solve.

One major strength of the multimethod approach to public policy should be noted. A substantial portion of the analysis examined policy outcomes. If political scientists are serious about studying public policy, they need to deal with policy outcomes. Explaining policy outputs only (that is, laws or even bureaucratic decisions) leaves the analyst with an explanation of only one-half of the policy process. Whether or not policies work strikes me as interesting in explaining why certain policies are adopted. Linking policy impact to decisions made in the design of public policies should be an integral part of political science.

In addition to these general theoretical findings, several more specific findings about public policy are demonstrated by this research. Although each of these findings will be noted only in the context of morality policy, in many cases they are probably relevant for all types of public policies. Each merits separate discussion.

Political Actors Are Autonomous

This study reinforces other scholarship that argues political actors, be they legislators, chief executives, or bureaucrats, have substantial policy autonomy. Political actors without a doubt are attentive to the demands of interest groups and the general public, but they are not dried leaves blown along by forces outside their control. Political actors have their own policy preferences on morality issues and exercise discretion in quest of these preferences. This study documented a variety of tools from legislation to reorganizations that political actors use to shape public policy. Despite the gap between adopted policies and implemented policies, laws and other similar policy adoptions often accomplish a great deal of what they are designed to do. The policy changes in implementation are interesting simply because they are deviations from intent rather than because policy intentions were never implemented. If political actors were simply registering the will of interest groups and the public, then the political and bureaucratic variables in this study would have had no predictive power. Not only was this not the case, but also in many policy models the predictive power of political forces exceeded those of industry and citizen forces.

This study assumed that citizen groups and industry groups influenced political actors but are not influenced by these political actors. Such an assumption maximizes the relative statistical impact of citizen and industry forces compared with the influence of political institutions. In reality, the relationships between political actors and both citizens and interest groups are reciprocal. Public opinion can be shaped by politicians, and interest groups can be urged by politicians to respond on key issues. Because one directional influence was specified in this study, some interesting public policy questions were not addressed. On the politics side (versus the impact side) of public policy, separating out this reciprocal influence is probably the most interesting issue that policy analysts can address.

The autonomy of political actors is complicated by the United States' preference for fragmented political power. Principal-agent theories of public policy that specify one principal controlling bureaucratic agents are simply wrong. Bureaucratic agents have many principals, each with the legitimate right to expect some responsiveness from the bureaucrats. Such relationships are further complicated by the federal system. With checks, counterchecks, divided authority, and policies working at cross-purposes, assessing political influence is difficult. Multiple principals are interacting with multiple agents (see Meier, 1993). Simply because the process is complex, however, does not mean that individual institutions or coalitions of institutions do not at times dominate the policy process; they do. Federal influences (especially the legislative and bureaucratic ones) on state implementation of illicit drug policies are an excellent example.

Citizens Influence Public Policy

Often in reaction to studies that claim politics does not matter, scholars spend a great deal of time demonstrating the influence of political institutions or interest groups and then contend that citizen preferences are unimportant. To find cases where citizens are able to influence public policy, the analyst needs to examine those policy areas where conditions facilitate citizen influence. Theoretically, a variety of scholars have argued that citizen influence is maximized in policies that are salient but not complex. Morality issues in general tend to be salient and easy to understand. Even though the specific measure of salience rarely has an independent impact, citizen forces are important in affecting the policies studied in this book. Such findings make sense because salience, theoretically, is a specifying hypothesis. When salience increases, citizens will have greater influence on public policy; the hypothesis says nothing about the relationship between salience per se and public policy.

The wide range of citizen impacts shown in these studies and the method of analysis have left open an interesting theoretical question. This study did not specify how citizen preferences are aggregated, and generally left them unaggregated in the empirical analysis (measures of race or church membership rather than measures of membership in race-related institutions or membership in specific antidrug or anti-alcohol groups). The interesting theoretical question is, Who aggregates these preferences? Is it done through the interest group process, or do politicians do it directly through the representational process? If elections, for example, facilitate the representation of citizen views on these morality policy issues, then interest groups are not needed to aggregate the citizen preferences independently. A politician who has a clear perception of citizen preferences on an issue really does not need an interest group to aggregate those preferences.

Industry Influence Is Minimal

Industry influence in drug policies, including the influence of the alcohol industries in alcohol regulatory policies, is fairly minimal. Morality policy is an area where one would expect industry to have little influence. Indeed in less salient policies (e.g., alcohol sales regulation), industry has more influence than in more salient policies (e.g., drunk driving). While this study addressed only morality issues, enough other studies of regulation exist to suggest that industry influence is generally overestimated in regulatory policy arenas (Quirk, 1981; Meier, 1988).

Industries need to overcome two problems inherent in U.S. politics to influence the policy process. First, they must overcome the problem of unity. Few industries have monolithic interests. This study demonstrated the difference in the interests of the alcohol production industry from those of the consumption industries. Brewers and distillers also have different interests. Such disunity is not uncommon in other policy areas (Meier, 1985). Second, industry must overcome the general populist orientation of many political elites. A substantial portion of the American public and its representatives distrust industry and will discount industry efforts at influencing public policy. Although some industries can prevail over these problems, the point of this discussion is that industries have to overcome some substantial disadvantages to be able to press for public policies that directly benefit the industry.

Morality Policies Are Often Poorly Designed

Two types of morality policy exist. One type concerns issues where active citizen interests exist on both sides (e.g., issues regarding the sale of alcohol, abortion, school prayer, gambling, etc.). Issues with competing citizen and political groups are classically redistributive, except that the redistribution concerns values rather than incomes. Such issues produce a distinctive pattern of politics; they are frequently partisan and tend to spawn two opposing advocacy coalitions that vie for influence with major political institutions (see Ripley and Franklin, 1991).

A second type of morality policy involves one-sided issues (e.g., drunk driving, drug abuse, murder, etc.). Such issues conform to what I call the politics of sin. Everyone is opposed to sin (especially if the costs of the associated policy are relatively small); as a result, there is universal opposition to drunk driving, to drug abuse (though not necessarily to drug access), to murder, and so on. The only opposition to this type of morality policy is clearly the work of Satan. One-sided morality issues tend to be dominated by entrepreneurs without the restraints of opposition. Individual politicians compete to be the most aggressive morality advocates. However, effective policymaking requires some opposition to point out the problems with policy proposals, to demand alternative proposals, or to slow the rapid rush to policy adoption. Morality policies pertaining to one-sided issues are rarely subjected to the expertise of bureaucrats; assessments of these morality policies are generally found only in academic journals, which no self-respecting politician would read. Even when bureaucratic expertise is available, it is often swept aside in the rush to Armageddon.[1] Such a policy process is much more likely to generate policies that will not work because the policy proposals have not been tempered by informed debate. Controlled-substance laws and most drunk driving laws are classic illustrations of this type of morality policy.

Policy Implementation Is the Real Policy

A truism of all public policy is that implementing the policy is as important as determining what policy is adopted. Policy implementation is especially important in morality policies because such policies are susceptible to symbolic politics. Sodomy laws, for example, are rarely enforced even though many states retain them on the books. The cross-sectional alcohol study (chapter 7) showed that the real drunk driving policy is the enforcement priority given to drunk driving by law enforcement agencies; the actual laws adopted have had no impact. Similarly the cross-sectional drugs study (chapter 4) showed that law enforcement officers have often moderated the impact of harsh marijuana laws by reducing the level of enforcement.

In morality policy, implementation cannot be separated from policy adoption; implementation often *is* the policy. The predictive ability of the policy theory used in the book is better for policy implementation than it is for policy adoption. The model should work better on implementation if implementation is where the real decisions are made. The key policy question in morality politics is rarely,

Should a law be passed? Rather, it is usually, What resources should be spent, if any, to enforce this law? The irony of morality politics, therefore, is that bureaucracies play almost no role in policy adoption, but the "real politics" of morality policy is bureaucratic politics. This suggests that great strides in understanding morality politics can be made by studying the ability of agencies to gain autonomy in policy implementation and the ability to acquire resources when the agency decides to enforce the law.

Substantive Conclusions

Whereas morality policies can be symbolic, those concerning drugs are not. Drug policies redistribute values. They impose costs on some persons and provide benefits to others. Drug abuse policies were selected as the topic of study because U.S. policies toward alcohol and other drugs have ranged from letting the free market operate to prohibition. The guiding question was, Given the relative harms of alcohol and illicit drugs, why is alcohol legal and regulated while marijuana, cocaine, and similar drugs are illegal? Examining both drug and alcohol policies from three different perspectives provides six different views of U.S. drug policy. On the basis of these views, we can see that some policies clearly work better than others. Although I am under no illusion that policymakers care what academics think about public policy issues, the social sciences are and should be concerned with how things might be rather than just with how things are (see Simon, 1969).

Illicit Drug Laws Do Not Work Especially Well

This analysis found little evidence that prohibiting drugs works well enough to justify the costs that it imposes. Alcohol prohibition was a limited success in that it reduced the consumption of alcohol, but alcohol is a unique drug. Prohibition did not eliminate alcohol consumption, and the illegal market shifted consumption to the more intoxicating and more profitable distilled spirits. Even distilled spirits are relatively bulky (compared with heroin or cocaine) and, thus, difficult to smuggle. This difficulty was reflected in prices. Much of the reduction in alcohol consumption might well have resulted from the increased costs that prohibition imposed on the price of alcohol.

Policies relating to drugs other than alcohol do not appear to work as well as the alcohol prohibition experiment did. Chapter 3 presented evidence that increased enforcement has little impact on the price of drugs (except for marijuana) and the amount of drug usage. Although this presentation is unique in the literature, the conclusions are similar to those of several other drug policy analysts. Perhaps the most interesting empirical finding is that drug usage appears to have a life cycle of its own. Musto (1987) noted a similar pattern among virtually all illicit drugs: usage would increase and then eventually decline on its own. In recent years, a variety of indicators show that drug usage for most drugs was declining before the current war on drugs started. The war itself has had little impact; something else (e.g., education programs, changes in values, etc.) has reduced the approval and the consumption of drugs.

Drug Prohibitions Impose Major Costs

The modest accomplishments of illicit drug policies must be considered in light of the costs they impose. Because the benefits and the costs can be assigned different values by rational persons with different perspectives, these individuals can disagree on whether or not drug policies have benefits exceeding the costs. The costs of current drug policies are substantial.

The direct costs of drug prohibition are the costs of enforcing the laws. Because drug policy is a morality policy with little opposition, policymakers have not demanded to know what the total direct costs of enforcing drug laws are. Information on many federal costs are available because they are contained in the federal budget, but the analogous costs of state and local governments are not available. The most obvious direct cost of drug prohibition is the salaries of police officers enforcing drug laws (these are opportunity costs, because if the money were not spent for drug enforcement it could be spent to enforce other laws or for other programs). Also fairly obvious are the costs of punishment; individuals convicted of drug crimes are frequently incarcerated, and additional prisoners generate more costs for corrections. Reasonably obvious, but without any method of assigning a value to them, are the costs that drug wars impose on the court systems. By overloading court systems, drug wars delay the justice process for other crimes and have an especially negative impact on the speed of the civil justice system. The inability of the court system to resolve complaints with dispatch cannot help but contribute to greater cynicism concerning government performance.

The obvious costs of current policies are probably not the largest costs involved in drug control policy, only the easiest to measure. Three generally incommensurable costs are those in terms of civil liberties, corruption, and violence. Every drug war fought in this century has seen aggressive law enforcement that pushed the envelope on criminal procedure. As documented in the individual chapters, courts generally acquiesce in these new interpretations of criminal procedure. In the 1980s' war on drugs, the U.S. Supreme Court upheld kidnaping of foreign citizens wanted on U.S. drug charges (*United States* v. *Alvarez-Machain*, 119 L. Ed. 2d 441, 1992), supported using low-flying aircraft to gather evidence of probable cause that drugs were being produced (*Florida* v. *Riley*, 488 U.S. 445, 1989), permitted searches of automobiles without warrants (*United States* v. *Ross*, 456 U.S. 798, 1982), allowed airport and highway searches on the basis of drug courier profiles (*Florida* v. *Royer*, 460 U.S. 491, 1983; *United States* v. *Montoya de Hernandez*, 473 U.S. 531, 1985) even though such profile-searches stop a disproportionate number of blacks and Hispanics (Johns, 1992: 91), granted search warrants of homes solely on the basis of anonymous tips (*Illinois* v. *Gates,* 462 U.S. 213, 1983), and permitted the search of trash without a warrant or probable cause (*California* v. *Greenwood,* 1988). Policies for drug-free workplaces perhaps even go beyond these criminal procedure cases in infringing on the privacy rights of individuals (see *NTEU* v. *Von Raab,* 489 U.S. 656, 1989). Putting a price tag on these costs is difficult, but in a nation built on the concept of limited government, they would have to be considered substantial.

The second major incommensurable is the costs of police corruption. Drug law enforcement and corruption have been bedfellows since the passage of the Harrison Act. The profitability of the illicit drug trade and the discretion vested in narcotics officers virtually guarantee that drug dealers will try to bribe police officers. Some of those attempts will succeed. The image of police corruption generated by drug wars brings public disrespect for law enforcement and cannot help but create problems for police officers when they enforce other laws.

The final incommensurable of drug control is crime and violence. This study provided a wide variety of empirical evidence that concludes that *drug law enforcement generates more crime and violence.* Illegal markets by their very nature are violent because individuals have no legal way to enforce contracts. Disrupting markets by arresting dealers creates a market vacuum; new dealers moving into that market vacuum will enforce their claims with additional violence. Property crimes will increase to cover the higher costs of illicit drugs. With few exceptions, drugs do not cause individuals to become violent and commit crimes that they would otherwise not commit. Making drugs illegal and enforcing those laws, however, has a direct causal relationship with increases in violence and in property crimes.

Drug Wars Involve Racial Targeting

A wealth of historical and empirical evidence has documented the racial dimension of America's drug policies. Drug laws are often proposed to prevent drug usage by immigrants, minorities, and foreigners. When laws become more restrictive and when enforcement of those laws increases, minorities and immigrants bear the brunt of enforcement efforts, even though their relative usage of drugs differs little from that of white citizens. Individuals arrested and convicted of drug violations must live in a system that restricts their economic and political rights. Ex-felons are denied the right to vote, and firms are less likely to hire them. Drug-free workplace policies exacerbate these restrictions because firms will probably perceive that past drug users might be more likely to use drugs in the future. The politics of race in the United States involves numerous political, economic, and social policies. Many of these policies are a sincere effort to improve the status of minority citizens and to create a more equitable political economy. Drug policies systematically undercut our policies of equity.

Drugs Make Good Politics But Bad Public Policy

Given the major costs of drug control policies and the general lack of their success, one wonders why drug crises are declared and drug wars launched. The obvious reason is that drug wars are good politics. Drug abuse is a universal bad. Even a cigarette smoker can feel moral about a crackdown on cocaine. Drugs are a safe electoral issue. People who are more likely to vote are also more likely to fear drugs. The election-year feeding frenzies of 1984, 1986, and 1988 confirm that politicians see drug abuse as a great political issue. Good politics, however, generates the same policies—more law enforcement with all its drawbacks.

A Policy Advantage of Legal and Regulated Drugs Is That More Policy-relevant Information Is Available

Because alcohol is a legal drug with recognized problems, a great deal of research is conducted on the social, economic, and medical consequences of its use. The corresponding information on illicit drugs is generally lacking. Reading the literature on licit and illicit drugs cannot help but convince the reader that our knowledge base for alcohol is far more extensive than our knowledge base for marijuana, cocaine, heroin, PCP, or other illegal drugs. Good public policies require information (even if policymakers ignore that information). Individuals also benefit from this information. Knowing that alcohol is linked to cirrhosis, suicides, accidents, and traffic fatalities means that such risks can be considered in deciding whether or not to drink alcohol. Lacking similar information about cocaine, or whatever the next drug of choice will be, is dangerous.

Part of the problem has been the tendency of the federal government to support the dissemination of propaganda rather than information. For many individuals, the National Institute on Drug Abuse and similar agencies lack credibility. Individuals who lived through the marijuana propaganda era and discovered that government information on the evil weed was generally wrong and usually overstated cannot help but be skeptical of government claims about other drugs. Even well-documented claims of the dangers of illicit drugs are often discounted because the source has been unreliable in the past. Nothing undercuts educational efforts on drugs and drug abuse more than the federal government's effort to avoid objective assessments of illicit drugs (see Bachman et al., 1988).

Morality Policies Have Limitations

All policies have limitations; that is, 100 percent compliance with a law is impossible. Pushing for greater enforcement or stricter laws in such circumstances can generate a backlash of resistance to the law and possibly a change in the policy itself. Just as the harsh penalties of the Jones Act ended public support for prohibition, the harsh marijuana penalties assessed in the 1960s triggered the decriminalization movement. Drunk driving policies might be at a similar junction. The absence of a solution to the problem has led interest group leaders to seek stronger and stronger laws. The current attempt to redefine drunk driving at an 0.08 percent blood alcohol level versus a 0.10 percent blood level might be just such an illustration. The major problem of drunk driving is unlikely to be persons with intoxication levels between 0.08 percent and 0.10 percent; the real problem appears to those who drive, and do so often, at far higher levels of intoxication than the defined minimum.

The support of law enforcement officers for greater enforcement also appears to have waned. After quadrupling between 1960 and 1983, drunk driving arrest rates dropped from 803.6 per 100,000 persons in 1983 to 666.8 per 100,000 in 1989, a drop of 17 percent. This drop is especially interesting because the only policy activity that appears to affect the rate of drunk driving (as measured by nighttime traffic fatalities) is the rate of enforcement.

Policymakers need to recognize these limits when designing public policies. Laws with harsh punishments may be moderated by implementation bureaucrats, or they might be ignored, or they might be enforced and trigger massive resistance to the public policy. Although these limits are not readily apparent to the observer, recognizing that limits exist would contribute to better policy design.

A Rational Drug Control Policy Is Needed

A person without any prior knowledge of U.S. drug control policies would be struck by the irrationality of overall policy. Nicotine, a highly dangerous and toxic drug, is legal and so lightly regulated that it is accessible to virtually everyone. Alcohol, a drug linked to serious health consequences, is legal but regulated with some degree of vigor. Americans spend approximately twice as much money on alcohol as they do on all illicit drugs combined (Kleiman, 1992: 204). Cocaine, heroin, and a variety of narcotics, although much less dangerous than either nicotine or alcohol, are illegal, and the laws are aggressively enforced. Marijuana, without question the safest drug discussed here, is illegal, but the federal government would like states to adopt stronger laws and be more aggressive in enforcing them. When viewed in their entirety, U.S. drug control policies are simply irrational.

On the basis of what is known about drugs and current drug policy, what would a rational drug control policy look like? First, a rational drug policy starts with the assumption that there is a general demand for intoxication. That demand might be influenced by education efforts but will always exist at some level greater than zero. A general demand for intoxication means that drugs can be substituted for each other; individual drugs need not be perfect substitutes for each other (that is, one can substitute something other than narcotics for heroin). When a drug user's favorite drug is unavailable, the user searches for the next best available alternative.

Second, a rational drug control policy accepts that prohibitions impose far more costs than benefits. At the same time a rational drug policy would not encourage citizens to spend their lives stoned; this requires a general policy of education and unbiased information so that individuals can assess the risks of drug use. Education programs appear to be successful in discouraging smoking; the proportion of Americans who smoke dropped from 43 percent in 1964 to 30 percent in 1980 at the same time that a national antismoking campaign was in existence (Glasser, 1991: 275). Bachman and colleagues (1988), in their of study marijuana use, also concluded that education programs have changed attitudes and decreased use (see also Jacobsen and Hanneman, 1992: 108, 110; and chapter 3).

Third, a rational drug policy treats each drug on a case-by-case basis to determine the relative risks of each. Alcohol should be compared with marijuana, each of these compared with cocaine, and so on. A rational drug policy then attempts to structure individual choices of intoxicants so that less dangerous forms are readily available and relatively inexpensive and more dangerous forms are less available and more expensive. The market should reinforce health concerns, not run counter to them. A rational drug control policy might conclude that some drugs are simply too dangerous to permit individuals to use. Restrictions in such cases could be prohibitive. With alternative available intoxicants, the demand for the more dangerous drugs should drop. This demand should drop further in response to factually based education campaigns that inform individuals of the risks of various drugs and generally discourage their use.

Fourth, a rational drug policy takes advantage of market systems to control use and demand. Dangerous drugs that are not banned should be priced much higher than less dangerous drugs. The intoxicants with the least risk should be priced as the cheapest (or taxed the least; given the relatively low price of marijuana, the tax on marijuana would probably be equal to the current market price). Pricing policy should be designed to funnel the demand for intoxication to the drugs with the least dangers. This might well result in a system where marijuana or some other currently illicit drug is encouraged as a substitute for alcohol. Such a process would also short-cut the perversities of the current process, which creates incentives for a more efficient delivery system for cocaine (i.e., crack) or marijuana with a higher THC content.

Fifth, production of legal intoxicating drugs must be rigidly regulated to eliminate problems with adulterants and impurities. Quality control should not be a major problem because such systems currently operate in the manufacture of medicinal drugs and to some extent in the manufacture of alcoholic beverages. Whether such controls should operate through a tort system or a regulatory system could be decided by the appropriate policymaking institutions.

Sixth, a rational drug control policy should take advantage of our federal system. Much of what we know about the impact of drug control laws is the result of variation among the states in this country. Variation in drug control systems is confusing to individuals and manufacturers; however, it could generate a great deal of information on what policies are effective in limiting the consequences of drug use and on what policies have no impact.

One promising drug control proposal is Mark Kleiman's (1992: 277) idea that access to drugs be controlled through a licensing system. Individuals would be issued a license allowing them to purchase up to a given quantity of whatever drugs are legal. Sales to individuals without licenses would be illegal. While all adults would qualify for a license, a license could be revoked or restricted for engaging in harmful behavior (e.g., driving while intoxicated, committing assault while under the influence, etc.). License actions would occur in addition to any legal actions. Such a process would limit licenses to individuals who demonstrate they can consume drugs without endangering themselves or others.

Although this proposed rational drug policy would not be costless, on its face it would impose fewer costs on society than the current policy. The one challenge to legalization proposals—and a rational drug policy would have to incorporate some drugs that could be legally consumed (even if the drug were a high-risk one, such as alcohol)—is that the number of users might skyrocket for any legalized drug. No one actually knows the extent of future use of drugs that are now illegal if they were suddenly to become legal; however, much scholarship suggests that consumption increases only moderately when prohibitions are ended. The increase in alcohol consumption after the end of Prohibition was moderate and continued below pre-Prohibition levels for many years (see Miron and Zweibel, 1991b: 6). Marijuana usage rates in states that decriminalized the possession of marijuana have moved in tandem with usage rates in other states (Morgan, 1991: 413–414; Wisotsky, 1990: 215).

Why We Probably Will Not Adopt a Rational Drug Policy

After completing this study of U.S. drug policies, the benefits of a rational drug policy as described above strike me as far exceeding the benefits of retaining the current policy. I am confident, however, that future policies will simply be a continuation of current policies. In a burst of insight we may experience a reduction in enforcement, but a shift to a full-fledged rational drug policy is unlikely. What motivates policymakers to support current drug policies is an interesting question. Three possibile answers come to mind.

First, individuals might sincerely believe that all currently illicit drugs are serious threats to the public's well-being. An individual might even believe that current policies, which encourage intoxication through alcohol rather than other drugs, are the best of a series of bad alternatives. The analysis presented in this book will not convince such an individual, but quite clearly such beliefs are difficult to reconcile with the evidence.

Second, individuals might support current drug policies because they are interested in the redistribution of values. Opposing drugs and seeking state sanction for that opposition is one way to certify that one's values are superior to another's. Drugs are probably a safer and easier vehicle for doing this than school prayer, abortion, or, heaven forbid, Murphy Brown. Such xenophobic objectives, however, can be driven only by a lack of confidence that the superiority of one's values is self-evident.

Third, drug wars could be a way to divert attention from other more pressing policy problems that require greater sacrifices. The decade of the 1980s saw national policymakers jump into the war on drugs with enthusiasm; at the same time chronic national debts, a sluggish economy, a health-care cost crisis, and a crumbling infrastructure were not addressed. Perhaps drug wars are the equivalent of those "splendid little wars" that serve to mobilize people and permit politicians to avoid addressing more serious political issues. Some have even argued that alcohol and tobacco interests, with their active support of the drug war, are participants in this conspiracy in order to protect their own legal markets and divert attention from the problems of legal drugs (see Johns, 1992). I am skeptical of such conspiracy theories of drug wars mostly because a conspiracy of this nature requires far more sophisticated reasoning and planning than has been demonstrated by our current political process.

Note

1. Drunk driving legislation is a classic case with some reasonable expertise built up (see Ross, 1982). We know a great deal about specific policies that do not work; however, this knowledge rarely ever informs public policy.

Bibliography

Aaron, Paul, and David Musto. 1981. "Temperance and Prohibition in America: A Historical Overview." In Moore and Gerstein, 1981, 127–181.

Advisory Commission on Intergovernmental Relations. 1987. *State Fiscal Capacity and Effort 1985.* Washington, DC: ACIR.

Advisory Commission on Intergovernmental Relations, 1990. *State Fiscal Capacity and Effort 1987.* Washington, DC: ACIR.

Allentuck, Samuel, and Karl Bowman. 1942. "The Psychiatric Aspects of Marijuana Intoxication." *American Journal of Psychiatry* 99: 248–250.

Anderson, James E. 1990. *Public Policymaking.* Boston: Houghton Mifflin.

Anderson, Patrick. 1981. *High in America: The True Story Behind NORML and the Politics of Marijuana.* New York: Viking Press.

Anglin, M. Douglas. 1983. "Drugs and Crime: Behavioral Aspects." In Kadish, 1983, 636–643.

Anslinger, Harry J. 1961. "We're Winning the War against Dope." *This Week Magazine,* April 16, 1961.

Anslinger, Harry J., with Courtney R. Cooper. 1937. "Marijuana: Assassin of Youth." *American Magazine,* July, 18ff.

Anslinger, Harry, and William F. Tompkins. 1953. *The Traffic In Narcotics.* New York: Funk and Wagnalls.

Appleton, Lynn M. 1985. "Explaining Laws' Making and Their Enforcement in the American States." *Social Science Quarterly* 66: 839–853.

Asch, Peter, and David T. Levy. 1987. "Does the Minimum Drinking Age Affect Traffic Fatalities?" *Journal of Policy Analysis and Management* 6: 180–192.

Bachman, Jerald G., Lloyd D. Johnston, Patrick M. O'Malley, and Ronald H. Humphrey. 1988. "Explaining the Recent Decline in Marijuana Use: Differentiating the Effects of Perceived Risks, Disapproval, and General Lifestyle Factors." *Journal of Health and Social Behavior* 29: 92–112.

Bagley, Bruce Michael. 1988a. "The New Hundred Years War? US National Security and the War on Drugs in Latin America." *Journal of Interamerican Studies and World Affairs* 30: 161–182.

Bagley, Bruce Michael. 1988b. "US Foreign Policy and the War on Drugs: Analysis of a Policy Failure." *Journal of Interamerican Studies and World Affairs* 30: 189–212.

Bakalar, James B., and Lester Grinspoon. 1985. *Drug Control in a Free Society.* New York: Cambridge University Press.

Barnett, Randy E. 1987. "Curing the Drug-Law Addiction: The Harmful Side Effects of Legal Prohibition." In Hamowy, 1987b, 73–102.

Baron, Stanley. 1962. *Brewed in America: A History of Beer and Ale in the United States.* Boston: Little, Brown.

Barrilleaux, Charles J., and Mark E. Miller. 1988. "The Political Economy of State Medicaid Policy." *American Political Science Review* 82: 1089–1107.

Bartlett, Randall. 1973. *Economic Foundations of Political Power.* New York: The Free Press.

Beauchamp, Dan E. 1980. *Beyond Alcoholism: Alcohol and Public Health Policy.* Philadelphia: Temple University Press.

Becker, Gary S. 1968. "Crime and Punishment: An Economic Approach." *Journal of Political Economy* 76: 169–217.

Becker, Howard S. 1963. *Outsiders: Studies in the Sociology of Deviance.* New York: The Free Press.

Bellis, David J. 1981. *Heroin and Politicians: The Failure of Public Policy to Control Addiction in America.* Westport, CT: Greenwood Press.

Berry, Frances Stokes, and William D. Berry. 1990. "State Lottery Adoptions as Policy Innovations: An Event History Analysis." *American Political Science Review* 84: 395–416.

Berry, William D. 1979. "Utility Regulation in the States: The Policy Effects of Professionalism and Salience to the Consumer." *American Journal of Political Science* 23: 263–277.

Berry, William D., and Stanley Feldman. 1987. *Multiple Regression in Practice.* Beverly Hills, CA: Sage Publications.

Bibby, John, Cornelius Cotter, James Gibson, and Robert Huckshorn. 1990. "Parties in State Politics." In *Politics in the American States,* 5th edition, ed. Virginia Gray, Herbert Jacobs, and Robert B. Albritton, 85–122. Glenview, IL: Scott, Foresman.

Biskupic, Joan. 1989. "Bush's Anti-Drug Campaign Emphasizes Enforcement." *Congressional Quarterly Weekly,* September 9, 2312–2315.

Block, Alan A., and John C. McWilliams. 1989. "On the Origins of American Counterintelligence: Building a Clandestine Network." *Journal of Policy History* 1: 353–373.

Blocker, Jack S. 1976. *Retreat from Reform: The Prohibition Movement in the United States 1890–1913.* Westport, CT: Greenwood Press.

Blocker, Jack S. 1989. *American Temperance Movements.* Boston: Twayne Publishers.

Bonnie, Richard J. 1985. "Regulating Conditions of Alcohol Availability: Possible Effective on Highway Safety." *Journal of Studies on Alcohol,* Supplement No. 10 (July): 129–143.

Bonnie, Richard J., and Charles H. Whitebread II. 1970. "The Forbidden Fruit and the Tree of Knowledge: An Inquiry into the Legal History of Marijuana Prohibition." *Virginia Law Review* 56: 971–1203.

Bonnie, Richard J., and Charles Whitebread II. 1974. *The Marihuana Conviction: A History of Marihuana in the United States.* Charlottesville: The University of Virginia Press.

Botvin, Gilbert J. 1990. "Substance Abuse Prevention: Theory, Practice, and Effectiveness." In Tonry and Wilson, 1990, 461–520.

Brazer, Harvey E., and Mary Walz. 1982a. "Miscellaneous Taxes." In Brazer and Laren, 1982b, 755–764.

Brazer, Harvey E., and Deborah S. Laren, eds. 1982b. *Michigan's Fiscal and Economic Structure.* Ann Arbor: University of Michigan Press.

Bromberg, Walter. 1934. "Marijuana Intoxication." *American Journal of Psychiatry* 91: 303–330.

Brunn, Kettil, Lynn Pan, and Ingemar Rexed. 1975. *The Gentlemen's Club: International Control of Drugs and Alcohol.* Chicago: University of Chicago Press.

Bureau of Justice Assistance. 1989. *Building Integrity and Reducing Drug Corruption in Police Departments.* Washington: U.S. Department of Justice.

Bureau of Justice Statistics. 1989. *Felony Sentences in State Courts, 1986.* Washington, DC: U.S. Department of Justice.

Bureau of Justice Statistics. 1990. *Federal Criminal Case Processing, 1980–87.* Washington, DC: U.S. Department of Justice.

Bureau of Labor Statistics. 1991. *Consumer Expenditure Survey: Results from 1990.* Washington, DC: Bureau of Labor Statistics.

Bureau of the Census. 1975. *Historical Statistics of the United States.* Washington, DC: U.S. Government Printing Office.

Bureau of the Census. Various years. *Statistical Abstract of the United States.* Washington, DC: U.S. Government Printing Office.

Burnham, J.C. 1968. "New Perspectives on the Prohibition 'Experiment' of the 1920s." *Journal of Social History* 2: 51–68.

Butynski, William, and Diane M. Canova. 1988. "Alcoholism Treatment Service Systems: A Health Services Research Perspective." *Public Health Reports* 103: 611–620.

Carmines, Edward G., and James A. Stimson. 1989. *Issue Evolution: Race and the Transformation of American Politics.* Princeton: Princeton University Press.

Carr, Robert R., and Erik J. Meyers. 1980. "Marijuana and Cocaine: The Process of Change in Drug Policy." In Drug Abuse Council, 1980, 153–189.

Chaiken, Jan M., and Marcia R. Chaiken. 1990. "Drugs and Predatory Crime." In Tonry and Wilson, 1990, 203–240.

Chauncey, Robert L. 1980. "New Careers for Moral Entrepreneurs: Teenage Drinking." *Journal of Drug Issues* 10: 45–70.

Chayet, Neil L. 1972. "The Legal Status of Marijuana." In National Commission on Marijuana and Drug Abuse, *Marijuana: A Signal of Misunderstanding,* volume I, 531–560. Washington, DC: U.S. Government Printing Office.

Chidsey, Donald Barr. 1969. *On and Off the Wagon: A Sober Analysis of the Temperance Movement from the Pilgrims to Prohibition.* New York: Cowles Book Company.

Clark, Jerry N., Keith O. Boyum, Samuel Krislov, and Roger C. Shaeffer. 1972. "Compliance, Obedience and Revolt: An Overview." In *Compliance and the Law,* ed. Samuel Krislov et al., 9–32. Beverly Hills, CA: Sage Publications.

Clausen, John A. 1977. "Early History of Narcotics Use and Narcotics Legislation in the United States." In *Drugs and Politics,* ed. Paul E. Rock. New Brunswick, NJ: Transaction Books.

Cloyd, Jerald W. 1982. *Drugs and Information Control.* Westport, CT: Greenwood Press.

Coakley, Judy F., and Sandie Johnson. 1978. *Alcohol Abuse and Alcoholism in the United States.* Working Paper No. 1. Washington, DC: National Institute on Alcohol Abuse and Alcoholism.

Coate, Douglas, and Michael Grossman. 1988. "Effects of Alcoholic Beverage Prices and Legal Drinking Ages on Youth Alcohol Use." *Journal of Law and Economics* 31: 145–171.

Cohen, Jeffrey A. 1985. "Congressional Oversight: A Test of Two Theories." Paper presented at the annual meeting of the American Political Science Association, New Orleans.

Cohen, Jeffrey A. 1991. "The Policy Implications of Bureaucratic Reorganizations." Paper presented at the annual meeting of the Midwest Political Science Association, Chicago.

Cohen, Jeffrey A. 1992. *The Politics of Telecommunications Regulation.* Armonk, NY: M. E. Sharpe Publishers.

Cohn, Bob, with Spencer Reiss. 1992. "Noriega: How the Feds Got Their Man." *Newsweek,* April 20, 37.

Collett, Merril. 1989. *The Cocaine Connection.* New York: Foreign Policy Association.

Colliver, J. D., and H. Malin. 1986. "State and National Trends in Alcohol Related Mortality: 1975–1982." *Alcohol Health and Research World* 10: 60–64, 75.

Cook, Philip J. 1981. "The Effect of Liquor Taxes on Drinking, Cirrhosis, and Auto Accidents." In Moore and Gerstein, 1981, 255–285.

Cook, Philip J. 1983. "Alcohol Taxes as a Public Health Measure." In Grant, Plant, and Williams, 1983, 190–200.

Cooper, Mary H. 1990. *The Business of Drugs*. Washington, DC: Congressional Quarterly Press.

Cooper, Philip J. 1988. *Public Law and Public Administration*. Palo Alto, CA: Mayfield Publishers.

Cooper, S. C. 1973. *Dismissal of Narcotics Arrests in the New York City Criminal Court*. Santa Monica, CA: Rand Corporation.

Copeland, Gary W., and Kenneth J. Meier. 1987. "Gaining Ground: The Impact of Medicaid and WIC on Infant Mortality." *American Politics Quarterly* 15: 254–273.

Dawson, Richard, and James A. Robinson. 1963. "Interparty Competition, Economic Variables, and Welfare Politics in the American States." *Journal of Politics* 25: 265–287.

Department of Justice. Various years. *Annual Report of the Attorney General of the United States*. Washington, DC: U.S. Government Printing Office.

Department of the Treasury. Various years. *Annual Report of the Secretary of the Treasury*. Washington, DC: U.S. Government Printing Office.

Derthick, Martha, and Paul J. Quirk. 1985. *The Politics of Deregulation*. Washington, DC: The Brookings Institution.

Dickson, Donald T. 1968. "Bureaucracy and Morality: An Organizational Perspective on a Moral Crusade." *Social Problems* 16: 143–156.

Distilled Spirits Council of the United States. 1985. *Summary of State Laws and Regulations Relating to Distilled Spirits*. Washington, DC: Distilled Spirits Council.

Distilled Spirits Council of the United States. 1991. *Summary of State Laws and Regulations Relating to Distilled Spirits*. Washington, DC: Distilled Spirits Council..

Dodge, Lowell. 1990. "Drug Crime and the Criminal Justice System." Testimony before the Permanent Subcommittee on Investigations, Committee on Governmental Affairs, United States Senate. March 19, Detroit, MI.

Downs, Anthony. 1957. *An Economic Theory of Democracy*. New York: Harper and Row.

Downs, Anthony. 1967. *Inside Bureaucracy*. Boston: Little, Brown.

Drug Abuse Council, ed. 1980. *The Facts about "Drug Abuse."* New York: The Free Press.

Drug Enforcement Administration. 1989. *1988 Domestic Cannabis Eradication Program*. Washington, DC: Department of Justice.

Dye, Thomas R. 1966. *Politics, Economics, and Public Policy*. Chicago: Rand McNally.

Dye, Thomas R. 1988. "Explaining Government Contraction." *Western Political Quarterly* 41: 779–790.

Eisner, Marc Allen, and Kenneth J. Meier. 1990. "Presidential Control versus Bureaucratic Power: Explaining the Reagan Revolution in Antitrust." *American Journal of Political Science* 34: 269–287.

Epstein, Edward J. 1977. *Agency of Fear, Opiates and Political Power in America*. New York: G. P. Putnam.

Etzioni, Amitai. 1988. *The Moral Dimension: Toward a New Economics*. New York: The Free Press.

Ewing, John A., and Beatrice Rouse, eds. 1978. *Drinking: Alcohol in American Society— Issues and Current Research*. Chicago: Nelson-Hall.

Fagan, Jeffrey. 1990. "Intoxication and Aggression." In Tonry and Wilson, 1990, 241–320.

Fairbanks, David. 1977. "Religious Forces and 'Morality' Policies in the American States." *Western Political Quarterly* 30: 411–417.

Farhi, Paul. 1990. "A Drug by Any Other Name." *Washington Post National Weekly Edition,* January 8, 31.

Federal Bureau of Investigation. Various years. *Uniform Crime Reports.* Washington, DC: FBI.

Feldman, Herman. 1930. *Prohibition: Its Economic and Industrial Aspects.* New York: Appleton.

Feldman, Laurence P. 1976. *Consumer Protection.* St. Paul, MN: West Publishing Company.

Fitzgerald, Gerry. 1990. "Dispatches from the Drug War." *Common Cause Magazine* 16: 13–19.

Flanagan, Timothy J., and Kathleen Maguire. 1992. *Source Book of Criminal Justice Statistics—1991.* Washington, DC: U.S. Government Printing Office.

Franke, James L., and Douglas Dobson. 1985. "Interest Groups: The Problem of Representation." *Western Political Quarterly* 38: 224–237.

Friedman, Milton. 1991. "The War We Are Losing." In Krauss and Lazear, 1991, 53–67.

Gaskins, Carla K. 1990. *Felony Case Processing in State Courts, 1986.* Washington, DC: Bureau of Justice Statistics.

General Accounting Office. 1990a. *Methadone Maintenance.* GAO/HRD–90–104. Washington, DC: GAO.

General Accounting Office. 1990b. *Drug Crime and the Criminal Justice System.* GAO/T-GGD–90–25. Washington, DC: GAO.

General Accounting Office. 1991. *The War on Drugs: Arrests Burdening Local Criminal Justice Systems.* GAO/GGD–91–40. Washington, DC: GAO.

Glasser, Ira. 1991. "Drug Prohibition as an Engine for Crime." In Krauss and Lazear, 1991, 271–282.

Gliksman, Louis, and Brian D. Rush. 1986. "Alcohol Availability, Alcohol Consumption and Alcohol-Related Damage. 2. The Role of Sociodemographic Factors." *Journal of Studies on Alcohol* 47: 11–18.

Godshaw, Gerald, et al. 1985. *Anti-Drug Law Enforcement Efforts and Their Impact.* Washington, DC: U.S. Government Printing Office.

Goldberg, Peter. 1980. "The Federal Government's Response to Illicit Drugs, 1969–1978." In Drug Abuse Council, 1980, 20–62.

Goldberg, Peter, and Erik J. Meyers. 1980. "The Influence of Public Attitudes and Understanding on Drug Education and Prevention." In Drug Abuse Council, 1980, 126–152.

Goldman, Albert. 1979. *Grass Roots: Marijuana in America Today.* New York: Harper and Row.

Goldstein, Paul J. 1989. "Drugs and Violent Crime." In *Pathways to Criminal Violence,* ed. Neil Alan Weiner and Marvin E. Wolfgang, 16–48. Newbury Park, CA: Sage Publications.

Gormley, William T. 1986. "Regulatory Issue Networks in a Federal System." *Polity* 18: 595–620.

Grad, Frank. 1978. "Legal Controls of Drinking, Public Drunkenness, and Alcoholism Treatment." In Ewing and Rouse, 1978, 307–336.

Grady, Dennis O. 1989. "Economic Development and Administrative Power Theory." *Policy Studies Review* 8: 322–339.

Grant, Marcus, Martin Plant, and Alan Williams, eds. 1983. *Economics and Alcohol.* New York: Gardner Press.

Grinspoon, Lester. 1971. *Marijuana Reconsidered.* Cambridge, MA: Harvard University Press.

Grinspoon, Lester. 1991. "Marijuana in a Time of Psychopharmacological McCarthyism." In Krauss and Lazear, 1991, 379–389.

Grinspoon, Lester, and James B. Bakalar. 1985. *Cocaine: A Drug and Its Social Evolution*. Revised edition. New York: Basic Books.

Gusfield, Joseph R. 1963. *Symbolic Crusade: Status Politics and the American Temperance Movement*. Urbana: University of Illinois Press.

Haberman, Paul W., and M. M. Baden. 1978. *Alcohol, Other Drugs, and Violent Death*. New York: Oxford University Press.

Hamowy, Ronald. 1987a. "Illicit Drugs and Government Control." In Hamowy, 1987b, 1–34.

Hamowy, Ronald, ed. 1987b. *Dealing with Drugs: Consequences of Government Control*. Lexington, MA: Lexington Books.

Hansen, Susan B. 1983. *The Politics of Taxation*. New York: Praeger Publishers.

Hanushek, Eric, and John Jackson. 1977. *Statistical Methods for Social Scientists*. New York: Academic Press.

Happen, Byron M., Edward Radford, Russel Fisher, and Yale Caplan. 1975. "A Fire Fatality Study." *Fire Journal* 69: 11–13.

Harrison, Leonard V., and Elizabeth Laine. 1936. *After Repeal: A Study of Liquor Control Administration*. New York: Harper and Brothers Publishers.

Hay, Joel W. 1991. "The Harm They Do to Others: A Primer on the External Costs of Drug Abuse." In Krauss and Lazear, 1991, 200–225.

Hellman, Arthur D. 1975. *Laws against Marijuana: The Price We Pay*. Urbana: University of Illinois Press.

Hellman, Daryl A. 1980. *The Economics of Crime*. New York: St. Martin's Press.

Helmer, John. 1975. *Drugs and Minority Oppression*. New York: Seabury Press.

Higham, John. 1963. "Beyond Consensus: The Historian and Moral Critic." *American Historical Review* 67: 610–625.

Himmelstein, Jerome L. 1983. *The Strange Career of Marihuana: Politics and Ideology of Drug Control in America*. Westport, CT: Greenwood Press.

Hofferbert, Richard I. 1969. *The Study of Public Policy*. Indianapolis: Bobbs-Merrill.

Holbrook-Provow, Thomas M., and Steven C. Poe. 1987. "Measuring State Political Ideology." *American Politics Quarterly* 15: 399–416.

Holden, Matthew, Jr. 1966. "'Imperialism' in Bureaucracy." *American Political Science Review* 60: 943–951.

Hunt, Dana E. 1990. "Drugs and Consensual Crimes." In Tonry and Wilson, 1990, 159–202.

Hutcheson, John, Jr., and George Taylor. 1973. "Religious Variables, Political System Characteristics and Policy Outputs in the American States." *American Journal of Political Science* 17: 414–421.

Innes, Christopher A. 1988. *Drug Use and Crime: State Prison Inmate Survey, 1986*. Washington, DC: Bureau of Justice Statistics.

Isikoff, Michael. 1990a. "Youths Deal a Snub to Drugs." *Washington Post National Weekly Edition*, February 19, 38.

Isikoff, Michael. 1990b. "Trafficking in Twilight Zone of Justice." *Washington Post National Weekly Edition*, May 7, 18.

Isikoff, Michael. 1992. "What Was Down Came Back Up." *Washington Post National Weekly Edition*, January 5, 32.

Jacobs, James B. 1989. *Drunk Driving: An American Dilemma*. Chicago: University of Chicago Press.

Jacobsen, Chanoch, and Robert A. Hanneman. 1992. "Illegal Drugs: Past, Present and Possible Futures." *Journal of Drug Issues* 22: 105–120.

Jellinek, E. M. 1960. *The Disease Concept of Alcoholism*. Highland Park, NJ: Hillhouse Press.

Jensen, Eric L., Jurg Gerber, and Ginna M. Babcock. 1991. "The New War on Drugs: Grass Roots Movement or Political Construction?" *Journal of Drug Issues* 21: 651–667.

Johns, Christina Jacqueline. 1992. *Power, Ideology, and the War on Drugs.* New York: Praeger.

Johnson, Bruce D., Terry Williams, Kojo A. Dei, and Harry Sanabria. 1990. "Drug Abuse in the Inner City." In Tonry and Wilson, 1990, 9–68.

Johnson, Cathy M., and Kenneth J. Meier. 1990. "The Wages of Sin: Taxing America's Legal Vices." *Western Political Quarterly* 43: 577–596.

Johnson, Charles A. 1976. "Political Culture in American States: Elazar's Formulation Examined." *American Journal of Political Science* 20: 491–509.

Johnson, James A., and Ernest H. Oksanen. 1977. "Estimation of Demand for Alcoholic Beverages in Canada." *Review of Economics and Statistics* 59: 113–118.

Johnson, Weldon T., and Robert Bogomolny. 1973. "Selective Justice: Drug Law Enforcement in Six American Cities." In National Commission on Marijuana and Drug Abuse, *Drug Use in America,* volume 3, 498–650. Washington, DC: U.S. Government Printing Office.

Johnston, J. 1972. *Econometric Methods.* 2nd edition. New York: McGraw-Hill.

Johnston, Lloyd D., Patrick M. O'Malley, and Jerald G. Bachman. 1989. *Illicit Drug Use, Smoking, and Drinking by America's High School Students, College Students and Young Adults, 1975–1987.* Washington, DC: National Institute on Drug Abuse.

Jones, Charles O. 1984. *An Introduction to the Study of Public Policy.* Monterey, CA: Brooks/Cole.

Kadish, Sanford K. 1983. *Encyclopedia of Crime and Justice.* New York: The Free Press.

Kaplan, John. 1970. *Marijuana—The New Prohibition.* New York: World Publishing.

Kaplan, John. 1983. "Drugs and Crime: Legal Aspects." In Kadish, 1983, 633–652.

Kaplan, John. 1988. "Taking Drugs Seriously." *Public Interest* 23: 32–50.

Katel, Peter. 1990. "Florida: Getting Caught in the Middle." *Newsweek* 115 (April 23), 20.

Keller, Mark H. 1985. "Alcohol Problems and Policies in Historical Perspective." In Kyvig, 1985b, 159–176.

Kemp, Kathleen 1981. "Symbolic and Strict Regulation in the American States," *Social Science Quarterly* 62: 516–526.

Kemp, Kathleen A. 1984. "Political Parties, Industrial Structures, and Political Support for Regulation." In *Policy Formation,* ed. Robert Eyestone, 151–184. Greenwich, CT: JAI Press.

Kemp, Kathleen A. 1987. "Growth in the Regulatory State: Social Regulation, Prosperity, and State Fragmentation." Paper presented at the annual meeting of the American Political Science Association, Chicago.

Kempe, Frederick. 1990. "The Noriega Files." *Newsweek* 115 (January 15): 19–28.

Kerr, K. Austin. 1985. *Organized for Prohibition: A New History of the Anti-Saloon League.* New Haven: Yale University Press.

Kessel, Reuben A. 1959. "Price Discrimination in Medicine." *Journal of Law and Economics* 1: 20–51.

Key, V. O., Jr. 1964. *Politics, Parties, and Pressure Groups.* 5th edition. New York: Thomas Y. Crowell.

Key, V. O., Jr. 1959. "Legislative Control." In *Elements of Public Administration,* ed. Fritz Morstein Marx, 312–336. Englewood Cliffs, NJ: Prentice-Hall.

Kinder, Douglas Clark. 1989. "Nativism, Cultural Conflict, Drug Control: United States and Latin American Antinarcotics Diplomacy through 1965." In Mabry, 1989b, 11–26.

Kinder, Douglas Clark. 1991. "Shutting Out the Evil: Nativism and Narcotics Control in the United States." *Journal of Policy History* 3: 468–494.

King, Rufus. 1953. "The Narcotics Bureau and the Harrison Act: Jailing the Healers and the Sick." *Yale Law Journal* 62: 736–750.

King, Rufus. 1972. *The Drug Hang-up: America's Fifty Year Folly.* New York: W. W. Norton.

Kleiman, Mark A. R. 1989. *Marijuana: Costs of Abuse, Costs of Control.* New York: Greenwood Press.

Kleiman, Mark A. R. 1992. *Against Excess: Drug Policy for Results.* New York: Basic Books.

Kleiman, Mark A. R., and Kerry D. Smith. 1990. "State and Local Drug Enforcement: In Search of a Strategy." In Tonry and Wilson, 1990, 69–108.

Kolb, Lawrence. 1962. *Drug Addiction: A Medical Problem.* Springfield, IL: Charles C. Thomas Publisher.

Kraus, Melvyn B., and Edward P. Lazear. 1991. *Searching for Alternatives: Drug-Control Policy in the United States.* Stanford, CA: Hoover Institution Press.

Krivanek, Jara. 1988. *Heroin: Myths and Reality.* Boston: Allen and Unwin.

Kyvig, David E. 1979. *Repealing National Prohibition.* Chicago: University of Chicago Press.

Kyvig, David E. 1985a. "Sober Thoughts: Myths and Realities of National Prohibition After Fifty Years." In Kyvig, 1985b, 3–20.

Kyvig, David E., ed. 1985b. *Law, Alcohol and Order: Perspectives on National Prohibition.* Westport, CT: Greenwood Press.

Lawrence, Christine C., and Stephen Gettinger. 1988. "Experts Skeptical of Congress' Anti-Drug Effort." *Congressional Quarterly Weekly,* June 25, 1711–1714.

Lee, Rensselaer W., III. 1985–86. "The Latin American Drug Connection." *Foreign Policy* 61: 142–159.

Lender, Mark Edward. 1985. "A Historian and Repeal." In Kyvig, 1985b, 177–205.

Lender, Mark Edward, and James Kirby Martin. 1987. *Drinking in America: A History.* New York: The Free Press.

Levine, Harry Gene. 1984. "What Is an Alcohol-Related Problem? (Or, What Are People Talking about When They Refer to Alcohol Problems?)" *Journal of Drug Issues* (Winter): 45–60.

Lewis, Alan. 1992. *The Psychology of Taxing.* Oxford: Robertson Press.

Lewis-Beck, Michael S. 1980. *Applied Regression: An Introduction.* Beverly Hills, CA: Sage Publications.

Lewis-Beck, Michael S. 1986. "Interrupted Time Series," In *New Tools for Social Scientists,* ed. William D. Berry and Michael S. Lewis-Beck, 209–240. Beverly Hills, CA: Sage Publications.

Lewis-Beck, Michael S., and John R. Alford. 1980. "Can Government Regulate Safety?" *American Political Science Review* 74: 745–756.

Lindesmith, Alfred R. 1965. *The Addict and the Law.* Bloomington, IN: University of Indiana Press.

Lindesmith, Alfred R. 1981. "The Case for Heroin Maintenance." In Lowinson and Ruiz, 1981, 339–343.

Loeb, Ben F. 1978. "Relationship of State Law to Per Capita Drinking." In Ewing and Rouse, 1978, 219–238.

Louis Harris and Associates. 1989. *Business Week/Harris Executive Poll.* August.

Lowery, David. 1987. "Electoral Stress and Revenue Structures in the American States: Searching for the Elusive Fiscal Illusion." *American Politics Quarterly* 15: 5–47.

Lowery, David, and Virginia Gray. 1990. "The Corporatist Foundations of State Industrial Policy." *Social Science Quarterly* 71: 3–24.

Lowery, David, and Lee Sigelman. 1981. "Understanding the Tax Revolt: Eight Explanations." *American Political Science Review* 75: 963–974.

Lowinger, Paul. 1981. "Why Do We Have Drug Abuse—Economic and Political Basis." In Lowinson and Ruiz, 1981, 614–618.

Lowinson, Joyce H., and Pedro Ruiz, eds. 1981. *Substance Abuse: Clinical Problems and Perspectives.* Baltimore: Williams and Wilkins.

Lund, Adrian K., and Arthur C. Wolfe. 1991. "Changes in the Incidence of Alcohol-Impaired Driving in the United States, 1973–1986." *Journal of Studies on Alcohol* 52: 293–301.

Luttbeg, Norman, and Harmon Zeigler. 1966. "Attitude Consensus and Conflict in an Interest Group." *American Political Science Review* 60: 655–665.

Mabry, Donald. 1988. "The US Military and the War on Drugs in Latin America." *Journal of Interamerican Studies and World Affairs* 30: 53–76.

Mabry, Donald J. 1989a. "Narcotics and National Security." In Mabry, 1989b, 3–10.

Mabry, Donald J., ed. 1989b. *The Latin American Narcotics Trade and U.S. National Security.* New York: Greenwood Press.

McCabe, John M. 1986. "Uniform State Laws: 1984–85." In *Book of the States.* 1986–87 edition, 324–331. Lexington, KY: Council of State Governments.

McCoy, Alfred W. 1972. *The Politics of Heroin in Southeast Asia.* New York: Harper and Row.

McCoy, Alfred W. 1974. "The Politics of the Poppy in Indochina." In Simmons and Said, 1974b, 113–138.

McShana, Larry. 1990. "Heroin Trail: US Seizures Indicate Mounting Traffic." *Milwaukee Journal,* May 6, J1, J8.

McWilliams, John C. 1990. *The Protectors: Harry J. Anslinger and the Federal Bureau of Narcotics, 1930–1962.* Newark: University of Delaware Press.

McWilliams, John C. 1991. "Through the Past Darkly: The Politics and Policies of America's Drug War." *Journal of Policy History* 3: 356–392.

Madison Capital Times. 1990. "US Likely to Sharply Hike Estimate of World Cocaine." February 17, 12.

Maguire, Kathleen, and Timothy J. Flanagan. 1991. *Source Book of Criminal Justice Statistics—1990.* Washington, DC: U.S. Government Printing Office.

Makowsky, Cheryl R., and Paul C. Whitehead. 1991. "Advertising and Alcohol Sales: A Legal Impact Study." *Journal of Studies on Alcohol* 52: 555–564.

Mann, Robert E., Reginald G. Smart, Lise Anglin, and Edward M. Adlaf. 1991. "Reductions in Cirrhosis Deaths in the United States: Associations with Per Capita Consumption and AA Membership." *Journal of Studies on Alcohol* 52: 361–365.

Marshall, Jonathan. 1987. "Drugs and United States Foreign Policy." In Hamowy, 1987b, 37–71.

Marshall, Jonathan. 1992. "Targeting the Drugs, Wounding the Cities." *Washington Post National Weekly Edition,* May 25, 23.

Martz, Larry. 1990. "A Dirty Drug Secret: Hyping Instant Addiction Doesn't Help." *Newsweek* 115 (February 19), 74–75.

Mathews, Mark. 1990. "Drug Agents Face, Fight Temptations." *Milwaukee Journal,* April 8, J1.

Mazmanian, Daniel A., and Paul A. Sabatier. 1989. *Implementation and Public Policy with a New Postscript.* New York: University Press of America.

Meier, Kenneth J. 1985. *Regulation: Politics, Bureaucracy, and Economics.* New York: St. Martin's Press.

Meier, Kenneth J. 1987. "The Political Economy of Consumer Protection." *Western Political Quarterly* 40: 343–360.

Meier, Kenneth J. 1988. *The Political Economy of Regulation: The Case of Insurance.* Albany: State University of New York Press.

Meier, Kenneth J. 1992. "The Politics of Drug Abuse: Laws, Implementation, Conse-
quences." *Western Political Quarterly* 45: 41–70.
Meier, Kenneth J. 1993. *Politics and the Bureaucracy.* 3rd Edition. Monterey, CA:
Brooks/Cole.
Meier, Kenneth J., and Cathy M. Johnson. 1990. "The Politics of Demon Rum." *Ameri-
can Politics Quarterly* 18: 404–429.
Meier, Kenneth J., and David R. Morgan. 1982. "Citizen Compliance with Public Policy:
The National Maximum Speed Law." *Western Political Quarterly* 25: 258–273.
Merz, Charles. 1931. *The Dry Decade.* Garden City, NY: Doubleday, Doran and Com-
pany.
Meyer, Donald B. 1960. *The Protestant Search for Political Realism, 1919–1941.* Berke-
ley: University of California Press.
Meyers, Erik J. 1980. "American Heroin Policy: Some Alternatives." In Drug Abuse
Council, 1980, 190–247.
Miles, Rufus E. 1978. "The Origin and Meaning of Miles' Law." *Public Administration
Review* 38: 399–403.
Miller, Mark. 1990. "Bennett's New Optimism: The Evidence is Mixed." *Newsweek* 115
(March 12), 32.
Miller, Robert M. 1958. *American Protestantism and Social Issues, 1919–1939.* Chapel
Hill: University of North Carolina Press.
Milwaukee Journal. 1989. "U.S. Steps Up Campaign against Drunken Driving." May 31,
A5.
Milwaukee Journal. 1990a. "Many Doubt Data on Declining Use of Cocaine." May 17,
A11.
Milwaukee Journal. 1990b. "Red Alert on Drugs: Lipstick Dye Can Kill Marijuana."
March 10, A1.
Milwaukee Journal. 1990c. "Teen Drug Use Still Declining." February 14, A8.
Milwaukee Journal. 1990d. "US Seizing More Assets in War against Drugs." April 15,
A13.
Milwaukee Journal. 1992a. "Drug Squad Takes Money from Drivers." June 15, A3.
Milwaukee Journal. 1992b. "Drug War Seen as War on Blacks." April 29, A14.
Milwaukee Journal. 1992c. "Mexico Praises Doctor's Acquittal: Camarena Case." De-
cember 15, A14.
Milwaukee Journal. 1992d. "Suspects' Kidnaping Ruled OK." June 15, A1, A9.
Milwaukee Sentinel. 1989. "US Seeks to Crack Down on Marijuana Production." October
2, 2.
Milwaukee Sentinel. 1990. "Purity of Cacaine Sold in US Down." May 22, 2.
Miron, Jeffrey A., and Jeffrey Zwiebel. 1991a. "Alcohol Consumption during Prohibi-
tion." *American Economic Review* 81: 240–247.
Miron, Jeffrey A., and Jeffrey Zwiebel. 1991b. "Alcohol Consumption during Prohibi-
tion." National Bureau of Economic Research, Inc., Working Paper No. 3675.
Mladenka, Kenneth R. 1981. "Citizen Demands and Urban Services." *American Journal
of Political Science* 24: 556–583.
Moe, Terry M. 1985. "Control and Feedback in Economic Regulation: The Case of the
NLRB." *American Political Science Review* 79: 1097–1117.
Moore, Mark H. 1990. "Supply Reduction and Drug Law Enforcement." In Tonry and
Wilson, 1990, 109–158.
Moore, Mark H., and Mark A. R. Kleiman. 1989. *The Police and Drugs.* Washington,
DC: National Institute of Justice.
Moore, Mark H., and Dean R. Gerstein, eds. 1981. *Alcohol and Public Policy.* New
York: Gardner Press.

Moore, W. John. 1987. "No Quick Fix." *National Journal* 19 (November 21): 2954–2959.

Moore, W. John. 1989. "Dissenters in the Drug War." *National Journal* 21 (November 4): 2692–2695.

Moore, W. John. 1990. "Why Drug Czar Turned Upbeat." *National Journal* 22 (February 3): 279.

Moore, W. John. 1992. "An Industry on the Rocks." *National Journal* 24 (January 4): 8–12.

Morgan, John P. 1991. "Prohibition Is Perverse Policy: What Was True in 1933 Is True Now." In Krauss and Lazear, 1991, 405–423.

Morgan, Patricia A. 1978. "The Legislation of Drug Law: Economic Crisis and Social Control." *Journal of Drug Issues* 8: 53–62.

Morganthau, Tom. 1990. "Uncivil Liberties?" *Newsweek* 115 (April 23), 18–20.

Murray, Robert K. 1955. *Red Scare: A Study of National Hysteria, 1919–1920.* Minneapolis: University of Minnesota Press.

Musto, David F. 1972. "The Marihuana Tax Act of 1937." *Archives of General Psychiatry* 26: 101–108.

Musto, David F. 1973. *The American Disease: Origins of Narcotic Control.* New Haven: Yale University Press.

Musto, David F. 1981. "Review of Narcotic Control Efforts in the United States." In Lowinson and Ruiz, 1981, 3–18.

Musto, David F. 1987. *The American Disease: Origins of Narcotic Control.* Revised edition. New Haven: Yale University Press.

Nadel, Mark V. 1971. *The Politics of Consumer Protection.* Indianapolis: Bobbs-Merrill.

Nadelmann, Ethan A. 1988. "The Case for Legalization." *Public Interest* 23: 3–31.

Nahas, Gabriel G. 1973. *Marihuana—Deceptive Weed.* New York: Raven Press.

Nannes, Allan S. 1974. "United Nations Activities in International Drug Control." In Simmons and Said, 1974b, 261–280.

National Highway Traffic Safety Administration. 1988. *Fatal Accident Reporting System 1986.* Washington, DC: Department of Transportation.

National Institute of Justice. 1990. *DUF: 1988 Drug Use Forecasting Annual Report.* Washington, DC: U.S. Department of Justice.

National Institute on Alcohol Abuse and Alcoholism. 1975. *The Economic Costs of Alcoholism.* Rockville, MD: NIAAA.

National Institute on Alcohol Abuse and Alcoholism (NIAAA). 1990. *Seventh Special Report to the U.S. Congress on Alcohol and Health.* Washington, DC: U.S. Department of Health and Human Services.

National Institute on Drug Abuse. Various years. *National Household Survey on Drug Abuse.* Washington, DC: NIDA.

Nelli, Humbert S. 1985. "American Syndicate Crime: A Legacy of Prohibition." In Kyvig, 1985b, 123–138.

Nice, David C. 1988. "State Deregulation of Intimate Behavior." *Social Science Quarterly* 69: 203–211.

Niskanen, William. 1971. *Bureaucracy and Representative Government.* Chicago: Aldine.

Noll, Roger G., and Bruce M. Owen. 1983. *The Political Economy of Deregulation.* Washington, DC: American Enterprise Institute.

Nordlinger, Eric A. 1981. *On the Autonomy of the Democratic State.* Cambridge, MA: MIT Press.

Odegard, Peter H. 1928. *Pressure Politics: The Story of the Anti-Saloon League.* New York: Columbia University Press.

Office of Justice Programs. 1988. *Sourcebook of Criminal Justice Statistics—1987.* Washington, DC: Department of Justice.

Office of Justice Programs. 1989. *Sourcebook of Criminal Justice Statistics—1988.* Washington, DC: Department of Justice, Office of Justice Programs, Bureau of Justice Statistics.

Olson, Mancur. 1965. *The Logic of Collective Action.* Cambridge, MA: Harvard University Press.

O'Malley, Patrick M., and Alexander C. Wagenaar. 1991. "Effects of Minimum Drinking Age Laws on Alcohol Use, Related Behaviors and Traffic Crash Involvement among American Youth: 1976–1987." *Journal of Studies on Alcohol* 52: 478–491.

Ornstein, Stanley I., and Dominique M. Hanssens. 1985. "Alcohol Control Laws and the Consumption of Distilled Spirits and Beer." *Journal of Consumer Research* 12: 200–213.

Ostrowski, James. 1989. "Thinking about Drug Legalization." *Cato Institute Policy Analysis.* Washington, DC: Cato Institute.

O'Toole, Lawrence J., and Robert S. Mountjoy. 1984. "Interorganizational Policy Implementation." *Public Administration Review* 44: 491–503.

Peat, Marwick, and Mitchell. 1977. *Marijuana: A Study of State Policies and Penalties.* Washington, DC: National Governors Conference.

Pekkanen, John R. 1980. "Drug Law Enforcement Efforts." In Drug Abuse Council, 1980, 63–94.

Peters, B. Guy. 1986. *American Public Policy.* Chatham, NJ: Chatham House Publishers.

Peters, B. Guy, and Brian W. Hogwood. 1985. "In Search of the Issue Attention Cycle." *Journal of Politics* 47: 238–253.

Pike, Thomas R. 1988. "Hearing Room Dreams and the Birth of the NIAAA." *Alcohol Health and Research World* 12: 268–269.

Pogue, Thomas F., and Larry G. Sgontz, 1989. "Taxing to Control Social Costs: The Case of Alcohol." *American Economic Review* 79: 235–243.

Popham, Robert, Wolfgang Schmidt, and Jan de Lint. 1978. "Government Control Measures to Prevent Hazardous Drinking." In Ewing and Rouse, 1978, 239–266.

Posner, Richard A. 1974. "Theories of Economic Regulation." *Bell Journal of Economics and Management Science* 5: 337–352.

Poveda, Tony. 1990. *The FBI in Transition: Lawlessness and Reform.* Pacific Grove, CA: Brooks/Cole.

Public Integrity Section. 1988. *Report to Congress.* Washington, DC: Public Integrity Section, Criminal Division, U.S. Department of Justice.

Public Opinion. 1989. "Attitudes about Alcohol." May/June, 30–34.

Quinn, Terry. 1974. "The Congressional Response to the International Drug Control Problem." In Simmons and Said, 1974b, 49–64.

Quirk, Paul J. 1981. *Industry Influence in Federal Regulatory Agencies.* Princeton: Princeton University Press.

Rachal, Patricia. 1982. *Federal Narcotics Enforcement: Reorganization and Reform.* Boston: Auburn House.

Reagan, Michael D. 1987. *Regulation: The Politics of Policy.* Boston: Little, Brown.

Reuter, Peter. 1984. "The (continued) Vitality of Mythical Numbers." *The Public Interest* 75: 135–147.

Reuter, Peter. 1988. "Can the Borders Be Sealed?" *The Public Interest* 123: 51–65.

Reuter, Peter, Gordon Crawford, and Jonathan Cave. 1988. *Sealing the Boarders: The Effects of Increased Military Participation in Drug Interdiction.* Santa Monica, CA: Rand Corporation.

Ripley, Randall B., and Grace A. Franklin. 1991. *Congress, the Bureaucracy, and Public Policy.* Pacific Grove, CA: Brooks/Cole.

Roizen, J. 1982. "Estimating Alcohol Involvement in Serious Events." In National Institute of Alcohol Abuse and Alcoholism, *Alcohol Consumption and Related Problems,* 179–219. Washington, DC: Department of Health and Human Services.

Room, Robin. 1978. "Evaluating the Effect of Drinking Laws on Drinking." In Ewing and Rouse, 1978, 267–289.

Rosenberg, Mark B. 1988. "Narcos and Politicos: The Politics of Drug Trafficking in Honduras." *Journal of Interamerican Studies and World Affairs* 30: 143–165.

Rosenthal, Michael P. 1977. "Legislative Response to Marihuana: When the Shoe Pinches Enough." *Journal of Drug Issues* 7: 61–77.

Ross, H. Laurence. 1982. *Deterring the Drinking Driver.* Lexington, MA: Lexington Books.

Rourke, Francis E. 1984. *Bureaucracy, Politics, and Public Policy.* 3rd edition. Boston: Little, Brown.

Rumbarger, John J. 1989. *Profits, Power, and Prohibition: Alcohol Reform and the Industrialization of America.* Albany: State University of New York Press.

Rupert, James, and Steve Coll. 1990. "Guerrillas for God, Heroin Dealers for Man." *Washington Post National Weekly Edition,* May 21, 15.

Rush, Brian D., Louis Gliksman, and Robert Brook. 1986. "Alcohol Availability, Alcohol Consumption and Alcohol-Related Damage. 1. The Distribution of Consumption Model." *Journal of Studies on Alcohol* 47: 1–10.

Sabatier, Paul A. 1988. "An Advocacy Coalition Framework of Policy Change and the Role of Policy-oriented Learning Therein." *Policy Sciences* 21: 129–68.

Sabatier, Paul A., and Susan M. McLaughlin. 1988. "Belief Congruence of Governmental and Interest Group Elites with Their Constituencies." *American Politics Quarterly* 16: 61–98.

Sabatier, Paul A., and Susan M. McLaughlin. 1990. "Belief Congruence between Interest Group Leaders and Members." *Journal of Politics* 52: 914–938.

Sabatier, Paul A., and Daniel Mazmanian. 1981. *Effective Policy Implementation.* Lexington, MA: Lexington Books.

Saffer, Henry, and Michael Grossman. 1987. "Drinking Age Laws and Highway Mortality Rates: Cause and Effect." *Economic Inquiry* 30: 403–417.

Salholz, Eloise. 1990. "The 'Walled Cities' of LA." *Newsweek* 115 (May 14), 24–25.

Schaller, Michael. 1973. "The Federal Prohibition of Marijuana." In *The Politics of Moral Behavior,* ed. K. Austin Kerr, 208–221. Reading, MA: Addison-Wesley Publishing Company.

Schmeckebier, Laurence F. 1929. *The Bureau of Prohibition.* Washington, DC: The Brookings Institution.

Schmidt, Wolfgang, and Jan de Lint. 1973. "The Mortality of Alcoholic People." *Alcohol and Health World.* Washington, DC: U.S Government Printing Office, 16–20.

Scholz, John T., and Feng Heng Wei. 1986. "Regulatory Enforcement in a Federalist System." *American Political Science Review* 80: 1249–1270.

Schwartz, John. 1988. *America's Hidden Success.* Revised edition. New York: Norton.

Schweitzer, Stuart O., Michael D. Intriligator, and Hossein Salehi. 1983. "Alcoholism: An Econometric Model of Its Causes, Its Effects and Its Control." In Grant, Plant, and Williams, 1983, 107–127.

Seidman, Harold, and Robert Gilmour. 1986. *Politics, Position, and Power.* Boston: Little, Brown.

Sells, S. B. 1983. "Drugs and Crime: Treatment and Rehabilitation." In Kadish, 1983, 652–663.

Sharp, Elaine B. 1992. "Interest Groups and Symbolic Policy Formation: The Case of Anti-Drug Policy." Mimeo, University of Kansas.

Shedler, Jonathan, and Jack Block. 1990. "Adolescent Drug Use and Psychological Health." *American Psychologist* 45: 612–630.

Simmons, Luiz R. S., and Abdul A. Said. 1974a. "The Politics of Addiction." In Simmons and Said, 1974b, 3–48.

Simmons, Luiz R. S., and Abdul A. Said, eds. 1974b. *Drugs, Politics, and Diplomacy: The International Connection.* Beverly Hills, CA: Sage Publications.

Simon, Herbert A. 1969. *Sciences of the Artificial.* Cambridge, MA: MIT Press.

Simon, Julian L. 1966. "The Economic Effects of State Monopoly of Packaged-Liquor Retailing." *Journal of Political Economy* 74: 188–194.

Singer, Max. 1971. "The Vitality of Mythical Numbers." *The Public Interest* 23: 3–9.

Single, Eric W. 1989. "The Impact of Marijuana Decriminalization: An Update." *Journal of Public Health Policy* (Winter): 456–466.

Skiba, Katherine M. 1990a. "Epilepsy Drug May Help Stave Off Cravings." *Milwaukee Journal,* May 9, A17.

Skiba, Katherine M. 1990b. "Scientists Seek Drugs That Work Like Those for Heroin Treatment." *Milwaukee Journal,* May 7, b5.

Skiba, Katherine M., and Joel Dresang. 1992. "Area Employers Win Praise from US Drug Czar." *Milwaukee Journal,* May 19, B1, B6.

Skocpol, Theda, and Kenneth Finegold. 1982. "State Capacity and Economic Intervention in the Early New Deal." *Political Science Quarterly* 97: 255–278.

Skowronek, Stephen. 1982. *Building a New American State.* Cambridge: Cambridge University Press.

Sloman, Larry. 1979. *Reefer Madness: The History of Marijuana in America.* Indianapolis: Bobbs-Merrill Company.

Smart, Reginald G. 1988. "Does Alcohol Advertising Affect Overall Consumption? A Review of Empirical Studies." *Journal of Studies on Alcohol* 49: 314–323.

Smart, Reginald G., and Robert E. Mann. 1991. "Factors in Recent Reductions in Liver Cirrhosis Deaths." *Journal of Studies on Alcohol* 52: 232–240.

Smith, Peter H. 1992. *Drug Policy in the Americas.* Boulder, CO: Westview Press.

Smithers, R. Brinkley. 1988. "Making It Happen: Advocacy for the Hughes Act." *Alcohol Health and Research World* 12: 271–272.

Solomon, Rayman L. 1985. "Regulating the Regulators: Prohibition Enforcement in the Seventh Circuit." In Kyvig, 1985b, 81–96.

Springen, Karen. 1990. "Have the Good Guys Gone Bad?" *Newsweek* 115 (May 14), 24.

Stellwagen, Lindsey D. 1985. *Use of Forfeiture Sanctions in Drug Cases.* Washington, DC: National Institute of Justice.

Stevens, Jan. 1988. *Storming Heaven: LSD and the American Dream.* New York: Harper and Row.

Stigler, George J. 1971. "The Theory of Economic Regulation." *Bell Journal of Economics and Management Science* 2: 3–21.

Stoil, Michael J. 1987. "Southern Peach Brandy versus Northern Hard Cider." *Alcohol Health and Research World* 11: 34–39.

Stone, Alan. 1982. *Regulation and Its Alternatives.* Washington, DC: Congressional Quarterly Press.

Stover, Robert V., and Don W. Brown. 1975. "Understanding Compliance and Noncompliance with the Law." *Social Science Quarterly* 56: 363–375.

Strickland, Donald E. 1983. "Advertising Exposure, Alcohol Consumption and the Misuse of Alcohol." In Grant, Plant, and Williams, 1983, 201–222.

Taylor, Paul. 1991a. "Still Our Drug of Choice." *Washington Post National Weekly Edition,* October 7, 37.

Taylor, Paul. 1991b. "Prohibition among the Young." *Washington Post National Weekly Edition,* November 11, 32.

Terris, Milton. 1967. "Epidemiology of Cirrhosis of the Liver: National Mortality Data." *American Journal of Public Health* 57: 2076–2088.

Thompson, Frank J., and Michael J. Scicchitano. 1987. "State Implementation and Federal Enforcement Priorities." *Administration and Society* 19: 95–124.

Thompson, James D. 1967. *Organizations in Action*. New York: McGraw-Hill.

Thornton, Mark. 1991. *The Economics of Prohibition*. Salt Lake City: University of Utah Press.

Timberlake, James H. 1963. *Prohibition and the Progressive Movement 1900–1920*. Cambridge, MA: Harvard University Press.

Tonry, Michael, and James Q. Wilson. 1990. *Drugs and Crime*. Chicago: University of Chicago Press.

Trebach, Arnold S. 1982. *The Heroin Solution*. New Haven: Yale University Press.

Tufte, Edward R. 1974. *Data Analysis for Politics and Policy*. Englewood Cliffs, NJ: Prentice-Hall.

U.S. Senate. 1990. *Hard-Core Cocaine Addicts: Measuring—and Fighting—the Epidemic*. Washington, DC: Committee on the Judiciary, S. Prt. 101–6.

Versfelt, David S. 1975. "The Impact of the Twenty-first Amendment on State Authority to Control Intoxicating Liquors." *Columbia Law Review* 1975: 1578–1610.

Viscusi, W. Kip. 1983. *Risk by Choice*. Cambridge, MA: Harvard University Press.

Viscusi, W. Kip. 1984. *Regulating Consumer Product Safety*. Washington, DC: American Enterprise Institute.

Wagenaar, Alexander C., and Harold D. Holder. 1991. "A Change from Public to Private Sale of Wine: Results from Natural Experiments in Iowa and West Virginia." *Journal of Studies on Alcohol* 52: 162–173.

Walker, William O., III. 1979. *Drug Control in the Americas*. Albuquerque: University of New Mexico Press.

Walker, William O., III. 1989. *Drug Control in the Americas*. Revised edition. Albuquerque: University of New Mexico Press.

Warburton, Clark. 1932. *The Economic Results of Prohibition*. New York: Columbia University Press.

Warner, Roger. 1986. *Invisible Hand: The Marijuana Business*. New York: Beech Tree Books.

Watts, Thomas D. 1982. "Three Traditions in Social Thought on Alcoholism." *International Journal of the Addictions* 17: 1231–1239.

Weingast, Barry R., and Mark J. Moran. 1983. "Bureaucratic Discretion or Congressional Control? Regulatory Policymaking by the Federal Trade Commission," *Journal of Political Economy* 91: 765–800.

Weinstein, Barbara. 1982. "The Michigan Liquor Control Commission and the Taxation of Alcoholic Beverages." In Brazer and Laren, 1982b, 720–755.

Weisner, Constance M. 1983. "The Alcohol Treatment System and Social Control: A Study in Institutional Change." *Journal of Drug Issues* (Winter): 117–133.

White House. 1990. *National Drug Control Strategy*. Washington, DC: White House.

Wickersham Commission. 1931. *U.S. National Commission on Law Observance and Enforcement. Enforcement of the Prohibition Laws of the United States*. 71st Congress, 3rd Session, House Document 722.

Wilson, James Q. 1966. "Corruption: The Shame of the States." *The Public Interest* 1: 28–38.

Wilson, James Q. 1980. *The Politics of Regulation*. New York: Basic Books.

Wilson, James Q. 1983. *Thinking about Crime*. New York: Basic Books.

Wish, Eric D., and Bruce D. Johnson. 1986. "The Impact of Substance Abuse on Criminal Careers." In *Criminal Careers and "Career Criminals,"* ed. Alfred Blumstein,

Jacqueline Cohen, Jeffrey A. Roth, and Christy A. Visher, 52–88. Washington, DC: National Academy Press.

Wisotsky, Steven. 1990. *Beyond the War on Drugs.* Buffalo, NY: Prometheus Books.

Wood, B. Dan. 1988. "Principals, Bureaucrats, and Responsiveness in Clean Air Enforcements." *American Political Science Review* 82: 213–234.

Wood, B. Dan. 1990. "Does Politics Make a Difference at the EEOC?" *American Journal of Political Science* 34: 503–530.

Wood, B. Dan, and James E. Anderson. 1991. "The Politics (or Unpolitics) of U.S. Antitrust Regulation." Paper presented at the annual meeting of the Midwest Political Science Association, Chicago.

Wood, B. Dan, and Richard W. Waterman. 1991. "The Dynamics of Political Control of the Bureaucracy." *American Political Science Review* 85: 801–828.

Woodiwiss, Michael. 1988. *Crime, Crusades, and Corruption: Prohibitions in the United States, 1900–1987.* London: Pinter Publishers.

Wright, Gerald C., Robert S. Erikson, and John. P. McIver. 1985. "Measuring State Partisanship and Ideology with Survey Data." *Journal of Politics* 47: 469–489.

Wright, Lynda. 1990. "Farrakhan's Mission: Fighting the Drug War—His Way." *Newsweek* 115 (March 19), 25.

Zador, Paul L., Adrian K. Lund, Michele Fields, and Karen Weinberg. 1989. "Fatal Crash Involvement and Laws against Alcohol-Impaired Driving." *Journal of Public Health Policy* (Winter): 467–475.

Zahn, Margaret A. 1980. "Homicide in the Twentieth Century United States." In *History and Crime: Implications for Criminal Justice Policy,* ed. James A. Inciardi and Charles E. Faupel, 111–131. Beverly Hills, CA: Sage Publications.

Zeese, Kevin B. 1991. "Drug War Forever?" In Krauss and Lazear, 1991, 251–270.

Zimring, Franklin E., and Gordon Hawkins. 1992. *The Search for Rational Drug Control.* New York: Cambridge University Press.

Index

Abuse of citizens: by drug control
agencies, 21, 47–8, 55; by Federal
Bureau of Narcotics, 40–1; under the
Harrison Act, 28–30; by Prohibition
Unit, 145
Administrative per se laws, 168
Alcohol consumption: and alcohol related
arrests, 191; and cirrhosis deaths,
166, 196; and crime, 198–204,
234–7; current levels of, 170–1;
determinants of, 187–90, 225–7;
impact on health, 209; lack of policy
impact on, 227; and murder rates,
201; and prison populations, 194,
233, 235; during prohibition, 148;
social costs of, 209; and suicide rates,
198; and status crimes, 201–3; and
traffic fatalities, 198; and violent
crimes 201, 202
Alcohol industries: conflict within, 10, 11,
191, 212, 246; definition of, 10, 71;
and drunk driving arrests, 223;
impact on alcohol taxes, 183; impact
on drug law enforcement, 116;
interest in drug policy, 104, 63n22;
lack of influence of, 246; and the
Marijuana Tax Act, 108; measures of,
178; opposition to prohibition, 137;
support for alcoholism as a disease, 163
Alcohol related arrests: determinants of,
223–5; impact on drunk driving, 231;
for drunk driving, 168; and suicide
rates, 198
Alcohol sales regulation: definition of,
213–4; determinants of, 216–8;
impact on drunk driving, 231; state
policies, 160–1

Alcohol tax policy: 16, 140, 214; and
alcohol consumption, 189; and
alcohol related arrests, 191;
determinants of, 181–4, 185; equity
of, 158; federal, 155–8; impact on
prisons, 194; state taxes, 157, 162,
183–4; impact on suicide rates, 229
Alcohol treatment policy, 162–5
Alcohol labeling programs, 169
Alcoholics anonymous, 9, 105, 162–3,
175n25, 212, 238n5
Alcoholism as a disease, 162–5
American Bar Association, 41, 153
American Federation of Labor, 153
American Legion, 153
American Medical Association, 41;
support for alcohol as a disease, 163
Anslinger, Harry: 14; appointment of, 32;
as bureaucratic leader, 72; as
entrepreneur, 103–4; forced
retirement of, 43; role in intelligence
networks, 63n17; role in Marijuana
Tax Act, 34–5; role in foreign policy,
42
Anti-Saloon League: 180, 189, 211, 212;
and the Jones Act, 146; and repeal,
148–9; role in prohibition movement,
136–8; as tool of capitalist elite,
173n1
Arrests: by type of drug, 57–9;
determinants of federal drug, 76–81;
determinants of state drug, 82, 84–6,
114–5; determinants of federal
marijuana, 78–9; determinants of
state marijuana, 84, 86; and drug
prices, 90; impact on state prison
population, 87; impact on federal

Arrests *(continued)*
prison population, 87; Harrison Act, 28–30. *See also* Alcohol related arrests
Asset seizures: 50; and civil rights, 55
Association Against the Prohibition Amendment, 150–1
Attitudes: toward alcohol use, 211; toward alcohol use, 70. *See also* Public opinion
Autonomy: Drug Enforcement Administrations's lack of, 71; of policy actors, 5, 244–5

Barbiturates: Anslinger declines control over, 39
Behavioral Risk Factor Surveillance System, 231–4
Bennett, William: 14, 72, 104; lobbying for stronger state laws, 109
Bias, Len, 10, 51, 70
Biden, Joseph: 54, 104; as drug policy entrepreneur, 69, 107
Boggs Act, 39
Boggs, Hale, as policy entrepreneur, 107
Boggs-Daniel Act, 40
Boole, Ella, 150
Bootlegging: after prohibition, 148, 149; currently, 227; during prohibition, 141
Bourne, Peter, 48
Brown, Edmund G., 42
Budgets: determinants of drug agency's, 73–4; as limit on bureaucracy, 68
Bureau leadership, impact on state drug arrests, 84
Bureau of Alcohol Tobacco and Firearms (BATF), 159, 170, 181
Bureaucracy: impact on controlled substance laws, 112; implementing the Harrison Act, 25–7; influence on public policy, 244; mediating the impact of harsh laws, 123; as political institution, 19n4; role in policy, 13
Bureaucratic competition: 15; and alcohol policy, 213
Bureaucratic imperialism, 21
Bush, George, 50, 107

Cannabis Eradication Program, 56
Cannon, James, 149
Capacity, bureaucratic, definition, 14
Capone, Al, 140
Carter, Jimmy, 48

Central Intelligence Agency, role in drug trafficking, 46, 64n36
Cherrington, Ernest, 149
China, Peoples Republic of: alleged source of drugs, 39, 46, 62n15
Choate, Joseph, 156
Churches: support for alcohol as a disease, 163; and alcohol policy, 177; in prohibition movement, 136, 137; role in interest aggregation, 9. *See also* Religion
Cirrhosis, 166; determinants of, 196–7, 228–30
Citizen forces: definition, 7; advantages in morality politics, 7; influence on morality policies, 245; measures of, 177
Citizen participation, lack of limits on, 5
Civil liberties, impact of drug wars on, 249–50
Clinton, Bill, 170
Cocaine: arrests as not a deterrent to use, 90; determinants of arrests, 116–7; determinants of use, 93; estimates of consumption, 131n2; medical uses, 23
Commission on Narcotic and Drug Abuse, 42
Comprehensive Drug Abuse Prevention and Control Act, 43
Congress: control of public policy, 67; influence on drug agency budgets, 74; influence on drug agency's personnel, 76; influence on drug penalties, 80; influence on federal drug arrest rates, 78; influence on federal prison populations, 87; influence on federal marijuana arrests, 78
Contras and drug trafficking, 65n47
Controlled substance laws, determinants of, 112–3
Conyers, John, 170
Corruption: and drug enforcement, 21, 47, 30, 32, 55–6, 250; and alcohol enforcement, 141, 144–5
Cost, of alcohol during prohibition, 141
Courts: acquiescence in drug wars, 41; as check on bureaucracy, 69; and the Harrison Act 26–7; impact on drug policy, 12; limiting prosecution, 30; supporting prohibition, 143

Crime: and drug use, 30, 39–40, 45, 95–6, 126–8, 134n30; impact of drug law enforcement on, 127–8; and marijuana use, 34
Cuba, as source of drugs, 51

Decriminalization of marijuana: 104; determinants of, 132n14; movement, 45; impact on use, 254
DeLorean, John, 54, 55
Demand for intoxication, 8, 252
Demand for alcohol: 177; measure of, 211
Design problems of morality policies, 246–7
Deterrence: and drunk driving, 168; impact on marijuana, 93–4; effect on alcohol arrests, 235; theory of, 16, 96, 126
Discretion, of law enforcement agencies, 67, 114
Distilled Spirits Council, 169, 170
Drug addicts: Anslinger's estimates of, 37; estimates in 1920s, 27; estimates in 1950s, 40; estimates in 1969–71, 45; current, 57; in early 20th century, 22, 23
Drug enforcement priorities, 58
Drug free workplace policy, 53
Drug law enforcement, as cause of crime, 250. See crime
Drug laws, failure of, 248–9
Drug policy: costs of, 249–50; as redistributive policy, 4
Drug trafficking, by American allies, 39, 51
Drug treatment clinics, government role in closing, 27
Drug use: determinants of, 91–3; impact on state marijuana laws, 110; state measure of, 105; and treatment clientele, 126
Drug Enforcement Administration (DEA): creation of, 47, 74; and drug penalties, 82; ineffectiveness of, 50; influence on federal marijuana arrests, 80; influence on personnel allocations, 76; as weak agency, 71
Drunk driving: arrests, determinants of, 191, 223–4; measures of, 215–6, 226; rise as a salient issue, 167–9;
Drunk driving policies: determinants of, 219–221; lack of impact on drunk driving, 231
Drunkenness, decriminalization of, 164

Economic theory of crime, 96, 127
Elections, and prohibition enforcement, 147
Employee assistance programs, 164
Enforcement. See Implementation
Entrepreneurial policies, lack of effectiveness, 222
Entrepreneurs: 10; Harry Anslinger as, 14; William Bennett as, 14; impact on controlled substance laws, 112; impact on drunk driving laws, 222; influence on decriminalization of marijuana, 64n35; lesson of prohibition for, 33; problems measuring, 244; as a residual hypothesis, 103, 210; and salient issues, 210; Hamilton Wright as, 24
Everard Breweries v. Day, 144

Federal Alcohol Control Administration, 156
Federal Alcohol Administration Act, 158–9
Federal Bureau of Investigation, role in drug enforcement, 50, 71
Federal Bureau of Narcotics, lost of influence, 42–5
Federalism: impact on drug policy, 15; federal influence on state governments, 30–1, 33, 39, 44, 84, 101n22, 116, 168; and policy experiments, 253; state impact on the federal government, 43, 142
Flexibility of current policy theory, 243
Ford, Gerald, 48
Foreign affairs and drug control: 21,31; and the Nixon drug war, 42, 46
Freud, Sigmund, 23

Glass, Carter, 149

Hague Convention, 24
Harrison Act, 24
Harrison, Francis, 24
Haynes, Roy, 138
Hearst, William Randolph, 153
Heroin arrests: as not a deterrent to use, 90, 93; determinants of, 116–7
Herrick, Myron, 137
Hoover, Herbert, 146, 154
Hoover, J. Edgar, 72
Hughes, Harold, 166
Hunt, Mary, 174n14

Illegal industries: role in politics, 10
Immigration: and alcohol taxes, 183; and drug policy, 70; impact on federal alcohol enforcement, 184; impact on federal drug arrests, 78; impact on state drug arrests, 84, impact on state marijuana arrests, 84; impact on state prison populations, 87
Implementation: 16; as actual policy, 247–8; and alcohol consumption, 189; alcohol laws after prohibition, 159; and bureau autonomy, 245; as changing the impact of laws, 114; determinants of federal alcohol policy implementation, 184–7; federal focus on drug trafficking, 90; of the Harrison Act, 27; impact of laws on drug policies, 119, 122–3; impact on alcohol policies, 176; 224–6; impact of alcohol industry on, 187; impact of partisanship, 187; of the Marijuana Tax Act, 37; need to study, 7; prohibition 142–5; of state alcohol laws, 189–93; of state drug laws 113–5
Income tax, support for prohibition, 139
Indian Hemp Commission, 34
Industrialists, support for prohibition, 137
Information distortion: 21; by Federal Bureau of Narcotics, 41, 42; in passing the Marijuana Tax Act, 34, 35, 36; by National Institute of Drug Abuse, 49
Information Needs, for good public policy, 251
Interdiction, as good politics, 50

Jackson, Jesse, 53
Japan, as alleged source of drugs, 64n30
Jellinek, E.M., 163
Jones Act, 146, 149
Jordan, Hamilton, 64n41
Just Say No campaign, 49
Juveniles, drug arrests of, 116–7

Kefauver hearings, 39
Kennedy John F., 42
Koller, Karl, 23
Kramer, John, 138
Kresge, S.S., 137

LaGuardia Commission, 36
Landon, Alf, 175n22
Law enforcement agencies: measure of, 108; impact on prison population, 125
Lawn, John C., 72
Leadership, bureaucratic, 14, 71–2, 244
Legislation: as control on public policy, 178–9; impact on drug policy, 12; impact on enforcement, 119, 122–3; as limit on bureaucracy, 67. See also Congress
License system of alcohol control, 161
Licensing system, for drug users, 254
Lightner, Candy, 167
Limitations, of morality policies, 251
Linder v. U.S., 26
Literary Digest, 154
Local government, as alcohol regulator, 136
Local option: policy on, 214; as prohibition strategy, 137

Mann, Marty, 163
Marijuana: arrests as deterrent to use, 90; decriminalization of, 45; determinants of use, 93; determinants of state laws on, 109–12; impact on moonshine industry, 160; implementation policies, 123; and the Harrison Act, 25; as medicine, 22, 64n40; misplaced priority on, 21; overemphasis on in Nixon drug war, 48; as political issue, 43
Marijuana arrests, determinants of, 116–7
Marijuana Tax Act: 32–7; provisions of, 35
Marketing, use in drug policy, 253
Martinez, Bob, 53
McCarthy, Joe, 63n28
Measurement, problems of, 243
Medical treatment, and Harrison Act, 25
Military, role in drug policy, 53
Minimum drinking age, 169–70
Misbranding drugs, 23
Monopoly system of alcohol control, 161
Morality policy, as place to find citizen influences, 245
Mothers Against Drunk Driving (MADD), 10 167–9, 170, 175n28, 210, 230
Multiple tests of theory, utility of, 242

Narcotics Division, budget, 31
National Commission on Marijuana and
    Drug Abuse, 44
National Council on Alcoholism (NCA)
    10, 105, 163, 167, 210, 212
National Industrial Recovery Act, 156
National Institute of Drug Abuse, 49, 251
National Institute of Mental Health, role in
    alcohol policy, 165, 166
National Institute on Alcohol Abuse and
    Alcoholism (NIAAA), 164, 166, 167,
    170
National Organization for the Reform of
    Marijuana Laws, 20, 45, 48, 107
National Prohibition Cases, 143
New public health view of alcohol, 167
Nicaragua, as source of drugs, 51
Nixon, Richard, 42; rejects partial
    prohibition of marijuana, 45; war on
    Heroin 45–8
Noriega, Manuel: and asset seizures, 55;
    cited for support in drug war, 51; as
    friend of George Bush, 53, 65n48
Novello, Antonia, 170

Oliphant Herman, 35
Olmstead v *U.S.*, 144
Operation Buccaneer, 46
Operation Intercept, 46
Opium smoking, 23
Opium Poppy Act, 37
Opium Wars, 24
Organized crime and illegal drugs, 56

Paraquat, 46, 48
Parent organizations, in drug policy, 49
Partisanship: and alcohol sales regulation,
    218; and alcohol taxes, 186, 218; and
    drug enforcement personnel, 76; and
    drug policy, 107; and elected chief
    executives, 179; and local option,
    218; as measure of values, 13, 68,
    179; and prohibition, 138; and
    prohibition repeal, 146, 150, 154; and
    treatment policy, 219; impact on state
    marijuana laws, 110; and support for
    law enforcement, 69
Party competition: definition, 13; and
    alcohol policies, 180; and alcohol
    related arrests, 191; and alcohol
    taxes, 183, 218; Anti-Saloon League
    use of, 137; impact on controlled

Party competition *(continued)*
    substance laws, 112; and drug law
    implementation, 116; and drug
    policy, 50–1, 69; and drunk driving
    arrests, 223; impact on state
    marijuana laws, 110
Patronage, and the prohibition agency,
    138, 141
Penalties for drug use, determinants of,
    80–82
Penalties for marijuana offenses,
    determinants of, 82–3
Penalties, in drunk driving cases, 221–2
Personnel: determinants of drug agency's,
    73–5; as prime determinants of
    arrests, 76
Physicians, and drugs 22
Plea bargaining: in alcohol cases, 142; in
    drug cases, 54
Policy entrepreneurs. *See* entrepreneurs
Policy outcomes: definition, 17;
    importance of, 244; need to study, 7
Political forces: definition, 11; measures
    of, 178
Political institutions, definition, 11
President's Commission on Drunk
    Driving, 168, 169
Presidents: control over bureaucracy,
    68–9; influence on public policy, 12;
    influence on federal marijuana
    arrests, 80; impact on state drug
    arrests, 84
Price elasticity, of alcohol, 187
Price of drugs, determinants of, 89–91
Principal agent theory, 67, 245
Prison population: the impact of alcohol
    consumption on, 194–5; affect of
    drug policy on, 86–89; impact of
    Harrison Act on, 30; impact of state
    drug arrests, 124–5
Procedural reform, in drunk driving cases,
    220–1
Progressive movement and prohibition,
    139
Prohibition, 181; adoption of, 135–40; and
    alcohol consumption, 187;
    enforcement of, 140; impact on
    implementation, 184; and murder
    rates, 201; reasons for passage,
    138–40; as salient issue, 177; at the
    state level, 137; state enforcement

Prohibition *(continued)*
  of prohibition, 142; and status crimes,
  203. *See also* Repeal of
  Prohibition
Prohibition Party, strategy of, 135–6, 138
Prohibition Unit: 30; budget controls on,
  179; implementation influence, 181
Proof, in drunk driving cases, 220–1
Public opinion: ability of politicians to
  manipulate, 243; on alcohol
  consumption, 170; alcohol taxes,
  218; on alcoholism as a disease, 163;
  approaches to, 4; on drugs, 66;
  measure of, 212; on prohibition, 138,
  139; on prohibition repeal, 153–4.
  See also Attitudes
Pure Food and Drug Act of 1906, 22–3

Race: and alcohol policy 178, 211; and
  drug agency resources, 73; and drug
  law enforcement, 78, 114–5, 118–22,
  250; and drug policy, 9, 21, 23, 25,
  37, 70, 106; and marijuana
  enforcement, 43; and the Marijuana
  Tax Act, 33, 34, 63n20; and
  prohibition, 174n12; and state drug
  arrests, 84; and state marijuana
  arrests, 84; and state marijuana laws,
  110
Radicalism, and prohibition, 139
Rascob, John, 150, 153
Rational drug control policy, outlined,
  252–3
Reagan, Ronald: war on drugs, 48–53
Redistributive policy, 4; redistributing
  values, 4
Reefer Madness, 34, 116
Referenda on prohibition, 137
Regulation, as alternative to prohibition,
  138
Regulation of alcohol. *See* state alcohol
  regulatory policies
Relationship between alcohol and illicit
  drugs, 62n14
Religion: and alcohol sales regulation,
  216; and alcohol related arrests, 191;
  and alcohol use, 211; and cirrhosis
  deaths, 196; and drug penalties, 82;
  and drug agency resources, 73; and
  drunk driving arrests, 223; and dry
  population areas, 218; and federal

Religion *(continued)*
  marijuana arrests, 80; impact on
  alcohol taxes, 183; impact on federal
  alcohol enforcement, 184; impact on
  prisons, 194; impact on state marijuana
  laws, 110; as measure of attitudes, 8,
  70, 105; and retail sales outlets, 219;
  and state drug law enforcement, 114; as
  substitute for drugs, 99n9; and
  treatment policy, 219
Remove Intoxicated Drivers, 168
Reorganization: as a control over bureaucracy,
  69; of Prohibition Unit, 145
Repeal of prohibition, 148–55; of state
  laws, 161; reasons for, 155
Restitution, in drunk driving cases, 220–1
Retail sales of alcohol: policies limiting,
  214; impact on cirrhosis, 229; impact
  on prison population, 233
Revenues collected, Harrison Act, 27
Robinson, Joseph, 154
Robinson v. *California*, 40
Rockefeller, John D., 137
Rockefeller, John D. Jr., 153, 160
Roosevelt, Franklin: 154; and drug policy,
  33; and prohibition, 153
Russell, Howard Hyde, 136
Russell Sage Foundation, 41

Sabin, Pauline Morton, 151
Salience: of alcohol, 152, 177; and alcohol
  taxes, 183; of drug issues, 5, 52, 70,
  104; of drunk driving, 167; as
  explanatory variable, 10; lack of
  impact of, 243; of marijuana, 43;
  impact on state drug arrests, 84
Saloon, as social institution, 136
Self-help groups: definition, 9, 105; and
  alcohol policy, 211; and drunk
  driving arrests, 223; impact on state
  marijuana laws, 110
Sin, definition of issue type, 247
Slack resources, role in drug policy, 70
Slayton, William, 150, 151
Smith, Alfred E., 142, 146, 149, 150, 153
Smith, Robert, 162
State of the drug war address, 54
Status politics, 9, 139, 177; and
  prohibition, 136
Suicide, determinants of, 196–9
Supply of drugs, 56

Thurmond, Strom, 169, 170
Tourism: and alcohol consumption, 213; and retail sales outlets, 219
Traffic fatalities: and alcohol, 171; determinants of, 198, 200, 229–231; and minimum drinking age, 169–70
Treatment bureaucracy: definition, 15; and alcohol consumption, 189; and alcohol policy, 181; and alcohol sales regulation, 218; interest in drug policy, 109; measure of, 213; impact on prison population, 125; impact on state alcohol taxes, 183; impact on state marijuana laws, 110
Treatment capacity: 215; and alcohol industries, 219; and law enforcement bureaucracies, 219; impact on suicide rates, 229
Turf battles, over drug policy, 52

U.S. v. Lanza, 144
U.S. Canal Zone Committee, 34
U.S. v. Jin Fuey Moy, 26
U.S. v. Doremus, 26
U.S. v. Behrman, 26

Values: deep core beliefs, 8; of politicians, 13
Vesco, Robert, 47
Violence, and prohibition, 141

Volstead Act, 138; modification of, 155
Voluntary Committee of Lawyers, 152–3, 154–5

War Production Board, and preferred status of beer, 160
Washington, George, as farmer, 22
Water faucet, metaphor for drug agency, 98
Webb et al. v. U.S., 26
Webb-Kenyon Act, 138
Wheeler, Wayne B., 136, 138, 149
White, George, 39
Wickersham Commission, 145, 146
Wilson, William, 162
Wilson, Woodrow, and war time prohibition, 138
Women's Christian Temperance Union, 140; and repeal, 149–50; strategy of, 135–6
Women's Organization for National Prohibition Reform, 151–2; as elite organization, 174n21; endorses Roosevelt, 153
Wright, Hamilton, 24

Yale plan clinics, 163
Yale University, role in alcohol policy, 163

Zero tolerance, Reagan policy of, 50

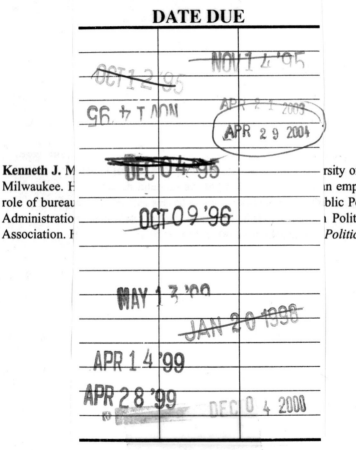

DATE DUE

NOV 1 4 '95

OCT 1 2 '95

NOV 1 4 '95

APR 2 1 2004

APR 2 9 2004

DEC 04 '95

OCT 09 '96

MAY 1 3 '99

JAN 2 0 1998

APR 1 4 '99

APR 2 8 '99

DEC 0 4 2000

Kenneth J. M ———————————————— rsity of Wisconsin–
Milwaukee. H   n emphasis on the
role of bureau   blic Policy, Public
Administratio   l Political Science
Association. F   *Political Science.*